Alexander Brändle

Volume Based Portfolio Strategies

GABLER RESEARCH

Alexander Brändle

Volume Based Portfolio Strategies

Analysis of the Relationship between Trading Activity and Expected Returns in the Cross-Section of Swiss Stocks

GABLER

RESEARCH

Bibliographic information published by the Deutsche Nationalbibliothek
The Deutsche Nationalbibliothek lists this publication in the Deutsche Nationalbibliografie; detailed bibliographic data are available in the Internet at http://dnb.d-nb.de.

Doctoral thesis, University of St. Gallen, Switzerland, 2010

1st Edition 2010

Editorial Office: Ute Wrasmann | Sabine Schöller

Gabler is part of the specialist publishing group Springer Science+Business Media.
www.gabler.de

Cover design: KünkelLopka Medienentwicklung, Heidelberg
Printed on acid-free paper
Printed in Germany

ISBN 978-3-8349-2106-2

Acknowledgements

Even though a dissertation is completed by an individual, it takes the support of many people and institutions for that individual to succeed. First of all, I want to thank my supervisor, Prof. Dr. Pascal Gantenbein. He granted me great freedom to pursue my interests as a researcher. He gave me exceptionally valuable and pragmatic advice whenever needed. Additionally, I am most grateful for his inspiring and motivating style – I always left his office feeling that I was working on a topic both important and fun. Thanks also to my co-supervisor, Prof. Dr. Klaus Spremann, for agreeing to support my research project and for continuously reminding me how important it was to ensure that my volume effect is independent of previously discovered stock return determinants.

I also thank Wegelin & Co. for being the welcoming, open-minded, and supportive organization that it is. Specific thanks goes to the following individuals: Dr. Magne Orgland agreed to support this dissertation and initiated my research interest in the chosen topic. Manuel Krieger and Reto Sonderegger helped me throughout this project and always knew the right person to contact within the organization regarding a particular issue. Finally, I am deeply indebted to Fabian Dori and Patrick Gander, who voluntarily spent many hours to support me with technical aspects of this dissertation. Fabian's profound Matlab programming skills helped me to improve the depth and quality of the analyses; Patrick introduced me to the world of econometrics and was an invaluable discussion partner concerning various aspects of this dissertation.

Next, thanks to my employer, McKinsey & Company, for the generous financial and technical support (particular thanks to Heath Williams for the latter). In addition, I want to thank my two mentors, Dr. Basil Heeb for putting me in contact with Wegelin & Co., and Thomas Wirth for introducing me to Prof. Dr. Pascal Gantenbein.

Many thanks also to Factset, in particular to Ernest Breitschwerdt, for the support regarding various data-related aspects of this dissertation, which is indispensable in all empirical work.

My appreciation to the Gabler Verlag Wiesbaden for publishing my dissertation. Many thanks particularly to Sabine Schöller for her congenial collaboration during the printing preparation phase.

I also want to thank my close friends for accompanying me on this journey, particularly Dr. Paul Beck and Dr. Michael Luhnen for the many enjoyable hours spent at the University, at the lunch table, or on the squash court.

Finally, my deepest gratitude goes to my parents, Margrith and Jost, and to my girlfriend Vera. It was invaluable to know that I always had their full support, even if the reasons for my ups and occasional downs during this work were not always comprehensible to them.

Zürich, November 2009

Alexander Brändle

Outline

Outline VII
Contents IX
Tables XV
Tables in Appendix XXII
Figures XXIII
Figures in Appendix XXIV
Abbreviations XXV
Abstract XXVII
1 Introduction 1
2 Review of Studies on the Relationship between Trading Volume and Stock Returns 6
3 Data and Methodology 47
4 Results: Trading Volume and the Cross-Sectional Variation of Stock Returns 98
5 Results: Time-Stability of Portfolio Returns 189
6 Results: Economic Significance of Volume-Return Relations 221
7 Summary and Conclusions 278
Appendix 289
References 309

Contents

Outline VII

Contents IX

Tables XV

Tables in Appendix XXII

Figures XXIII

Figures in Appendix XXIV

Abbreviations XXV

Abstract XXVII

1 Introduction 1

1.1 Motivation 1
1.2 Objectives and Own Contribution 3
1.3 Definitions 4
1.4 Structure 5

2 Review of Studies on the Relationship between Trading Volume and Stock Returns 6

2.1 Lagged Volume-Return Relationship 6
2.1.1 Volume Level 7
2.1.1.1 Empirical Findings 7
2.1.1.2 Liquidity Premium Hypothesis 10
2.1.1.3 Misperception of Future Earnings Hypothesis 15
2.1.2 Change in Volume 15
2.1.2.1 Short-Term Studies 16
2.1.2.1.1 Empirical Findings 16
2.1.2.1.2 Investor Visibility Hypothesis 18
2.1.2.2 Longer-Term Studies 18
2.1.2.2.1 Empirical Findings 18
2.1.2.2.2 Potential Interpretations 19
2.1.3 Variability in Volume 20
2.2 Trading Volume and Return Autocorrelations 21
2.2.1 Longer-Term Studies 21
2.2.1.1 Empirical Findings 22

2.2.1.2 Momentum Life Cycle Hypothesis and Other Potential Explanations *23*
2.2.2 Shorter-Term Studies 25
2.2.2.1 Empirical Findings *26*
2.2.2.2 Market Structure Models Explaining Short-Term Return Autocorrelations *27*
2.3 Contemporaneous Volume-Return Relation 29
2.3.1 Correlation between Volume and Absolute Returns 30
2.3.1.1 Empirical Findings *30*
2.3.1.2 Potential Explanations of Positive Volume-Absolute Return Correlation *32*
2.3.2 Correlation between Volume and Returns 33
2.3.2.1 Empirical Findings *33*
2.3.2.2 Costly Short Sales Hypothesis *36*
2.4 Lagged Return-Volume Relationship 36
2.4.1 Overconfidence Hypothesis 37
2.4.2 Attention Hypothesis 39
2.5 Dynamic Volume-Return Relation 40
2.5.1 Vector Autoregressive Models (VARs) 40
2.5.2 Empirical Findings and Interpretations 41
2.5.2.1 Research on Individual Stocks *41*
2.5.2.2 Research on Aggregate Stock Markets *44*
2.6 Chapter Summary 45

3 Data and Methodology 47

3.1 Research Questions 47
3.2 Data 49
3.3 Methodology along Research Questions 52
3.3.1 Trading Volume and the Cross-Sectional Variation of Stock Returns 52
3.3.1.1 Regression Analysis *52*
3.3.1.1.1 Empirical Model *52*
3.3.1.1.2 Trading Volume and Other Analyzed Firm Characteristics .. *55*
3.3.1.1.3 Robustness Checks *64*
3.3.1.2 Portfolio Strategies *67*
3.3.1.2.1 One-Way Sorts *67*
3.3.1.2.2 Two-Way Sorts *68*

3.3.1.2.3 Multi-Month Holding Periods ... *70*
3.3.2 Time-Stability of Portfolio Strategies ... 71
3.3.2.1 Dependence on Few Months with Extreme Returns ... *71*
3.3.2.2 Dependence on Returns of Single Calendar Months ... *71*
3.3.2.3 Definition of Market Regimes ... *72*
3.3.2.3.1 Sub-Periods ... *72*
3.3.2.3.2 Market Phases ... *72*
3.3.2.3.3 Market Volatility ... *75*
3.3.2.3.4 Market Volume ... *77*
3.3.3 Economic Significance of Volume-Return Relations ... 79
3.3.3.1 Portfolio Returns in a More Practical Setting ... *79*
3.3.3.2 Risk-Based Analysis ... *85*
3.3.3.3 Investability ... *88*
3.3.3.4 Performance in Selected Market States ... *92*
3.4 Research Hypotheses ... 93
3.5 Differentiation from Existing Literature ... 95

4 Results: Trading Volume and the Cross-Sectional Variation of Stock Returns ... 98

4.1 Regression Analysis ... 98
4.1.1 Base Results ... 98
4.1.1.1 Volume Level ... *99*
4.1.1.2 Abnormal Volume ... *102*
4.1.1.3 Volume Growth ... *105*
4.1.1.4 Variability in Volume ... *107*
4.1.1.5 Combined Volume Measures ... *110*
4.1.2 Results of Robustness Checks ... 113
4.1.2.1 Volume Level ... *114*
4.1.2.2 Abnormal Volume ... *126*
4.1.2.3 Volume Growth ... *136*
4.1.2.4 Variability in Volume ... *145*
4.1.3 Summary of Regression Analysis ... 150
4.2 Base Portfolio Strategies ... 152
4.2.1 Volume Level ... 153
4.2.2 Abnormal Volume ... 161
4.2.3 Volume Growth ... 175
4.2.4 Variability in Volume ... 182

4.3 Chapter Summary **187**

5 Results: Time-Stability of Portfolio Returns **189**

5.1 Abnormal Volume **189**
5.1.1 Dependence on Few Months with Extreme Returns 190
5.1.2 Dependence on Returns of Single Calendar Months 193
5.1.3 Portfolio Returns across Market Regimes 198
5.1.3.1 Sub-Periods *198*
5.1.3.2 Market Phases *200*
5.1.3.3 Market Volatility *204*
5.1.3.4 Market Volume *209*
5.2 Other Volume Measures **210**
5.2.1 Volume Level 211
5.2.2 Volume Growth 214
5.2.3 Variability in Volume 217
5.3 Chapter Summary **219**

6 Results: Economic Significance of Volume-Return Relations **221**

6.1 Abnormal Volume **221**
6.1.1 Portfolio Returns in a Practical Setting 222
6.1.2 Risk-Based Analysis 234
6.1.2.1 Risk-Adjusted Portfolio Returns *234*
6.1.2.2 Risk and Performance Analysis *239*
6.1.3 Investability 242
6.1.3.1 Inclusion of Transaction Costs *242*
6.1.3.2 Scalability Tests *247*
6.1.3.3 More Realistic Calculation of Long-Short Profits in Multi-Month Setting *250*
6.1.4 Performance in Selected Market States 253
6.1.4.1 Robustness Check of Time-Stability of Portfolio Returns *253*
6.1.4.2 Outlook: Dynamic Portfolio Strategies *257*
6.1.4.3 Stress-Test: 2008 Results *263*
6.2 Other Volume Measures **266**
6.2.1 Volume Level 266
6.2.2 Volume Growth 270
6.2.3 Variability in Volume 273

6.3 Chapter Summary 275

7 Summary and Conclusions 278

Appendix 289

References 309

Tables

Table 2.1: Selected Studies on Relationship between Volume Level and Expected Returns 9
Table 2.2: Selected Studies on Relationship between Liquidity and Expected Returns 14
Table 2.3: Selected Studies on Relationship between Short-Term Change in Volume and Expected Returns 17
Table 2.4: Selected Studies on Relationship between Long-Term Change in Volume and Expected Returns 19
Table 2.5: Selected Studies on Relationship between Variability in Volume and Expected Returns 20
Table 2.6: Selected Studies on Influence of Volume on Momentum Strategies 22
Table 2.7: Selected Studies on Influence of Volume on Short-Term Return Autocorrelations 26
Table 2.8: Selected Studies on Contemporaneous Relationship between Volume and Absolute Returns 31
Table 2.9: Selected Studies on Contemporaneous Relationship between Volume and Returns (Individual Stocks) 34
Table 2.10: Selected Studies on Contemporaneous Relationship between Volume and Returns (Aggregate Markets) 35
Table 2.11: Selected Studies on Relation between Returns and Subsequent Trading Volume 37
Table 2.12: Relationship between Price Extremes and Subsequent Trading Volume 39
Table 2.13: Selected Studies on Dynamic Volume-Return Interactions 43
Table 3.1: Yearly Number of Companies Included in the Database 50
Table 3.2: Summary Statistics 59
Table 3.3: Correlation Matrix of Analyzed Firm Characteristics (Formation Period J = 1 Month; Part 1) 60
Table 3.4: Correlation Matrix of Analyzed Firm Characteristics (Formation Period J = 1 Month; Part 2) 61
Table 3.5: Correlation Matrix of Analyzed Firm Characteristics (Formation Period J = 12 Months) 64

Table 3.6: Transparency on Delistings in the Database ... 83
Table 4.1: Fama-MacBeth Regression Estimates, Using Share Turnover ... 99
Table 4.2: FM Regression Estimates, Using Swiss Franc Volume ... 101
Table 4.3: FM Regression Estimates, Using Abnormal Turnover ... 103
Table 4.4: FM Regression Estimates, Using Abnormal Swiss Franc Volume ... 104
Table 4.5: FM Regression Estimates, Using Turnover Growth ... 105
Table 4.6: FM Regression Estimates, Using Swiss Franc Volume Growth ... 106
Table 4.7: FM Regression Estimates, Using Variability in Turnover ... 108
Table 4.8: FM Regression Estimates, Using Variability in Swiss Franc Volume ... 109
Table 4.9: FM Regression Estimates, Using a Combination of Turnover Measures ... 111
Table 4.10: FM Regression Estimates, Using a Combination of Swiss Franc Volume Measures ... 112
Table 4.11: FM Regression Estimates, Including 1-Month Lag in Volume Variable (Turnover) ... 115
Table 4.12: FM Regression Estimates, Excluding Different Levels of Outliers (Turnover) ... 117
Table 4.13: FM Regression Estimates, Excluding Different Size Groups (Turnover) ... 118
Table 4.14: FM Regression Estimates in Different Sub-Periods (Turnover) ... 120
Table 4.15: FM Regression Estimates, Comparing Free-Float Adjusted and Non-Free-Float Adjusted Measures (Turnover) ... 121
Table 4.16: FM Regression Estimates, Excluding Different Free-Float Groups (Turnover) ... 123
Table 4.17: FM Regression Estimates, Using Different Empirical Methods (Turnover) ... 124
Table 4.18: FM Regression Estimates over Longer Return Horizons (Turnover) ... 125
Table 4.19: FM Regression Estimates, Including 1-Month Lag in Volume Variable (Abnormal Turnover) ... 127
Table 4.20: FM Regression Estimates over Longer Return Horizons (Abnormal Turnover) ... 128
Table 4.21: FM Regression Estimates, Excluding Different Levels of Outliers (Abnormal Turnover) ... 130

Table 4.22: FM Regression Estimates, Excluding Different Size Groups (Using Abnormal Turnover) ... 131
Table 4.23: FM Regression Estimates in Different Sub-Periods (Abnormal Turnover) ... 133
Table 4.24: FM Regression Estimates, Excluding Different Free-Float Groups, (Abnormal Turnover) ... 134
Table 4.25: FM Regression Estimates, Using Different Empirical Methods (Abnormal Turnover) ... 135
Table 4.26: FM Regression Estimates, Including 1-Month Lag in Volume Variable (Turnover Growth) ... 137
Table 4.27: FM Regression Estimates, Excluding Different Levels of Outliers (Turnover Growth) ... 138
Table 4.28: FM Regression Estimates, Excluding Different Size Groups (Turnover Growth) ... 139
Table 4.29: FM Regression Estimates in Different Sub-Periods (Turnover Growth) 141
Table 4.30: FM Regression Estimates, Excluding Different Free-Float Groups (Turnover Growth) ... 142
Table 4.31: FM Regression Estimates, Using Different Empirical Methods (Turnover Growth) ... 143
Table 4.32: FM Regression Estimates over Longer Return Horizons (Turnover Growth) ... 144
Table 4.33: FM Regression Estimates, Robustness Checks, Part 1 (Coefficient of Variation in Turnover) ... 146
Table 4.34: FM Regression Estimates, Robustness Checks, Part 2 (Coefficient of Variation in Turnover) ... 148
Table 4.35: FM Regression Estimates over Longer Return Horizons (Coefficient of Variation in Turnover) ... 149
Table 4.36: Monthly Returns to Portfolios Sorted on Share Turnover ... 155
Table 4.37: Returns to Turnover Portfolios Averaged over 3 Quantiles of the Control Variable ... 157
Table 4.38: Returns to Turnover Portfolios Averaged over 3 Size Quantiles ... 158
Table 4.39: Returns to Portfolios Sorted on Turnover, Multi-Month Holding Periods ... 160
Table 4.40: Monthly Returns to Portfolios Sorted on Abnormal Turnover ... 163

Table 4.41: Returns to Abnormal Turnover Portfolios Averaged over 3 Quantiles of the Control Variable 164
Table 4.42: Returns to Abnormal Turnover Portfolios Averaged over 3 Size Quantiles 166
Table 4.43: Returns to Abnormal Turnover Portfolios Averaged over 3 Book-to-Market Quantiles 168
Table 4.44: Returns to Abnormal Turnover Portfolios Averaged over 3 Past Return Quantiles 169
Table 4.45: Returns to Abnormal Turnover Portfolios Averaged over 4 Industry Quantiles 171
Table 4.46: Returns to Portfolios Sorted on Abnormal Turnover, Multi-Month Holding Periods 173
Table 4.47: Returns to Abnormal Turnover Portfolios Averaged over 3 Quantiles of the Control Variable, Multi-Month Holding Periods 174
Table 4.48: Returns to Portfolios Sorted on Turnover Growth 176
Table 4.49: Returns to Turnover Growth Portfolios Averaged over 3 Quantiles of the Control Variable 178
Table 4.50: Returns to Turnover Growth Portfolios Averaged over 3 Size Quantiles 179
Table 4.51: Returns to Portfolios Sorted on Turnover Growth, Multi-Month Holding Periods 180
Table 4.52: Returns to Portfolios Sorted on Coefficient of Variation in Turnover .. 183
Table 4.53: Returns to Coefficient of Variation in Turnover Portfolios Averaged over 3 Quantiles of the Control Variable 184
Table 4.54: Returns to Coefficient of Variation in Turnover Portfolios Averaged over 3 Size Quantiles 185
Table 4.55: Returns to Portfolios Sorted on Coefficient of Variation in Turnover, Multi-Month Holding Periods 186
Table 5.1: Returns to Abnormal Turnover Portfolios after Excluding Highest Monthly Values 191
Table 5.2: Returns to Two-Way Sorted Abnormal Turnover Portfolios after Excluding Highest Monthly Values 192
Table 5.3: Returns to Abnormal Turnover Portfolios, Excluding December and January 194

Table 5.4: Returns to Two-Way Sorted Abnormal Turnover Portfolios, Excluding December and January ... 195
Table 5.5: Returns to Abnormal Turnover Portfolios in Different Return Months 196
Table 5.6: Returns to Two-Way Sorted Abnormal Turnover Portfolios in Different Return Months ... 197
Table 5.7: Returns to Abnormal Turnover Portfolios in Different Sub-Periods ... 199
Table 5.8: Returns to Abnormal Turnover Portfolios in Different Market Phases. 201
Table 5.9: Returns to Abnormal Turnover Portfolios in Down Market States, Averaged over 4 Industry Groups ... 203
Table 5.10: Returns to Abnormal Turnover Portfolios in Different Volatility Regimes ... 206
Table 5.11: Returns to Abnormal Turnover Portfolios in High Volatility Phases, Averaged over 4 Industry Groups ... 207
Table 5.12: Returns to Abnormal Turnover Portfolios in Different Volume Regimes ... 209
Table 5.13: Returns to Turnover Portfolios in Different Market Phases (J = 1 Month) ... 212
Table 5.14: Returns to Turnover Portfolios in Different Market Phases (J = 12 Months) ... 213
Table 5.15: Returns to Turnover Growth Portfolios in Different Market Phases (J = 3 Months) ... 214
Table 5.16: Returns to Turnover Growth Portfolios in Different Market Phases (J = 12 Months) ... 215
Table 5.17: Returns to Turnover Growth Portfolios in Different Market Phases, Averaged over 3 Size Quantiles ... 216
Table 5.18: Returns to Coefficient of Variation in Turnover Portfolios in Different Market Phases ... 218
Table 6.1: Returns to Abnormal Turnover Portfolios in a Practical Setting ... 223
Table 6.2: Returns to Abnormal Turnover Portfolios Averaged over 3 Quantiles of the Control Variable, Practical Setting ... 226
Table 6.3: Returns to Two-Way Sorted Abnormal Turnover Portfolios in Practical Setting ... 229
Table 6.4: Time-Series Regression Alphas of Abnormal Turnover Portfolios ... 235

Table 6.5: Time-Series Regression Coefficients of Abnormal Turnover Arbitrage Strategies 237
Table 6.6: Time-Series Regression Alphas of Two-Way Sorted Abnormal Turnover Portfolios 238
Table 6.7: Risk and Performance Analysis of Abnormal Turnover Decile Portfolios 240
Table 6.8: Risk and Performance Analysis of Two-Way Sorted Abnormal Turnover Arbitrage Strategies 241
Table 6.9: Inclusion of Transaction Costs to Abnormal Turnover Decile Portfolios 243
Table 6.10: Inclusion of Transaction Costs to Two-Way Sorted Abnormal Turnover Arbitrage Strategies 246
Table 6.11: Abnormal Turnover Decile Portfolios in Practical Setting, Value-Weighted 248
Table 6.12: Abnormal Turnover Decile Portfolios in Practical Setting, Exclusion of Micro Cap Stocks 249
Table 6.13: More Realistic Long-Short Calculation of Abnormal Turnover Decile Strategies 252
Table 6.14: Abnormal Turnover Portfolios in Practical Setting, Performance across Market Regimes (Part 1) 254
Table 6.15: Abnormal Turnover Portfolios in Practical Setting, Performance across Market Regimes (Part 2) 255
Table 6.16: Abnormal Turnover Portfolios in Practical Setting, Selected Risk-Adjusted Returns 257
Table 6.17: Evaluation of Dynamic Down Market Strategy (Reference Index: EW)258
Table 6.18: Evaluation of Dynamic High Forecasted Volatility Strategy (Reference Index: EW) 261
Table 6.19: Inclusion of Transaction Costs to Dynamic Strategies (EW-Based) 262
Table 6.20: 2008 Performance of Abnormal Turnover Portfolios in Practical Setting (K = 1 Month) 264
Table 6.21: 2008 Performance of Abnormal Turnover Portfolios in Practical Setting (K = 12 Months) 265
Table 6.22: Returns to Turnover Portfolios in Practical Setting (J = 1 Month)........ 267

Table 6.23: Time-Series Regression Coefficients of Turnover Arbitrage Strategies (J = 1 Month) 269

Table 6.24: Returns to Turnover Growth Portfolios in Practical Setting (J = 12 Months) 271

Table 6.25: Time-Series Regression Coefficients of Turnover Growth Arbitrage Strategies (J =12 Months) 272

Table 6.26: Returns to Coefficient of Variation in Turnover Portfolios in Practical Setting 274

Table 6.27: Time-Series Regression Coefficients of Coefficient of Variation in Turnover Arbitrage Strategies 275

Tables in Appendix

Table A1: Returns to Two-Way Sorted Abnormal Turnover Portfolios in Different Sub-Periods 289

Table A2: Returns to Two-Way Sorted Abnormal Turnover Portfolios in Different Market Phases 290

Table A3: Returns to Two-Way Sorted Abnormal Turnover Portfolios in Different Volatility Regimes 291

Table A4: Returns to Two-Way Sorted Abnormal Turnover Portfolios in Different Volume Regimes 292

Table A5: Time-Series Regression Coefficients of Abnormal Turnover Arbitrage Strategies, Small Companies 293

Table A6: Time-Series Regression Coefficients of Abnormal Turnover Arbitrage Strategies, Low Book-to-Market Companies 294

Table A7: Time-Series Regression Coefficients of Abnormal Turnover Arbitrage Strategies, Loser Stocks 295

Table A8: Risk and Performance Analysis of Two-Way Sorted Abnormal Turnover Arbitrage Strategies (K = 12 Months) 296

Table A9: Risk and Performance Analysis of Long-Only Abnormal Turnover Decile Portfolios 297

Table A10: Inclusion of Transaction Costs to Abnormal Turnover Arbitrage Strategies, Small Companies 298

Table A11: Evaluation of Dynamic Down Market Strategy (Reference Index: SPI)299

Table A12: Evaluation of Dynamic High Forecasted Volatility Strategy (Reference Index: SPI) 301

Table A13: Inclusion of Transaction Costs to Dynamic Strategies (SPI-Based)...... 303

Table A14: Returns to Turnover Portfolios in Practical Setting (J = 12 Months) 305

Table A15: Time-Series Regression Coefficients of Turnover Arbitrage Strategies (J = 12 Months) 306

Table A16: Returns to Turnover Growth Portfolios in Practical Setting (J = 3 Months) 307

Table A17: Time-Series Regression Coefficients of Turnover Growth Arbitrage Strategies (J = 3 Months) 308

Figures

Figure 2.1: Momentum Life Cycle Hypothesis 25
Figure 3.1: Development of SPI and Value-Weighted Index Constructed from Database 51
Figure 3.2: Correlation between Swiss Franc Volume and Size 62
Figure 3.3: Correlation between Share Turnover and Size 63
Figure 3.4: Bull and Bear Markets SPI 73
Figure 3.5: Up and Down Markets SPI 74
Figure 3.6: VCL Clariden Leu Swiss Equity Volatility Index 75
Figure 3.7: Forecasted Volatility Regimes 76
Figure 3.8: Total Market Trading Volume, De-Trended and Season-Adjusted (CHF Million) 77
Figure 3.9: Average Market Turnover, Season-Adjusted (Percent) 79
Figure 3.10: 'Base' Versus 'Practical' Portfolio Strategies 80
Figure 3.11: Main Differences Between Own Investigation and Kaniel et al. (2007). 96
Figure 6.1: NAVs of Abnormal Turnover Arbitrage Strategies (V1-V10) 231
Figure 6.2: NAVs of Long-Only Abnormal Turnover Portfolios (Deciles) 233
Figure 6.3: NAVs of Dynamic Down Market Strategy and Benchmarks (EW-Based) 259
Figure 6.4: NAVs of Dynamic High Forecasted Volatility Strategy and Benchmarks (EW-Based) 260

Figures in Appendix

Figure A1: NAVs of Dynamic Down Market Strategy and Benchmarks (SPI-Based)........ 300
Figure A2: NAVs of Dynamic High Forecasted Volatility Strategy and Benchmarks (SPI-Based)........ 302
Figure A3: Market Trading Volume, De-Trended and Season-Adjusted (CHF Million), incl. 2008........ 304
Figure A4: Average Market Turnover, Season-Adjusted (Percent), incl. 2008....... 304

Abbreviations

Adj	Adjusted
AMEX	American Stock Exchange
Ann.	Annualized
BM	Firm book-to-market ratio
Bps	Basis points
CAPM	Capital Asset Pricing Model
CHF	Swiss franc
CHFVOL	Swiss franc volume
CRSP	Center for Research in Security Prices
CVTURN	Coefficient of Variation in (share) turnover
CVVOL	Coefficient of Variation in Swiss franc volume
DAX	Deutscher Aktien IndeX
DELTATURN A	Abnormal (share) turnover
DELTATURN B	(Share) Turnover growth
DELTAVOL A	Abnormal Swiss franc volume
DELTAVOL B	Swiss franc volume growth
Dyna	Dynamic
E.g.	For example
Eq.	Equation
Et al.	Et alii (and others)
Etc.	Et cetera (and so on)
EUREX	European Exchange
EW	Equal-Weighted Index
FF3	Fama-French three-factor model
FM	Fama-MacBeth
FTSE	Financial Times Stock Exchange
HML	High Minus Low ('Value factor')
I.e.	Id est (that is)
J	Formation / reference period length (in months)
K	Holding period length (in months)
LIBOR	London Interbank Offered Rate
Manuf	Manufacturing

MIT	Massachusetts Insititue of Technology
NASDAQ	National Association of Securities Dealers Automated Quotations
NAV	Net Asset Value
NBER	National Bureau of Economic Research
NYSE	New York Stock Exchange
OLS	Ordinary Least Squares
Q4	Fourth quarter
RET2-12	Past one-year stock return (with the exception of the last month)
RMRF	Market factor
S&P	Standard & Poor's
SIX	SIX Swiss Exchange
SIZE	Firm market capitalization
SMB	Small Minus Big ('Size factor')
SPI	Swiss Performance Index
Std. Dev.	Standard Deviation
STDTURN	Standard Deviation of (share) turnover
STDVOL	Standard Deviation of Swiss franc volume
TOPIX	Tokyo Stock Exchange Price Index
TURN	(Share) Turnover
UMD	Up Minus Down ('Momentum factor')
US	United States
USD	US dollar
V1	Portfolio containing stocks with highest volume
VAR	Vector Autoregressive Model
Vola	Volatility

Abstract

The presented dissertation investigates whether different measures of trading volume play an important role in explaining the variation of returns across Swiss stocks. It is discovered that recent abnormal volume, defined as the percentage change of last month's trading volume versus the average trading volume in the preceding three to twelve months, relates positively to expected returns in the cross-section of Swiss stocks. In other words, stocks with unusual trading volume in a given month experience systematically higher subsequent returns. The presented abnormal volume premium is interpreted as a consequence of increased visibility of a stock leading to increased subsequent demand and price for that stock (investor visibility hypothesis by MILLER (1977)).

The effect is strongest in the month immediately following the abnormal volume, but it is shown that portfolios containing high abnormal volume stocks continue to systematically outperform portfolios with low abnormal volume stocks for the next twelve months. The relationship between abnormal volume and expected returns is stable to controlling for various previously discovered cross-sectional effects including company size, book-to-market ratio, momentum, liquidity, market beta, and industry affiliation. The subsequent investigation of the stability of the abnormal volume premium across time and different market regimes reveals that the effect is particularly strong in a market environment that is characterized by poor recent performance and high volatility.

Finally, tests on the economic significance of abnormal volume based portfolio strategies find mixed results. On the one hand, the trading-intensive one-month holding period setting, which is found to be the most attractive throughout the analysis, is most probably not profitably marketable due to the high level of transaction costs involved. Returns to simple dynamic portfolio strategies that only invest in abnormal volume portfolios in ex-ante known market regimes, on the other hand, are promising.

The other volume measures analyzed, namely volume level, volume growth and variability in volume, do not seem to be systematically related to the cross-section of Swiss stocks.

1 Introduction

In this introductory chapter, we first introduce the topic of this project and its relevance to research and practice. After the statement of the main objectives, we formulate its research questions and contributions. Following some important definitions, we conclude this introduction by outlining the structure of this project report.

1.1 Motivation

For a long time, the predominant view in finance was that the variation of returns across stocks could be explained by their sensitivities (i.e., betas) to a single factor, the excess return of the market portfolio. This classical view, reflected in the Capital Asset Pricing Model (CAPM), implies that no portfolio strategy selecting stocks on the basis of other factors is able to consistently outperform a passive 'buy and hold' strategy (reflecting the market capitalization-weighted investment universe). Later research, however, found that other factors also play an important role in the cross-sectional variation of stock returns. Especially observed stock attributes such as past returns, market capitalization, or book-to-market ratio, were found to have a high explanatory power. Subsequent research even proved the existence of profitable portfolio strategies formed on the basis of such stock attributes, which led to their practical implementation and offering by professional investment firms. These quantitative strategies have since become increasingly popular, especially as a means to diversify investments (which is particularly helpful in case of a low correlation between a strategy's return and the development of the market).

It was a discussion with representatives of a provider of such quantitative portfolio strategies, Wegelin & Co., which initiated the research interest for this project. The specialists told the author that while several investment professionals had successfully implemented quantitative strategies on the basis of value attributes (for example a firm's book-to-market ratio), or momentum (exploiting the empirical phenomenon of intermediate-term return continuation in stock prices), they had not yet seen publicly available *trading volume based* portfolio strategies.

There were two initial hypotheses to explain this fact: first, there exists no previous literature on the relationship between volume and expected returns, which would be surprising given the easy accessibility of volume data and the common use of this variable in technical chart analysis. And second, there is no relation between volume and expected returns that could be exploited via quantitative portfolio strategies, which is not improbable. Initial research revealed the existence of both a considerable body of literature on trading volume as well as evidence of a relationship between trading volume and the cross-sectional variation of stock returns, at least in the US markets. Nevertheless, existing literature exhibits some important gaps:

First, there exists very limited trading volume research in the context of Swiss (and other developed European countries') stock market data. However, the Swiss market is of special interest for at least two reasons:[1] it is among the largest stock markets by market capitalization worldwide, which makes it important to study similarities and differences with other markets. And existing research, for example by FAMA/FRENCH (1998), shows that previously identified relations between stock attributes and stock returns are country-specific.

In addition, little emphasis has been given so far to the practicability of volume based portfolio strategies. This includes the analysis of portfolio returns net of transaction costs, performance analyses of these active strategies compared to their respective benchmarks, and the in-depth investigation of the time-stability of strategy returns (particularly in light of different market regimes). Especially the consideration of transaction costs is critical, however, since many potential strategies fail to consistently outperform the market once transaction costs are considered.

In this project report, we address both these gaps.

[1] See AMMANN/STEINER (2008), 2.

1.2 Objectives and Own Contribution

The main objective of this research project is to investigate the relationship between trading volume and expected returns in the cross-section of Swiss stocks, with a particular emphasis on the practicability of portfolio strategies formed on the basis of past trading volume.

Answers to the following four research questions help us to achieve this goal (described in detail below, 3.1):

[1] Do different measures of trading volume play an important role in the cross-sectional variation of expected returns in the Swiss stock market?

[2] How robust are the portfolio returns across time and different market regimes?

[3] Are the discovered volume-return relations economically significant?

[4] How sensitive are the results to changes in the experimental design?

The main contributions of this research project are:

Empirical results in the Swiss stock market. To our knowledge there exists no systematic analysis of the volume-return relation based on Swiss stock market data.

Particular focus on the economic significance respectively practicability of volume based portfolio strategies to analyze whether such strategies are able to outperform the market net of transaction costs and across time respectively market regimes.

Systematization and overview of trading volume literature: in chapter 2 we show the existence of a considerable body of trading volume literature. By grouping these studies in a logical way, we help to better integrate this and future research efforts into existing literature.

Multiple facets of trading volume investigated: much of existing research focuses on some aspects of trading volume. We include four different measures of trading volume in our analyses, namely volume level, abnormal volume, volume growth, and variability in volume.

Individual stock and portfolio-based empirical tests: existing literature predominantly tests the volume-return relation based on the analysis of either individual stocks or stock portfolios. We apply both approaches on a single dataset, resulting in a more powerful test of the volume-return relation.

Investigation based on a very recent dataset: finally, we include data until August 2008 in our empirical analysis. As a stress test of our results, we even expand the time-series to the fourth quarter of 2008, which was a particularly challenging market environment.

1.3 Definitions

Volume/trading volume: umbrella term for (measures of) trading activity. Depending on the specific context, this can be *volume level*, *abnormal volume*, *volume growth*, or *variability in volume*.

(Share) turnover: number of shares traded in a given stock divided by the number of shares outstanding of that stock (is used as a measure of *volume level*).

Swiss franc/dollar volume: number of shares traded in a given stock multiplied by the corresponding transaction price (is used as an alternative measure of *volume level*).

Abnormal volume: percentage change of last month's share turnover (Swiss franc/dollar volume) versus the average monthly share turnover (Swiss franc/dollar volume) in the preceding three to twelve months.

Volume growth: average monthly percentage change in share turnover (Swiss franc/dollar volume) in the last one to twelve months.

Coefficient of variation in share turnover (Swiss franc/dollar volume): standard deviation of share turnover (Swiss franc/dollar volume) divided by its time-series mean (is used as a measure of *variability in volume*).

1.4 Structure

Following these introductory remarks, chapter 2 provides a review of existing literature on the relationship between trading volume and stock returns.

Chapter 3 starts with a detailed description of the research questions. This is followed by the outline of the methodology to answer each research question including data used in the empirical tests. The chapter concludes with the statement of the main research hypotheses and the differentiation from existing literature.

Chapters 4 to 6 present results of the empirical tests conducted to answer the research questions.

Finally, chapter 7 summarizes the main findings and proposes topics for future research.

2 Review of Studies on the Relationship between Trading Volume and Stock Returns

Trading volume has attracted researchers' attention for years, resulting in voluminous existing literature. LO/WANG (2000) report to have found 190 articles from various fields of study including economics, finance and accounting. Within the finance literature, studies exist mainly on volume-return relations, market microstructure, volume-return volatility relations, and models of asymmetric information.

Following the objectives of the research project, the focus of this literature overview is placed on volume-return relations, with selective inclusion of market microstructure and asymmetric information models as potential explanations of observed empirical evidence. Studies on volume-return volatility relations, however, are out of scope of this review.[2]

The structure of the chapter follows the direction of the relationship between volume and returns studied, for example lagged volume-return or contemporaneous volume-return relations.[3] Within these categories, the discussion includes both a summary of previous empirical findings as well as potential theoretical explanations thereof. Note, however, that existing literature is vast, even within the defined focus area. As a result, this review can only include a selection of the most important articles.

2.1 Lagged Volume-Return Relationship

The first area of research analyzes whether different measures of lagged trading volume relate to subsequent returns (in other words, whether there exists a relation between trading volume and expected returns). The articles presented are divided into three parts based on whether the object of the investigation is the volume level, change in volume, or the variability in volume.

2 One exception is the correlation between volume and absolute returns. In some studies, squared stock returns are used as a measure of realized return volatility. See below, 2.3.1.

3 We are aware that not all of these relations are directly related to our research questions. However, a detailed overview of previous volume-return research helps to integrate the contribution of this project into existing literature.

2.1.1 Volume Level

There is strong evidence in US stock market data that different types of volume level relate negatively to expected returns. A possible theoretical explanation for this empirical phenomenon is that different types of trading volume proxy for liquidity, with illiquidity being a priced factor in the stock markets. However, not all empirical results support this view.

2.1.1.1 Empirical Findings

Table 2.1 summarizes results of empirical studies on the relationship between different types of trading volume level and expected returns, divided into studies on US and international stock market data.

Several researchers apply Fama-MacBeth type regressions or variations thereof:[4] HAUGEN/BAKER (1996) run regressions of stock returns on over 40 firm characteristics related to risk, liquidity, price level, growth potential and price history. They report a statistically significant negative relationship between the ratio of dollar volume to market capitalization and returns for stocks in the Russell 3000 stock index. Several authors confirm the existence of a negative relation between volume level and expected returns in the major US stock markets applying different measures of trading volume such as dollar trading volume or share turnover.[5] In addition, BRENNAN ET AL. (1998) and CHORDIA ET AL. (2001) find the trading volume effect to be persistent even in risk-adjusted returns.[6] Finally, HU (1997) confirms the existence of a negative relationship between lagged share turnover and returns in the Tokyo stock exchange.

[4] See FAMA/MACBETH (1973) and 3.3.1.1.1 for background on this methodology.

[5] See BRENNAN ET AL. (1998), CHORDIA ET AL. (2001), DATAR ET AL. (1998).

[6] In BRENNAN ET AL. (1998), excess returns are adjusted using both the principal components approach of CONNOR/KORAJCZYK (1988) and the FAMA/FRENCH (1993) factors.

Portfolio-based tests yield similar results for individual US stocks: LEE/SWAMINATHAN (2000) form portfolios of all NYSE/AMEX stocks based on past share turnover and past returns and find that firms with high past turnover ratios earn lower future returns while firms with low past turnover ratios earn higher future returns. This effect is long-lived, i.e., observable over three to five years following portfolio formation. AGGARWAL/SUN (2003) confirm this result, but only for stocks of small size. Finally, KEENE/PETERSON (2007) construct a factor-mimicking portfolio for different measures of volume using FAMA/FRENCH (1993) methodology.[7] The authors conclude that this factor is important in affecting portfolio returns, alongside market beta, size, book-to-market ratio, and momentum (i.e., past stock returns).

While the above studies all confirm a significantly negative relationship between volume level and expected returns, results of portfolio-based tests in international markets are less conclusive: ROUWENHORST (1999) finds little evidence of a difference between average returns of high and low share turnover portfolios in a study of 20 emerging markets. In fact, when forming portfolios by ranking stocks based on prior share turnover, the return on high turnover portfolios even exceeds the return on low turnover portfolios in 12 of the 20 countries studied (including the three European countries in the sample, Greece, Portugal, and Turkey). However, the absolute value of the t-statistics for the equality of means exceeds two in only one of these countries. CHAN/FAFF (2005) on the other hand, again analyzing the issue by constructing factor-mimicking portfolios, confirm the existence of a negative relationship between turnover and expected returns on the Australian stock exchange. Finally, WANG/CHIN (2004) also find the presence of a negative relationship between share turnover and expected returns in a portfolio-based test on the Chinese stock markets, although the difference in mean returns is hardly significant, even at the 10% level.

Let us summarize these empirical findings: there is strong evidence in US stock market data that different measures of trading volume play an important role in the cross-sectional variation of stock returns above well-studied effects such as size, book-to-market ratio, and momentum. Results of previous studies on international stock markets, however, are somewhat mixed.

---

[7] The Fama-French methodology is touched upon in 3.3.3.2.

Table 2.1: Selected Studies on Relationship between Volume Level and Expected Returns

Author(s)	Sample Data	Sample Period	Type of Volume	Frequency	Negative Relationship Lagged Volume-Return?
HAUGEN/BAKER (1996)	Stocks in Russell 3000 stock index	1979-1993	Dollar volume to market capitalization	Monthly	Yes
BRENNAN/ CHORDIA/ SUBRAHMANYAM (1998)	Sample of non-financial US commons stocks (~2500)	1966-1995	Dollar trading volume	Monthly	Yes
DATAR/NAIK/ RADCLIFFE (1998)	All non-financial firms on NYSE	1962-1991	Share turnover	Monthly	Yes
LEE/ SWAMINATHAN (2000)	All firms on NYSE and AMEX	1965-1995	Share turnover	Monthly	Yes
CHORDIA/ SUBRAHMANYAM/ ANSHUMAN (2001)	Sample of common stock of NYSE/AMEX, NASDAQ-listed companies	1966-1995	Dollar trading volume, share turnover	Monthly	Yes
AGGARWAL/SUN (2003)	NYSE and AMEX stocks	1962-2000	Share turnover	Monthly	Yes (for small stocks)
KEENE/PETERSON (2007)	Individual US stocks	1963-2002	Dollar trading volume, share turnover	Monthly/ Yearly	Yes
HU (1997)	Individual securities traded on the Tokyo Stock Exchange	1976-1993	Share turnover	Monthly	Yes
ROUWENHORST (1999)	Individual stocks in 20 emerging markets	1987-1992	Share turnover	Monthly	No
MARSHALL/ YOUNG (2003)	Individual stocks listed on Australian Stock Exchange	1994-1998	Share turnover	Monthly	Yes
WANG/CHIN (2004)	All A-shares traded on Shanghai and Shenzhen stock exchanges	1994-2000	Share turnover	Monthly	(Yes)
CHAN/FAFF (2005)	Individual stocks listed on Australian Stock Exchange	1990-1998	Share turnover	Monthly	Yes

2.1.1.2 Liquidity Premium Hypothesis

At the starting point of the discussion whether above empirical findings could be explained by the fact that different measures of trading volume proxy for liquidity (with less liquid stocks generating higher expected returns), it is important to get a common understanding of what liquidity entails. Because there exists not one generally accepted definition for liquidity, different views are shared and common elements extracted:

KEYNES (1930) proposes that 'an asset is more liquid than another if it is more certainly realizable at short notice without loss'. AVRAMOV ET AL. (2006) state that 'most market participants agree that liquidity generally reflects the ability to buy or sell sufficient quantities quickly, at low trading cost, and without impacting the market price too much'. Finally, LIU (2006) defines liquidity as 'the ability to trade large quantities quickly at low cost with little price impact'. These different descriptions entail four elements of liquidity, namely *trading quantity*, *trading speed*, *trading cost*, and *price impact*. Although the *prime interest of this project lies in the trading quantity element* of liquidity, it is important not to analyze this in an isolated way but in the context of the other elements.

The intuitive explanation why liquidity might affect expected returns is 'that investors can reasonably expect to be compensated with larger returns for the risk that they will not be able to sell a stock in a timely fashion without undue loss[8]'. In addition, as investors are interested in holding period returns *net of trading costs*, more costly to trade (i.e., less liquid) assets must provide higher gross returns than more liquid assets.[9] This trading cost aspect of liquidity was the first element to be formally investigated, namely by AMIHUD/MENDELSON (1986). The authors show that, in equilibrium, illiquid assets are held by investors with longer investment horizons, resulting in observed asset returns being an increasing and concave function of transaction costs. Testing their model using quoted bid-ask spread as a measure of liquidity, the authors find that risk-adjusted returns for NYSE/AMEX stocks decrease with liquidity. According to the authors, this evidence confirms the notion of a liquidity premium.

---

8 MARSHALL/YOUNG (2003), 187.

9 See DATAR ET AL. (1998), 204.

However, results of subsequent empirical tests on the return-spread relationship are mixed: ELESWARAPU/REINGANUM (1993), in a longer-horizon study, report a statistically significant return-spread relationship only in the month of January. ELESWARAPU (1997), on the other hand, confirms the initial results for NASDAQ stocks. Finally, CHALMERS/KADLEC (1998) criticize the fact that previous studies focus solely on the magnitude of the spread, not considering the length of investors' holding periods over which the spreads are amortized. Therefore, the authors introduce a new liquidity measure, amortized spread, which they define as 'the product of the effective spread and the number of shares traded summed over all trades for each day and expressed as an annualized fraction of equity value[10]'. Applying FAMA/MACBETH (1973) methodology (see 3.3.1.1.1), the authors find a significant positive relationship between amortized spread and excess return when market beta, size, book-to-market equity, and standard deviation of monthly returns are included as control variables. However, no statistically significant relationship is found when subsets of control variables are used.[11] MARSHALL/YOUNG (2003), testing the two previously defined spread measures using Australian stock exchange data, find no relationship between return and amortized spread and even a negative relationship between return and the bid-ask spread.

Because of the inconclusive empirical evidence on the return-spread relationship researchers switched their focus from trading costs to different potential measures of liquidity related to *trading quantity*. A first measure widely used is share turnover. DATAR ET AL. (1998) state two main advantages of using share turnover as a proxy for liquidity: first, AMIHUD/MENDELSON (1986) prove that in equilibrium liquidity is correlated with trading frequency, and second, data on share turnover is easier to obtain than spreads, which enables to observe liquidity effects over long periods of time and across a large number of stocks. In addition, CHORDIA ET AL. (2001) state that share turnover is related to a representative investor's holding period, thereby linking it to liquidity in AMIHUD/MENDELSON (1986) and CHALMERS/KADLEC (1998). Another measure of trading volume widely used in empirical studies of the liquidity premium, dollar trading volume, is positively related to liquidity in STOLL (1978). In

[10] See CHALMERS/KADLEC (1998), 160.

[11] Nevertheless, the authors argue that the amortized spread is a superior liquidity proxy than the spread, because the spread shows no statistical significance at all.

addition, CHORDIA ET AL. (2000) show a strong cross-sectional relationship between dollar trading volume and bid-ask spread measures.

As shown above (section 2.1.1.1, in particular Table 2.1), there is strong evidence for a negative cross-sectional relationship between these measures of trading volume and returns in US stock market data, generally supporting a liquidity premium hypothesis. However, other empirical studies challenge this explanation of the observed negative trading volume-return relationship:

Some findings question *the role of share turnover as a liquidity proxy*: as SUBRAHMANYAM (2005) argues, for share turnover to be a priced measure of liquidity, it should have a consistent effect on expected returns in the cross-section. LEE/SWAMINATHAN (2000), however, find that high volume stocks earn higher average returns in each of five years prior to portfolio formation, while low volume stocks earn lower average returns. In addition, the authors show that share turnover is only weakly correlated with traditional liquidity proxies such as firm size, stock price, and relative spread. CHORDIA ET AL. (2001), on the other hand, report a persistently negative cross-sectional relationship between share turnover and returns even after controlling for past performance in their Fama-MacBeth cross-sectional regressions, thereby providing evidence in favor of turnover-liquidity relations. However, more recent results cast further doubt on the role of share turnover as a liquidity proxy: AGGARWAL/SUN (2003) show that share turnover is significantly negatively related to expected returns only for small capitalization stocks, while SUBRAHMANYAM (2005) finds this relation to be restricted to stocks with abnormally low stock price performance in the recent past. Finally, ROUWENHORST (1999) finds no evidence of a relation between expected returns and turnover in emerging markets and concludes that return premiums do not reflect a compensation for illiquidity.

Another study by CHAN/FAFF (2005) questions the appropriateness of using dollar volume as a liquidity proxy because of a potential size bias.

These empirical challenges to the liquidity premium hypothesis and the role of different measures of trading volume therein entail two consequences: first, the chosen measures of trading volume might not be a good proxy for liquidity and need to be replaced by different proxies. Secondly, there might exist different explanations for the vast empirical evidence of a negative relationship between trading volume and expected returns. Solutions to the former issue are outlined subsequently, while the latter will be discussed in the next section.

So far only two elements of liquidity were considered, namely *trading quantity* and *trading cost*. More recent empirical studies on the liquidity premium hypothesis focus on the other two aspects, *price impact* and *trading speed*.

Price impact: AMIHUD (2002) introduces an 'illiquidity ratio', defined as the average daily absolute price change per dollar of trading volume, and finds a significant negative effect of liquidity on expected returns over a 34-year period, even after controlling for size, beta, and momentum.

Trading speed: LIU (2006) introduces an additional liquidity measure defined as the standardized share turnover-adjusted number of zero daily trading volumes over the prior 12 months. While the focus of the measure is on trading speed, mainly the potential delay or difficulty in executing an order, the author claims to also capture aspects of trading quantity and trading cost.[12] This new measure supports the liquidity premium hypothesis with the least liquid decile stocks significantly outperforming the most liquid decile stocks over a 12-month holding period.[13]

Measure for order-driven markets: evidence on Australian stock exchange data is inconclusive. While MARSHALL/YOUNG (2003) find a negative relationship between share turnover and returns (indicating a positive liquidity premium), they at the same time find a negative spread-return relationship (indicating a negative liquidity premium). A potential explanation for this empirical phenomenon is given by MARSHALL (2006), suggesting that liquidity proxies in large hybrid quote-driven markets might yield inconsistent results in tests of the return-liquidity relationship on small pure order-driven markets.[14] Thus, the author develops a new measure for order-driven markets, 'Weighted Order Value', incorporating bid-ask spreads as well as market depth, and

---

[12] LIU (2006) shows that the new measure is highly correlated with other commonly used liquidity measures such as the bid-ask spread and share turnover.

[13] The results are robust to various controls for firm characteristics associated with stock returns.

[14] The author builds on AITKEN/WINN (1997) who report almost 70 measures of liquidity used in the literature with little or no correlation between many of them.

reports a significant liquidity-return relationship when controlling for beta, size, book-to-market equity, and return on equity.

Table 2.2: Selected Studies on Relationship between Liquidity and Expected Returns

Author(s)	Sample Data	Sample Period	Type of Liquidity	Frequency	Negative Relationship Lagged Liquidity-Return?
AMIHUD/ MENDELSON (1986)	Individual NYSE/AMEX stocks	1961-1980	Bid-ask spread (trading cost)	Monthly/ Yearly	Yes
ELESWARAPU/ REINGANUM (1993)	Individual NYSE stocks	1961-1990	Bid-ask spread (trading cost)	Monthly	January only
ELESWARAPU (1997)	Individual NASDAQ stocks	1973-1990	Bid-ask spread (trading cost)	Monthly	Yes
CHALMERS/ KADLEC (1998)	US domiciled NYSE/AMEX stocks	1983-1992	Amortized spread (trading cost)	Yearly	Inconclusive
MARSHALL/ YOUNG (2003)	Individual stocks listed on Australian Stock Exchange	1994-1998	Monthly bid-ask spread, amortized spread (trading cost)	Monthly	No
AMIHUD (2002)	Individual NYSE stocks	1963-1997	Average of daily absolute price change per dollar of daily trading volume (price impact)	Monthly	Yes
LIU (2006)	Individual NYSE/ AMEX, NASDAQ stocks	1960-2003	Number of zero daily trading volumes over the prior 12 months (*trading speed*, trading quantity, trading cost)	Monthly/ Yearly	Yes
MARSHALL (2006)	Individual stocks listed on Australian Stock Exchange	1991-2002	Weighted order value	Monthly	Yes

Sensitivity to market-wide liquidity: finally, PASTOR/STAMBAUGH (2003) find that stocks with high sensitivities to market-wide liquidity (i.e., with higher 'liquidity betas') have higher expected returns. Their monthly aggregate liquidity measure is a cross-sectional average of individual-stock liquidity measures, defined as the average effect that a given volume on day *d* has on the return for day *d+1*.

This section concludes with a table summarizing selected empirical studies on the relationship between liquidity measures and expected returns, sorted by the type or element of liquidity studied (Table 2.2). Literature on the *trading quantity* aspect of liquidity is omitted to avoid duplication with studies reported in Table 2.1. The next section provides an alternative explanation for the empirically established negative cross-sectional volume-return relationship in light of the doubts around the liquidity premium hypothesis and the role of different measures of trading volume therein.

2.1.1.3 Misperception of Future Earnings Hypothesis

LEE/SWAMINATHAN (2000) provide a behavioral explanation for the fact that *low turnover stocks experience higher future returns* while at the same time *systematically earning lower average returns in the five years prior to portfolio formation.*[15] The authors show that analysts provide lower long-term earnings growth forecasts for low volume stocks. But these firms experience significantly better future operating performance and report significantly positive short-window earnings announcements over the next eight quarters. Low volume firms seem to surprise the market with these systematically higher future earnings, a phenomenon LEE/SWAMINATHAN (2000) label 'investor misperceptions about future earnings'.

2.1.2 Change in Volume

Having discussed previous research on volume levels, we now present studies on the relationship between different measures of change in volume and subsequent stock returns.

Focusing on unusual short-term volume, there is strong evidence in both US and international stock market data of a positive correlation between 'volume shocks' and expected returns. The dominant theoretical explanation for such a high-volume return premium is

[15] For simplicity, only the relation between low turnover stocks and subsequent returns is reported here. However, all findings are valid for high turnover stocks as well, in the opposite direction.

the notion of increased investor visibility. When studying longer-term relationships, however, evidence is not as clear with different measures yielding different results.

2.1.2.1 Short-Term Studies

2.1.2.1.1 Empirical Findings

Table 2.3 summarizes results of important empirical studies on the relationship between short-term change in volume (i.e., day / week) and subsequent stock returns. First, YING (1966), analyzing stock index data, finds that increases in daily trading volume on the NYSE are followed by a rise in the price of the S&P 500 Composite Index.[16]

GERVAIS ET AL. (2001) extend Ying's analysis by studying 'unusual' volume effects for individual NYSE stocks over a 34-year time period. In their *daily sample*, the authors split the time-interval into intervals of 50 trading days, using the first 49 days as the reference period and the last day of the interval as the formation period. The *weekly sample* is constructed in a similar way.[17] At the end of each interval, stocks are labeled 'high volume stocks' if the formation period volume is among the top 5 out of 50 daily volumes (i.e., top 10%), 'low volume stocks' if the formation period volume is among the bottom 5 out of 50 daily volumes, and 'normal volume stocks' otherwise. Using portfolio-based tests, the authors show that stocks experiencing *unusually high trading volume* over a day or a week ('high volume stocks') *appreciate in the following month* while stocks experiencing *unusually low trading volume* ('low volume stocks') have a particularly weak performance in the following month.[18] This basic result, which the authors label 'high-volume return premium', remains unchanged when controlling for size (although the premium decreases in firm size), return autocorrelations, firm announcements, market risk, and liquidity (measured by bid-ask spreads), as well as when

[16] And vice versa, i.e., decreases in daily trading volume on the NYSE are followed by a fall in the S&P 500 price.

[17] The total time-interval is split into trading intervals of 10 weeks, the first 9 weeks being used as reference period and the last week as formation period.

[18] GERVAIS ET AL. (2001) use two different portfolio formation strategies, *zero investment portfolios* (taking long positions in high volume stocks and short positions in low volume stocks) and *reference return portfolios* (adjusting the weight given to trading intervals according to the number of high or low volume stocks in the interval).

applying different measures of trading volume.[19] In the daily sample, profits level off for longer-term returns, i.e., holding periods of 50 and 100 trading days. Positive returns based on weekly volume shocks, however, persist up to the 100-day test period.

Table 2.3: Selected Studies on Relationship between Short-Term Change in Volume and Expected Returns

Author(s)	Sample Data	Sample Period	Type of Volume	Time horizon	Positive Relationship Lagged Volume Change-Return?
YING (1966)	NYSE/ S&P 500 index	1957-1962	Number of shares traded	Short-term	Yes
GERVAIS/ KANIEL/ MINGELGRIN (2001)	Individual NYSE stocks	1963-1996	Number of shares traded, dollar volume, detrended volume, further measures	Short-term	Yes
AGGARWAL/ SUN (2003)	NYSE and AMEX stocks	1962-2000	Daily share turnover	Short-term	Yes (for small stocks)
KANIEL/LI/ STARKS (2007)	Individual stocks in 41 countries	1963-2001	Number of shares traded	Short-term	Yes

AGGARWAL/SUN (2003) confirm the existence of a 'high-volume return premium' in US markets, but only for stocks of small size. Finally, KANIEL ET AL. (2007) extend the analysis of a potential high-volume return premium to 41 countries and also confirm previous results for most of these markets.[20] Note that the sample periods in KANIEL ET AL. (2007) vary in different countries based on stock market data availability. In Switzerland, for example, the sample period comprises years 1989-2001 with an average of 65 stocks included in the analysis. The average return for zero-investment portfolios in the Swiss stock market held for 20 days is 0.65%, significant at the 1% level.[21]

---

[19] Besides *number of shares traded* and *dollar volume* measures, the authors also use *de-trended volume*, *firm specific volume*, and *day of the week corrected volume*. *De-trended volume* applies a weighting scheme putting more weight on the days closer to the formation period, *firm specific volume* uses the ratio of a stock's daily trading volume over that of the market, and *day of the week corrected volume* multiplies a stock's daily volume by a factor adjusting for differences in expected volume across days of the week.

[20] The authors use 70-day trading intervals with a 49-day reference period, a 1-day formation period, and a 20-day holding period.

[21] See KANIEL ET AL. (2007), tables 1 and 3.

2.1.2.1.2 Investor Visibility Hypothesis

GERVAIS ET AL. (2001) interpret the high-volume return premium caused by short-term volume shocks as a consequence of increased visibility of a stock leading to increased subsequent demand and price for that stock.

This *investor visibility hypothesis* goes back to MILLER (1977). The author claims that any shock attracting the attention of investors towards a given stock should lead to a price increase, because this additional attention increases the number of potential buyers (who did not have that stock on their 'radar' before[22]), while the number of potential sellers is mostly restricted to current stockholders.[23] In other words, the reluctance to make short sales[24] – or the existence of institutional constraints on short-selling – limits the response of most non-owners (to the additional visibility) to purchasing the stock or doing nothing, thereby increasing the demand for that stock and subsequently its price. Note that already MILLER (1977) explicitly refers to trading volume: 'if the [high] volume does attract attention and cause more people to look at a stock, some are likely to persuade themselves that the stock should be bought'. BARBER/ODEAN (2008) confirm the hypothesis that individual investors are net buyers of 'attention-grabbing stocks' due to the difficulty that investors have searching all stocks that they can potentially buy. Among other (non-volume based) attention measures, these authors use one-day unusual trading volume in their empirical tests.

2.1.2.2 Longer-Term Studies

2.1.2.2.1 Empirical Findings

The results are not as consistent when studying longer-term relationships between change in trading volume and expected returns (Table 2.4). However, one has to bear in mind that these studies use different measures of changes in trading volume: as mentioned previously, HAUGEN/BAKER (1996) run Fama-MacBeth type regressions of

[22] MILLER (1977) notes that realistically there are more securities available than the typical investor can evaluate.

[23] Similarly, MERTON (1987) develops a general equilibrium model in which stocks ignored by a large fraction of investors tend to sell at a discount. An additional related paper is written by MAYSHAR (1983).

[24] BARBER/ODEAN (2008) find that only 0.29% of positions (representing 0.78% of total value) of investors in their large discount brokerage dataset are short positions.

stock returns in the Russell 3000 stock index on over 40 firm characteristics. Besides reporting a statistically significant negative relationship between the ratio of dollar volume to market capitalization and returns, the authors also find a significant *negative relationship* between trading volume trend and monthly returns. This time trend is computed as the trailing five-year time trend divided by the five-year average trading volume for each stock. LEE/SWAMINATHAN (2000) form portfolios of NYSE/AMEX stocks based on change in trading volume as a measure of unusual trading volume. They find that firms whose *recent volume is higher (lower)* than the volume four years ago yield *significantly lower (higher) future returns* in the next 5 years.[25] Finally, WATKINS (2007), using quintile portfolios sorted on mean volume growth, finds that stocks with *high-mean volume growth* in the past 12 months experience *higher returns* over the next one to 60 months.

Table 2.4: Selected Studies on Relationship between Long-Term Change in Volume and Expected Returns

Author(s)	Sample Data	Sample Period	Type of Volume	Time horizon	Positive Relationship Lagged Volume Change-Return?
HAUGEN/BAKER (1996)	Stocks in Russell 3000 stock index	1979-1993	Dollar trading volume trend	Long-term	No
LEE/ SWAMINATHAN (2000)	All firms on NYSE and AMEX	1965-1995	Increase in share turnover	Long-term	No
WATKINS (2007)	NYSE/AMEX, and NASDAQ stocks	1963-1999	Mean share turnover growth	Long-term	Yes

2.1.2.2.2 Potential Interpretations

WATKINS (2007) interprets the *positive relationship* between high-mean turnover growth and subsequent returns as a long-horizon confirmation of GERVAIS ET AL. (2001). It is important to note, however, that the author uses a different measure of volume, namely turnover growth instead of 'volume shocks', which makes direct comparisons between the two studies difficult. HAUGEN/BAKER (1996), on the other hand,

[25] The exact definition of this volume measure is described in LEE/SWAMINATHAN (2000), 2059.

find that stocks characterized by growing levels of trading volume sell at prices that produce lower expected returns and interpret this finding as additional evidence for a liquidity premium. This is in direct contradiction with LEE/SWAMINATHAN (2000). These authors compare the predictive power of change in trading volume and lagged trading volume (for the latter see above, 2.1.1) and find that most of the long-term predictive power of trading volume (i.e., over the next five years) is attributable to recent changes in the level of trading volume rather than lagged volume. The authors interpret this finding as evidence supporting the argument that past turnover is a measure of fluctuating investor sentiment rather than a liquidity proxy.

2.1.3 Variability in Volume

An additional result by CHORDIA ET AL. (2001) needs further investigation, the *negative cross-sectional relationship of variability in trading volume* (measured either as the standard deviation of dollar volume / share turnover or the 'coefficient of variation' in dollar volume / share turnover) *and expected returns*, which is confirmed by KEENE/PETERSON (2007) (see Table 2.5). Intuitively, CHORDIA ET AL. (2001) expect investors to be risk averse and dislike variability in liquidity, resulting in stocks with greater variability commanding higher expected returns. The authors' data, however, does not support this hypothesis.

Table 2.5: Selected Studies on Relationship between Variability in Volume and Expected Returns

Author	Sample Data	Sample Period	Type of Volume	Frequency	Negative Relationship Lagged Variability in Volume-Return?
CHORDIA/ SUBRAHMANYAM/ ANSHUMAN (2001)	Common NYSE/ AMEX stocks, NASDAQ-listed companies	1966-1995	Volatility of trading volume/ turnover	Monthly	Yes
KEENE/PETERSON (2007)	Individual US stocks	1963-2002	Volatility of trading volume/ turnover	Monthly/ Yearly	Yes

Clientele effect hypothesis as a potential explanation: CHORDIA ET AL. (2001) refer to MERTON (1987), who shows that stocks with greater investor following should command lower expected returns, and suggest that volatility of trading volume might proxy for heterogeneity of clientele holding a stock. If high volatility implies a shift towards a more heterogeneous group of potential investors interested in a particular stock, such a shift would result in lower required returns, as indicated by their empirical results. However, when the number of analysts following a company is added to the Fama-MacBeth regressions, the effect of volatility of trading volume on expected returns remains strongly significant. In that sense, this clientele effect hypothesis is unable to consistently explain the nature of a potentially negative relationship between variability in volume and expected returns.

2.2 Trading Volume and Return Autocorrelations

A second area of research on volume-return relations focuses on the joint influence of past trading volume and past return on the cross-section of stock returns. Because different time-horizons studied exhibit different dynamics, previous research presented is divided into longer-term and shorter-term studies.

2.2.1 Longer-Term Studies

Recent research documents the existence of a price momentum effect in stock returns, meaning that stocks outperforming the average stock market during the past months tend to sustain this outperformance over the next months. JEGADEESH/TITMAN (1993), for example, find that for the US market (NYSE/AMEX stocks) zero-cost momentum portfolios with long positions in past winners and short positions in past losers yield significant average profits over the 1965-1989 time period. This finding is confirmed by numerous other studies across different markets and time periods.[26] While the momentum effect is mainly observed in the intermediate time-horizon (3 to 12 months), other research shows that this effect reverses in the long-run, i.e., over investment periods of three to five years.[27] DE BONDT/THALER (1985), for example, find that prior losers

[26] See REY/SCHMID (2007) for a recent study using Switzerland's largest blue-chip stocks.

[27] See for example DE BONDT/THALER (1985), FAMA/FRENCH (1988), and BALVERS ET AL. (2000).

outperform prior winners by about 25% 36 months after portfolio formation (strategies exploiting this price reversal are denoted 'contrarian strategies').[28] Our main interest here lies on the influence of trading volume on these medium- and long-term momentum / reversal dynamics.

2.2.1.1 Empirical Findings

Table 2.6 provides a summary of empirical results of previous studies on the influence of trading volume on intermediate-term momentum strategies.

Table 2.6: Selected Studies on Influence of Volume on Momentum Strategies

Author(s)	Sample Data	Sample Period	Type of Volume	Positive Relationship Volume/Momentum?
LEE/ SWAMINATHAN (2000)	All firms on NYSE and AMEX	1965-1995	Share turnover	Yes
HAMEED/ KUSNADI (2002)	Individual securities (>1,000) traded on six Asian markets	1981-1994	Share turnover	(Yes)
GLASER/WEBER (2003)	446 companies listed on the Frankfurt Stock Exchange	1988-2001	Share turnover	Yes
WANG/CHIN (2004)	All A-shares traded on Shanghai and Shenzhen stock exchanges	1994-2000	Share turnover	No
SUBRAHMANYAM (2005)	Individual NYSE/AMEX and NASDAQ stocks	NYSE/AMEX: 1962-2004 NASDAQ: 1982-2004	Share turnover	Yes

Using portfolio-based tests, most researchers find that the *momentum effect* is *stronger among high volume stocks*. LEE/SWAMINATHAN (2000), in a study on US stock market data, find that portfolios which are long in high volume winners and short in high volume losers yield significantly higher returns than portfolios which are long in

[28] DE BONDT/THALER (1985) study portfolios based on NYSE common stocks in the 1926-1982 time period.

low volume winners and short in low volume losers. The authors find that this result is primarily driven by high volume losers.[29] Note, however, that the authors find an even more profitable portfolio strategy with a *long-position in low volume winners and a short-position in high volume losers*. GLASER/WEBER (2003) confirm the finding that momentum strategies are more profitable among high turnover stocks in a similar study using German stock market data. But their result is mainly driven by high volume winners, i.e., the return differential in the winner portfolio. HAMEED/KUSNADI (2002) also find weak evidence in favor of the above relation in emerging stock markets. While low turnover stocks do not exhibit momentum in any of six Asian stock markets studied, momentum strategies are profitable among high turnover stocks in two out of six countries (namely Malaysia and South Korea). WANG/CHIN (2004), however, find contradicting evidence. These authors report that low volume momentum strategies outperform high volume momentum strategies in the Chinese stock markets.[30]

Not much focus has been given to studying the influence of trading volume on return autocorrelations over time-horizons above one year.[31] One exception is LEE/ SWAMINATHAN (2000). These authors confirm the existence of long-term price reversal in US stock market data (i.e., price momentum effects reverse over the next five years), with high volume winners and low volume losers experiencing faster reversal.

2.2.1.2 Momentum Life Cycle Hypothesis and Other Potential Explanations

Several authors, for example GLASER/WEBER (2003) or LEE/SWAMINATHAN (2000), adjust returns for known risk factors (e.g., size, book-to-market ratio) or other effects known to affect momentum profits (e.g., industry effects). While this reduces both magnitude of returns and significance of results, indicating that the results are to some extent a size, book-to-market and industry effect, the basic effects hold even when using adjusted returns. Therefore, the authors try to align their evidence with existing behavioral models on the influence of trading volume on return autocorrelations:

---

[29] The authors find that low volume losers rebound strongly in the next 12 months relative to high volume losers.

[30] However, the authors also note that the difference in mean returns is significant at the 10% level only for the 3-month formation period.

[31] This might be primarily driven by data availability constraints outside the US.

A first model by HONG/STEIN (1999) predicts larger momentum profits for stocks with slower information diffusion (i.e., initial market underreaction). If a low level of trading volume serves as a proxy for slow information diffusion, the model predicts greater momentum for low volume stocks. However, this is not supported by most empirical evidence (one exception is the study by WANG/CHIN (2004) on the Chinese stock markets).

A second model by DANIEL ET AL. (1998) argues that stocks that are more difficult to value (e.g., growth stocks) tend to generate greater overconfidence among investors which leads to an initial market overreaction to news about fundamentals. Because LEE/SWAMINATHAN (2000) find that high volume stocks behave more like growth stocks in their sample, this model entails the implicit assumption that high trading volume 'fuels' momentum.[32] This is generally in line with most of the existing evidence that momentum is more pronounced among high volume stocks. LEE/SWAMINATHAN (2000), however, show that this effect is only true for losers. While high volume losers continue to lose (i.e., momentum effect), returns to portfolios consisting of low volume losers revert quickly. The opposite is true for winners (high volume winners experience fast reversals while low volume winners exhibit momentum).

As a result, LEE/SWAMINATHAN (2000) present another model incorporating the role of trading volume as an important empirical link between intermediate-horizon return continuation and long-horizon return reversal. Before outlining the 'momentum life cycle hypothesis', let us quickly summarize their most important empirical findings:

1. *Low volume winners* and *high volume losers* exhibit most *momentum* in the intermediate term.

2. High volume winners and low volume losers experience fastest reversal.

3. Momentum strategies are more profitable among high volume stocks.

[32] The authors find that high volume stocks have smaller loadings on the FAMA/FRENCH (1993) HML factor.

Figure 2.1: Momentum Life Cycle Hypothesis[33]

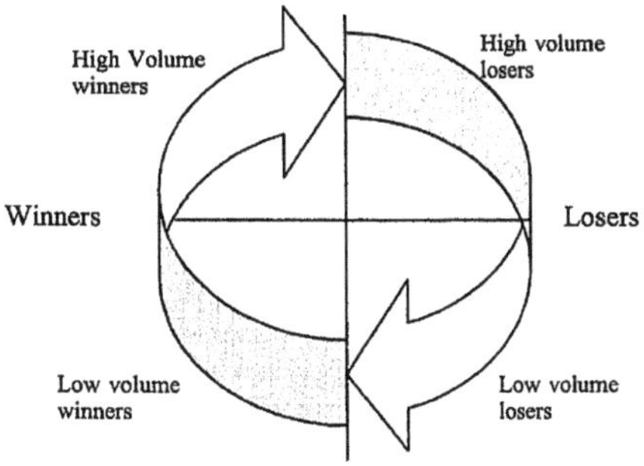

According to the momentum life cycle hypothesis illustrated in Figure 2.1, stocks undergo intervals of glamour and neglect with trading volume being the indicator of the level of investor interest in a stock. Taking low volume winners as an example, these stocks are in an early stage move from neglect to glamour. Thus, they are expected to have higher subsequent returns than high volume winners, which are nearly through the interval of glamour and are expected to subsequently reverse. Because of the dynamics illustrated in Figure 2.1 low volume winners and high volume losers are labeled early stage momentum stocks, while high volume winners and low volume losers are late stage momentum stocks. This model helps to incorporate the first two empirical findings in LEE/SWAMINATHAN (2000). What the model fails to address, however, is the third empirical finding that momentum strategies are generally more profitable among high volume stocks.[34]

2.2.2 Shorter-Term Studies

While previous research finds that prices revert in the long-run, i.e., over investment periods of three to five years, the same negative return autocorrelations have been observed over very short (daily / weekly) time horizons. JEGADEESH (1990) for example

[33] LEE/SWAMINATHAN (2000), 2063 p.

[34] In addition, these authors point out that the momentum life cycle is based on empirical findings on the portfolio level. For individual stocks, the dynamics are less deterministic.

shows that strategies exploiting short-run return reversals in individual stocks generate abnormal returns of 2.5% per month. Next, the potential role of trading volume on these short-term dynamics is described.

2.2.2.1 Empirical Findings

Table 2.7 summarizes results of selected studies on the influence of trading volume on short-term return autocorrelations, sorted based on the discovered relationship between volume and return autocorrelation.

Table 2.7: Selected Studies on Influence of Volume on Short-Term Return Autocorrelations

Author(s)	Sample Data	Sample Period	Type of Volume	Frequency	Relationship Volume/Return Autocorrelation?
CONRAD/ HAMEED/ NIDEN (1994)	Individual stocks listed on NASDAQ	1983-1990	Growth in number of transactions	Weekly	-
AVRAMOV/ CHORDIA/ GOYAL (2006)	Individual NYSE/AMEX stocks	1962-2002	Share turnover	Weekly	-
MCMILLAN (2007)	Stock indices in UK, US, France and Japan	1990-2004	Number of shares traded	Daily	-
STICKEL/ VERRECCHIA (1994)	Individual NYSE/AMEX and NASDAQ firms	1982-1990	Abnormal share turnover	Daily	+
COOPER (1999)	300 largest NYSE/AMEX stocks	1962-1993	Share turnover growth	Weekly	+
CHAN/ HAMEED/ TONG (2000)	Stock market indices from 17 countries	1980-1995	Change in dollar volume/share turnover	Weekly	+
LLORENTE/ MICHAELY/ SAAR/WANG (2002)	Individual NYSE/AMEX common stocks	1993-1998	Share turnover growth	Daily	o

Explanation of different types of relationships: '+' indicates that volume *increases (reduces) positive (negative) return autocorrelation*, '-' indicates that volume *reduces (increases) positive (negative) return autocorrelation, and 'o'* indicates that additional variables influence the relationship between volume and return autocorrelation.

The table shows that previous empirical studies on both individual stock and aggregate market levels find somewhat contradicting evidence regarding the influence of trading volume on short-term return autocorrelations:

One set of studies finds that volume *increases negative return autocorrelations* and / or *reduces positive return autocorrelations*. In other words, prices of heavily traded stocks tend to revert while prices of less traded stocks tend to experience momentum. CONRAD ET AL. (1994), for example, in a study of individual NASDAQ stocks, find that reversal profitability increases with trading volume, while less traded stocks exhibit return continuation. AVRAMOV ET AL. (2006) confirm that high turnover stocks exhibit higher negative serial correlation than low turnover stocks in a sample of NYSE/AMEX stocks. And in a study of four stock indices, MCMILLAN (2007) finds that returns exhibit positive serial correlation when volume is low, while returns tend to exhibit random behavior or weak reversion when volume is high.

Other studies find evidence of exactly the opposite relationship: STICKEL/ VERRECCHIA (1994), for example, find that price changes on earnings announcement days with weak volume support tend to revert, while price increases with strong volume support tend to be followed by another price increase the next day.[35] COOPER (1999), in a sample of large NYSE/AMEX stocks, also finds that trading volume reduces negative return autocorrelations and even makes them positive in some cases. And CHAN ET AL. (2000) find higher weekly momentum profits for portfolios of countries with high lagged trading volume in a study of stock market indices from 17 countries.

2.2.2.2 Market Structure Models Explaining Short-Term Return Autocorrelations

There exist several market structure models to explain the different evidence outlined above. CAMPBELL ET AL. (1993) propose a model with two groups of investors, 'noninformational' / 'liquidity' traders desiring to sell a stock for exogenous reasons, and 'market makers' accommodating this selling pressure if rewarded in form of a lower stock price and a higher expected return. As a result of this higher expected return required by the risk-averse utility maximizing 'market makers', non-informational trading

35 STICKEL/VERRECCHIA (1994) show that their results are robust to replication on non-announcement days.

causes price movements to revert. The authors then use stock market trading volume as an indicator of such non-informational trading and show that non-informed trading is accompanied by high trading volume. Informed trading, on the other hand, is accompanied by little trading volume, because the arrival of public information results in the fact that all investors adjust their valuation of the stock market. In sum, the model implies that price changes on days with high trading volume should revert, while price changes on days with low trading volume should not. Empirical findings by CONRAD ET AL. (1994) and AVRAMOV ET AL. (2006) are consistent with this model.

While the model by CAMPBELL ET AL. (1993) assumes an economy with symmetric information, WANG (1994) assumes a world of asymmetric information with two types of investors: uninformed investors (who trade for noninformational purposes, see above) and investors with superior information who trade both for informational and noninformational purposes. WANG (1994) then hypothesizes that when informed investors condition trades on private information, high returns are expected to continue when accompanied by high trading volume. The intuition behind this relation is that in a world of asymmetric information, uninformed investors do not know a priori whether they trade against uninformed investors or against informed investors' private information. When informational trading dominates, high realized returns signal to uninformed investors that they underestimated the value of the stock and thus underinvested in the stock. As a result, these uninformed investors subsequently buy more shares and expected future returns increase.

COOPER (1999) tests whether the effect of symmetric information and liquidity trading or asymmetric information and informed trading dominates in a dataset of large-capitalization stocks. His results support WANG'S (1994) asymmetric information model. COOPER (1999) then compares this to results of CONRAD ET AL. (1994) in a sample of relatively smaller NASDAQ stocks. One possible explanation for the opposite results is the following: in periods of large price movements, high volume for larger stocks might indicate a higher percentage of informed traders in WANG'S (1994) model (resulting in price continuation). High volume for smaller stocks, on the other hand, might represent a higher percentage of liquidity traders (resulting in price reversal).

However, the model and empirical evidence of LLORENTE ET AL. (2002) do not confirm COOPER'S (1999) intuition: these authors develop a simple equilibrium model similar to that of WANG (1994). In their model, returns generated by speculative trades tend to continue themselves, while returns generated by risk-sharing trades tend to reverse themselves. The empirical evidence then reveals that returns to stocks of smaller firms or stocks with higher bid-ask spreads (which the authors suggest to be proxies for a high degree of speculative trading) tend to continue following high volume days. The opposite is true for the returns of stocks of larger firms / market indices or stocks with smaller bid-ask spreads (which indicates low information asymmetry according to the authors).

2.3 Contemporaneous Volume-Return Relation

The so far discussed areas of research deal with the relationship between different measures of *trading volume* (as an isolated factor or in interaction with returns) and subsequent returns. However, much of the early research focused on the *contemporaneous* relationship between volume and returns. KARPOFF (1987), in a review article of previous studies in this specific field, examines two 'stylized' facts:

1. Existence of a positive relationship between volume and the *absolute value of the price change.*
2. Existence of a positive relationship between volume and the *price change per se.*

The following explanations are divided according to these two relationships.[36]

[36] Note that we focus on studies within equity markets. For research on bond and futures markets the interested reader is referred to the original paper (KARPOFF (1987)).

2.3.1 Correlation between Volume and Absolute Returns

There exists an old saying on Wall Street that 'it takes volume to make prices move[37]'. The implied positive correlation between volume and absolute returns has been strongly confirmed by prior research (note, however, that 'correlation' says little about the asserted casualty[38]). Two alternative explanations for this empirical phenomenon are the *sequential information arrival model* and the *mixture of distributions hypothesis (MDH).*

2.3.1.1 Empirical Findings

Table 2.8 provides a summary of selected previous studies on the contemporaneous relationship between volume and absolute returns, sorted by the time of study.

The table shows that prior research almost unanimously confirms the hypothesized positive correlation between volume and absolute returns across various frequencies, aggregation levels and sample periods: CROUCH (1970a, 1970b) finds a positive correlation between absolute values of daily price changes and daily volumes for both individual stocks and market indices. JAIN/JOH (1988) confirm this finding over one-hour intervals using market index data. LEE/SWAMINATHAN (2000) find share turnover to be positively correlated with absolute returns in a study using monthly data on a more than 30 year time-period. And COMISKEY ET AL. (1987) find the hypothesized correlation even in yearly data on individual stocks. HARRIS (1983, 1986, 1987) investigates the relationship between volume and the square of price change in individual stocks and also finds a positive correlation (this correlation is weaker for transaction data). GURGUL ET AL. (2007), finally, confirm this positive correlation between volume and squared stock returns in daily data of individual stocks.[39]

[37] KARPOFF (1987), 112.

[38] See KARPOFF (1987), 112.

[39] GURGUL ET AL. (2007) include squared stock returns in their analyses as a measure of realized return volatility.

Table 2.8: Selected Studies on Contemporaneous Relationship between Volume and Absolute Returns[40]

Author(s)	Sample Data	Sample Period	Frequency	Positive Volume-Absolute Return Correlation?
GODFREY/ GRANGER MORGENSTERN (1964)	Stock market *aggregates*	1959-1962	Transactions, daily, weekly	No
	3 common stocks	1951-1953, 1963	Transactions, daily, weekly	No
CROUCH (1970a)	5 common stocks	1963-1967	Daily	Yes
CROUCH (1970b)	Stock market *aggregates*, 3 common stocks	1966-1968	Hourly, daily	Yes
HARRIS (1983)	16 common stocks	1968-1969	Daily	Yes
HARRIS (1986)	479 common stocks	1976-1977	Daily	Yes
COMISKEY/ WALKLING/ WEEKS (1987)	211 common stocks	1976-1979	Yearly	Yes
HARRIS (1987)	50 common stocks	1981-1983	Transactions, daily	Yes
JAIN/JOH (1988)	S&P 500 index	1979-1983	Hourly	Yes
LEE/ SWAMINATHAN (2000)	Stocks on NYSE and AMEX	1965-1995	Monthly	Yes
GURGUL/ MAJDOSZ/ MESTEL (2007)	Individual DAX stocks	1994-2005	Daily	Yes

[40] For all studies prior to 1987, see KARPOFF (1987), 113.

2.3.1.2 Potential Explanations of Positive Volume-Absolute Return Correlation[41]

Two competing theoretical explanations for the observed positive volume-absolute return correlation are the *'sequential information arrival model'* and the *'mixture of distributions hypothesis'*. Below follows a brief outline of these models. For a more detailed overview as well as model extensions, the interested reader is referred to KARPOFF (1987).

Sequential information arrival model: COPELAND (1976, 1977) develops a model in which information is disseminated sequentially (i.e., one trader at a time) rather than simultaneously, which implies a positive volume-absolute return correlation. The information causes a one-time upward shift in each 'optimist's' demand curve by a fixed amount δ and a downshift of δ in each 'pessimist's' demand curve, thereby initiating a trade after each trader receives information. This results in a sequence of transitional equilibria accompanied by high trading volume. One major criticism of the model, addressed by KARPOFF (1987), is Copeland's assumption that uninformed traders do not learn about the information from informed traders' actions.

Mixture of distributions hypothesis (MDH): an alternative strand of literature analyzes the distribution of speculative assets. At the outset lies the observation that the daily price changes of speculative assets seem uncorrelated with each other and symmetrically distributed, but the distribution is in fact kurtotic relative to the normal distribution. One explanation for this phenomenon, the *mixture of distributions hypothesis (MDH),* is that daily returns are sampled from a set of distributions with different variances. EPPS/EPPS (1976) develop a MDH model in which the variance of the price change on single transactions is conditional on the volume of that transaction (which implies that transaction price changes are then mixtures of distributions with volume as mixing variable). As a result, these models imply the observed contemporaneous positive correlation between volume and absolute returns.[42]

---

[41] See KARPOFF (1987), 113 pp.

[42] Strictly speaking, the model implies a positive correlation between volume and the *variance of returns*. However, absolute returns as expressed by the squared value of stock returns are often used as a proxy of realized return volatility. See for example GURGUL ET AL. (2007).

Note that EPPS/EPPS' (1976) model cannot be mutually consistent with COPELAND (1976, 1977), since it requires all investors to receive information simultaneously. More specifically, Copeland's model implies a negative volume-absolute return correlation when simultaneous information arrival is imposed. One general drawback of both types of models is that they do not imply a relation between volume and returns (i.e., the price change per se), which is inconsistent with below evidence.[43]

2.3.2 Correlation between Volume and Returns

A second popular Wall Street saying is that 'volume is relatively heavy in bull markets and light in bear markets[44]', implying a positive correlation between volume and returns. While some empirical findings are inconsistent with such a correlation between volume and returns, most research generally supports the hypothesis. One possible explanation for a positive volume-return correlation is the relatively large cost of short-selling.

2.3.2.1 Empirical Findings

Table 2.9 and Table 2.10 provide a summary of selected previous empirical studies on the contemporaneous relationship between volume and returns, thereby illustrating the somewhat mixed results. Previous studies are sorted based on whether the author(s) investigated individual stocks or aggregate stock markets / indices.

Individual stocks (Table 2.9): EPPS (1977) shows that the ratio of volume to return is greater for *transactions* in which the price ticks up than for transactions on downticks. WOOD ET AL. (1985), however, find this ratio to be larger on downticks. Directly analyzing the relationship between volume and returns, HARRIS (1986, 1987) finds a positive correlation in both *transactions* and *daily* data. In a very recent empirical study of individual stocks in the German DAX index, however, GURGUL ET AL. (2007) find no correlation between *daily* volume and returns. Investigating *longer-term* relations, COMISKEY ET AL. (1987) find a positive correlation using *annual* measures of share turnover and returns in a study of 211 common stocks. LEE/SWAMINATHAN (2000), finally, build portfolios based on past share turnover and returns using *monthly* data.

---

43 See KARPOFF (1987), 116.

44 KARPOFF (1987), 117.

They find that extreme winners have higher turnover than extreme losers, thereby supporting the hypothesis of a positive contemporaneous correlation between volume and returns.

Table 2.9: Selected Studies on Contemporaneous Relationship between Volume and Returns (Individual Stocks)[45]

Author(s)	Sample Data	Sample Period	Frequency	Positive Volume-Return Correlation?
GODFREY/GRANGER MORGENSTERN (1964)	3 common stocks	1951-1953, 1963	Transactions, daily, weekly	No
EPPS (1977)	20 common stocks	Jan 1971	Transactions, daily	Yes
JAMES/EDMISTER (1983)	500 common stocks	1975, 1977-1979	Daily	No
WOOD/MCINISH/ORD (1985)	946 common stocks	1971-1972	Minutes	No
	1138 common stocks	1982		
HARRIS (1986)	479 common stocks	1976-1977	Daily	Yes
COMISKEY/WALKLING/ WEEKS (1987)	211 common stocks	1976-1979	Yearly	Yes
HARRIS (1987)	50 common stocks	1981-1983	Transactions, daily	Yes
LEE/SWAMINATHAN (2000)	Stocks on NYSE and AMEX	1965-1995	Monthly	Yes
GURGUL/ MAJDOSZ/ MESTEL (2007)	Individual DAX stocks	1994-2005	Daily	No

45 For studies prior to 1987 see KARPOFF (1987), 118.

Aggregate stock markets (Table 2.10): it was reported earlier (see above, 2.3.1.1) that JAIN/JOH (1988) find volume to be positively related to the magnitude of return over one-hour intervals using S&P 500 index data. In addition, the authors find volume to be more sensitive to positive than negative returns. LEE/RUI (2000) also find a positive contemporaneous relationship between trading volume and returns in all four of China's stock markets, even after taking into account heteroskedasticity.[46] Finally, LEE/RUI (2002) confirm a positive volume-return relationship in a study of three stock market indices in New York, Tokyo and London.

Table 2.10: Selected Studies on Contemporaneous Relationship between Volume and Returns (Aggregate Markets) [47]

Author(s)	Sample Data	Sample Period	Frequency	Positive Volume-Return Correlation?
GODFREY/ GRANGER MORGENSTERN (1964)	Stock market *aggregates*	1959-1962	Transactions, daily, weekly	No
JAIN/JOH (1988)	S&P 500 index	1979-1983	Hourly	Yes
LEE/RUI (2000)	*Aggregates* from China's 4 stock markets	Shanghai A: 1990-1997 Shanghai B, Shenzhen A, Shenzhen B: 1992-1997	Daily	Yes
LEE/RUI (2002)	3 stock market *indices* (S&P 500 index, Tokyo Stock Exchange Price Index, Financial Times-Stock Exchange 100)	S&P 500: 1973-1999 TOPIX: 1974-1999 FT-SE 100: 1986-1999	Daily	Yes

46 The authors control for non-normality of error distribution (non-constant variance) by means of a GARCH (1,1) model. For an introduction to GARCH models see for example BROOKS (2002), 452 pp.

47 For studies prior to 1987 see KARPOFF (1987), 118.

2.3.2.2 Costly Short Sales Hypothesis[48]

In COPELAND'S (1976, 1977) sequential information arrival model (see above, 2.3.1.2), short selling is prohibited. JENNINGS ET AL. (1981) therefore extend this model to allow for short selling. Short sales, however, are generally more costly than long positions, which restricts some investors' ability to trade on new information. As a result, JENNINGS ET AL. (1981) show that, in general, volume is smaller when a previously uninformed trader interprets new information pessimistically than when the trader is an optimist. Because the price increases with an optimist who buys and decreases with a pessimist who sells, it is then inferred that volume is relatively high when prices increase (i.e., positive returns) and relatively low when prices decrease (i.e., negative returns). The *costly short sales hypothesis* is supported by the lack of empirical evidence of a positive correlation between volume and returns in futures markets, where costs of taking long and short positions are symmetric.

2.4 Lagged Return-Volume Relationship

The so far discussed volume-return research focuses either on the relationship between lagged trading volume and subsequent returns (i.e., the influence of volume on returns) or on contemporaneous volume-return relations. This section complements previous discussions by focusing on the *influence of returns on trading volume*. We present two empirical findings:

1. There exists a positive relationship between *returns* and *subsequent trading volume*.
2. There exists a positive relationship between *price extremes and subsequent trading volume*.

Possible explanations of these findings are the *'overconfidence hypothesis'* (first finding) and the *'attention hypothesis'* (second finding). This section is divided according to the two findings and their respective explanations.

[48] See KARPOFF (1987), 118 p.

2.4.1 Overconfidence Hypothesis

Table 2.11 summarizes three empirical studies on the relationship between stock returns and subsequent trading volume. All three studies find this relationship to be positive.

Table 2.11: Selected Studies on Relation between Returns and Subsequent Trading Volume

Author(s)	Sample Data	Sample Period	Type of Volume	Frequency	Positive Relationship Lagged Return-Volume?
GALLANT/ ROSSI/ TAUCHEN (1992)	S&P composite stock index	1928-1985	Number of shares traded on NYSE	Daily	Yes
BARBER/ ODEAN (2002)	1,600 individual investors	1991-1996	Stock portfolio turnover	Monthly	Yes
GLASER/ WEBER (2005)	3,000 individual investors	1997-2001	Stock portfolio turnover, number of stock transactions	Monthly	Yes

GALLANT ET AL. (1992), in a study of US aggregate stock market data, find that price changes lead to volume movements. BARBER/ODEAN (2002) use an event-based approach to test whether past performance induces subsequent trading. From a sample of 78,000 households with brokerage accounts at large discount brokers the authors select those 1,600 investors who switched from phone-based to online trading during a 7-year sample period (with 'time of switching' as the event). In addition, the authors employ a matched-pair research design to compare online and phone-based traders by size-matching each online investor to an investor whose market value of common stocks is the closest to that of the online trader.[49] The authors confirm the existence of a positive relationship between past returns and subsequent trading volume based on two pieces of evidence: first, they show that the average online investor outperforms both the market and the average size-matched investor by roughly 2% prior to switching to online trading.[50] And second, trading volume significantly increases after switching to online trad-

[49] Size matching is performed in the month preceding the online investor's first online trade.

[50] This figure represents annualized portfolio returns net of trading costs.

ing, an effect persisting at least over the following two years.[51] GLASER/WEBER (2005) analyze the relationship between returns and subsequent trading volume studying 3,000 individual investors over a 51-month period using panel regressions. They find that both past market returns and past portfolio returns are significantly positively related to subsequent trading volume (at four lags).[52]

Results of the presented studies are consistent with theoretical models of *investor overconfidence.*[53] In short, these models propose that high returns make investors overconfident, leading to higher subsequent trading. DANIEL ET AL. (1998) develop a model in which *overconfidence*, modeled as the degree of the underestimation of the variance of signals, is *a function of past investment success*.[54] The authors' modeling assumption is based on models of a self-attribution bias, which means that people overestimate the degree to which they are responsible for their own success.[55] In a stock market investment context, self-attribution bias means that high market returns make some investors overconfident about the precision of their information. Because these investors attribute gains in wealth to their personal ability to pick stocks, they underestimate the variance of stock returns. Overconfidence models by ODEAN (1998a) and GERVAIS/ODEAN (2001) build on these assumptions and establish a link between past returns and trading volume. GERVAIS/ODEAN (2001), for example, develop a multi-period market model describing the process by which traders learn about their ability and how self-attribution in this learning creates overconfident traders. The model predicts both that overconfidence is higher after gains (and lower after losses), and that overconfident traders will increase their trading volume because of inappropriately tight error bounds around return forecasts. GLASER/WEBER (2005) note, however, that this model analyzes an economy with only one risky asset, which means that total market return and portfolio

---

51 The trading volume measure used is an investor's monthly turnover, which is one-half the total value of purchases and sales divided by the sum of month-end position statements.

52 Trading volume is measured by *monthly stock portfolio turnover* (i.e., the sum of absolute values of purchases and sales per month divided by the respective end-of-month stock portfolio position), the *number of stock transactions over the whole sample period*, and the *probability to trade stocks in a given month*.

53 To be precise, this is not entirely true for GALLANT ET AL. (1992). As noted by STATMAN ET AL. (2006), the nonparametric methodology used by these authors does not yield interpretations relevant to the overconfidence hypothesis.

54 This model was already mentioned in the context of potential explanations for volume-momentum interactions. See 2.2.1.2.

55 See GLASER/WEBER (2005) for an overview of psychological studies on this self-attribution bias.

returns are identical. As a result, the GERVAIS/ODEAN (2001) model makes no prediction which past returns affect overconfidence and thus trading volume. As reported in their empirical findings, GLASER/WEBER (2005) show that both the market return and portfolio returns are significantly positively related to subsequent trading volume.

2.4.2 Attention Hypothesis

In addition to previous research on the relationship between returns and subsequent trading volume, there also exists a study on the relationship between price extremes and subsequent trading volume. HUDDART ET AL. (2006) examine the relation between a stock's trading volume and its price relative to the 52-week high / low trading range and find a substantial increase in trading volume after a stock's price exits this range (i.e., when the stock trades above the highest or below the lowest price of the benchmark period).[56] This result is robust to controlling for contemporaneous and past returns as well as news arrivals. The authors consider the attention hypothesis by BARBER/ODEAN (2008), which is also mentioned in 2.1.2.1.2, as a potential explanation for their results. In this model, investors considering a buying decision face an overwhelming range of potential stocks and focus on the subset that has caught their attention.[57] [58] HUDDART ET AL. (2006) consider the breach of a prior trading range as such an event triggering investor attention.

Table 2.12: Relationship between Price Extremes and Subsequent Trading Volume

Author(s)	Sample Data	Sample Period	Type of Volume	Frequency	Positive Relationship Price Extreme-Volume?
HUDDART/ YETMAN/ LANG (2006)	Random sample of 2,000 common stocks listed on NYSE, AMEX or NASDAQ	1982-2006	Share turnover (individual, aggregate)	Weekly	Yes

[56] The 52-week benchmark period ends 20 trading days before the last day of the observation week.

[57] As noted in HUDDART ET AL. (2006), the effect of the attention hypothesis is less pronounced for investors considering a selling decision because these investors focus on a limited universe, i.e., the stocks currently in their portfolios.

[58] Note the similarity to the investor visibility hypothesis as a potential explanation for the observed high-volume return premium caused by short-term abnormal trading volume (see above, 2.1.2.1.2).

2.5 Dynamic Volume-Return Relation

2.5.1 Vector Autoregressive Models (VARs)

A final and more recent area of research discussed here investigates the joint dynamics between stock returns and trading volume using vector autoregressive models (VARs). There are mainly two differences between these models and previously discussed research: first, VARs study *pure time-series, not cross-sectional data*. And second, VARs are dynamic models. In below volume-return context, this means that the models *at the same time investigate the influence of volume on returns as well as the influence of returns on volume*. For a better understanding of empirical results presented, we provide a brief explanation of basic methodologies used:

Vector autoregressive models (VARs):[59] The simplest case of a VAR model is a bivariate model with two variables y_{1t} and y_{2t}, each of whose current values depend on different combinations of previous k values of both variables and error terms:

$$y_{1t} = \beta_{10} + \beta_{11} y_{1t-1} + ... + \beta_{1k} y_{1t-k} + \alpha_{11} y_{2t-1} + ... + \alpha_{1k} y_{2t-k} + u_{1t} \tag{2.1}$$

$$y_{2t} = \beta_{20} + \beta_{21} y_{2t-1} + ... + \beta_{2k} y_{2t-k} + \alpha_{21} y_{1t-1} + ... + \alpha_{2k} y_{1t-k} + u_{2t} \tag{2.2}$$

In our context, y_{1t} could represent current trading volume and y_{2t} the stock return of an individual stock or an aggregate stock market index.

An important feature in the context of VARs are *Granger-casualties* introduced by GRANGER (1969):[60] a Granger-casualty is a correlation between the current value of one variable and past values of other variables. In other words, Granger-casualties answer questions such as whether 'changes in y_1 (e.g., trading volume) cause changes in y_2 (e.g., stock return).' If yes, lags in y_1 should be significant in y_2. If this is the case, but not vice versa, y_1 is said to 'Granger-cause' y_2.[61]

---

59 For a more detailed description of VAR models see for example BROOKS (2002), 330 pp.

60 See BROOKS (2002), 338 pp.

61 If both sets of lags are significant, there is a *'bi-directional casualty'* or *'bi-directional feedback'*. If, however, neither sets of lags are statistically significant in the equation for the other variable, it is said that y_1 and y_2 are *independent*. See BROOKS (2002), 340.

2.5.2 Empirical Findings and Interpretations

Previous research analyzes dynamic relations between trading volume and returns using time-series data of either *individual stocks* or aggregate stock market *indices*. Table 2.13 provides a summary of these studies, sorted based on whether the authors analyzed time-series of individual stocks or of aggregate market data.[62]

2.5.2.1 Research on Individual Stocks

Studies on individual stocks find very *little evidence of time-series relations between past trading volume and stock returns* over different time horizons: STATMAN ET AL. (2006), in a study of nearly 2,000 US stocks, find no significant association between lagged share turnover and *monthly* returns over a 40-year sample. CHUANG/LEE (2006) share this finding after analyzing the relation between lagged share turnover and *weekly* returns using a comparable dataset. Similarly, GURGUL ET AL. (2007), in a study using *daily* data of 29 DAX companies, find that lagged trading volume has very limited impact on current stock returns (in fact, only in one of the 29 cases do the authors find any significant parameters on the lags of trading volume at the 5% level). The authors conclude that this evidence is in line with the efficient market hypothesis, since short-run forecasts of current or future stock returns cannot be improved via knowledge of recent volume data (and vice versa). Finally, BRAUNEIS/MESTEL (2007), while also studying daily time-series data of individual DAX companies, apply a slightly adapted, namely event based methodology: for each date (and individual stock), the authors identify the level of returns and volume and categorize days into different events (in terms of signaling certain market states). Then, they apply VAR models as well as Granger-casualty analyses separately for each cluster, using a 20-days ‘post-event’ window. The authors find that *high volume* tends to result in positive stock returns and interpret this as a confirmation of the existence of a high-volume return premium (see above, 2.1.2.1).

[62] Note: we only report *dynamic relations* between trading volume and stock returns. Some studies, for example LEE/RUI (2002), additionally investigate *contemporaneous relations* between trading volume and stock returns. For a discussion of empirical findings see 2.3 above. Other studies, for example GURGUL ET AL. (2007), also add return volatility as a variable in their VAR models.

Unlike the relationship between past trading volume and stock returns, studies on individual US stocks find significant *time-series relations between past (stock / market) returns and subsequent stock trading volume.*

STATMAN ET AL. (2006) interpret the reported positive relation between lagged *security returns* and trading volume as evidence of the disposition effect of SHEFRIN/ STATMAN (1985). This disposition effect describes the tendency of investors to sell winning investments too soon in order to realize gains, but to hold on to losing investments too long.[63]

The positive relation between lagged *market returns* and trading volume, on the other hand, is interpreted as evidence of investor overconfidence by both STATMAN ET AL. (2006) and CHUANG/LEE (2006). See above, 2.4.1, for an explanation of the overconfidence hypothesis in this context.

The two studies on German DAX stocks, however, find only a limited impact of lagged stock returns on trading volume: GURGUL ET AL. (2007) report that in 22 out of 29 stocks, none of the estimated parameters on any considered lag of stock returns are significant at the 5% level. And BRAUNEIS/MESTEL (2007) find no increased casualty of security returns on subsequent trading volume in high return clusters. However, the authors also find that joint high returns and high volume result in positive volume, but this relationship is not significant at the 5% level in most cases. One potential explanation for the weak statistical significance of the relationship as given by the authors could be the specific dataset of the most liquid German stocks.

---

63 ODEAN (1998b) tests the disposition effect by analyzing trading records for 10,000 accounts at large discount brokerage houses and confirms its existence.

Table 2.13: Selected Studies on Dynamic Volume-Return Interactions

Author(s)	Sample Data	Sample Period	Type of Volume	Frequency of data sample	Direction of Volume-Return Relationship Identified: Vol→Ret?	Ret→Vol?
STATMAN/ THORLEY/ VORKINK (2006)	Individual NYSE/AMEX common stocks	1962-2002	Share turnover	Monthly	o	+
CHUANG/ LEE (2006)	All firms on NYSE/AMEX	1963-2001	Share turnover	Weekly	o	+
GURGUL/ MAJDOSZ/ MESTEL (2007)	*Individual* DAX stocks	1994-2005	Number of shares traded	Daily	o	(+)
BRAUNEIS/ MESTEL (2007)	*28 individual* DAX companies	1994-2007	Number of shares traded	Daily	+	(+)
LEE/RUI (2000)	Data from China's 4 *stock exchanges*	Shanghai A: 1990-1997 Shanghai B, Shenzhen A, Shenzhen B: 1992-1997	Number of shares traded	Daily	o	+
LEE/RUI (2002)	3 stock market *indices* (S&P 500 index, Tokyo Stock Exchange Price Index, Financial Times-Stock Exchange 100)	S&P 500: 1973-1999 TOPIX: 1974-1999 FTSE 100: 1986-1999	Number of shares traded	Daily	o	N/A
GRIFFIN/ NARDARI/ STULZ (2004)	46 stock market *indices*	1993-2003	Dollar trading volume to market value, market-wide share turnover	Weekly	o	+
STATMAN/ THORLEY/ VORKINK (2006)	NYSE/AMEX market	1962-2002	Market-wide share turnover	Monthly	o	+

Explanation of signs used in the table: '+' denotes a positive relation, 'o' no / limited relation, and 'N/A' no results reported.

2.5.2.2 Research on Aggregate Stock Markets

Similar to findings of studies on individual stocks, previous *research on aggregate stock market indices* finds no time-series relations between past trading volume and stock returns. Examples are LEE/RUI (2000, 2002) or STATMAN ET AL. (2006).[64] On the other hand, most of these studies report a statistically significant *positive relation between past returns and trading volume:* STATMAN ET AL. (2006), in their US data sample, find a positive relation between lagged market returns and market-wide turnover using *monthly* data and again interpret this finding as evidence of investor overconfidence. LEE/RUI (2000), in a study of China's four stock exchanges, find that *daily* stock returns Granger-cause trading volume on each of these markets. In addition, these authors study cross-market casual relationships and find that while the information contained in volume and returns from financial markets in the US / Hong Kong have very weak predictive power for Chinese financial market variables, some feedback relationships exist in China's stock markets (e.g., Shanghai A-volume Granger-causes stock return on Shenzhen B).[65] LEE/RUI (2000) do not provide an interpretation of these findings but generally state that it confirms GALLANT ET AL. (1992) that more can be learned about stock markets by studying the joint dynamics of stock prices and trading volume than by focusing only on univariate dynamics of stock prices. Finally, GRIFFIN ET AL. (2004), in an extensive study of dynamic relations between weekly returns and turnover in 46 stock markets (incl. Switzerland), also confirm a positive relation between turnover and past returns. The reported magnitude of this relation varies widely across markets and is stronger for developing countries. This substantial variation across countries allows the authors to thoroughly investigate potential explanations for this relation.[66] Overall, they find their evidence to be most consistent with *models of investor*

---

[64] GRIFFIN ET AL. (2004) do not explicitly report results but state that the effect of volume on subsequent returns is both mixed and weak in their sample.

[65] In a similar study on the stock market indices in New York, Tokyo, and London, the same authors find that US trading volume contains extensive predictive power for UK and Japanese financial market variables (see LEE/RUI (2002)).

[66] The authors test the following hypotheses explaining a positive return-turnover relation: liquidity, investor protection, short-sales, participation, over-confidence and disposition, foreign 'hot-money'. For more details see GRIFFIN ET AL. (2004), 15 pp, 27 pp & 46.

participation, and at least *partially inconsistent with models of overconfidence / disposition effect and other explanations*:[67]

- *Investor participation*: in participation models, there exists a group of sidelined investors not trading due to costs of participation (e.g., information and trading costs). These investors will be prompted to trade following high past returns. As a result, effects of past returns on volume should be stronger in markets with high costs of participation and more sidelined investors. The authors claim investors to regard participation as more costly in markets that are less informationally efficient. Using the market-model R^2 by MORCK ET AL. (2000) as a proxy for efficiency of markets (with a high R^2 indicating less efficient markets) they find evidence in favor of investor participation models.

- *Overconfidence and disposition*: at first, prevailing evidence seems in line with overconfidence and disposition models, because these hypotheses predict the strength of the return-turnover relation to be positively related to a country's market-model R^2 as well.[68] At the same time, however, overconfidence and disposition effects should be stronger in periods of long-term bull markets, i.e., the 1990s, which is inconsistent with the data.

2.6 Chapter Summary

We conclude this literature review by summarizing the main empirical results of previous studies on the relation between trading volume and stock returns, again structured based on the direction of this relationship.

Lagged volume-return relationship: there is considerable evidence of a negative relationship between the *level of trading volume* and expected returns in US, but not in international stock markets. When analyzing the relationship between *change in trading*

[67] See GRIFFIN ET AL. (2004), 15 pp & 27 pp.

[68] A low correlation among security returns in a market generally leads to variation in portfolio returns among investors. This results in past market returns being less informative about trading incentives of investors. On the other hand, if most security returns within a market move together (i.e., high market-model R^2), portfolios of investors will move similarly as well. This results in a stronger positive relation between past market returns and future volume. See GRIFFIN ET AL. (2004), 18.

volume and expected returns, the evidence is less conclusive: while there is strong evidence for a positive volume-return correlation over short horizons, empirical evidence over long horizons is ambiguous. Finally, previous research in US stock markets finds a significantly negative relationship between variability in volume and expected returns.

Trading volume and return autocorrelations: most existing research on the influence of trading volume on *intermediate-term* return continuation finds this momentum effect to be stronger among high volume stocks. Previous evidence on the effect of trading volume on *short-term* return reversals, on the other hand, suggests a less direct relationship: some studies find that volume increases negative return autocorrelations, while other research reports exactly the opposite evidence.

Contemporaneous volume-return relationship: prior research provides strong evidence of a positive contemporaneous correlation between *volume and absolute returns*, thereby supporting an old Wall Street saying that it 'takes volume to make prices move'. Most literature also generally supports another saying that 'volume is relatively heavy in bull markets and light in bear markets', implying a positive correlation between *volume and returns*.

Lagged return-volume relationship: existing literature on the influence of return on trading volume finds a positive relationship between returns and subsequent trading volume as well as between price extremes and subsequent trading volume.

Dynamic volume-return relations: Finally, vector autoregressive models find no relationship between trading volume and subsequent returns in both the time-series of individual stocks and aggregate market indices. At the same time, these models mostly confirm the existence of significant time-series relations between returns and subsequent trading volume.

3 Data and Methodology

After the overview of previous research on the relationship between trading volume and stock returns, this chapter presents the research project's methodology. We start by describing the research questions. We then outline the data used in the empirical tests. This is followed by a detailed description of the methodology applied to answer each research question. The chapter ends with the statement of the main research hypotheses and the differentiation from existing literature.

3.1 Research Questions

As noted earlier, the main objective of this research project is to investigate the relationship between trading volume and expected returns in the cross-section of Swiss stocks, with a particular emphasis on the practicability of portfolio strategies formed on the basis of past trading volume. This is reflected in the following four research questions:

[1] Do different measures of trading volume play an important role in the cross-sectional variation of expected returns in the Swiss stock market?

Previous research on US and selected international stock market data finds various significant relationships between different trading volume measures and expected returns. We test whether and in what direction such relationships exist in the Swiss stock market. While much of existing literature focuses on some aspects of trading volume, we include four types of trading volume variables in our analysis, namely volume level, abnormal volume, volume growth, and variability in volume. In addition, to improve the power of our conclusions, we conduct both individual stock (i.e., regression analysis) and portfolio-based empirical tests. Finally, to increase the probability of finding *economically significant* portfolio strategies based on volume-return relations, we restrict our analysis to relationships of at least one month.

[2] How robust are the portfolio returns across time and different market regimes?

If above tests find significant relationships between measures of trading volume and the cross-sectional variation of expected returns in the Swiss stock market, we then focus on the practicability of volume based portfolio strategies. As a first step, we investigate whether the discovered relations are stable across time by analyzing possible portfolio return differences depending on the time period considered or the prevailing market regime (e.g., bull versus bear market phases).

[3] Are the discovered volume-return relations economically significant?

Finally, we analyze whether investors would have actually earned money in the past by implementing investment strategies based on the relationship between trading volume and expected returns in the Swiss stock market. This includes a more realistic return calculation than in much of previous literature as well as the investigation of the strategy performance after the inclusion of transaction costs. In addition, we test whether the portfolio returns remain significant after being adjusted for their sensitivities to previously discovered risk factors in the cross-section of Swiss stocks (e.g., market beta).

[4] How sensitive are the results to changes in the experimental design?

Throughout the empirical analysis (i.e., research questions [1]-[3]), we investigate the sensitivity of our results to some key assumptions. This includes for example the exclusion of micro caps, the comparison of results across various formation and holding periods, or differences between the chosen equally-weighted portfolio return calculation and a value-weighted alternative.

3.2 Data

The empirical investigation uses survivorship bias neutral end-of-month data from January 1996 to August 2008 for all companies listed on the Swiss Performance Index (SPI).[69] Factset is the data provider for all share prices, dividend payments[70], number of shares traded, number of shares outstanding[71], and company book values.[72] 1-month CHF LIBOR and VCL Clariden Leu Swiss Equity Volatility Index are provided by Bloomberg, and monthly Swiss risk factors are made available by Manuel Ammann and Michael Steiner.[73] Each stock has to fulfill the following requirements to be included in the sample in a given month (to a large extent these requirements are a direct consequence of the different analyses outlined in 3.3 below):

- It has to *belong to the SPI* at the end of the month.
- It has to represent a company's *main class of stock*[74]
- It is not an investment company.[75]
- Sufficient data is available to calculate all firm characteristics, i.e., *market capitalization* (as of the previous month), *positive book-to-market ratio* (using book value of equity as of six months ago (to avoid a look-ahead bias[76]) and market capitalization as of the previous month).
- Sufficient data is available to calculate all volume measures used in empirical tests, i.e., CHF trading volume (daily *number of shares traded* and associated

---

69 Prior to 1996, there is no (reliable) volume data available for SPI stocks.

70 All returns in this empirical investigation are total returns.

71 Starting in October 2001, we use free-float adjusted shares outstanding to calculate share turnover (previously not available).

72 There are mainly two reasons why we choose Factset as the data provider: *data availability* and the fact that its data is *survivorship bias neutral* (which means that each month, only those stocks are selected that are actually part of the SPI at that point of time).

73 See AMMANN/STEINER (2008). The website of the authors' data library is www.ammannsteiner.ch.

74 For example common versus preferred stock. For the calculation of market capitalization and book-to-market ratios, however, multiple classes are integrated into the main class of stock.

75 This is only relevant prior to July 1999. At this date, investment companies were eliminated from the SPI universe and transferred to a separate index.

76 To ensure that the book-values are available to the public at the beginning of t, when investment decisions are taken (for more details on this see 3.3.1.1.2).

share price for the last 14 months) and share turnover (daily number of shares traded and *number of shares outstanding* for the last 14 months).

- Its return is available for the last 12 months as well as for the next $K = 1, 3, 6, or 12$ months (depending on the time horizon studied; see 3.3 below for more details).[77]

These data requirements result in a first cross-sectional regression respectively the beginning of the first portfolio holding period in March 1997 using data of companies providing volume data since January 1996. Table 3.1 shows the number of companies included in the database at the end of February each year.

Table 3.1: Yearly Number of Companies Included in the Database

Year	Number of stocks in SPI	- Adjustments	- Non-main class stocks	- Stocks with missing data	Stocks in database in February of each year
1997	331	20	40	137	134
1998	322	24	32	115	151
1999	292	6	25	95	166
2000	274	6	20	72	176
2001	282	7	21	65	189
2002	276	4	19	43	210
2003	243	3	13	29	198
2004	232	2	12	24	194
2005	226	2	10	14	200
2006	226	2	7	21	196
2007	223	3	7	10	203
2008	225	4	7	12	202

This table reports the number of stocks included in the database at the end of February each year (in the case of monthly rebalancing, i.e., $K = 1$). This number is set in relation to the complete universe of all stocks included in the SPI at each point of time as obtained from the SIX homepage, www.six-swiss-exchange.com. First, we adjust for minor discrepancies between Factset and the SPI constituent list and remove investment companies from the database (note that the large drop in necessary adjustments between 1998 and 1999 is due to the fact that investment companies were transferred to a separate index as of July 1999). The remaining difference between the database and the SPI constituent list can be explained by the elimination of non-main class stocks and stocks with missing data.

[77] If the stock is excluded from the SPI in the holding period, it remains in the sample except if it is delisted from the SIX Swiss Exchange altogether (i.e., no full return series available).

The total number of stocks in our database is marginally smaller than in AMMANN/ STEINER (2008), which is the result of our more stringent data requirements. At the same time, our data base is larger than samples used in most other related studies using Swiss stock market data.[78] In addition, the table shows that the quality of the data improves over time as indicated by the substantial reduction of stocks with missing data. This finding is confirmed when comparing the returns of the Swiss Performance Index with a hypothetical, value-weighted index constructed from the stocks included in the database.[79] While the correlation between the two returns is 0.972 in the first half of the sample period (from March 1997 to November 2002), it becomes as high as 0.999 in the second, more recent sub-period (from December 2002 to August 2008). Figure 3.1 illustrates the strong correlation between the two indices.

Figure 3.1: Development of SPI and Value-Weighted Index Constructed from Database

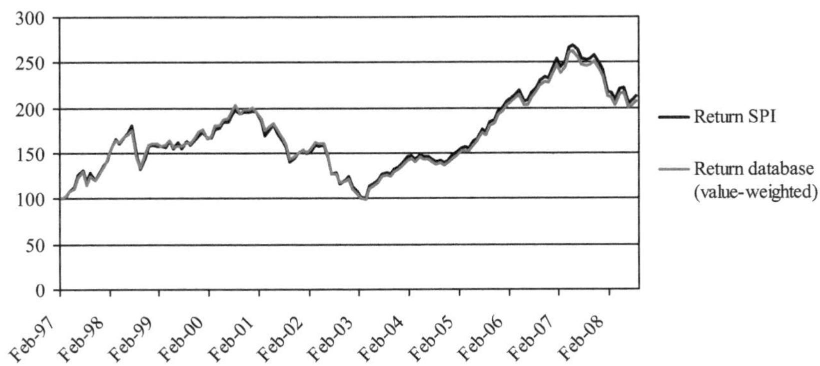

As a final remark, note that any deviations from the data requirements outlined here are specifically mentioned at the relevant positions in the text.

[78] For example FAMA/FRENCH (1998), LIEW/VASSALOU (2000) or KANIEL ET AL. (2007).

[79] Based on monthly returns, with monthly adjustment for members.

3.3 Methodology along Research Questions

In this section, we separately describe the methodology to answer each research question. Note that there is no separate sub-section regarding research question [4] (sensitivity of results to changes in the experimental design), since the different robustness tests are relevant throughout the entire empirical analysis. As a result, we describe the different tests at the relevant positions.

3.3.1 Trading Volume and the Cross-Sectional Variation of Stock Returns

As previously mentioned, we apply both regression analysis and portfolio-based empirical tests to answer the question whether different measures of trading volume play an important role in the cross-sectional variation of expected returns in the Swiss stock market. These two different methodologies are separately described below.

3.3.1.1 Regression Analysis

3.3.1.1.1 Empirical Model

To assess the role of trading volume in the cross-sectional variation of expected returns, we first follow the FAMA/MACBETH (1973) method based on ordinary least-squares (OLS) regressions: each month *t*, we estimate an empirical model of the form

$$r_i = f_0 + \sum_{g=1}^{G} f_g x_{gi} + e_i, \qquad i = 1,2,\ldots N, \;\; g = 1,2,\ldots,G, \tag{3.1}$$

where r_i is the return on stock i, and x_{gi} is the firm characteristic g (such as the volume measures investigated and other variables hypothesized to explain expected returns) of stock i.[80] The coefficient f_g measures the effect of firm characteristic g on expected returns, and e_i is the error term. Finally, N denotes the total number of securities, which can vary from month to month. The monthly regressions of model (3.1) over the full sample period produce T estimates of each coefficient f_{gt}, $t = 1,2,\ldots,T$. These monthly estimates are averaged,

80 To be precise: firm characteristic g stems from a previous period and is known to investors at the beginning of month t (when they make their investment decisions).

$$\hat{f}_g = \frac{1}{T}\sum_{t=1}^{T}\hat{f}_{gt}\,, \tag{3.2}$$

and tests of statistical significance performed. This standard Fama-MacBeth regression methodology is used widely in the analysis of the cross-section of stock returns.[81]

Small methodological remark on the above: the pooled structure of our dataset allows us to contemporaneously execute steps 1 (eq. 3.1) and 2 (eq. 3.2) using Pooled OLS estimation procedure. The formula for the estimator is then given by

$$\hat{f} = \left(\sum_{i=1}^{N}\sum_{t=1}^{T} x_{it}'x_{it}\right)^{-1}\left(\sum_{i=1}^{N}\sum_{t=1}^{T} x_{it}'r_{it}\right), \tag{3.3}$$

where x_{it} is a $(G+1) \times 1$ vector of explanatory variables (including the constant) and $\hat{f}$ is the $(G+1) \times 1$ vector of coefficients. Note one additional point: to mitigate a potential heteroskedasticity respectively serial correlation problem, we follow ANG ET AL. (2006) among others and calculate t-statistics using NEWEY-WEST (1987) adjusted, heteroskedasticity and serial correlation robust standard errors.[82]

Next, assume that the error term, e_{it}, contains an unobserved, cross-sectionally constant variable c_t, called unobserved effect, so that $e_{it} = c_t + u_{it}$.[83] Recall that a central assumption in OLS models is that the error in each cross-section and time period is conditionally independent from the explanatory variables in that same cross-section and time period, i.e., $E(x'e) = 0$.[84] If, however, an unobserved effect c_t, which is included in the error term, correlates with any regressor x_{gi}, this assumption is violated. As a result, the (Pooled) OLS estimator might not be consistent anymore.

81 See 2.1.1.1 above for an overview of studies applying Fama-MacBeth methodology or variations thereof in a volume-return context. Additional studies applying this methodology include FAMA/FRENCH (1992) and AMIHUD (2002).

82 See QUANTITATIVE MICRO SOFTWARE (2004), 853.

83 See WOOLDRIDGE (2002), 247 pp., for more details on the following explanations (note that WOOLDRIDGE analyzes the case of a time constant unobserved effect).

84 Population orthogonality condition, see WOOLDRIDGE (2002), 52.

One way to deal with this potential issue is the *fixed effects transformation*, also called *within transformation*: consider the linear unobserved effects model,

$$r_{it} = f_{it} x_{it} + c_i + u_{it} \qquad t = 1,2,\ldots,T,\ i = 1,2,\ldots,N, \tag{3.4}$$

where f_{it} is a $(G+1) \times 1$ vector of coefficients and x_{it} is a $(G+1) \times 1$ vector of explanatory variables (including the constant). If we de-mean each cross-section t by removing cross-section averages from the dependent variable and exogenous regressors per cross-section t, the individual unobserved cross-sectionally constant effect is removed, since $c_t - \overline{c}_t = 0$. Our transformed model is then given by

$$(r_{it} - \overline{r}_t) = f_{it}(x_{it} - \overline{x}_t) + (u_{it} - \overline{u}_t), \qquad t = 1,2,\ldots,T, \tag{3.5}$$

and the resulting formula for the fixed effects estimator is

$$\hat{f} = \left(\sum_{i=1}^{N} \sum_{t=1}^{T} \widetilde{x}_{it}' \widetilde{x}_{it} \right)^{-1} \left(\sum_{i=1}^{N} \sum_{t=1}^{T} \widetilde{x}_{it}' \widetilde{r}_{it} \right), \tag{3.6}$$

where $\widetilde{}$ (e.g., $\widetilde{x}_{it}$) denotes the de-meaned variable ($x_{it} - \overline{x}_t$).

As a result, the fixed effects method is again consistent with the assumption that the error in each cross-section is conditionally independent from the explanatory variables in the same cross-section.

To conclude, when analyzing the question whether different measures of trading volume play a role in the cross-sectional variation of expected returns in the Swiss stock market using regression analysis, we follow a two-step approach. First, we apply standard Fama-MacBeth regression methodology using Pooled OLS estimation procedure as shown in equation (3.3).[85] In a second step, we perform the described fixed effects transformation as a robustness check of our base results.[86]

3.3.1.1.2 Trading Volume and Other Analyzed Firm Characteristics

While a stock's return[87] in any given ($K = 1$) month serves as dependent variable in our monthly Fama-MacBeth (FM) regressions, we include the following firm characteristics as independent variables:

A first set of firm characteristics used are the *different volume measures hypothesized to play a role in the cross-sectional variation of expected returns* (i.e., volume level, abnormal volume, volume growth, and variability in volume), namely:

TURN: the natural logarithm of average monthly share turnover in the stock (measured by the total number of shares traded in a month divided by the average number of shares outstanding) in the last $J = 1, 3, 6, 12$ months.

DELTATURN A: the percentage change of last month's share turnover versus the average monthly share turnover in the preceding $J = 3, 6, 12$ months. The idea is that this variable measures *abnormal volume.*

DELTATURN B: the average monthly percentage change in share turnover in the last $J = 1, 3, 6, 12$ months. This second 'change in volume' variable measures *volume growth.*

STDTURN: the natural logarithm of the standard deviation of monthly share turnover calculated over the past 12 months.

---

85 The main 'technical' advantage of Pooled OLS is the fact that it is efficient in our (linear) setting, i.e., the estimator with the smallest variance. In other words, Pooled OLS is a more appropriate estimation procedure than fixed effects transformation if the linear model without unobserved effects is correctly specified or if there exists an unobserved effect, but with the following property: $E(x'c) = 0$, i.e., the unobserved effect is not correlated with any regressor.

86 Again we calculate t-statistics using Newey-West (1987) adjusted, heteroskedasticity and serial correlation robust standard errors.

87 We use discrete returns, because investors do not earn continuous returns from holding a stock. We thank Weimin Liu for the following illustration: if an investor invests $10 in a stock and a month later he only gets $1 back, his return per dollar in that month is -90%, which is the discrete return. The corresponding continuously compounded return, however, is -230.26%, which does not make any economic sense.

CVTURN: the natural logarithm of the coefficient of variation in share turnover, i.e., the standard deviation of monthly share turnover over the past 12 months divided by the average monthly share turnover over the past 12 months.[88] The big advantage of the coefficient of variation versus the standard deviation as a measure of variability in volume is that the former is a dimensionless quantity while the latter strongly correlates with the volume level, TURN (see below, Table 3.3 to Table 3.5, for time-series averages of cross-sectional correlations between different volume measures).

CHFVOL: the natural logarithm of average monthly Swiss franc million volume of trading in the stock in the last $J = 1, 3, 6, 12$ months.[89]

DELTAVOL A: the percentage change of last month's Swiss franc million volume versus the average monthly Swiss franc million volume in the preceding $J = 3, 6, 12$ months.

DELTAVOL B: the average monthly percentage change in Swiss franc million volume in the last $J = 1, 3, 6, 12$ months.

STDVOL: the natural logarithm of the standard deviation of monthly Swiss franc million volume calculated over the past 12 months.

CVVOL: the natural logarithm of the coefficient of variation in Swiss franc million volume calculated over the past 12 months.

In addition to these volume measures, we include the following firm characteristics as independent variables in our FM regressions to control for previously documented return determinants:

SIZE: the natural logarithm of the market value of equity of the firm as of the end of the second to last month. The origin of the size effect goes back to BANZ (1981) who documents that companies with a small market capitalization significantly outperform

---

88 CHORDIA ET AL. (2001) calculate CVTURN each month *over the past 36 months* in their main empirical test. As a robustness check, these authors also use 12-month formation periods and find that their main results do not change. Because we only have a 12-year time period for our empirical tests, we therefore use a 12-month formation period.

89 Due to the lack of availability of consistent monthly CHF volume data, we use the *sum of daily number of shares traded in a stock* times the *average daily share price*, 0.5 x $(p_{t-1} + p_t)$; p_{t-1} and p_t are daily closing prices.

companies with a large market capitalization. FAMA/FRENCH (1992) confirm a significant relation between a company's market capitalization and its returns for US stocks. The significance of the size effect is less clear in the cross-section of Swiss stocks. AMMANN/STEINER (2008) find indication of a negative size effect between 1990 and 2005 (but not significantly from zero). However, this result is not constant over time. Restricting the analysis to the second sub-period from 1998 to 2005, which is closer to the time-series analyzed here, the authors find a positive size effect (but again not significantly from zero). Despite this uncertainty regarding the true relationship between firm size and expected returns in the Swiss stock market, we see no clear disadvantage of including this variable in our regression analysis.

BM: the natural logarithm of the ratio of the book value of equity (using end of the previous year accounting data with a lag of six months) to the market value of equity of the firm (at the end of the second to last month). The lag of six months in accounting data implies that we use end-of-year book values from year *y-1* no earlier than at the end of June of year *y*. This lag is necessary to avoid a look-ahead bias.[90] Using a six-month lag is conservative and in accordance with FAMA/FRENCH (1992) and AMMANN/ STEINER (2008). In our decision to include the book-to-market ratio as a proxy for the value effect as documented by STATTMAN (1980) and confirmed by FAMA/FRENCH (1992) for US as well as by AMMANN/STEINER (2008) for Swiss stock returns, we follow the rationale in AMMANN/STEINER (2008).[91]

RET2-12: the cumulative return over the 11 months ending at the end of the second to last month. This measure of past return serves as a proxy for the momentum effect as documented by JEGADEESH/TITMAN (1993) and confirmed by AMMANN/ STEINER (2008) for the Swiss stock market.[92]

Some additional comments about the variables used: we do not include a firm's market beta in our FM regressions for the following three reasons, *data availability*, *errors-in-variables problem*, and *previous results*. First, the Fama-MacBeth approach applied in FAMA/FRENCH (1992) uses up to five years of previous stock returns to estimate mar-

---

[90] To ensure that the book values are available to the public at the beginning of *t*, when investment decisions are taken.

[91] Alternative measures could be price-earnings ratio, cash-flow-to-price ratio, or dividend yield.

[92] See 2.2.1 for an introduction to momentum.

ket beta. Because of data availability issues we only have a 12-year time period for our empirical tests. Using up to five years of previous returns does not seem sensible in light of this fact. Second, the estimation of market betas comes at the cost of measurement errors, which would need to be specifically dealt with. We do not face such a measurement problem with the other firm characteristics used in our FM regressions, because they are measured precisely and do not stem from a first-stage estimation. And third, previous results show that the inclusion of market beta in FM regressions of stock returns on other firm characteristics such as share turnover, book-to-market ratio, or firm size, do not substantially alter sign, level, or significance of coefficients on these other firm characteristics.[93] In addition, we account for market betas on a portfolio level as part of research question [3], namely in the regressions of monthly excess returns of volume portfolios on Swiss risk factors (see below, 3.3.3.2).

We follow BRENNAN ET AL. (1998) and CHORDIA ET AL. (2001) and lag all control variables (SIZE, BM, RET2-12) by one month. For the past return variable, the exclusion of the most recent month is based on the reported negative autocorrelations of one-month stock returns due to microstructure issues such as the bid-ask bounce.[94] We also lag SIZE and BM for consistency reasons.

Table 3.2 provides time-series averages of cross-sectional means of the main firm characteristics (calculated for the $J = 1$ month formation period[95]) analyzed over the full 1997 to 2008 time period. Most variables display considerable skewness. BRENNAN ET AL. (1998) and CHORDIA ET AL. (2001) deal with this issue by employing logarithmic transformations of all variables used in FM regressions except momentum (which may be zero). We follow these authors by using natural logarithms of all firm characteristics except past return and change in volume measures in our FM regressions.

93 See for example DATAR ET AL. (1998).

94 See for example JEGADEESH (1990), ASNESS (1994) and the discussion above, 2.2.2.

95 We choose the $J = 1$ time horizon to be able to compare our results to CHORDIA ET AL'S (2001) table 1.

Table 3.2: Summary Statistics

Variable	Mean	Median	Std. Dev.	Skew-ness
Firm size (CHF billion)	4.91	0.51	19.44	6.23
Book-to-market ratio	1.04	0.62	3.99	8.60
Share turnover (%)	4.93	2.90	6.25	3.13
Standard deviation of share turnover (%)	2.76	1.80	4.05	4.34
Coefficient of variation in turnover	0.62	0.56	0.32	1.54
Change in turnover (%)	62.36	0.95	382.23	6.31
CHF trading volume (CHF million per month)	357.94	8.16	1'434.64	5.55
Standard deviation of CHF trading volume (CHF million)	93.82	5.73	353.13	5.53
Coefficient of variation in CHF trading volume	0.65	0.59	0.34	1.51
Change in CHF volume (%)	65.08	1.15	389.78	6.53

This table reports the time-series averages of cross-sectional statistics for an average of 190 stocks over 138 months from February 1997 through July 2008. Each stock satisfies the following criteria: (1) it is part of the SPI at the end of the current month; (2) it is a company's main class of stock; (3) it is not an investment company; (4) sufficient data is available to calculate all firm characteristics; and (5) its return is available for the last 12 months as well as for the next month. Statistics on share turnover, change in turnover, CHF trading volume, and change in CHF trading volume are calculated for the $J = 1$ month formation period.

In addition, we compare our summary statistics to previous research as a small cross-check of data consistency. In fact, CHORDIA ET AL. (2001), in a study of US stock market data from 1966-1995, report a mean (median) dollar trading volume of approximately USD 30 (4) million per month and average (median) monthly share turnover of approximately 4% (3%). Our data seems generally in line regarding share turnover. Our CHF trading volume figures, on the other hand, are substantially higher. However, this seems mainly driven by the fact that mean (median) firm size in CHORDIA ET AL'S (2001) sample is only USD billion 0.7 (0.1) compared to CHF billion 4.9 (0.5) in our more recent Swiss stock market data.

Finally, we discuss correlations between the firm characteristics used in the FM regressions. (see Table 3.3 and Table 3.4 for the $J = 1$ month formation period and Table 3.5 for the $J = 12$ months formation period).[96]

Table 3.3: Correlation Matrix of Analyzed Firm Characteristics (Formation Period J = 1 Month; Part 1)

	SIZE	BM	TURN	STD TURN	CV TURN	DELTA TURN
SIZE	1.000	-0.424	**0.385**	0.077	-0.635	-0.116
BM	-0.424	1.000	-0.254	-0.184	0.229	0.048
TURN	0.385	-0.254	1.000	0.711	-0.323	0.125
STDTURN	0.077	-0.184	**0.711**	1.000	0.198	-0.011
CVTURN	-0.635	0.229	**-0.323**	0.198	1.000	0.170
DELTATURN	-0.116	0.048	0.125	-0.011	0.170	1.000
CHFVOL	0.854	-0.385	0.776	0.416	-0.616	-0.027
STDVOL	0.831	-0.386	0.699	0.558	-0.468	-0.107
CVVOL	-0.628	0.215	-0.282	0.205	0.945	0.165
DELTAVOL	-0.116	0.048	0.128	-0.007	0.171	0.977
RETURN2-12	0.106	-0.280	0.052	0.097	0.016	-0.041

This table reports time-series averages of monthly cross-sectional correlations between the firm characteristics used in Fama-MacBeth pricing regressions. The variables relate to an average of 190 stocks over 138 months from February 1997 through July 2008. The control variables and the volume variables (the latter are calculated over the $J = 1$ month formation period) are defined at the beginning of this section, 3.3.1.1.2.

[96] The criteria for a stock to be in the sample in a given month are the same as in Table 3.2.

There are several interesting observations in Table 3.3 and Table 3.4. First, recall above discussion on the most appropriate measure of variability in volume. The average month by month cross-sectional correlation between the standard deviation of Swiss franc volume (share turnover) and the level of Swiss franc volume (share turnover) is very high at 0.943 (0.711). The correlation between the coefficient of variation of Swiss franc volume (share turnover) and the respective measures of volume level, on the other hand, is substantially lower, namely -0.586 (-0.323). The coefficient of variation in volume thus seems the more appropriate measure of variability in volume. We compare regression results using either measure in chapter 4.

Table 3.4: Correlation Matrix of Analyzed Firm Characteristics (Formation Period J = 1 Month; Part 2)

	CHF VOL	STD VOL	CV VOL	DELTA VOL	RETURN 2-12
SIZE	**0.854**	0.831	-0.628	-0.116	0.106
BM	-0.385	-0.386	0.215	0.048	-0.280
TURN	0.776	0.699	-0.282	0.128	0.052
STDTURN	0.416	0.558	0.205	-0.007	0.097
CVTURN	-0.616	-0.468	0.945	0.171	0.016
DELTATURN	-0.027	-0.107	0.165	0.977	-0.041
CHFVOL	1.000	0.943	-0.586	-0.022	0.087
STDVOL	**0.943**	1.000	-0.428	-0.104	0.078
CVVOL	**-0.586**	-0.428	1.000	0.172	0.046
DELTAVOL	-0.022	-0.104	0.172	1.000	-0.031
RETURN2-12	0.087	0.078	0.046	-0.031	1.000

This table reports time-series averages of monthly cross-sectional correlations between the firm characteristics used in Fama-MacBeth pricing regressions. The variables relate to an average of 190 stocks over 138 months from February 1997 through July 2008. The control variables and the volume variables (the latter are calculated over the J = 1 month formation period) are defined at the beginning of this section, 3.3.1.1.2.

The second interesting result in Table 3.3 and Table 3.4 is the correlation between volume level and company size. Intuitively, we expect a rather high correlation between the absolute value of trading volume (i.e., CHFVOL) and company size. The data supports this intuition – the actual correlation is 0.854. In Figure 3.2, we plot pairs of Swiss franc volume and market capitalization across all stocks and cross-sections (approximately 26,000 observations).[97] The positive correlation between Swiss franc volume and company size is clearly visible.

Figure 3.2: Correlation between Swiss Franc Volume and Size

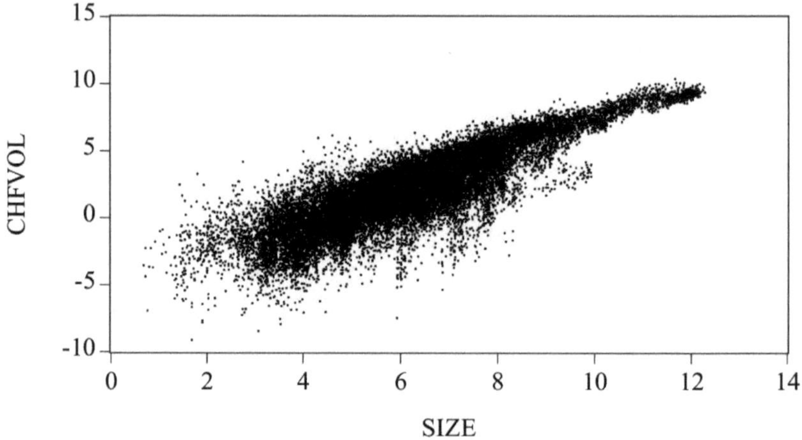

When setting the number of shares traded in a stock in relation to the total number of outstanding shares of that stock (i.e., TURN) we can at least partially neutralize this size-dependence of trading volume. The resulting correlation between share turnover and size is 0.385. We again plot pairs of share turnover and market capitalization across all stocks and cross-sections (see Figure 3.3).[98] Interestingly, the level of share turnover is quite independent from a company's size for small and medium stocks. All stocks above a market capitalization of approximately CHF 3 billion (which corresponds to 8

[97] The presented firm characteristics are logarithmically transformed.
[98] The presented firm characteristics are again logarithmically transformed.

in logarithmic form), however, have at least a base level of share turnover. In fact, almost no large stock has a turnover level below 1% (i.e., 0 in logarithmic form).

As a result of this volume-size correlation analysis we generally prefer share turnover as a measure of trading volume. However, we conduct base regressions using both volume measures to analyze the influence of different levels of size-dependence on the relationship between trading volume and expected returns.

Figure 3.3: Correlation between Share Turnover and Size

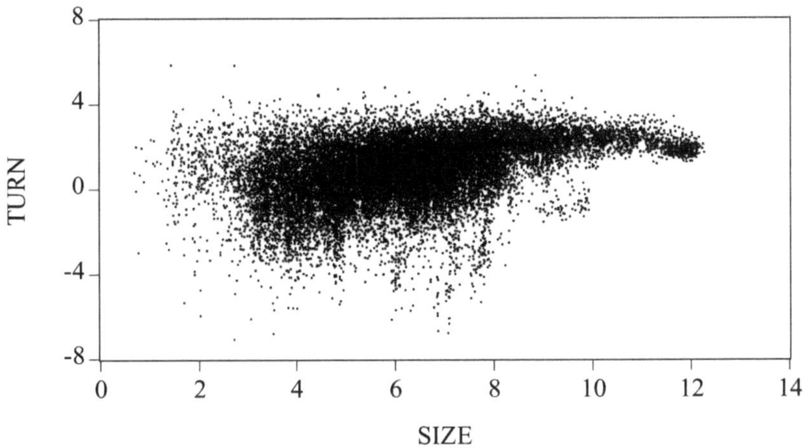

As a final analysis, we briefly discuss correlations between selected firm characteristics formed over the 12-month formation period (instead of the one-month formation period reported in Table 3.3 and Table 3.4). Results reported in Table 3.5 indicate that the two measures of 'change in volume', DELTA A and DELTA B, have quite different dynamics, which justifies the separate inclusion of both measures in our analysis. Note the low correlation between DELTATURN 12A (DELTAVOL 12A) and DELTATURN 12B (DELTAVOL 12B) of 0.141 (0.146).

Table 3.5: Correlation Matrix of Analyzed Firm Characteristics (Formation Period J = 12 Months)

	DELTA TURN 12A	DELTA TURN 12B	**DELTA VOL 12A**	DELTA VOL 12B
SIZE	0.004	-0.297	0.024	-0.296
BM	0.020	0.096	-0.030	0.077
TURN12	-0.016	-0.195	0.005	-0.165
STDTURN	0.024	-0.005	0.043	0.029
CVTURN	0.084	0.427	0.079	0.438
DELTATURN 12A	1.000	0.141	0.928	0.145
DELTATURN 12B	**0.141**	1.000	0.124	0.924
CHFVOL12	0.000	-0.329	0.012	-0.316
STDVOL	0.021	-0.277	0.038	-0.259
CVVOL	0.095	0.410	0.111	0.432
DELTAVOL 12A	0.928	0.124	1.000	0.146
DELTAVOL 12B	0.145	0.924	**0.146**	1.000
RETURN2-12	-0.042	0.003	0.100	0.069

This table reports time-series averages of monthly cross-sectional correlations between the firm characteristics used in Fama-MacBeth pricing regressions. The variables relate to an average of 190 stocks over 138 months from February 1997 through July 2008. The control variables and the volume variables (the latter are calculated over the $J = 12$ months formation period) are defined at the beginning of this section, 3.3.1.1.2.

3.3.1.1.3 Robustness Checks

Following the regression analysis outlined above, we perform several robustness checks to investigate the sensitivity of our results to some key assumptions. In addition, we hope that the outcome of these tests will also serve as a first step in the interpretation of our results.

First, we introduce a *one-month lead-lag* interval between the volume measures used as independent regressors and the dependent variable in our regressions. Let us illustrate this with the regression of a stock's return in any given month on Swiss franc volume. In this robustness test, CHFVOL represents the natural logarithm of average monthly Swiss franc million volume of trading in the stock in the $J = 1, 3, 6, 12$ months *ending in the second to last month* (instead of Swiss franc volume of trading in the stock *in the last* $J = 1, 3, 6, 12$ *months*). The introduction of a one-month lead-lag interval serves two purposes. On the one hand, we can check whether discovered volume-return relationships are driven by the immediate last month. On the other hand, it allows us to compare our results to BRENNAN ET AL (1998) and CHORDIA ET AL (2001).

Second, we perform an *outlier analysis* to investigate the sensitivity of the regression results to extreme observations. We execute this outlier analysis by discarding the lowest 1% (5%) and highest 1% (5%) of the different volume measures in our complete dataset.[99]

Third, potentially discovered relations between trading volume and expected returns could be *limited to stocks of certain size*. In addition, the inclusion of micro caps could bias the results through inefficiencies in the market microstructure such as the bid-ask spread, as noted by AMMANN/STEINER (2008). Therefore, we repeat above regressions discarding all companies with a market capitalization below CHF 50 million (approximately 10% of stocks[100]) or CHF 200 million (approximately 30% of stocks[101]).

Fourth, we check the robustness of regression results over time by dividing the sample into *two sub-periods* of roughly equal length. The first return series runs from March 1997 to November 2002 and the second return series from December 2002 to August 2008.

We generally use free-float adjusted shares outstanding for the share turnover variable, because this represents a more accurate measure of trading volume in a stock. However, free-float adjusted figures are only available after 2001.[102] Therefore, as a fifth robust-

[99] We do not perform a separate outlier analysis for control variables, because AMMANN/STEINER (2008) show that the Swiss risk factors do not result from extreme observations.

[100] This number varies rather substantially across cross-sections. Depending on the month of observation, it can be as low as 5% or as high as 20%.

[101] This number again varies across cross-sections. Depending on the month of observation, it can be as low as 20% or as high as 50%.

[102] In October 2001, the SIX Swiss Exchange (formerly SWX Swiss Exchange) introduced free-float adjusted market capitalizations to calculate index weights of individual stocks.

ness check, we investigate the *influence of free-float adjustment on the turnover-return relationship* by comparing results in the second sub-period (December 2002 to August 2008) using either free-float adjusted or non-free-float adjusted share turnovers.

Sixth, potential deviations in the volume-return relationship between the US and Swiss stock markets could be caused by differences in firm ownership structures as proxied by a stock's free-float factor. Since the average free-float factor is higher in the US in our sample period, we suspect a convergence of results when excluding stocks with a low free-float in our Swiss sample. Therefore, we repeat above regressions in the second sub-period (December 2002 to August 2008) *discarding all stocks with a free-float below 30%* (approximately 8% of stocks) *respectively 60%* (approximately 35% of stocks).

Next, we repeat the base Pooled OLS regressions using the *fixed effects method* as outlined in the description of the empirical model (see above, 3.3.1.1.1).

Finally, we check the robustness of results over longer return horizons. Recall that up to this point a stock's return in a given $(K = 1)$ month serves as dependent variable in the FM regressions. In this test, we increase the return period to $K = 3, 6, 12$ months to investigate longer-term relationships between the different volume measures investigated and expected returns. Increasing the return period to $K > 1$ month, however, introduces overlapping return observations into the regressions. As noted by HJALMARSSON (2008) and BRITTEN-JONES/NEUBERGER (2004), this causes severe serial correlation in the regression residuals. One way to potentially deal with this issue is the use of an auto-correlation robust estimation of standard errors, for example NEWEY/WEST (1987) (the approach followed in our empirical tests for the non-overlapping $K = 1$ month return period). However, simulation studies by HJALMARSSON (2008) and BRITTEN-JONES/NEUBERGER (2004) show that the estimates of standard errors using the Newey-West adjustment are severely biased down, particularly when using long-return horizons. Our unreported initial regression results for long return horizons using the Newey-West adjustment confirm this. HJALMARSSON (2008), thus, proposes an alternative approach to allow for improved inference in long-horizon regressions. In fact, the author finds that the standard t-statistic divided by the square root of the forecasting (return) horizon corrects for the overlap in the data. Due to its ease of implementation, we thus follow HJALMARSSON (2008) for the purpose of this final robustness check.[103]

The results of all the analyses presented in this section give us first insights as to whether (and if yes which) measures of trading volume play an important role in the cross-sectional variation of expected returns in the Swiss stock market.

3.3.1.2 Portfolio Strategies

Next, we analyze whether portfolio strategies that are built on the basis of the insights gained in the Fama-MacBeth regressions of stock returns on different measures of trading volume yield profitable returns.

3.3.1.2.1 One-Way Sorts

In a first step, we form portfolios based on a single trading volume measure applying the following methodology:[104] at the beginning of each month t, all eligible stocks are assigned to five (ten) equal-weighted quintile (decile) portfolios based on their trading volume in the previous $J = 1, 3, 6, 12$ months. We then calculate monthly returns for these portfolios in month t (i.e., holding period $K = 1$ month with monthly rebalancing). Finally, we report time-series average returns over the total sample period for long positions in each volume quintile (decile) as well as for zero-cost arbitrage strategies consisting of long positions in high volume (i.e., first quantile) stocks and short positions of equal size in low volume (i.e., last quantile) stocks.

Further methodological remarks:

Data: to ensure consistency with the FM regressions we use the same time-series. This means that the first holding period is March 1997 using data of companies providing volume data since January 1996. The last portfolio holding period is August 2008.

Selection of volume measures: based on the regression results, we decide which of the initial volume measures (3.3.1.1.2) to include in the portfolio-based tests.

[103] HJALMARSSON (2008) develops his solution in a time-series setup. However, the author agrees with our line of reasoning that this approach is likely to apply in our panel setup as well.

[104] See for example JEGADEESH/TITMAN (1993), LEE/SWAMINATHAN (2000), or REY/SCHMID (2007).

Return calculation within portfolio: we generally use equal-weighted portfolios, which means that we invest the same amount in each stock within a portfolio. As a result, the monthly return of a portfolio is calculated as the arithmetic mean return of its constituent stocks. In our decision, we follow VAIHEKOSKI (2004) who states that equal-weighting highlights the cross-sectional variety of all available assets. At the same time, we acknowledge that value-weighted investing might increase the practicability of the analyzed portfolio strategy. Therefore, we conduct a robustness check using value-weighted return calculation as part of the investigation of the economic significance of volume-return relations.

Return calculation over the entire time-series: based on the assumption that monthly observations are equally likely to occur, we calculate the *arithmetic mean* of all monthly returns. This approach follows most of the relevant literature such as JEGADEESH/ TITMAN (1993), LEE/SWAMINATHAN (2000), or LIU/STRONG (2008).

3.3.1.2.2 Two-Way Sorts

Having completed the analysis of portfolios constructed on the basis of a single trading volume measure, we then form portfolios based on a two-way sort of a control variable and a volume measure. The main goal of this second step is to ensure that a potentially discovered volume-effect is not simply the result of another, previously discovered cross-sectional effect.[105] Another objective is to potentially identify even more profitable portfolio strategies, which might be important regarding the economic significance of volume-return relations (see research question [3]).

Control variables used: we include the same three control variables used in the FM regressions, namely company size, book-to-market ratio and past return (see above, 3.3.1.1.2). As a further robustness test, we additionally control for different industry groups (according to the sector classification provided by Factset) to make sure that a

[105] Illustration: assume that the results of the one-way sort indicate that low volume stocks generally outperform high volume stocks. If, however, low volume stocks have systematically higher book-to-market ratios, there exists the possibility that such a *'low volume premium'* is just a manifestation of the previously documented *value effect*, not an independent volume effect.

potentially discovered volume effect is not simply caused by industry affiliation. The industry groups are:[106]

- *Manufacturing – sectors included:* Non-Energy Minerals, Producer Manufacturing, Energy Minerals, Process Industries, Industrial Services, Utilities;
- *Technology & Health:* Electronic Technology, Health Technology, Technology Services, Health Services, Communications;
- *Finance;*
- *Consumer:* Consumer Durables, Consumer Non-Durables, Commercial Services, Distribution Services, Consumer Services, Retail Trade, Transportation, Miscellaneous.

Return calculation: the methodology applied to calculate two-way sorted portfolio returns follows ANG ET AL. (2006): at the beginning of each month t, we sort stocks into three terciles based on the examined control variable (e.g., past returns). Then, within each tercile, we sort stocks based on the investigated trading volume measure (e.g., share turnover). The portfolios are rebalanced monthly (holding period $K = 1$ month) and equal-weighted. We then average the returns of each volume quantile over the three corresponding control portfolios per month and calculate time-series average returns. The resulting averaged volume portfolios thus control for differences in the specific control variable.

Sequential versus independent sorting: we use sequential sorting, which means that we first sort stocks into control variable portfolios, and *within these quantiles* into volume portfolios. An alternative approach used in the literature, for example by LEE/ SWAMINATHAN (2000), is independent sorting.[107] However, following this approach in our setting would result in undiversified portfolios. In fact, while VAIHEKOSKI

[106] We merge the different sectors into four industries (of roughly equal number of constituents) to ensure a minimum level of diversification.

[107] Illustration for independent sorting using past return as the control variable and share turnover as the volume variable: at the beginning of each month, all eligible stocks are sorted based on the past J months' share turnover and divided into equal-weighted volume portfolios. Stocks are then *independently* sorted based on the past J months' return and also divided into equal-weighted momentum portfolios. Stocks at the *intersection* of the two sorts are then grouped together to form portfolios based on past share turnover and past returns.

(2004) recommends at least five or more assets in a portfolio, our unreported analysis finds that some portfolios would even be empty (i.e., contain no stock at all) at specific formation months. Sequential 3x3 sorting, on the other hand, results in well-diversified portfolios containing at least 10 stocks at each point of time.

3.3.1.2.3 Multi-Month Holding Periods

Next, we increase the holding period from $K = 1$ month to $K = 3, 6, 12$ months. This is particularly important with regards to the practical implementation, because a monthly rebalancing is likely to strongly reduce a portfolio strategy's profitability due to a high level of transaction costs.

Approach: at the beginning of each month t, we sort stocks into quantiles based on the value of the investigated measure(s) and hold the resulting (equal-weighted) portfolios for $K = 3, 6, 12$ months. This methodology implies overlapping holding periods on a monthly basis, because we invest in parallel in K different investment cohorts each month. To calculate the nonoverlapping monthly portfolio returns over the full time-series from March 1997 to August 2008, we apply the technique by JEGADEESH/ TITMAN (1993) and LEE/SWAMINATHAN (2000): the monthly return for a K-month holding period is the equal-weighted average of portfolio returns from strategies (i.e., investment cohorts) implemented in the current month and in the previous $K-1$ months.[108] Illustration for $K = 3$ months: the monthly return in t is the equal-weighted average of portfolio returns from strategies implemented in t, $t-1$, and $t-2$.[109] Note that by applying this 'rolling portfolio' approach we avoid the problems of serial correlation outlined above in a regression context (3.3.1.1.3).

The completion of all (regression and portfolio-based) empirical tests presented in this section should enable us to answer the first research question whether and, if yes, which measures of trading volume play an important role in the cross-sectional variation of expected returns in the Swiss stock market.

[108] From a practical perspective, this approach means that we revise approximately $1/K$ of the invested asset value per portfolio each month.

[109] To calculate the return over the entire time-series we again take the arithmetic mean of all monthly returns.

3.3.2 Time-Stability of Portfolio Strategies

In a next step, we investigate whether the returns to the discovered volume strategies are stable across time and different market regimes. This analysis is important for several reasons: first, it is a further robustness check to ensure that a potentially discovered volume effect is not just a manifestation of a previously documented effect (e.g., the January seasonality). Second, it helps to better understand the dynamics of the volume-return relationship, also in the sense of an interpretation of results. Finally, the analysis is important regarding the practical implementation of volume based portfolio strategies. Some points of particular practical interest are:

- To investigate whether an effect is driven by only a few months;
- To analyze whether an effect is only significant at the beginning of the time-series, but not in more recent times;
- To get a first indication regarding a possible dynamic implementation of volume based portfolio strategies (in the sense that we might invest in a given strategy only in certain market regimes).

The analysis of time-stability contains three elements, the *dependence of results on few months with extreme returns*, the *dependence of results on returns of single calendar months*, and the analysis of *portfolio returns across market regimes*. We describe each of these elements in the following sections.

3.3.2.1 Dependence on Few Months with Extreme Returns

Inspired by REY/SCHMID (2007), we investigate the changes of results and statistical inference of a given strategy when removing the $p = 1, 2, 3, 5$ highest monthly portfolio returns from the time-series.

3.3.2.2 Dependence on Returns of Single Calendar Months

Next, we want to make sure that our results are not driven by single calendar months, especially not by the well-known December (see e.g., CHEN/SINGAL (2003)) and January seasonality (see e.g., KEIM (1983)). Therefore, we separately analyze average monthly portfolio returns of a given strategy per individual calendar month as well as after excluding the return month of January respectively the return months of December and January.

3.3.2.3 Definition of Market Regimes

As a third analysis in research question [2], we investigate the performance of volume based portfolio strategies in different market regimes by restricting the time-series of monthly portfolio returns to specific months with certain characteristics. We now separately outline the definition of each of these market regimes, namely sub-periods, market phases, market volatility, and market volume.

3.3.2.3.1 Sub-Periods

To ensure consistency with the corresponding robustness check in the Fama-MacBeth regressions we divide the time-series into two sub-periods.

- Sub-period 1: return series from March 1997 to November 2002.
- Sub-period 2: return series from December 2002 to August 2008.

3.3.2.3.2 Market Phases

A second definition of regimes is based on the performance of an underlying market index. In our specific case, this reference index is the Swiss Performance Index (SPI), because our portfolio strategies are formed on the basis of its constituent stocks. We distinguish between three different classifications of market phases, *bull markets versus bear markets*, *up and down markets*, and *positive and negative markets*.

Bull markets versus bear markets: the full time-series of portfolio returns is divided into two bull market phases (1: March 1997 to August 2000; 2: April 2003 to May 2007) and two bear market phases (1: September 2000 to March 2003; 2: June 2007 to August 2008). This segmentation is straightforward considering Figure 3.4 below, which plots the development of the SPI over time (indexed to 100 at the end of February 1997). The only discussion point evolves around the market correction in August / September 1998. We decided, however, to concentrate on the main structural breaks in the time-series.

Thus, we include this correction in the overall bull market between March 1997 and August 2000.

Figure 3.4: Bull and Bear Markets SPI

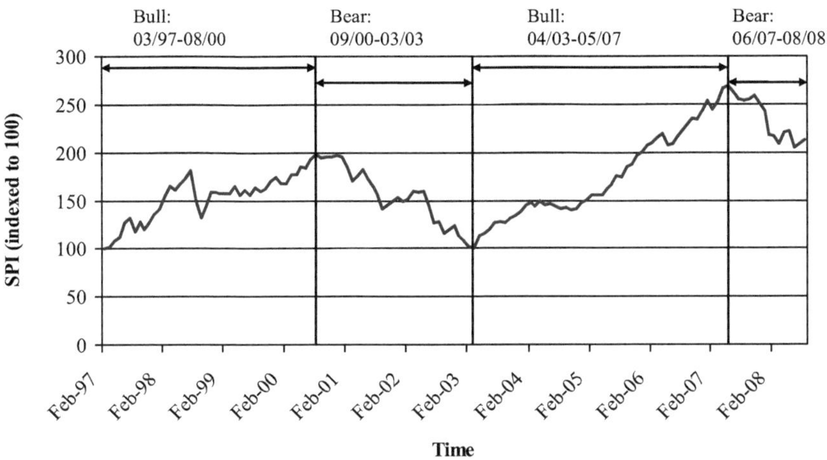

Up and down markets: in a second classification of market phases, following COOPER ET AL. (2004), we distinguish between up and down markets based on rolling 12-month index performance. Let us illustrate this approach with an example: if the index value at a specific point in time (e.g., at the end of January 2000) is higher than 12 months ago (in this example at the end of January 1999) the next return month (February 2000) is considered as being part of an up market. Otherwise we are in a down market. For a definition of up and down markets in our concrete data set see Figure 3.5 (note that a state indicator of "1" corresponds to an up market while a "-1" corresponds to a down market). When comparing this classification with the above bull and bear market phases in Figure 3.4 we see that the definition of up and down markets follows the 'true' development of the market with a lag of approximately six months.

An advantage of this classification of the time-series compared to the bull and bear market definition is that the state of the market is known ex-ante (i.e., at the beginning of month t when investment decisions are taken). Depending on the test results, this might enable us to define dynamic strategies, e.g., a 'volume based' investment only in up markets or down markets.

Figure 3.5: Up and Down Markets SPI

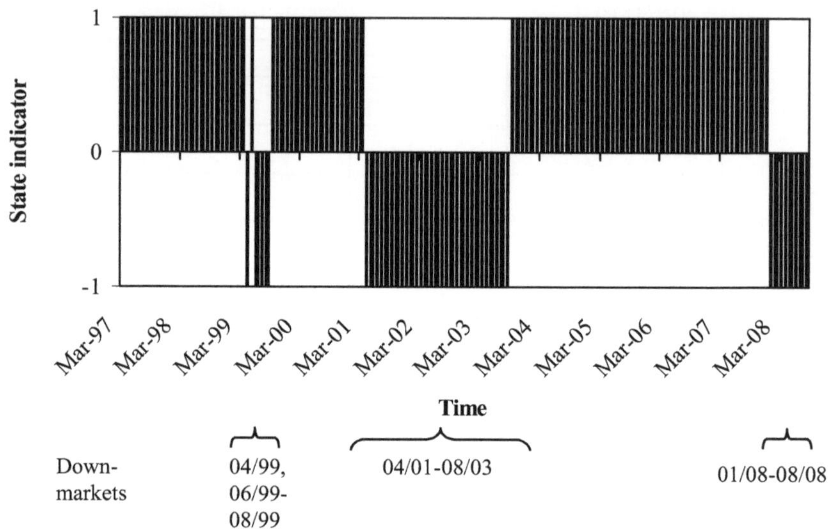

As a final remark regarding this classification, we should point out the possibility to define up and down markets according to longer time-horizons, e.g., rolling 24- or 36-month windows.[110] However, we find (in unreported tests) that the described lag versus the true market development increases substantially with the length of this time-horizon.[111] We thus limit the analysis to the 12-month horizon.

Positive and negative market return months: finally, we distinguish between months with positive market returns and months with negative market returns. Of the 138 SPI return months from March 1997 to August 2008, market returns were positive in 88 months and negative in 50 months.

[110] See COOPER ET AL. (2004).

[111] Illustration: in the case of rolling 36-month windows, August 2008 is still classified as an up market, although the SPI has been in a bear market since June 2007.

3.3.2.3.3 Market Volatility

The relationship between trading volume and expected returns could also differ depending on the aggregate volatility of the stock market.[112] In this analysis, we take the VCL Clariden Leu Swiss Equity Volatility Index as a measure of market volatility.[113] The VCL was first calculated in January 1996 and measures the implied volatility of EUREX (a major futures and options exchange) options (on most important Swiss stocks), thereby serving as an indicator for the risk evaluation of market participants. In the market volatility time-series displayed in Figure 3.6, we calculate the monthly index value (in points) as an average of daily values in the respective month. We define three different volatility regimes, *high volatility* (approximately the top 30% of monthly values), *low volatility* (approximately the bottom 30% of daily values), and *normal volatility*.

Figure 3.6: VCL Clariden Leu Swiss Equity Volatility Index

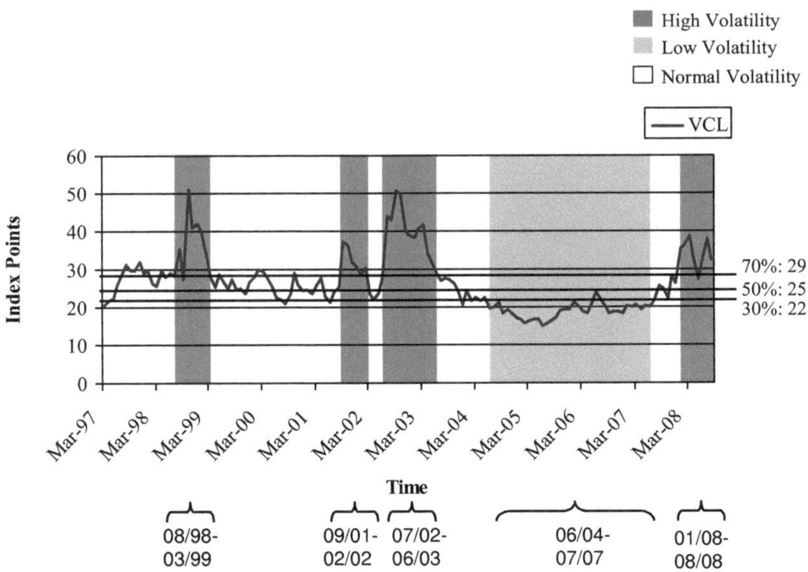

[112] The regime definition based on market volatility is inspired by ANG ET AL. (2006).

[113] See www.claridenleu.ch.

One interesting finding in Figure 3.6 is the fact that different volatility phases are rather persistent (note that the existence of so-called 'volatility clusters' is a phenomenon that has been known for a long time, see for example the seminal work by MANDELBROT (1963)). This allows us to build a 'naïve' volatility forecasting model, which might again prove useful with regard to defining dynamic investment strategies (see above, 3.3.2.3.2).

This forecasting model is based on the following rules:

- *'High forecasted volatility regime'* in month *t*, if the average VCL index value is above 30 in *t-1;*
- *'Low forecasted volatility regime'* in month *t*, if the average VCL index value is below 20 in *t-1;*
- *'Normal forecasted volatility regime'* in month *t*, if the average VCL index value is between 20 and 30 in *t-1*.

Figure 3.7 shows the resulting forecasted volatility regimes in our time-series (note that values of *1*, *-1*, and *0* correspond to *high*, *low*, and *normal* forecasted volatility).

Figure 3.7: Forecasted Volatility Regimes

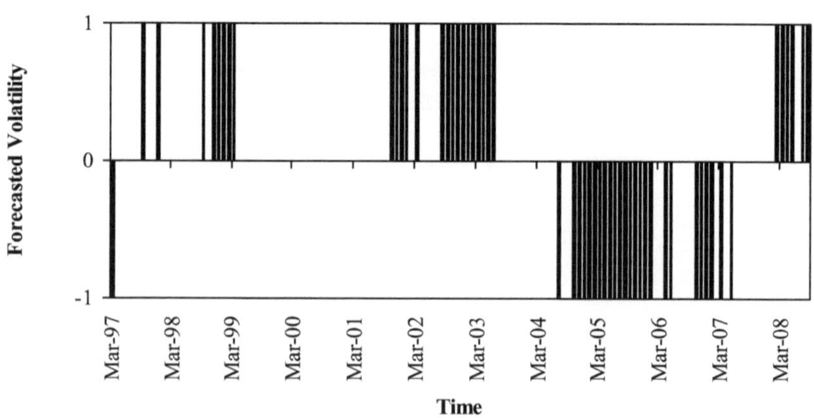

When testing the accuracy of the forecasting model we find that it correctly identifies approximately 75% of the true high- and low-volatility months. This is not surprising given the fact that the volatility regimes are relatively persistent as shown in Figure 3.6. Despite this positive result, it is important to note that the forecasting model is only a very rough approximation. Developing a more elaborate forecasting model, however, is out of scope of this research project.

3.3.2.3.4 Market Volume

Recall that the main objective of this research project is to investigate the relationship between *trading volume* and expected returns. It is thus interesting to see whether the *level of market volume* has an influence on the direction or strength of this relation. We consider two alternative definitions of volume regimes based on either *total Swiss franc volume of trading* or market *average share turnover*.

Total Swiss franc volume of trading: as shown in Figure 3.8, the time-series is divided into two parts, namely a normal volume regime from March 1997 to January 2007 and a high volume regime from February 2007 onwards.

Figure 3.8: Total Market Trading Volume, De-Trended and Season-Adjusted (CHF Million)

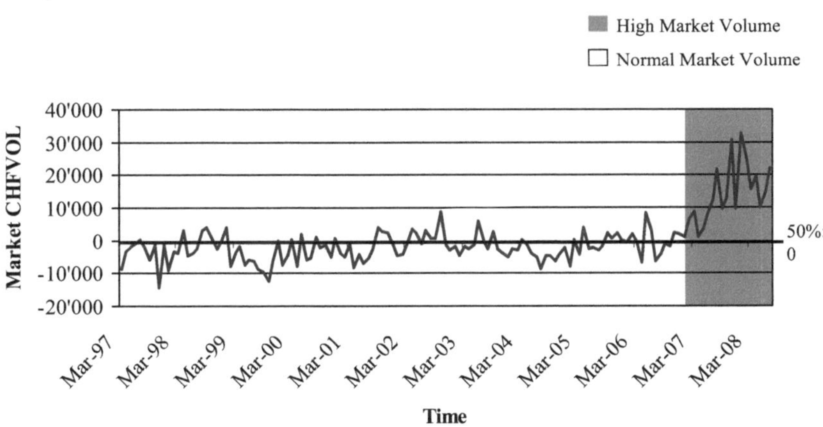

Note that numbers presented in Figure 3.8 do not correspond to absolute traded amounts (i.e., the sum of Swiss franc volume of all stocks included in the database in a given month). Rather, the raw figures are adjusted to account for two (potential) biases. First, the volume series contains a *time-trend,* because market capitalizations generally increase over time, which also inflates the Swiss franc trading volume. We follow AMIHUD (2002) and adjust for this trend by multiplying the raw amount of total Swiss franc volume of trading in a given month *t* by the ratio of (Total market cap $_{\text{Mar 1997}}$ / Total market cap $_{t-1}$). Thus, we make sure that the substantial increase in volume towards the end of the time-series in Figure 3.8 is not just a result of higher market capitalizations. Second, there could be a *seasonal-trend* in the volume time-series, i.e., systematically higher or lower market volume in a given calendar month. We neutralize this potential calendar effect by subtracting the average volume of the respective calendar month from the 'time-trend adjusted total volume' in any given month *t*.[114]

Average share turnover: we again divide the time-series into two parts, a normal share turnover phase from March 1997 to January 2005 and a high share turnover regime from February 2005 onwards (see Figure 3.9). The presented turnover figures are constructed in two steps. First, we calculate the average (equal-weighted) share turnover across all stocks included in the database in a given month. And second, we again adjust for a potential calendar effect applying the same methodology described above. Since share turnover is a relative and not an absolute measure, we abstain from additionally detrending the time-series.[115]

Final remark regarding volume regimes: in 3.3.2.3.2, we show ways to ex-ante define the prevailing regime (i.e., up and down markets). Unfortunately, we do not see any similar approach regarding volume regimes. As a result, we concentrate on the ex-post definition described in this section.

[114] The general pattern of the 'non-adjusted volume series' does not substantially differ from the presented 'time-trend and season-adjusted market volume'.

[115] The general pattern of the turnover time-series does not substantially change when using alternative construction methods (i.e., no season-adjustment or value-weighting of individual stock's share turnover ratios in a given month).

Figure 3.9: Average Market Turnover, Season-Adjusted (Percent)

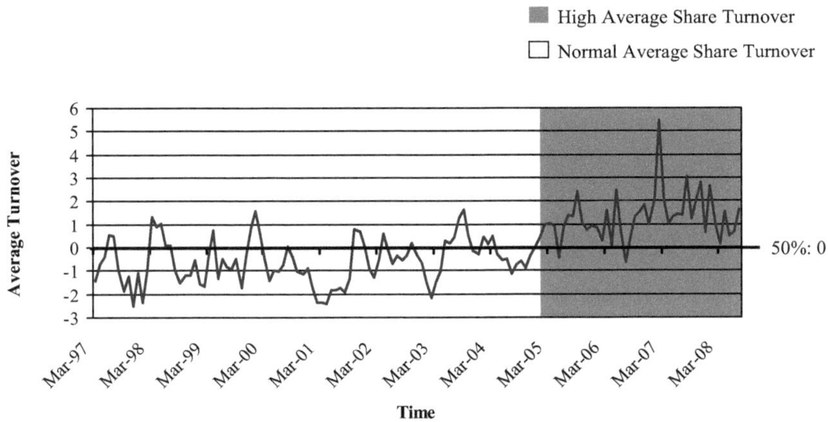

3.3.3 Economic Significance of Volume-Return Relations

A third and final set of empirical tests is designed to answer research question [3] whether discovered volume-return relations are economically significant. The main objective is to analyze whether volume-return relations also exist in a setting that is more realistic for an investor than the simplified base strategy scenario. This is reflected in the following four sub-analyses: *calculation of portfolio returns in a more practical setting*, *risk-based analysis*, investigation of *investability of volume based portfolio strategies*, and *performance in selected market states / regimes*. Each of these analyses are outlined next.

3.3.3.1 Portfolio Returns in a More Practical Setting

As a first step, we repeat selected previous portfolio-based analyses (labeled 'base strategies') in a more realistic setting (labeled 'practical strategies'). Figure 3.10 shows a comparison between main construction principles of these two types of strategies.

Figure 3.10: 'Base' Versus 'Practical' Portfolio Strategies

	Base strategies	**Practical strategies**
Data		
• Return series	• 03/1997 – 08/2008	• 02/1998 – 08/2008
• Data requirements	• Availability of complete return series over holding period (K = *1, 3, 6, 12* months)	• Availability of next month's return only
Return calculation		
• Within portfolio	• Arithmetic mean return of constituent stocks	• Weighted average based on each *stock*'s performance over previous holding period months
• Across all K cohorts	• Equal-weighted average	• Weighted average based on each *portfolio*'s performance over previous holding period months
• Over entire time-series	• Arithmetic mean of monthly returns	• Arithmetic mean of monthly returns

Return series: in the base strategies, the first holding period month is March 1997 (using data of companies providing volume data since January 1996) and the last portfolio holding period is August 2008. We choose March 1997 as a first holding period month for two reasons: first, this is consistent with the regression analysis and enables us to directly compare results. And second, it is in line with VAIHEKOSKI (2004) who states that 'all data should be used as efficiently as possible, especially in small markets'. We thus use the longest time-series possible (given the limited availability of volume data) to answer the question whether trading volume plays a role in the cross-sectional variation of expected returns in the Swiss stock market.

In a multi-month holding period setting (i.e., $K > 1$ month), however, there is a 'practicability downside' to using portfolio return months as early as March 1997. Namely, we cannot invest in all K investment cohorts in parallel at the beginning of the time-series due to data availability.[116] Let us illustrate this issue for the $K = 12$ months holding pe-

[116] Recall from above discussion (3.3.1.2.3) that we are in parallel invested in K different strategies / investment cohorts, since we form portfolios each month t, not only every K months.

riod: in March 1997, we should preferably invest in strategies (i.e., investment cohorts) implemented in the current month (March 1997) and in the previous K - 1 months (i.e., from April 1996 onwards). However, we do not have enough previous data to construct the early portfolios for high formation periods J. In the most extreme case of $J = 12$ months, the portfolio implemented in April 1996 would be based on data from as early as February 1995 (depending on the volume measure investigated), but we only have volume data available starting in January 1996. To eliminate this problem we *discard the first 11 holding period months* from the sample for the practicability test. As a result, the first holding period is February 1998 (the last holding period remains August 2008). This ensures that for every combination of volume measures, formation period lengths, and holding period lengths, we can directly invest in all K investment cohorts from the beginning, which improves the practicability of the test. Note that in the base strategies we circumvent this data availability issue by not investing in K different strategies / cohorts from the beginning. Rather, we only invest in one first cohort in March 1997, a second one in April 1997, and so on. This means that we are 'fully' invested in the K cohorts only after K-1 months.[117]

Data requirements: in the regression analysis, it is by construction necessary that an individual stock's return is available for the next $K = 1, 3, 6, 12$ months. Otherwise the stock cannot be included in the sample in a given month. We apply the same rule for the base portfolio strategies in research questions [1]&[2], again to be consistent with the regressions (which ensures the comparability of results). However, from an investor's point of view it is possible that a stock included in a particular portfolio is delisted from the stock exchange during the holding period (from a database perspective this means that the return series is incomplete). Therefore, we adjust the data requirement for the practicability test: to be included in the sample in a given month only a stock's one-month return is necessary, regardless of the length of the holding periods, K.

[117] Note that we face the same problem of data availability in a multi-month holding period setting at the end of the time-series, because not all necessary returns are yet available in August 2008. In the base strategies we ensure being able to use the complete time-series until August 2008 (consistent with regressions) by investing in K parallel strategies only until month 'August 2008 minus K-1'. Afterwards, we do not start a new strategy anymore due to data availability. This means that in the final month we are only invested in one last cohort (started in 'August 2008 minus K-1'). In the more practical setting (chapter 6), the adjustment of the data requirements (next paragraph) enable us to remain invested in K parallel strategies until the end of the time-series.

Two additional remarks regarding delistings: first, if a stock is delisted during the holding period, we assume a post-delisting return of 0 for the rest of the holding period months.[118] The second remark deals with the delisting return itself (i.e., the last reported stock return). SHUMWAY (1997) and SHUMWAY/WARTHER (1999) point out that in case of a performance-related delisting the final return included in financial databases is often missing / not available, which potentially creates a bias. The authors of these papers find that performance-related delistings are often unanticipated, which implies that a stock is probably not traded anymore after the announcement of a delisting. In such a case, however, the last return reported in a database is not the return for an investor who holds the specific stock, which can be as low as -100%. But, even though this issue might also concern our data, we do not see a large potential bias for the following reasons: SHUMWAY/WARTHER (1999) find that an annual average of roughly 5.6% of all Nasdaq stocks have been delisted for performance reasons between 1973 and 1995. The corresponding number for NYSE/AMEX stocks is 1.2% according to SHUMWAY (1997). In an analysis of all delistings of stocks included in our database, however, we find this number to be as low as 0.3% (see Table 3.6).[119] This shows that the issue of delisting returns is smaller in our database. In addition, we did not find any striking commonalities regarding past volume measures of the six performance-related delistings. Thus, we do not see the need to systematically adjust our data.

[118] An alternative approach is to take the risk-free rate instead of 0. The difference to our approach should be marginal given the rather low historical risk-free rates in Switzerland. Even in the US, LIU/STRONG (2008) report similar results for both methods.

[119] These results are based on a web-search, in particular the website of the Swiss stock exchange, www.six-swiss-exchange.com, and www.google.ch.

Table 3.6: Transparency on Delistings in the Database

Year	Number of Firms in Database	Number of Delistings	Percentage Delisted	Performance-related Delistings	Percentage Delisted (Performance-related)
1997	142	2	1.4	0	0.0
1998	158	3	1.9	0	0.0
1999	170	4	2.4	0	0.0
2000	181	3	1.7	0	0.0
2001	198	4	2.0	0	0.0
2002	207	3	1.4	1	0.5
2003	192	10	5.2	4	2.1
2004	196	3	1.5	0	0.0
2005	199	6	3.0	1	0.5
2006	199	8	4.0	0	0.0
2007	203	3	1.5	0	0.0
2008	202	2	1.0	0	0.0
Average	**187**	**4**	**2.3**	**0.5**	**0.3**

Number of firms in database is average of monthly constituent list (end of month; in 1997 only Feb-Dec; in 2008 only Jan-Jul). Number of delistings is the number of stocks with an incomplete monthly return series in the respective year. Performance-related delistings are all delistings where reason is not merger / takeover / going private or a pre-announced liquidation.

Return calculation within portfolio: in the base strategies, we follow the approach used in most of the relevant literature including JEGADEESH/TITMAN (1993) and LEE/SWAMINATHAN (2000).[120] More concretely, we calculate monthly portfolio returns as the arithmetic mean return of individual stocks included. For the $K = 1$ month holding period this approach is correct, even from an investor's perspective. For multi-month holding periods (i.e., $K > 1$), however, this calculation assumes a monthly rebalancing of the portfolio to equal weights. As noted by LIU/STRONG (2008), this simplification is unrealistic because it most likely involves prohibitive transaction costs. More realistically, the portfolio returns in a given holding period month should reflect each constituent stock's performance over previous holding period months. Let us illustrate this with

[120] See LIU/STRONG (2008), table 1, for a more complete list of recently published papers using this method.

a portfolio consisting of two stocks, A and B. Assume we invest CHF 1 in each stock at the beginning of month t. Given month t performance of stocks A and B of 100% respectively 0%, the Net Asset Value (NAV) of the portfolio (disregarding transaction costs) increases to CHF 3 at the end of t (NAV A: CHF 2; NAV B: CHF 1). As a result, the weights given to stocks A and B for the calculation of the portfolio return in month $t+1$ should be 2/3 respectively 1/3. Assuming month $t+1$ returns for stocks A and B of 20% and 50%, this results in a portfolio return of 30% (i.e., 2/3 x 0.2 + 1/3 x 0.5) in month $t+1$. The equal-weighted performance followed in most of the relevant literature as well as in our base strategies, however, would be 35% (i.e., 1/2 x 0.2 + 1/2 x 0.5).

In the practicability test, we thus follow a more realistic weighting scheme. More formally, we apply the following formulas for the return to an equally-weighted portfolio in an individual month τ from a K-month holding period:[121]

$$r_{P1}^{ew} = \frac{1}{N}\sum_{i=1}^{N} r_{i1},$$

$$r_{p\tau}^{ew} = \sum_{i=1}^{N} \frac{\prod_{t=1}^{\tau-1}(1+r_{it})}{\sum_{j=1}^{N}\prod_{t=1}^{\tau-1}(1+r_{jt})} r_{i\tau}, \qquad \tau = 2,\dots,K; \qquad (3.7)$$

Note again that the return in the first month of the holding period is the arithmetic average of individual stock returns. As a result, this adjusted calculation method does not affect the return calculation of $K = 1$ month strategies.

Return calculation across all K cohorts: recall that we invest in parallel in K different strategies / investment cohorts. In the base strategies, we follow the simplified approach of JEGADEESH/TITMAN (1993) and LEE/SWAMINATHAN (2000) to calculate monthly returns across these investment cohorts. More concretely, we calculate the monthly return for a K-month holding period in month t as the equal-weighted average of portfolio returns from strategies implemented in the current and in the previous $K-1$ months (see 3.3.1.2.3 above). Unless we rebalance all investment cohorts to equal-weights at the end of every month (which might entail prohibitive transaction costs), this technique is again not entirely correct from an investor's perspective. This is caused by

[121] See LIU/STRONG (2008), formula (4).

the fact that the individual cohorts' NAVs differ depending on past portfolio performance within each cohort.

The solution used for our practicability test is similar to the 'within portfolio' case: at the beginning of the first holding period, February 1998, we invest equal amounts (e.g., CHF 1) in each cohort. We then record changes in the NAVs of different cohorts each period depending on respective portfolio returns. Finally, the monthly return across all K cohorts is simply the percentage change in total NAV (which is the sum of the K individual cohorts' NAVs). Note that for the $K = 1$ month holding period this calculation is not necessary, since we are only invested in one cohort each month. As a result, portfolio returns equal total monthly returns.

Return calculation over entire time-series: finally, the average return over the entire time-series equals the arithmetic average of all monthly returns, both in the base strategies (see 3.3.1.2.1) and in the practicability test. This approach allows us to calculate conventional (two-sided) t-statistics for the statistical tests.[122] As one additional robustness check, however, we also report geometric mean returns.

3.3.3.2 Risk-Based Analysis

A further test of economic significance is the question of analyzing risk-adjusted portfolio returns. We execute this analysis by taking into account several risk factors shown to explain an important part of stock return variations, which has become a standard in our research context.

CAPM: The origin of all risk factor-based analyses is the *Capital Asset Pricing Model* (CAPM) developed by SHARPE (1964), LINTNER (1965) and MOSSIN (1966). This model is based on a single risk factor, the excess return of the market portfolio over the risk-free rate. As noted earlier, the CAPM states that the variation of returns across stocks can be explained solely by their sensitivities (i.e., betas) to this market factor.

[122] REY/SCHMID (2007), who report geometric mean returns, have to conduct Monte Carlo simulations to test the statistical significance of their portfolio strategies.

To account for market risk, we regress monthly excess returns to our (practical) volume based portfolio strategies on the time-series of monthly excess returns on the market portfolio, i.e.,

$$r_{p,t} - rf_t = a_T + b_T RMRF_t + e_t; \tag{3.8}$$

$r_{p,t}$ is the return of the respective portfolio at time t, rf_t is the monthly CHF risk-free rate, and $RMRF_t$ is the excess return of the Swiss market portfolio over the CHF call money rate at time t. Note that the estimated intercept coefficient, a_T, is interpretable as the risk-adjusted portfolio return relative to the CAPM. If this intercept coefficient is significantly different from zero in our estimates, this implies that the risk factor-based model (CAPM) cannot fully explain excess returns generated by volume-sorted portfolio strategies.

Later research documents empirical contradictions and anomalies that strongly question the validity of the CAPM. See particularly FAMA/MACBETH (1973) and FAMA/FRENCH (1992). This evidence led to the extension of the CAPM to multifactor models to explain stock returns.[123] We thus include two additional standard risk factor-based models in our analysis, namely the *Fama-French three-factor model* and the *Carhart four-factor model.*

Fama-French three-factor model: as previously described (see above, 3.3.1.1.2), two observed stock attributes shown to affect the cross-section of returns are market capitalization (i.e., 'size effect') and book-to-market ratio (i.e., 'value effect'). FAMA/FRENCH (1993) thus construct factor mimicking portfolios based on firm size and book-to-market ratios, which account for risks additional to the market risk represented in the CAPM. More precisely, the authors incorporate two additional risk factors in their model, labeled SMB and HML. SMB stands for 'Small Minus Big' and represents the time-series of returns on a zero-cost arbitrage portfolio that is long in *small* stocks and short in large ('*big*') stocks (based on market capitalizations). HML on the other hand stands for 'High Minus Low' and represents the time-series of returns on a zero-cost

[123] We focus on fundamental multifactor models (instead of macroeconomic and statistical factor models) because CONNOR (1995) shows that those have the highest explanatory power, which results in a high relevance both in theory and practice.

arbitrage portfolio that is long in stocks with *high* book-to-market ratios and short in stocks with *low* book-to-market ratios.

In a second step, we thus follow FAMA/FRENCH (1993) and regress monthly excess returns to our (practical) volume based portfolio strategies on the time-series of Swiss factor premiums RMRF, SMB, and HML, i.e.,

$$r_{p,t} - rf_t = a_T + b_T RMRF_t + s_T SMB_t + v_T HML_t + e_t . \quad (3.9)$$

Carhart four-factor model: FAMA/FRENCH (1996) show that their model captures returns to portfolios formed on many other empirical anomalies such as earnings-price ratio or reversal of long-term returns. However, the previously mentioned phenomenon of intermediate-term return continuation documented by JEGADEESH/TITMAN (1993) is unexplained by their three-factor model. As a result, CARHART (1995, 1997) extends the Fama-French model by an additional momentum factor, UMD. UMD stands for 'Up Minus Down' and represents the time-series of returns on a zero-cost arbitrage portfolio that is long in stocks with high one-year past returns (*'up'*) and short in stocks with low one-year past returns (*'down'*).

Thus, as a final risk-adjustment, we apply the Carhart-model and regress monthly excess returns to our (practical) volume based portfolio strategies on the four Swiss factor premiums RMRF, SMB, HML, and UMD[124], i.e.,

$$r_{p,t} - rf_t = a_T + b_T RMRF_t + s_T SMB_t + v_T HML_t + u_T UMD_t + e_t . \quad (3.10)$$

Besides the estimation of risk-adjusted portfolio returns, the analysis in this section includes a comparison of risk and performance attributes (e.g., returns, standard deviations, Sharpe ratios) of volume based portfolio strategies compared to relevant index returns. The indices considered are the Swiss Performance Index (which is a value-weighted index) and a hypothetical equal-weighted index constructed from all stocks included in our database each month (for details regarding data requirements, see above, 3.2).

[124] All four Swiss factor premiums are provided by Manuel Ammann and Michael Steiner (see www.ammannsteiner.ch).

3.3.3.3 Investability

The first set of analyses within the chapter on economic significance is designed to establish a setting that is more practical from an investor's perspective. On the basis of these more realistic construction principles we then test the investability of volume based portfolio strategies. This means to investigate whether investors would have actually earned money in the past by implementing portfolio strategies based on the relationship between trading volume and expected returns in the cross-section of Swiss stocks. The analysis entails the *inclusion of transaction costs*, some *further robustness checks regarding scalability*, as well as a *more realistic calculation of profits of long-short strategies over multi-month holding periods*.

Inclusion of transaction costs: this first analysis includes two components, the calculation of transaction costs and the appropriate level of transaction costs.

Calculation of transaction costs: the chosen approach is inspired by LIU/STRONG (2008) and works on the basis of adjusting monthly returns of individual stocks in those months when a transaction occurs. Given the transaction-cost-adjusted monthly returns for individual stocks we can again calculate portfolio returns applying the same methodology described above for the practical strategies (3.3.3.1, particularly equation (3.7)).

Recall that we investigate both long-only portfolio strategies as well as zero-cost arbitrage strategies consisting of long positions and short positions of equal size. We first show the calculation of transaction-cost-adjusted monthly returns for stocks in the long portfolio:

(1) Transaction-cost-adjusted returns: long portfolio, buying

In the long portfolio, a first transaction is needed at the beginning of each holding period *h*. When investing in a new portfolio, we buy a specific quantity of stock *i*. This lowers the return on stock *i* in the first holding period month, r_{i1} , which we incorporate through the following equation,

$$r_{adj_{i1}} = \frac{(1+r_{i1})}{(1+tc_{long})} - 1, \tag{3.11}$$

where tc_{long} is the transaction cost for the long portfolio (in percent of the invested quantity). It is important to note that this return-adjustment is only needed if a stock is included in a specific portfolio in holding period *h*, but not in holding period *h-1*. If the stock, however, remains in the same portfolio for two consecutive holding periods, no transaction is necessary.[125]

(2) Transaction-cost-adjusted returns: long portfolio, selling

At the end of holding period *h*, a further transaction is needed when liquidating the portfolio. We incorporate the costs of selling by adjusting the return of stock i in holding period month *K*, r_{iK} ,

$$r_{adj_{iK}} = ((1+r_{iK})(1-tc_{long}))-1; \tag{3.12}$$

Here, the return-adjustment is only necessary if the stock is included in a portfolio in holding period *h* but not in holding period *h+1*. Special case for holding periods of *K* = *1* month length: if a stock is bought at the beginning of the month and sold at the end of the (same) month, r_{iK} in equation (3.12) corresponds to the 'buying-cost-adjusted' return from (3.11).

The transaction-cost-adjustments for the short portfolio are very similar, only in the opposite direction:

(3) Transaction-cost-adjusted returns: short portfolio, selling[126]

$$r_{adj_{i1}} = \frac{(1+r_{i1})}{(1-tc_{short})} - 1, \tag{3.13}$$

where tc_{short} is the transaction cost for the short portfolio (in percent of the quantity sold short at the beginning of holding period *h*).

[125] This is a simplification; in reality, a small rebalancing is necessary at the end of holding period *h-1* to restore equal weights at the beginning of *h*. We do not feel that this should significantly alter our results.

[126] i.e., at the beginning of holding period *h*, if the stock is not included in the same short portfolio in holding period *h-1*.

(4) Transaction-cost-adjusted returns: short portfolio, buying[127]

$$r_{adj_{iK}} = ((1 + r_{iK})(1 + tc_{short})) - 1. \tag{3.14}$$

Transaction cost level: we acknowledge that different investors (e.g., private, institutional) face different levels of trading costs. But since we want our results to be useful for all types of traders, we conduct this analysis for various levels of transaction costs. First, we apply costs for buying respectively selling of 30 basis points each (i.e., round-trip costs of 60 basis points). This follows DOMOWITZ ET AL. (2001) who report this level of explicit costs for institutional traders in Swiss stocks (between 1996 and 1998). This is also the same level used by KANIEL ET AL. (2007), thereby ensuring comparability of results (see above, 2.1.2.1.1). Further buying / selling costs considered are 50, 100, and 150 basis points (corresponding to round-trip costs of 100, 150, and 300 basis points).

Note that we apply the same level of transaction costs for all stocks in our analysis, regardless of company size, which is of course a simplification. Nevertheless, we feel that the various levels of transaction costs considered give a good overview of how much costs a specific strategy can bear before its returns become insignificant respectively zero.

Further robustness checks regarding scalability: a strategy's scalability is another concern that needs to be addressed, particularly for institutional investors:

Value-weighting: above, 3.3.1.2.1, we state that we generally apply an equal-weighted investing of stocks within a portfolio, which means that we allocate equal CHF amounts to each stock in a portfolio at the beginning of a specific holding period *h*. The advantage of this approach is that it highlights the cross-sectional variety of all available assets.[128] On the other hand, however, it is possible that an investor cannot allocate the theoretically desired amount in a particular stock due to its (small) overall market capitalization. Therefore, as noted above, we conduct a robustness check where initial CHF allocation to each stock in a portfolio depends on the weight of its market capitalization

127 i.e., at the end of the last month of holding period *h*, if the stock is included in the short portfolio in holding period *h* but not in holding period *h+1*.

128 See VAIHEKOSKI (2004).

in relation to the total market capitalization of all stocks in the respective portfolio. Technically, we directly incorporate these weights into equation (3.7) by adding initial weights equaling the relative market values, i.e.,[129]

$$r_{P1}^{vw} = \sum_{i=1}^{N} w_i r_{i1},$$

$$r_{p\tau}^{vw} = \sum_{i=1}^{N} \frac{w_i \prod_{t=1}^{\tau-1}(1+r_{it})}{\sum_{j=1}^{N} w_j \prod_{t=1}^{\tau-1}(1+r_{jt})} r_{i\tau}, \quad \tau = 2,\ldots,K. \tag{3.15}$$

Exclusion of micro cap stocks: additionally, we want to make sure that the returns of volume based portfolio strategies are not exclusively driven by the smallest stocks. Thus, we selectively repeat the practical strategies excluding different levels of market capitalizations, namely CHF 50 million and CHF 100 million.

More realistic calculation of profits of long-short strategies for multi-month holding periods: so far, in both the base strategies as well as in the practicability test, monthly returns to zero-cost arbitrage strategies (also called 'long-short strategies') are calculated as the simple return difference between the long portfolio[130] and the short portfolio[131] in that month, i.e.,

$$LS_\tau = r_{L,\tau} - r_{S,\tau}, \qquad \tau = 1,\ldots,K; \tag{3.16}$$

This calculation method has different advantages. First, it is the approach followed by most of the relevant existing empirical studies including JEGADEESH/TITMAN (1993) and LEE/SWAMINATHAN (2000), thereby ensuring comparability. Besides, it is easily comprehensible for a reader and it helps to analyze the dynamics of a particular (in our case 'volume') effect in the cross-section of stock returns. In a multi-month holding period setting (i.e., $K > 1$ month), however, this calculation does not precisely track a real investor's return. This is caused by the fact that, as LIU/STRONG (2008) put it, 'the initial investment of \$1 in the long and short sides increases or decreases with changes in the market values of the long and short portfolios.' Thus, as a final test concerning

[129] See LIU/STRONG (2008), formula (3).

[130] e.g., high volume stocks.

[131] e.g., low volume stocks.

investability, we follow LIU/STRONG (2008) to account for these changes in the market values of the long and short portfolios:[132] suppose a strategy is long CHF 1 in portfolio L for K months, and at the same time it is short CHF 1 in portfolio S for the same K months. The monthly profits of this long-short strategy over the K-month holding period are

$$LS_1 = r_{L,1} - r_{S,1},$$

$$LS_\tau = r_{L,\tau}\prod_{t=1}^{\tau-1}(1+r_{L,t}) - r_{S,\tau}\prod_{t=1}^{\tau-1}(1+r_{S,t}), \quad \tau = 2,\ldots,K; \tag{3.17}$$

Note that the first holding period month corresponds to formula (3.16). As a result, this adjusted methodology does not affect the return calculation of long-short strategies for the $K = 1$ month holding period case.[133] As LIU/STRONG (2008) report, formula (3.16) generally underestimates the true profits if the phenomenon under examination holds. In that sense an additional advantage of following (3.16) up to this point is that it is more conservative. This helps not to jump to conclusions about potential volume-return relations too quickly.

3.3.3.4 Performance in Selected Market States

A final set of tests based on the more realistic portfolio construction and return calculation principles is the analysis of the performance of these 'practical strategies' in selected market states.

First, we perform a general *robustness check of the time-stability of portfolio returns* to make sure that the dynamics identified as part of research question [2] (chapter 5) remain unchanged in the practical setting (which we hypothesize to be the case).

Second, as previously mentioned, we test the *feasibility of simple dynamic portfolio strategies*, e.g., the combination of long-short volume strategies (in specific, ex-ante known market regimes) with long-only index investments.

---

[132] See LIU/STRONG (2008), formula (11).

[133] Because the previous calculation method already corresponds to a real investor's return.

And finally, we perform a *stress test of our results in a particular market environment*. Recall that our return time-series ends in August 2008. However, following the collapse of the US investment bank Lehman Brothers in September 2008 stock markets around the world got into serious turmoil until (at least) the end of that year. To make sure that this turmoil did not fundamentally change the investigated relationship between trading volume and expected returns, we thus individually analyze the performance of our volume based portfolio strategies in 2008, with a particular emphasis on the last four months.[134]

3.4 Research Hypotheses

On the basis of the literature review, the description of the research questions, and the detailed outline of the methodology applied to answer them, we now state the main hypotheses that guide us in the empirical part of this research project. We define a set of testable main hypotheses for each investigated volume measure.

Volume Level (VL): based on considerable evidence in US and other developed stock markets (see above, Table 2.1), we expect a *negative relationship between the level of trading volume and expected returns* in the cross-section of Swiss stocks. While we acknowledge the inconclusive volume level-return evidence by ROUWENHORST (1999), we hypothesize his study of 20 emerging markets to be less relevant in our context of the developed Swiss stock market. Technically, we investigate the relationship between volume level and expected returns through the following hypotheses, both in regression analyses and portfolio-based tests:

> *[VL-H0]: There is no relationship between the level of trading volume and expected returns in the cross-section of Swiss stocks.*

> *[VL-H1]: There is a (positive / negative) relationship between the level of trading volume and expected returns in the cross-section of Swiss stocks.*

Abnormal Volume (AV): although we introduce a new measure of abnormal volume, we hypothesize our findings to be in line with the high-volume return premium of

[134] This means that we extend the time-series by four months for that test.

GERVAIS ET AL. (2001) for the US and of KANIEL ET AL. (2007) for international stock markets. Thus, we expect a *positive relationship between abnormal volume and expected returns* in the cross-section of Swiss stocks, in line with the investor visibility hypothesis by MILLER (1977). Technically, we again transform this to two testable hypotheses, namely:

> *[AV-H0]: There is no relationship between abnormal trading volume and expected returns in the cross-section of Swiss stocks.*

> *[AV-H1]: There is a (positive / negative) relationship between abnormal trading volume and expected returns in the cross-section of Swiss stocks.*

Volume Growth (VG): previous (empirical and theoretical) research is scarce regarding volume growth. The only lead is a study by WATKINS (2007) who applies a similar measure of volume growth in the US stock markets. Based on these results, we rather expect a *positive relationship between volume growth and expected returns* in the cross-section of Swiss stocks. Technically, we again test the relationship via the two following hypotheses:

> *[VG-H0]: There is no relationship between volume growth and expected returns in the cross-section of Swiss stocks.*

> *[VG-H1]: There is a (positive / negative) relationship between volume growth and expected returns in the cross-section of Swiss stocks.*

Variability in Volume (VV): again based on evidence from the US stock markets, namely by CHORDIA ET AL. (2001) and KEENE/PETERSON (2007), we expect a *negative relationship between variability in volume and expected returns* in the cross-section of Swiss stocks. The corresponding testable hypotheses are:

> *[VV-H0]: There is no relationship between variability in volume and expected returns in the cross-section of Swiss stocks.*

> *[VV-H1]: There is a (positive / negative) relationship between variability in volume and expected returns in the cross-section of Swiss stocks.*

3.5 Differentiation from Existing Literature

We finish the chapter by relating the outlined methodology applied in this empirical investigation to existing literature, with a particular emphasis on previous studies on Swiss stock market data.

This research project mainly relates to the lagged volume-return relationship outlined in chapter 2.1. Additionally, we marginally touch upon the relationship between lagged trading volume / returns and subsequent returns (outlined in chapter 2.2) when controlling for previously documented return determinants in the Swiss stock market, namely past one-year returns (i.e., momentum).

The other volume-return relations presented in chapter 2 are not subject to this investigation for the following reasons:

- Knowledge about contemporaneous relationships between volume and returns (chapter 2.3) does not help in the development of profitable portfolio strategies, because we cannot infer any information about future returns.

- Since we are interested in the cross-sectional variation of returns and not in the cross-sectional variation of trading volume, we also abstain from studying relationships between lagged returns and subsequent volume (chapter 3.4).

- Finally, dynamic vector-autoregressive volume-return models (chapter 3.5) are not in scope because they study time-series, not cross-sectional data. As a result, information obtained from these models cannot be transferred to quantile-based portfolio strategies.

To our knowledge, there exists only one empirical study on the relationship between trading volume and expected returns in a Swiss stock market context, namely by KANIEL ET AL. (2007), who analyze the existence of a high-volume return premium in 41 countries including Switzerland (see above, 2.1.2.1). Figure 3.11 outlines the main differences between our own investigation and the paper by KANIEL ET AL. (2007).

Figure 3.11: Main Differences Between Own Investigation and Kaniel et al. (2007)

	Brändle (2009)	**Kaniel et al. (2007)**
Volume measures	• 4 volume measures • Own measure of 'abnormal volume': percentage change of last month's volume vs. average volume in preceding *J = 3, 6, 12* months	• Only 'high volume shocks' • 'High volume shock' if last day's trading volume among top 20% of trading volumes in past 50 days
Sample	• More recent data – up to 2008 • More complete universe – all SPI stocks (average: 190 stocks)	• Data only up to 2001 • Average of 65 stocks
Data	• Survivorship bias neutral data from Factset	• Datastream (survivorship bias?)
Time horizons	• Focus on longer-term relations – Formation period: 1 month – Reference period: 3-12 months – Holding period: 1-12 months	• Focus on short-term relations – Formation period: 1 day – Reference period: 50 days – Holding period: 20 days
Test procedure	• Construction of volume measure allows to apply standard cross-sectional tests	• Standard tests not easily applicable (since number of stocks assigned to high / normal / low volume portfolios varies each month)

Volume measures: KANIEL ET AL. (2007) investigate only one volume measure, high volume shocks. A high volume shock exists if a stock's last day trading volume is among the top 20% of the past 50 days' trading volume. Our empirical investigation, on the other hand, uses a different measure labeled 'abnormal volume', defined as the percentage change of last month's volume versus the average volume in the preceding $J = 3, 6, 12$ months. On top, we include three additional volume measures, namely volume level, volume growth, and variability in volume.

Sample: KANIEL ET AL'S (2007) Swiss stock market data only comprises an average of 65 stocks. Our sample, on the other hand, includes all SPI stocks that comply with certain data requirements, which is an average of 190 stocks. In addition, our data is more recent. While the final return month in our study is August 2008 (or even December 2008 for some tests), the time-series studied in KANIEL ET AL. (2007) ends in 2001.

Data: as described in chapter 3.2, this project uses survivorship bias neutral data from Factset, which means that only those stocks are selected each month that were actually part of the SPI at that point of time. KANIEL ET AL. (2007), on the other hand, use data from Datastream. As pointed out by INCE/PORTER (2006), however, classification errors in Datastream might induce a survivorship bias.

Time horizons: while KANIEL ET AL. (2007) focus on short-term relations between volume and expected returns, we also study longer-term relations, both regarding portfolio formation and holding periods.

Test procedure: finally, the construction of our volume measures allows us to apply standard tests of the cross-sectional variation of returns (as ANG ET AL. (2006) put it, 'it allows to easily control for other cross-sectional effects'), namely Fama-MacBeth regressions and portfolio-based tests using quantile-sorts. The relationship between KANIEL ET AL'S (2007) measure of volume shocks and expected returns, however, cannot be easily investigated via standard cross-section tests. This is due to the fact that, by definition, the number of stocks assigned to the different portfolios varies each month, which prevents the construction of quantile-sorted portfolios.

4 Results: Trading Volume and the Cross-Sectional Variation of Stock Returns

This chapter commences the empirical part of the research project. It presents results of tests designed to answer the first research question *whether different measures of trading volume play an important role in the cross-sectional variation of expected returns in the Swiss stock market*. The empirical analyses are divided into two parts, *regression analysis* and *portfolio-based tests*. The methodology applied is described in detail in the previous chapter (namely in 3.3.1). However, for ease of understanding we repeat the most important aspects of the approach at the relevant places.

4.1 Regression Analysis

We start by reporting coefficient estimates of Fama-MacBeth (FM) regressions of stock returns on the various volume measures hypothesized to have explanatory power in the cross-section. First, we outline results of the base analyses conducted on the entire dataset. Then, we test the sensitivity of these results to some key assumptions through various robustness checks.

4.1.1 Base Results

We investigate the role of volume in the cross-sectional variation of stock returns using four different measures, namely *volume level*, *abnormal volume*, *volume growth*, and *variability in volume*. Results of the FM regressions are reported according to this classification. Within each measure, we first present results of *share turnover based* volume variables, followed by *Swiss franc volume* based variables. This order is chosen because share turnover is less correlated with a company's size (see above, 3.3.1.1.2).

4.1.1.1 Volume Level

Table 4.1 reports average coefficient estimates of Pooled OLS-based FM regressions of stock returns on share turnover over different formation horizons.

Table 4.1: Fama-MacBeth Regression Estimates, Using Share Turnover

	Formation period *J* (months)			
Variable	1	3	6	12
Panel A: Share turnover				
Intercept	0.700 (11.135)***	0.810 (11.877)***	0.911 (12.349)***	0.941 (12.545)***
TURN	**0.309** **(5.761)*** **	**0.158** **(2.686)*** **	**0.051** **(0.789)**	**0.021** **(0.303)**
Panel B: Share turnover, controlled				
Intercept	1.665 (5.504)***	1.441 (4.869)***	1.355 (4.591)***	1.332 (4.551)***
TURN	**0.415** **(6.424)*** **	**0.232** **(3.234)*** **	**0.100** **(1.252)**	**0.071** **(0.842)**
SIZE	-0.154 (-3.134)***	-0.100 (-2.092)**	-0.069 (-1.429)	-0.062 (-1.262)
BM	0.511 (4.506)***	0.488 (4.242)***	0.469 (4.052)***	0.465 (4.032)***
RET2-12	0.013 (6.043)***	0.013 (6.059)***	0.013 (6.144)***	0.013 (6.199)***

This table reports coefficient estimates of Pooled OLS regressions over a return series from March 1997 to August 2008. The dependent variable is a stock's return in a given month. The independent variables are defined as follows: TURN is the logarithm of average monthly share turnover in the stock in the preceding *J = 1, 3, 6, 12* months. SIZE is the logarithm of a company's market capitalization at the beginning of the previous month. BM is the logarithm of the ratio of book value of equity to market capitalization at the beginning of the previous month. RET2-12 is the stock's cumulative return over the 11 months ending at the beginning of the previous month. ***/**/* Denotes statistical significance at the 1%/5%/10% level. T-statistics (in parentheses) are calculated using Newey-West (1987) adjusted, heteroskedasticity and serial correlation robust standard errors.

In Panel A, we find a positive relationship between share turnover and expected returns, even at significant levels for the shorter-term formation lengths (i.e., $J = 1, 3$ months). This relationship remains practically unchanged when additionally controlling for size, value and momentum measures (Table 4.1, Panel B). Note that the coefficients on the control variables in Panel B show the expected signs, i.e., positive for value and momentum, negative for size, and mostly at significant levels.

When repeating above regressions using Swiss franc volume as the only independent variable, however, the relationship between volume and expected returns is mostly negative, even at significant levels for longer-term formation periods (see Table 4.2, Panel A). But the results in Table 4.2, Panel B, show that once we additionally control for size, value, and momentum, this relationship becomes again significantly positive for shorter-term formation lengths ($J = 1, 3$ months) and non-significantly negative for longer-term formations ($J = 6, 12$ months). The nearby explanation for this phenomenon is the strong correlation between Swiss franc volume and size. In other words, the negative relation between size and expected returns (i.e., the size effect) dominates the positive relation between Swiss franc volume and expected returns (i.e., the potential volume level effect) in Table 4.2, Panel A.

In sum, the results so far suggest a positive relationship between different short-term measures of volume level and expected returns in the Swiss stock market (i.e., high volume stocks have higher expected returns). The evidence of a rather positive volume-return relationship is surprising when considering the results of previous studies. In fact, to our knowledge all existing FM regression based empirical tests suggest a negative relationship (see above, 2.1.1.1, and particularly Table 2.1). The only indication for a potential positive 'volume level'-return relationship in the context of European stock markets are ROUWENHORST'S (1999) portfolio-based test results. In that study, the return on high turnover portfolios exceeds the return on low turnover portfolios in all three European 'emerging markets' analyzed (Greece, Portugal, Turkey), however at statistically insignificant levels.[135]

[135] Note that ROUWENHORST (1999) only analyzes the $J = 1$ month formation period.

Table 4.2: FM Regression Estimates, Using Swiss Franc Volume

	Formation period *J*			
Variable	1	3	6	12
Panel A: Swiss franc volume				
Intercept	0.915 (10.892)***	1.021 (11.539)***	1.100 (12.278)***	1.152 (13.007)***
CHFVOL	**0.023** **(0.899)**	**-0.026** **(-0.963)**	**-0.060** **(-2.170)****	**-0.081** **(-2.878)*****
Panel B: Swiss franc volume, controlled				
Intercept	2.999 (6.261)***	1.988 (4.090)***	1.281 (2.480)**	1.042 (1.952)*
CHFVOL	**0.281** **(5.231)*****	**0.119** **(2.003)****	**-0.006** **(-0.094)**	**-0.052** **(-0.727)**
SIZE	-0.409 (-4.727)***	-0.197 (-2.221)**	-0.041 (-0.427)	0.014 (0.135)
BM	0.474 (4.205)***	0.463 (4.074)***	0.452 (3.961)***	0.448 (3.930)***
RET2-12	0.013 (6.056)***	0.013 (6.177)***	0.013 (6.309)***	0.013 (6.353)***

This table reports coefficient estimates of Pooled OLS regressions over a return series from March 1997 to August 2008. The dependent variable is a stock's return in a given month. The independent variables are defined as follows: CHFVOL is the logarithm of average monthly Swiss franc volume of trading in the stock in the preceding $J = 1, 3, 6, 12$ months. SIZE is the logarithm of a company's market capitalization at the beginning of the previous month. BM is the logarithm of the ratio of book value of equity to market capitalization at the beginning of the previous month. RET2-12 is the stock's cumulative return over the 11 months ending at the beginning of the previous month. ***/**/* Denotes statistical significance at the 1%/5%/10% level. T-statistics (in parentheses) are calculated using Newey-West (1987) adjusted, heteroskedasticity and serial correlation robust standard errors.

4.1.1.2 Abnormal Volume

Recall from above that we use two different measures of *'change in volume'* in our analyses. The first, DELTA A, is the percentage change of last month's volume versus the average monthly volume in the preceding J = *3, 6, 12* months, thereby measuring *abnormal volume*. Table 4.3 reports average coefficient estimates of Fama-MacBeth (FM) regressions of stock returns on abnormal turnover. In Panel A, we find a *systematically significant positive relationship between abnormal volume and expected returns* over all reference periods analyzed (J = *3, 6, 12* months). This finding is confirmed when additionally controlling for size, value, and momentum variables (Panel B). When repeating the regressions on the basis of Swiss franc volume instead of share turnover, the results remain qualitatively the same. The significance levels, however, are generally lower (see Table 4.4).

To summarize, we find a positive relationship between abnormal volume and expected returns (i.e., high abnormal volume stocks have higher expected returns). This effect is more pronounced using share turnover than Swiss franc volume. The positive 'abnormal volume'-return relation is not surprising given existing literature presented above, 2.1.2.1.[136] However, there are methodological differences to take into account; one is that previous studies define 'volume shocks' based on a *single day's respectively week's* trading volume in relation to a reference period of 20 to 240 trading days.[137] Here, on the other hand, we define abnormal volume based on a *month's trading volume* in relation to a similar reference period (three to twelve months).

[136] The only contradicting evidence stems from LEE/SWAMINATHAN (2000) who report a negative relationship between abnormal volume and expected returns. But their analysis is hardly comparable to our study (the authors investigate a stock's average daily turnover over the past six months in relation to the average daily turnover four years ago).

[137] See GERVAIS ET AL. (2001) and AGGARWAL/SUN (2003).

Table 4.3: FM Regression Estimates, Using Abnormal Turnover

	Reference period *J*		
Variable	3	6	12
Panel A: Abnormal share turnover			
Intercept	0.921 (14.041)***	0.933 (14.497)***	0.938 (14.631)***
DELTATURN A	**0.169** **(3.154)*****	**0.161** **(2.765)*****	**0.171** **(2.617)*****
Panel B: Abnormal share turnover, controlled			
Intercept	1.189 (4.068)***	1.232 (4.265)***	1.265 (4.403)***
DELTATURN A	**0.175** **(3.192)*****	**0.167** **(2.806)*****	**0.174** **(2.649)*****
SIZE	-0.036 (-0.810)	-0.041 (-0.924)	-0.046 (-1.028)
BM	0.454 (4.008)***	0.453 (4.009)***	0.448 (3.976)***
RET2-12	0.014 (6.494)***	0.014 (6.479)***	0.014 (6.427)***

This table reports coefficient estimates of Pooled OLS regressions over a return series from March 1997 to August 2008. The dependent variable is a stock's return in a given month. The independent variables are defined as follows: DELTATURN A is the percentage change of last month's turnover versus the average turnover in the preceding $J = 3, 6, 12$ months. SIZE is the logarithm of a company's market capitalization at the beginning of the previous month. BM is the logarithm of the ratio of book value of equity to market capitalization at the beginning of the previous month. RET2-12 is the stock's cumulative return over the 11 months ending at the beginning of the previous month. ***/**/* Denotes statistical significance at the 1%/5%/10% level. T-statistics (in parentheses) are calculated using Newey-West (1987) adjusted, heteroskedasticity and serial correlation robust standard errors.

Table 4.4: FM Regression Estimates, Using Abnormal Swiss Franc Volume

	Reference period *J*		
Variable	3	6	12
Panel A: Abnormal Swiss franc volume			
Intercept	0.941	0.938	0.925
	(14.113)***	(14.416)***	(14.446)***
DELTAVOL A	**0.080**	**0.111**	**0.188**
	(1.450)	**(2.143)****	**(2.820)*****
Panel B: Abnormal Swiss franc volume, controlled			
Intercept	1.246	1.247	1.257
	(4.271)***	(4.314)***	(4.395)***
DELTAVOL A	**0.077**	**0.104**	**0.160**
	(1.419)	**(2.118)****	**(2.621)*****
SIZE	-0.041	-0.041	-0.043
	(-0.920)	(-0.927)	(-0.975)
BM	0.455	0.456	0.456
	(4.023)***	(4.035)***	(4.033)***
RET2-12	0.013	0.013	0.013
	(6.365)***	(6.303)***	(6.012)***

This table reports coefficient estimates of Pooled OLS regressions over a return series from March 1997 to August 2008. The dependent variable is a stock's return in a given month. The independent variables are defined as follows: DELTAVOL A is the percentage change of last month's Swiss franc volume versus the average Swiss franc volume in the preceding *J = 3, 6, 12* months. SIZE is the logarithm of a company's market capitalization at the beginning of the previous month. BM is the logarithm of the ratio of book value of equity to market capitalization at the beginning of the previous month. RET2-12 is the stock's cumulative return over the 11 months ending at the beginning of the previous month. ***/**/* Denotes statistical significance at the 1%/5%/10% level. T-statistics (in parentheses) are calculated using Newey-West (1987) adjusted, heteroskedasticity and serial correlation robust standard errors.

4.1.1.3 Volume Growth

The second measure of *'change in volume'* is *volume growth*, labeled DELTA B. This variable is defined as the average monthly percentage change in the volume variable (share turnover, Swiss franc volume) in the previous $J = 1, 3, 6, 12$ months. Table 4.5, Panel A, reports average coefficient estimates of the Fama-MacBeth (FM) regressions of stock returns on share turnover growth.

Table 4.5: FM Regression Estimates, Using Turnover Growth

	Formation period *J*			
Variable	1	3	6	12
Panel A: Share turnover growth				
Intercept	0.963 (15.153)***	0.969 (15.145)***	0.980 (15.112)***	0.974 (14.595)***
DELTATURN B	**0.000** **(0.036)**	**-0.009** **(-0.959)**	**-0.026** **(-1.890)***	**-0.018** **(-0.475)**
Panel B: Share turnover growth, controlled				
Intercept	1.315 (4.567)***	1.338 (4.608)***	1.383 (4.676)***	1.390 (4.702)***
DELTATURN B	**0.000** **(0.043)**	**-0.010** **(-1.052)**	**-0.031** **(-2.136)****	**-0.036** **(-0.971)**
SIZE	-0.049 (-1.095)	-0.051 (-1.150)	-0.057 (-1.246)	-0.057 (-1.270)***
BM	0.453 (4.001)***	0.452 (3.992)***	0.450 (3.973)***	0.451 (3.980)***
RET2-12	0.013 (6.355)***	0.013 (6.343)***	0.013 (6.347)***	0.013 (6.370)***

This table reports coefficient estimates of Pooled OLS regressions over a return series from March 1997 to August 2008. The dependent variable is a stock's return in a given month. The independent variables are defined as follows: DELTATURN B is the average monthly percentage change in turnover in the preceding $J = 1, 3, 6, 12$ months. SIZE is the logarithm of a company's market capitalization at the beginning of the previous month. BM is the logarithm of the ratio of book value of equity to market capitalization at the beginning of the previous month. RET2-12 is the stock's cumulative return over the 11 months ending at the beginning of the previous month. ***/**/* Denotes statistical significance at the 1%/5%/10% level. T-statistics (in parentheses) are calculated using Newey-West (1987) adjusted, heteroskedasticity and serial correlation robust standard errors.

While this relation is mostly negative, it is also mostly insignificant (we find only one coefficient estimate that is significant at the 10% level, namely for the $J = 6$ months horizon). Although being slightly more significant the results remain qualitatively the same when additionally controlling for size, value, and momentum variables (Table 4.5, Panel B). The same (negative, but mostly at insignificant levels) is true when repeating the regressions on the basis of Swiss franc volume as reported in Table 4.6.

Table 4.6: FM Regression Estimates, Using Swiss Franc Volume Growth

	Formation period *J*			
Variable	1	3	6	12
Panel A: Swiss franc volume growth				
Intercept	0.970 (15.081)***	0.973 (14.924)***	0.980 (14.793)***	0.937 (11.615)***
DELTAVOL B	**-0.010** **(-0.808)**	**-0.015** **(-1.026)**	**-0.026** **(-1.342)**	**0.040** **(0.450)**
Panel B: Swiss franc volume growth, controlled				
Intercept	1.341 (4.643)***	1.365 (4.645)***	1.418 (4.692)***	1.337 (4.479)***
DELTAVOL B	**-0.011** **(-0.842)**	**-0.021** **(-1.337)**	**-0.045** **(-2.119)****	**-0.010** **(-0.119)**
SIZE	-0.052 (-1.165)	-0.055 (-1.217)	-0.061 (-1.326)	-0.051 (-1.178)
BM	0.451 (3.995)***	0.450 (3.985)***	0.448 (3.960)***	0.452 (4.041)***
RET2-12	0.013 (6.342)***	0.013 (6.373)***	0.014 (6.457)***	0.013 (6.165)***

This table reports coefficient estimates of Pooled OLS regressions over a return series from March 1997 to August 2008. The dependent variable is a stock's return in a given month. The independent variables are defined as follows: DELTAVOL B is the average monthly percentage change in Swiss franc volume in the preceding $J = 1, 3, 6, 12$ months. SIZE is the logarithm of a company's market capitalization at the beginning of the previous month. BM is the logarithm of the ratio of book value of equity to market capitalization at the beginning of the previous month. RET2-12 is the stock's cumulative return over the 11 months ending at the beginning of the previous month. ***/**/* Denotes statistical significance at the 1%/5%/10% level. T-statistics (in parentheses) are calculated using Newey-West (1987) adjusted, heteroskedasticity and serial correlation robust standard errors.

It is difficult to compare these results to previous literature, since we know of only one related study. However, it is interesting to note for now that our findings are not in line with WATKINS (2007), who finds that stocks with high-mean turnover growth in the past 12 months experience higher subsequent returns. But this finding is based on a portfolio-based test environment, which we replicate later in this chapter.

4.1.1.4 Variability in Volume

In chapter 3, we presented two measures of variability in volume, the *standard deviation of volume* and the *coefficient of variation in volume*, both calculated over the past 12 months. Intuitively, we prefer the latter measure, which is a dimensionless quantity[138], while the former strongly correlates with the volume level. Our results support this intuition.

Table 4.7 reports average coefficient estimates of the Fama-MacBeth (FM) regressions of stock returns on variability in share turnover. Panel A finds a negative relation between the coefficient of variation in turnover and expected returns, which becomes significant when controlling for size, value, and momentum variables. Note that additional, unreported analysis shows that the insignificant results in the first column are mainly driven by the strong negative correlation of CVTURN and company size of -0.635 (see Table 3.3 in 3.3.1.1.2). The coefficient on the standard deviation of share turnover, on the other hand, is insignificant, even if controlled for size, value, and momentum variables (Table 4.7, Panel B). But this is caused by the strong correlation of the standard deviation of turnover with the level of turnover (particularly at $J = 12$ months), which can be shown by additionally controlling for the volume level. Under these circumstances (not reported in a table), the coefficient on the standard deviation of share turnover also becomes significantly negative at the 1% level.

The bias in the standard deviation measure becomes even clearer when using Swiss franc volume based variables. In Table 4.8, Panel A, we again find a negative relationship between the coefficient of variation in volume and expected returns, which becomes significant when controlling for size, value, and momentum variables. The coef-

[138] Recall that the coefficient of variation in volume is defined as the standard deviation of monthly volume over the past 12 months divided by the average monthly volume over the past 12 months, thereby eliminating level effects.

ficient on the standard deviation of Swiss franc volume, however, is significantly negative when used as the only independent regressor in the FM regressions, and becomes insignificant when controlled for size, value, and momentum (Table 4.8, Panel B). But these coefficient estimates are very similar to the corresponding volume level estimates for the $J = 12$ months formation period (see Table 4.2 above).

Table 4.7: FM Regression Estimates, Using Variability in Turnover

	Panel A: Coefficient of variation in share turnover		Panel B: Standard deviation of share turnover	
Variable	Volume only	Controlled	Volume only	Controlled
Intercept	0.869 (7.485)***	1.655 (5.606)***	0.968 (17.098)***	1.322 (4.702)***
STDTURN			**-0.011** **(-0.143)**	**-0.028** **(-0.351)**
CVTURN	**-0.153** **(-1.052)**	**-0.693** **(-4.082)*****		
SIZE		-0.173 (-3.330)***		-0.049 (-1.092)
BM		0.438 (3.892)***		0.447 (3.881)***
RET2-12		0.014 (6.434)***		0.013 (6.272)***

This table reports coefficient estimates of Pooled OLS regressions over a return series from March 1997 to August 2008. The dependent variable is a stock's return in a given month. The independent variables are defined as follows: STDTURN is the logarithm of the standard deviation of monthly share turnover (calculated over the past 12 months). CVTURN is the logarithm of the coefficient of variation in share turnover (calculated over the past 12 months). SIZE is the logarithm of a company's market capitalization at the beginning of the previous month. BM is the logarithm of the ratio of book value of equity to market capitalization at the beginning of the previous month. RET2-12 is the stock's cumulative return over the 11 months ending at the beginning of the previous month. ***/**/* Denotes statistical significance at the 1%/5%/10% level. T-statistics (in parentheses) are calculated using Newey-West (1987) adjusted, heteroskedasticity and serial correlation robust standard errors.

Table 4.8: FM Regression Estimates, Using Variability in Swiss Franc Volume

	Panel A: Coefficient of variation in Swiss franc volume		Panel B: Standard deviation of Swiss franc volume	
Variable	Volume only	Controlled	Volume only	Controlled
Intercept	0.940 (8.139)***	1.633 (5.642)***	1.142 (14.353)***	0.817 (1.629)
STDVOL			**-0.101** **(-3.227)*****	**-0.105** **(-1.490)**
CVVOL	**-0.041** **(-0.274)**	**-0.604** **(-3.606)*****		
SIZE		-0.157 (-3.113)***		0.059 (0.655)
BM		0.439 (3.894)***		0.441 (3.862)***
RET2-12		0.014 (6.591)***		0.013 (6.342)***

This table reports coefficient estimates of Pooled OLS regressions over a return series from March 1997 to August 2008. The dependent variable is a stock's return in a given month. The independent variables are defined as follows: STDVOL is the logarithm of the standard deviation of monthly Swiss franc volume (calculated over the past 12 months). CVVOL is the logarithm of the coefficient of variation in Swiss franc volume (calculated over the past 12 months). SIZE is the logarithm of a company's market capitalization at the beginning of the previous month. BM is the logarithm of the ratio of book value of equity to market capitalization at the beginning of the previous month. RET2-12 is the stock's cumulative return over the 11 months ending at the beginning of the previous month. ***/**/* Denotes statistical significance at the 1%/5%/10% level. T-statistics (in parentheses) are calculated using Newey-West (1987) adjusted, heteroskedasticity and serial correlation robust standard errors.

In sum, our results yield three preliminary insights about the role of variability in volume in the cross-sectional variation of Swiss stock returns: first, the high correlation between the standard deviation and the volume level contaminates results, which is the expected outcome. Therefore, we use the coefficient of variation as the only measure of variability in volume going forward. Second, there is a significantly negative relationship between variability in volume and expected returns, once we control for previously documented return determinants. This result is in line with previous literature, i.e.,

CHORDIA ET AL. (2001), and KEENE/PETERSON (2007). And finally, this negative 'variability in volume'-return relation can probably not be exploited via one-way sorted portfolio strategies. The reason is that it only becomes significant once controlled for size, book-to-market ratio, and momentum (particularly size).

4.1.1.5 Combined Volume Measures

Our results so far suggest the following:

- A positive relationship between short-term volume level and expected returns;
- A systematically positive relationship between abnormal volume and expected returns;
- A negative but mostly insignificant relationship between volume growth and expected returns; and
- A significantly negative relationship between variability in volume and expected returns.

In this section, we test whether these effects are independent from one another by estimating regressions that jointly include the different volume measures. Results are reported in Table 4.9 for share turnover based variables and in Table 4.10 for Swiss franc volume based variables.

Before we compare results for each volume measure with above findings, there is an important methodological note on Table 4.9 and Table 4.10. At $J = 12$, the coefficient of variation in volume (e.g., CVTURN) contains another variable included in the same regression, namely the volume level (TURN).[139] Given the close relationship between the two variables, multicollinearity issues could arise, thereby diluting the precision of the coefficient estimates at $J = 12$.[140] However, the results appear consistent with $J = 1$,

[139] Recall that the coefficient of variation in share turnover is defined as the standard deviation of monthly share turnover over the past 12 months divided by the average monthly share turnover over the past 12 months (i.e., TURN at $J = 12$).

[140] When replacing the coefficient of variation in volume by the standard deviation of volume, the coefficient estimates on intercept, variability in volume measure, and control variables remain identical.

3, 6 months formation periods as well as with findings from regressions of stock returns on single volume measures reported above (4.1.1.1 to 4.1.1.4).

Table 4.9: FM Regression Estimates, Using a Combination of Turnover Measures

	Formation/reference period *J*			
Variable	1	3	6	12
Intercept	1.889 (6.149)***	1.693 (5.524)***	1.700 (5.571)***	1.705 (5.699)***
TURN	**0.391** **(5.861)*** **	**0.179** **(2.424)** **	**0.061** **(0.755)**	**0.047** **(0.563)**
DELTATURN A		**0.211** **(3.506)*** **	**0.198** **(3.117)*** **	**0.202** **(2.823)*** **
DELTATURN B	**-0.001** **(-0.164)**	**-0.030** **(-2.371)** **	**-0.038** **(-2.105)** **	**-0.022** **(-0.554)**
CVTURN	**-0.492** **(-2.791)*** **	**-0.744** **(-4.288)*** **	**-0.771** **(-4.431)*** **	**-0.800** **(-4.448)*** **
SIZE	-0.236 (-4.345)***	-0.214 (-4.000)***	-0.199 (-3.699)***	-0.202 (-3.714)***
BM	0.497 (4.392)***	0.463 (4.037)***	0.443 (3.858)***	0.437 (3.840)***
RET2-12	0.013 (6.107)***	0.014 (6.319)***	0.014 (6.400)***	0.014 (6.401)***

This table reports coefficient estimates of Pooled OLS regressions over a return series from March 1997 to August 2008. The dependent variable is a stock's return in a given month. The independent variables are defined as follows: TURN is the logarithm of average monthly turnover in the stock in the preceding *J = 1, 3, 6, 12* months. DELTATURN A is the percentage change of last month's turnover versus the average turnover in the preceding *J = 3, 6, 12* months. DELTATURN B is the average monthly percentage change in turnover in the last *J = 1, 3, 6, 12* months. CVTURN is the logarithm of the coefficient of variation in turnover (calculated over the past 12 months for all formation periods). SIZE is the logarithm of a company's market capitalization at the beginning of the previous month. BM is the logarithm of the ratio of book value of equity to market capitalization at the beginning of the previous month. RET2-12 is the stock's cumulative return over the 11 months ending at the beginning of the previous month.

***/**/* Denotes statistical significance at the 1%/5%/10% level. T-statistics (in parentheses) are calculated using Newey-West (1987) adjusted, heteroskedasticity and serial correlation robust standard errors.

Table 4.10: FM Regression Estimates, Using a Combination of Swiss Franc Volume Measures

	Formation/reference period *J*			
Variable	1	3	6	12
Intercept	3.187 (6.669)***	2.119 (4.292)***	1.495 (2.887)***	1.290 (2.480)**
CHFVOL	**0.269** **(4.790)*** **	**0.087** **(1.416)**	**-0.037** **(-0.543)**	**-0.069** **(-0.946)**
DELTAVOL A		**0.104** **(1.929)* **	**0.128** **(2.331)** **	**0.183** **(2.768)*** **
DELTAVOL B	**-0.012** **(-0.969)**	**-0.039** **(-2.496)** **	**-0.055** **(-2.218)** **	**-0.001** **(-0.016)**
CVVOL	**-0.448** **(-2.578)*** **	**-0.602** **(-3.417)*** **	**-0.648** **(-3.605)*** **	**-0.758** **(-3.951)*** **
SIZE	-0.476 (-5.584)***	-0.264 (-2.998)***	-0.125 (-1.313)	-0.095 (-0.951)
BM	0.461 (4.104)***	0.445 (3.936)***	0.433 (3.817)***	0.434 (3.852)***
RET2-12	0.013 (6.207)***	0.014 (6.465)***	0.014 (6.627)***	0.013 (6.101)***

This table reports coefficient estimates of Pooled OLS regressions over a return series from March 1997 to August 2008. The dependent variable is a stock's return in a given month. The independent variables are defined as follows: CHFVOL is the logarithm of average monthly Swiss franc volume of trading in the stock in the preceding *J* = *1, 3, 6, 12* months. DELTAVOL A is the percentage change of last month's Swiss franc volume versus the average Swiss franc volume in the preceding *J* = *3, 6, 12* months. DELTAVOL B is the average monthly percentage change in Swiss franc volume in the last *J* = *1, 3, 6, 12* months. CVVOL is the logarithm of the coefficient of variation in Swiss franc volume (calculated over the past 12 months for all formation periods). SIZE is the logarithm of a company's market capitalization at the beginning of the previous month. BM is the logarithm of the ratio of book value of equity to market capitalization at the beginning of the previous month. RET2-12 is the stock's cumulative return over the 11 months ending at the beginning of the previous month.

***/**/* Denotes statistical significance at the 1%/5%/10% level. T-statistics (in parentheses) are calculated using Newey-West (1987) adjusted, heteroskedasticity and serial correlation robust standard errors.

Discussion of results:

- *Volume level:* while the coefficients on the volume level variables show slightly lower significance levels, the conclusions remain unchanged;
- *Abnormal volume:* the coefficients on the abnormal volume variables are even more significantly positive and the conclusions remain unchanged;
- *Volume growth:* the coefficients on the volume growth variables remain negative, at slightly higher significance levels (i.e., statistically significant at formation periods of $J = 3$ and $J = 6$ months, whereas this was only the case at $J = 6$ before);
- *Variability in* volume: Table 4.9 and Table 4.10 confirm previous findings of a negative relation between the coefficient of variation in volume and expected returns.

In sum, our results suggest that the relationships between the four different volume measures analyzed and expected returns are mostly independent in the cross-section of Swiss stocks.

4.1.2 Results of Robustness Checks

We now report results of robustness checks conducted to investigate the sensitivity of our findings to some key assumptions.[141] The section is again divided into the four volume-return relations investigated (based on *volume level*, *volume growth*, *abnormal volume*, and *variability in volume*), which seems sensible given that these are mostly independent measures.

Some additional comments about the *variables used* in the robustness checks: because of the qualitatively similar but stronger results using *share turnover* instead of Swiss franc volume, especially when investigating potential volume level effects (caused by the strong correlation between Swiss franc volume and size), we limit the following tests to the former variables. And second, as previously noted, we only use the *coefficient of variation as a measure of variability in volume.*

---

[141] See 3.3.1.1.3 above for a detailed overview of the different tests.

The findings reported in the last section show the importance of controlling for size and other variables known to influence the cross-section of stock returns. Thus, we only report results of robustness checks based on regressions that control for these variables (namely size, book-to-market ratio, and momentum).[142]

4.1.2.1 Volume Level

In the previous section, we identify a positive relationship between volume level and expected returns in the Swiss stock market. This effect is statistically significant for short-term volume variables, i.e., average volume in the last respectively last three months (formation period $J = 1$ and $J = 3$).

As a first robustness check, we introduce a one-month lead-lag interval between the volume measures used as independent regressors and the stock returns representing the dependent variable in our regressions. Table 4.11 reports average coefficient estimates of Fama-MacBeth (FM) regressions of stock returns on share turnover. Panel A repeats the base results and Panel B reports results of regressions including the one-month lag in turnover variables. Although the turnover coefficients remain positive across all formation periods in Panel B, significance levels are strongly reduced, indicating the *importance of the immediate last month* for the reported effects. Nevertheless, the *relationship between $J = 1$ month share turnover and expected returns remains statistically significantly positive*, which is in sharp contrast with BRENNAN ET AL. (1998) and CHORDIA ET AL. (2001). These authors find a significantly negative relationship for US stock market data using the methodology applied in this test (i.e., inclusion of a one-month lead-lag interval).[143]

[142] Except for the robustness check over longer return horizons where we also report coefficient estimates of FM regressions on volume measures alone.

[143] Note that these authors only analyze the $J = 1$ formation period.

Table 4.11: FM Regression Estimates, Including 1-Month Lag in Volume Variable (Turnover)

	Formation period *J* (months)			
Variable	1	3	6	12
Panel A: No lag in volume variable				
Intercept	1.665	1.441	1.355	1.332
	(5.504)***	(4.869)***	(4.591)***	(4.551)***
TURN	**0.415**	**0.232**	**0.100**	**0.071**
	(6.424)*	**(3.234)***	**(1.252)**	**(0.842)**
SIZE	-0.154	-0.100	-0.069	-0.062
	(-3.134)***	(-2.092)**	(-1.429)	(-1.262)
BM	0.511	0.488	0.469	0.465
	(4.506)***	(4.242)***	(4.052)***	(4.032)***
RET2-12	0.013	0.013	0.013	0.013
	(6.043)***	(6.059)***	(6.144)***	(6.199)***
Panel B: 1-month lag in volume variable				
Intercept	1.454	1.345	1.318	1.323
	(4.841)***	(4.530)***	(4.459)***	(4.520)***
TURN	**0.161**	**0.051**	**0.002**	**0.023**
	(2.534)	**(0.715)**	**(0.028)**	**(0.280)**
SIZE	-0.090	-0.060	-0.050	-0.054
	(-1.890)*	(-1.268)	(-1.024)	(-1.091)
BM	0.476	0.460	0.452	0.456
	(4.143)***	(3.979)***	(3.906)***	(3.956)***
RET2-12	0.013	0.013	0.013	0.013
	(6.104)***	(6.195)***	(6.236)***	(6.255)***

This table compares coefficient estimates of Pooled OLS regressions with and without the inclusion of a one-month lead-lag interval between the volume variable and returns (return series from March 1997 to August 2008). The dependent variable is a stock's return in a given month. In *Panel A*, TURN is the logarithm of average monthly share turnover in a stock *in the last* $J = 1, 3, 6, 12$ months. In *Panel B*, TURN is the logarithm of monthly share turnover in the stock in the $J = 1, 3, 6, 12$ *months ending in the second to last month.* Definition of the independent control variables: SIZE is the logarithm of a company's market capitalization at the beginning of the previous month. BM is the logarithm of the ratio of book value of equity to market capitalization at the beginning of the previous month. RET2-12 is the stock's cumulative return over the 11 months ending at the beginning of the previous month. ***/**/* Denotes statistical significance at the 1%/5%/10% level. T-statistics (in parentheses) are calculated using Newey-West (1987) adjusted, heteroskedasticity and serial correlation robust standard errors.

Second, we investigate the sensitivity of the regression results to extreme volume observations. In Table 4.12, Panel A, we exclude outliers at the 2% level (by eliminating stocks with the lowest 1% and the highest 1% share turnover values per cross-section), in Panel B at the 10% level (eliminating the lowest 5% and the highest 5% values). This exclusion of the most extreme volume observations even increases significance levels of the turnover coefficients. Thus, the positive relationship between volume level and expected returns does not result from outliers. Note that, while this is generally a positive result regarding the stability of the relationship between volume level and returns, it also indicates potential difficulties regarding volume based portfolio strategies (discussed below, 4.2.1). This is particularly true for the zero-cost arbitrage strategies consisting of long and short positions investing in the most extreme volume observations.

Third, we analyze whether the so far discovered volume level effect is limited to the smallest stocks. In Table 4.13, Panel A, we discard all companies with a market capitalization below CHF 50 million, in Panel B all companies with a market capitalization below CHF 200 million. The three most important findings in Table 4.13 are: first, the *basic conclusion of a positive relationship between short-term volume level and expected returns does not change*, even when excluding all small stocks (approximately 30% of the sample). Second, the *inclusion of micro caps in our base regressions does not bias the results* through inefficiencies in the market microstructure. In fact, our results remain almost identical when excluding micro caps. However, and this is the third finding, the *positive relationship between (short-term) volume level and expected returns is much stronger among small stocks*. At the same time Swiss stocks are generally smaller than US stocks (while the time-series average of monthly mean firm size in our sample is 4.9 billion Swiss francs[144], the average NYSE/AMEX company has a market capitalization of 9.7 billion Swiss francs[145] over the same sample period). One possible explanation for the different results of previous (mainly US) studies could thus be that the Swiss stocks are smaller (i.e., have a lower market capitalization). However, AGGARWAL/SUN (2003) find the negative relationship between the volume level and expected returns in US data to be most pronounced for small stocks as well, not for large stocks.

[144] See Table 3.2 above (3.3.1.1.2).

[145] This number represents the time-series average of monthly mean market capitalizations of all main class NYSE/AMEX stocks over the 138 months from February 1997 through July 2008.

Table 4.12: FM Regression Estimates, Excluding Different Levels of Outliers (Turnover)

	Formation period *J*			
Variable	1	3	6	12
Panel A: Exclusion of outliers at 2% level				
Intercept	1.657	1.563	1.431	1.456
	(5.372)***	(5.464)***	(4.956)***	(5.010)***
TURN	**0.477**	**0.305**	**0.141**	**0.147**
	(6.762)* **	**(4.318)*** **	**(1.813)***	**(1.699)***
SIZE	-0.170	-0.126	-0.089	-0.091
	(-3.338)***	(-2.678)***	(-1.838)*	(-1.797)*
BM	0.473	0.495	0.432	0.467
	(4.352)***	(4.529)***	(4.036)***	(4.326)***
RET2-12	0.015	0.013	0.012	0.014
	(7.459)***	(6.049)***	(4.970)***	(6.008)***
Panel B: Exclusion of outliers at 10% level				
Intercept	1.635	1.689	1.650	1.542
	(5.264)***	(5.528)***	(5.467)***	(5.302)***
TURN	**0.596**	**0.376**	**0.199**	**0.174**
	(7.195)* **	**(4.467)*** **	**(2.103)** **	**(1.741)***
SIZE	-0.169	-0.149	-0.123	-0.113
	(-3.256)***	(-2.929)***	(-2.444)**	(-2.238)**
BM	0.580	0.573	0.512	0.484
	(5.052)***	(5.059)***	(4.452)***	(4.146)***
RET2-12	0.014	0.016	0.015	0.016
	(6.008)***	(6.476)***	(6.430)***	(6.776)***

This table shows the robustness of the coefficient estimates of Pooled OLS regressions to outliers (return series from March 1997 to August 2008). In *Panel A (B)*, the 1% (5%) highest and 1% (5%) lowest TURN observations have been eliminated per cross-section. The independent variables are defined as follows: TURN is the logarithm of average monthly share turnover in the stock in the preceding *J = 1, 3, 6, 12* months. SIZE is the logarithm of a company's market capitalization at the beginning of the previous month. BM is the logarithm of the ratio of book value of equity to market capitalization at the beginning of the previous month. RET2-12 is the stock's cumulative return over the 11 months ending at the beginning of the previous month. ***/**/* Denotes statistical significance at the 1%/5%/10% level. T-statistics (in parentheses) are calculated using Newey-West (1987) adjusted, heteroskedasticity and serial correlation robust standard errors.

Table 4.13: FM Regression Estimates, Excluding Different Size Groups (Turnover)

	Formation period *J*			
Variable	1	3	6	12
Panel A: Exclusion of micro caps				
Intercept	1.674	1.405	1.291	1.257
	(5.138)***	(4.405)***	(4.071)***	(4.030)***
TURN	**0.409**	**0.215**	**0.082**	**0.037**
	(6.424)* **	**(2.903)*** **	**(0.982)**	**(0.421)**
SIZE	-0.154	-0.093	-0.059	-0.047
	(-2.894)***	(-1.775)**	(-1.102)	(-0.894)
BM	0.508	0.474	0.449	0.441
	(4.529)***	(4.193)***	(3.966)***	(3.903)***
RET2-12	0.013	0.013	0.014	0.014
	(5.884)***	(5.913)***	(5.986)***	(6.048)***
Panel B: Exclusion of small caps				
Intercept	1.538	1.342	1.266	1.246
	(3.787)***	(3.346)***	(3.173)***	(3.150)***
TURN	**0.274**	**0.105**	**-0.002**	**-0.049**
	(3.716)* **	**(1.323)**	**(-0.019)**	**(-0.517)**
SIZE	-0.114	-0.066	-0.041	-0.032
	(-1.835)*	(-1.074)	(-0.660)	(-0.505)
BM	0.550	0.508	0.481	0.468
	(4.409)***	(4.078)***	(3.854)***	(3.774)***
RET2-12	0.015	0.015	0.015	0.015
	(6.377)***	(6.378)***	(6.405)***	(6.433)***

This table reports coefficient estimates of Pooled OLS regressions when excluding stocks with low market capitalizations (return series from March 1997 to August 2008). In *Panel A (B)*, all stocks with firm market capitalization below CHF 50 (200) million have been elminated in each cross-section. The dependent variable is a stock's return in a given month. The independent variables are defined as follows: TURN is the logarithm of average monthly share turnover in the stock in the preceding *J = 1, 3, 6, 12* months. SIZE is the logarithm of a company's market capitalization at the beginning of the previous month. BM is the logarithm of the ratio of book value of equity to market capitalization at the beginning of the previous month. RET2-12 is the stock's cumulative return over the 11 months ending at the beginning of the previous month. ***/**/* Denotes statistical significance at the 1%/5%/10% level. T-statistics (in parentheses) are calculated using Newey-West (1987) adjusted, heteroskedasticity and serial correlation robust standard errors.

As a fourth robustness check we test the stability of the base regression results over time by dividing the sample into two sub-periods (see Table 4.14). The coefficient on the very short-term ($J = 1$ month) turnover measure is *strongly significantly positive in both sub-periods*. However, the previously discovered relationship between volume level and expected returns is much stronger in the second sub-period from December 2002 to August 2008 (Panel B). One possibility for the differences in the two sub-periods could be the presence of varying underlying market regimes displaying different 'volume level'-return dynamics (e.g., bear vs. bull markets). This point is further examined in chapter 5. Another possibility for the generally more significant volume-return relations in the recent sub-period could be the improvement of the quality of our data over time (which would be promising for the practical implementation of portfolio strategies). The substantial reduction of stocks with missing data over time is a first indication (see above, Table 3.1). Additionally, only the analyses in the second sub-period were conducted using free-float adjusted share turnover, which is a more precise measure of trading volume.[146] Therefore, as a fifth robustness check, we investigate the influence of free-float adjustment on the turnover-return relationship.

Table 4.15 compares regression results in the second sub-period using either free-float adjusted (Panel A) or non-free-float adjusted (Panel B) share turnover. As expected, turnover coefficients are more significant when using free-float adjusted measures.[147] However, these differences cannot fully explain the variations in the two sub-periods as reported in Table 4.14.

[146] Free-float adjusted shares outstanding figures were not available in the first sub-period.

[147] This is an additional explanation for the fact that results are generally stronger when using share turnover instead of Swiss franc volume, because Swiss franc volume is non-free-float adjusted throughout the whole sample period.

Table 4.14: FM Regression Estimates in Different Sub-Periods (Turnover)

	Formation period *J*			
Variable	1	3	6	12
Panel A: Return series 03/1997-11/2002				
Intercept	0.662	0.399	0.299	0.315
	(1.254)	(0.781)	(0.590)	(0.626)
TURN	**0.294**	**0.061**	**-0.111**	**-0.119**
	(3.286)* **	**(0.616)**	**(-1.016)**	**(-1.020)**
SIZE	-0.073	-0.012	0.023	0.022
	(-0.846)	(-0.146)	(0.275)	(0.262)
BM	0.504	0.477	0.455	0.452
	(2.993)***	(2.813)***	(2.687)***	(2.683)***
RET2-12	0.018	0.018	0.018	0.018
	(6.637)***	(6.697)***	(6.770)***	(6.769)***
Panel B: Return series 12/2002-08/2008				
Intercept	2.686	2.522	2.462	2.418
	(7.372)***	(7.002)***	(6.871)***	(6.808)***
TURN	**0.454**	**0.322**	**0.237**	**0.155**
	(4.480)* **	**(2.979)*** **	**(2.082)** **	**(1.290)**
SIZE	-0.225	-0.183	-0.161	-0.141
	(-3.810)***	(-3.118)***	(-2.740)***	(-2.375)**
BM	0.485	0.466	0.452	0.436
	(3.315)***	(3.135)***	(3.013)***	(2.901)***
RET2-12	0.003	0.003	0.003	0.003
	(1.302)	(1.312)	(1.366)	(1.477)

This table reports coefficient estimates of Pooled OLS regressions over two sub-periods. The first return series from March 1997 to November 2002 is reported in *Panel A. T*he second return series from December 2002 to August 2008 is reported in *Panel B*. The dependent variable is a stock's return in a given month. The independent variables are defined as follows: TURN is the logarithm of average monthly share turnover in the stock in the preceding *J = 1, 3, 6, 12* months. SIZE is the logarithm of a company's market capitalization at the beginning of the previous month. BM is the logarithm of the ratio of book value of equity to market capitalization at the beginning of the previous month. RET2-12 is the stock's cumulative return over the 11 months ending at the beginning of the previous month. ***/**/* Denotes statistical significance at the 1%/5%/10% level. T-statistics (in parentheses) are calculated using Newey-West (1987) adjusted, heteroskedasticity and serial correlation robust standard errors.

Table 4.15: FM Regression Estimates, Comparing Free-Float Adjusted and Non-Free-Float Adjusted Measures (Turnover)

	Formation period *J*			
Variable	1	3	6	12
Panel A: Free-float adjusted share turnover				
Intercept	2.686 (7.372)***	2.522 (7.002)***	2.462 (6.871)***	2.418 (6.808)***
TURN	**0.454** **(4.480)*** **	**0.322** **(2.979)*** **	**0.237** **(2.082)** **	**0.155** **(1.290)**
SIZE	-0.225 (-3.810)***	-0.183 (-3.118)***	-0.161 (-2.740)***	-0.141 (-2.375)**
BM	0.485 (3.315)***	0.466 (3.135)***	0.452 (3.013)***	0.436 (2.901)***
RET2-12	0.003 (1.302)	0.003 (1.312)	0.003 (1.366)	0.003 (1.477)
Panel B: Non-free float adjusted share turnover				
Intercept	2.831 (7.637)***	2.623 (7.163)***	2.538 (6.956)***	2.467 (6.718)***
TURN	**0.321** **(3.810)*** **	**0.208** **(2.398)** **	**0.147** **(1.622)**	**0.087** **(0.904)**
SIZE	-0.207 (-3.596)***	-0.167 (-2.942)***	-0.149 (-2.610)***	-0.132 (-2.265)**
BM	0.444 (3.228)***	0.433 (3.120)***	0.426 (3.055)***	0.417 (2.992)***
RET2-12	0.003 (1.349)	0.003 (1.369)	0.003 (1.406)	0.004 (1.472)

This table reports coefficient estimates of Pooled OLS regressions (only second sub-period from December 2002 to August 2008). The dependent variable is a stock's return in a given month. The independent volume variable is defined as follows: In *Panel A*, TURN is the logarithm of average monthly turnover in the stock in the last $J = 1, 3, 6, 12$ months, measured by the total number of shares traded in a month divided by the average number of *free-float adjusted shares outstanding*. This is the method applied in the previous analyses. In *Panel B*, TURN is the logarithm of average monthly turnover in the stock in the last $J = 1, 3, 6, 12$ months, measured by the total number of shares traded in a month divided by the average number of *total shares outstanding*. Definition of the independent control variables: SIZE is the logarithm of a company's market capitalization at the beginning of the previous month. BM is the logarithm of the ratio of book value of equity to market capitalization at the beginning of the previous month. RET2-12 is the stock's cumulative return over the 11 months ending at the beginning of the previous month.

***/**/* Denotes statistical significance at the 1%/5%/10% level. T-statistics (in parentheses) are calculated using Newey-West (1987) adjusted, heteroskedasticity and serial correlation robust standard errors.

Sixth, deviations in the volume level-return relationship between the US and Swiss stock markets could also be caused by differences in firm ownership structures as proxied by a stock's free-float. In the second sub-period from December 2002 to August 2008, the average (median) free-float factor of NYSE/AMEX stocks is 0.76 (0.83) while the corresponding numbers in the Swiss data set are 0.70 (0.73).[148] Although the difference is relatively small, it is still possible that test results in the two markets converge when discarding stocks with a low free-float in the Swiss sample. We therefore repeat above (Swiss) regressions in the second sub-period while excluding all stocks with a free-float below 30 respectively 60%. To confirm above presumption, the relationship between volume level and expected returns should become negative when discarding Swiss stocks with a low free-float. The results reported in Table 4.16 show that this is not the case. Although the significance levels are reduced when discarding stocks with a free-float below 60% (Panel B), the relationship between short-term turnover and expected returns remains significantly positive at the 5% level. At the same time, the turnover coefficient does not even nearly become significantly negative in any formation horizon. It is important, however, to recognize that this test is only indicative. Specifically, a stock's free-float does not fully represent ownership structure if a company has several share classes, mostly with different free-floats and attached voting rights. But this only affects approximately 5% of our sample.

As a seventh test for the robustness of volume level results we repeat the base Pooled OLS regressions using the fixed effects method.[149] Table 4.17 reports average coefficient estimates of regressions of stock returns on share turnover (and control variables) over the entire return series. While Panel A repeats the base Pooled OLS results, Panel B reports regression results estimated via fixed effects transformation. The significance levels of share turnover coefficients are smaller in the fixed effects estimation, but the basic conclusions do not change. Specifically, the coefficient of the very short-term ($J = 1$ month) turnover measure is strongly significantly positive using both estimation methods.

---

[148] These numbers represent time-series averages of cross-sectional statistics.

[149] See above, 3.3.1.1.1, for a detailed description of the fixed effects methodology.

Table 4.16: FM Regression Estimates, Excluding Different Free-Float Groups (Turnover)

	Formation period *J*			
Variable	1	3	6	12
Panel A: Exclusion of stocks with free-float below 30%				
Intercept	2.766	2.600	2.535	2.485
	(6.246)***	(6.008)***	(5.942)***	(5.939)***
TURN	**0.494**	**0.372**	**0.288**	**0.207**
	(4.398)* **	**(2.950)*** **	**(2.118)** **	**(1.533)**
SIZE	-0.246	-0.204	-0.181	-0.161
	(-3.390)***	(-2.794)***	(-2.477)**	(-2.212)**
BM	0.488	0.472	0.460	0.445
	(3.165)***	(3.025)***	(2.921)***	(2.827)**
RET2-12	0.003	0.003	0.003	0.003
	(1.022)	(1.015)	(1.063)	(1.182)
Panel B: Exclusion of stocks with free-float below 60%				
Intercept	2.327	2.236	2.206	2.203
	(4.855)***	(4.721)***	(4.707)***	(4.782)***
TURN	**0.267**	**0.119**	**0.009**	**-0.095**
	(2.030) **	**(0.821)**	**(0.057)**	**(-0.632)**
SIZE	-0.159	-0.119	-0.093	-0.072
	(-2.118)**	(-1.558)	(-1.215)	(-0.963)
BM	0.329	0.311	0.296	0.280
	(1.938)*	(1.804)*	(1.701)*	(1.613)
RET2-12	0.001	0.001	0.001	0.001
	(0.361)	(0.378)	(0.416)	(0.440)

This table reports coefficient estimates of Pooled OLS regressions when excluding stocks with low free-floats (only second sub-period from December 2002 to August 2008). In *Panel A (B)*, all stocks with a free-float factor below 30% (60%) have been elminated in each cross-section. The dependent variable is a stock's return in a given month. The independent variables are defined as follows: TURN is the logarithm of average monthly share turnover in the stock in the preceding $J = 1, 3, 6, 12$ months. SIZE is the logarithm of a company's market capitalization at the beginning of the previous month. BM is the logarithm of the ratio of book value of equity to market capitalization at the beginning of the previous month. RET2-12 is the stock's cumulative return over the 11 months ending at the beginning of the previous month. ***/**/* Denotes statistical significance at the 1%/5%/10% level. T-statistics (in parentheses) are calculated using Newey-West (1987) adjusted, heteroskedasticity and serial correlation robust standard errors.

Table 4.17: FM Regression Estimates, Using Different Empirical Methods (Turnover)

	Formation period *J*			
Variable	1	3	6	12
Panel A: Pooled OLS method				
Intercept	1.665	1.441	1.355	1.332
	(5.504)***	(4.869)***	(4.591)***	(4.551)***
TURN	**0.415**	**0.232**	**0.100**	**0.071**
	(6.424)***	**(3.234)*****	**(1.252)**	**(0.842)**
SIZE	-0.154	-0.100	-0.069	-0.062
	(-3.134)***	(-2.092)**	(-1.429)	(-1.262)
BM	0.511	0.488	0.469	0.465
	(4.506)***	(4.242)***	(4.052)***	(4.032)***
RET2-12	0.013	0.013	0.013	0.013
	(6.043)***	(6.059)***	(6.144)***	(6.199)***
Panel B: Fixed effects method				
Intercept	1.341	1.247	1.206	1.193
	(4.723)***	(4.492)***	(4.368)***	(4.358)***
TURN	**0.175**	**0.093**	**0.018**	**-0.029**
	(2.833)***	**(1.400)**	**(0.254)**	**(-0.395)**
SIZE	-0.084	-0.061	-0.044	-0.035
	(-1.826)*	(-1.353)	(-0.976)	(-0.772)
BM	0.302	0.289	0.277	0.268
	(2.856)***	(2.715)***	(2.593)***	(2.519)**
RET2-12	0.011	0.011	0.011	0.011
	(5.156)***	(5.133)***	(5.170)***	(5.206)***

This table compares coefficient estimates of Fama-MacBeth regressions using two different econometric methods (return series from March 1997 to August 2008). In *Panel A*, coefficients were estimated by applying the Pooled OLS method. This is the estimation procedure applied in all previous analyses. In *Panel B*, coefficients were estimated by using fixed effects transformation methodology. The dependent variable is a stock's return in a given month. The independent variables are defined as follows: TURN is the logarithm of average monthly share turnover in the stock in the preceding $J = 1, 3, 6, 12$ months. SIZE is the logarithm of a company's market capitalization at the beginning of the previous month. BM is the logarithm of the ratio of book value of equity to market capitalization at the beginning of the previous month. RET2-12 is the stock's cumulative return over the 11 months ending at the beginning of the previous month. ***/**/* Denotes statistical significance at the 1%/5%/10% level. T-statistics (in parentheses) are calculated using Newey-West (1987) adjusted, heteroskedasticity and serial correlation robust standard errors.

Table 4.18: FM Regression Estimates over Longer Return Horizons (Turnover)

	Formation period *J*			
Holding period K	1 month	3 months	6 months	12 months
Panel A: Share turnover (TURN) coefficient				
1 month	**0.309**	**0.158**	0.051	0.021
	(5.761)* **	**(2.686)*** **	(0.789)	(0.303)
3 months	**0.493**	0.220	0.045	0.035
	(3.115)* **	(1.260)	(0.243)	(0.180)
6 months	**0.707**	0.474	0.420	0.374
	**(1.936)* **	(1.176)	(0.991)	(0.841)
12 months	**2.066**	**1.976**	1.845	1.891
	(2.078) **	**(1.799)* **	(1.603)	(1.569)
Panel B: Share turnover (TURN) coefficient, controlled for Size, Book-to-market, and Momentum				
1 month	**0.415**	**0.232**	0.100	0.071
	(6.424)* **	**(3.234)*** **	(1.252)	(0.842)
3 months	**0.794**	**0.468**	0.252	0.263
	(4.627)* **	**(2.455)** **	(1.258)	(1.252)
6 months	**1.497**	**1.273**	**1.224**	**1.218**
	(3.793)* **	**(2.906)*** **	**(2.661)*** **	**(2.531)** **
12 months	**4.100**	**4.232**	**4.190**	**4.334**
	(3.834)* **	**(3.566)*** **	**(3.362)*** **	**(3.328)*** **

This table reports coefficient estimates of TURN (logarithm of average monthly share turnover in a stock in the last $J = 1, 3, 6, 12$ months) in Pooled OLS regressions over a return series from March 1997 to August 2008. The dependent variable is a stock's return over $K = 1, 3, 6, 12$ months. In *Panel A*, TURN is the only independent variable. In *Panel B*, we additionally include SIZE, BM and RET2-12 as control variables. ***/**/* Denotes statistical significance at the 1%/5%/10% level. For the $K = 1$ month return horizon, t-statistics (in parentheses) are calculated using Newey-West (1987) adjusted, heteroskedasticity and serial correlation robust standard errors. For the $K > 1$ month return horizon, reported t-statistics are calculated using the Hjalmarsson (2008) adjustment methodology, i.e., by dividing the standard t-statistic by the square root of the forecasting (return) horizon K.

As a final robustness check, we analyze the results over longer return horizons. Table 4.18, Panel A, reports share turnover coefficient estimates of Fama-MacBeth regressions of stock returns on volume level alone, over different formation *and* return horizons. Results show that the very short-term turnover measure (i.e., $J = 1$ month) is significantly positively related to expected returns over all horizons investigated (i.e., in the next $K = 1, 3, 6, 12$ months). Interestingly, once we additionally control for size, book-to-market ratio, and momentum (Panel B), even the coefficients of the longer-term turnover measures (*J = 6, 12*) become significantly positive over longer return horizons. This result is surprising at first. Recall, however, that we need to adjust the t-statistics for multi-month holding periods (i.e., *K > 1* month) in Table 4.18. This is due to the severe serial correlation in the regression residuals induced by overlapping return observations.[150] We must therefore not ignore the possibility that the surprisingly significant long-horizon results are driven by some remaining serial correlation that could not entirely be eliminated by the HJALMARSSON (2008) adjustment procedure. Results of portfolio strategies over longer return horizons give us more clarity regarding this point (see below, 4.2.1).

4.1.2.2 Abnormal Volume

Having tested the stability of volume level effects we now perform robustness checks of the significantly positive relationship between abnormal volume and expected returns.

First, we again introduce a one-month lag between volume variables and stock returns (see Table 4.19). Panel A repeats the previously discussed base results, while Panel B reports results of regressions including the one-month lag in abnormal volume variables. It is found that the *positive relationship with expected returns is largely driven by abnormal volume in the immediate last month.* In fact, the positive effect completely vanishes in Panel B and the relationship between abnormal volume and expected returns is driven to zero.

As a consequence of these results, we expect the abnormal volume effect to be short-lived. We test this presumption by analyzing regression results over longer return horizons, i.e., *K > 1*. Results in Table 4.20 confirm our intuition. In fact, abnormal volume coefficients are only significantly positive in the next month (*K = 1*). This finding is in line with related literature, e.g., GERVAIS ET AL. (2001), who report the existence of a relatively short-lived 'high-volume return premium'. Note, however, that these authors use portfolio-based tests. Thus, a meaningful comparison is only possible once we conduct portfolio-based tests ourselves (see below, 4.2.2).

---

[150] See 3.3.1.1.3 for more details.

Table 4.19: FM Regression Estimates, Including 1-Month Lag in Volume Variable (Abnormal Turnover)

	Reference period *J*		
Variable	3	6	12
Panel A: No lag in volume variable			
Intercept	1.189	1.232	1.265
	(4.068)***	(4.265)***	(4.403)***
DELTATURN A	**0.175**	**0.167**	**0.174**
	(3.192)***	**(2.806)*****	**(2.649)*****
SIZE	-0.036	-0.041	-0.046
	(-0.810)	(-0.924)	(-1.028)
BM	0.454	0.453	0.448
	(4.008)***	(4.009)***	(3.976)***
RET2-12	0.014	0.014	0.014
	(6.494)***	(6.479)***	(6.427)***
Panel B: 1-month lag in volume variable			
Intercept	1.314	1.315	1.319
	(4.559)***	(4.566)***	(4.591)***
DELTATURN A	**0.005**	**0.004**	**-0.006**
	(0.180)	**(0.158)**	**(-0.278)**
SIZE	-0.049	-0.049	-0.049
	(-1.096)	(-1.101)	(-1.110)
BM	0.452	0.452	0.452
	(3.993)***	(3.993)***	(4.000)***
RET2-12	0.013	0.013	0.013
	(6.357)***	(6.357)***	(6.365)***

This table compares coefficient estimates of Pooled OLS regressions with and without the inclusion of a one-month lead-lag interval between the volume variable and returns (return series from March 1997 to August 2008). The dependent variable is a stock's return in a given month. In *Panel A*, DELTATURN A is the *percentage change of last month's turnover* versus the average turnover in the preceding *J = 3, 6, 12 months*. In *Panel B*, DELTATURN A is the *percentage change of the second to last month's turnover* versus the average turnover in the preceding *J = 3, 6, 12* months. Definition of the independent control variables: SIZE is the logarithm of a company's market capitalization at the beginning of the previous month. BM is the logarithm of the ratio of book value of equity to market capitalization at the beginning of the previous month. RET2-12 is the stock's cumulative return over the 11 months ending at the beginning of the previous month. ***/**/* Denotes statistical significance at the 1%/5%/10% level. T-statistics (in parentheses) are calculated using Newey-West (1987) adjusted, heteroskedasticity and serial correlation robust standard errors.

Table 4.20: FM Regression Estimates over Longer Return Horizons (Abnormal Turnover)

	Reference period *J*		
Holding period K	3 months	6 months	12 months
Panel A: Abnormal turnover (DELTATURN A) coefficient			
1 month	**0.169**	**0.161**	**0.171**
	(3.154)* **	**(2.765)*** **	**(2.617)*** **
3 months	0.153	0.158	0.143
	(1.460)	(1.501)	(1.259)
6 months	0.035	0.013	0.044
	(0.145)	(0.056)	(0.167)
12 months	0.031	0.023	0.040
	(0.048)	(0.035)	(0.057)
Panel B: Abnormal turnover (DELTATURN A) coefficient, controlled for Size, Book-to-market, and Momentum			
1 month	**0.175**	**0.167**	**0.174**
	(3.192)* **	**(2.806)*** **	**(2.649)*** **
3 months	0.161	0.169	0.148
	(1.541)	(1.618)	(1.307)
6 months	0.016	0.010	0.035
	(0.066)	(0.043)	(0.136)
12 months	-0.106	-0.070	-0.041
	(-0.166)	(-0.110)	(-0.060)

This table reports coefficient estimates of DELTATURN A (percentage change of last month's turnover versus the average turnover in the preceding $J = 3, 6, 12$ months) in Pooled OLS regressions over a return series from March 1997 to August 2008. The dependent variable is a stock's return over $K = 1, 3, 6, 12$ months. In *Panel A*, DELTATURN A is the only independent variable. In *Panel B*, we additionally include SIZE, BM and RET2-12 as control variables. ***/**/* Denotes statistical significance at the 1%/5%/10% level. For the $K = 1$ month return horizon, t-statistics (in parentheses) are calculated using Newey-West (1987) adjusted, heteroskedasticity and serial correlation robust standard errors. For the $K > 1$ month return horizon, reported t-statistics are calculated using the Hjalmarsson (2008) adjustment methodology, i.e., by dividing the standard t-statistic by the square root of the forecasting (return) horizon K.

Results of the outlier analysis are reported in Table 4.21. The numbers show that the previously identified effect is not a result of outliers. The positive relationship between abnormal volume and expected returns even becomes more significant upon the exclusion of extreme abnormal volume values. We report below (section 4.2.2) whether this finding has a negative effect on the profitability of volume based portfolio strategies (particularly in the case of zero-cost arbitrage strategies consisting of long and short positions in the most extreme abnormal volume observations).

As a further robustness check, we again analyze whether the discovered abnormal volume effect is limited to the smallest stocks. In Table 4.22, Panel A (B), all companies with a market capitalization below CHF 50 (200) million are discarded. Similar to the discussion regarding volume level the table shows that the *inclusion of micro caps in the regressions does not bias the results* through inefficiencies in the market microstructure. In fact, the results are only marginally affected by the exclusion of micro caps. In addition, the *basic conclusion of a positive relationship between abnormal volume and expected returns does not change*, even when excluding all small stocks. However, the *positive relationship between abnormal volume and expected returns is stronger among small stocks*. While the abnormal volume coefficients are statistically significant at the 1% level in the full sample, the significance level drops to 10% once all small stocks are excluded. This finding of a stronger relation between abnormal volume and expected returns for small stocks is in line with results reported by AGGARWAL/SUN (2003) for US stocks, using a similar volume measure (see 2.1.2.1.1 above). But these authors find their 'high-volume return premium' to exist exclusively in stocks of small size, while our results suggest the existence of an 'abnormal volume premium' also for non-small stocks, only at lower levels. A more meaningful comparison with AGGARWAL/SUN'S (2003) portfolio analysis is again only possible when applying the same methodology (see below, 4.2.2).

Table 4.21: FM Regression Estimates, Excluding Different Levels of Outliers (Abnormal Turnover)

	Reference period J		
Variable	3	6	12
Panel A: Exclusion of outliers at 2% level			
Intercept	1.001 (3.332)***	1.096 (3.731)***	1.270 (4.429)***
DELTATURN A	**0.725** **(8.002)*****	**0.760** **(9.055)*****	**0.700** **(7.854)*****
SIZE	-0.017 (-0.353)	-0.029 (-0.628)	-0.050 (-1.134)
BM	0.468 (3.934)***	0.459 (3.940)***	0.433 (3.870)***
RET2-12	0.014 (6.908)***	0.014 (6.970)***	0.014 (6.676)***
Panel B: Exclusion of outliers at 10% level			
Intercept	0.891 (2.914)***	1.221 (4.057)***	1.490 (4.922)***
DELTATURN A	**1.268** **(11.133)*****	**1.445** **(11.557)*****	**1.175** **(8.497)*****
SIZE	0.003 (0.060)	-0.042 (-0.910)	-0.078 (-1.699)*
BM	0.502 (3.896)***	0.436 (3.458)***	0.421 (3.485)***
RET2-12	0.015 (7.377)***	0.015 (7.246)***	0.014 (7.001)***

This table shows the robustness of the coefficient estimates of Pooled OLS regressions to outliers (return series from March 1997 to August 2008). In *Panel A (B)*, the 1% (5%) highest and 1% (5%) lowest DELTATURN A observations have been eliminated per cross-section. The independent variables are defined as follows: DELTATURN A is the precentage change of last month's turnover versus the average turnover in the preceding $J = 3, 6, 12$ months. SIZE is the logarithm of a company's market capitalization at the beginning of the previous month. BM is the logarithm of the ratio of book value of equity to market capitalization at the beginning of the previous month. RET2-12 is the stock's cumulative return over the 11 months ending at the beginning of the previous month. ***/**/* Denotes statistical significance at the 1%/5%/10% level. T-statistics (in parentheses) are calculated using Newey-West (1987) adjusted, heteroskedasticity and serial correlation robust standard errors.

Table 4.22: FM Regression Estimates, Excluding Different Size Groups (Using Abnormal Turnover)

	Reference period *J*		
Variable	3	6	12
Panel A: Exclusion of micro caps			
Intercept	1.130	1.173	1.206
	(3.770)***	(3.944)***	(4.074)***
DELTATURN A	**0.191**	**0.163**	**0.160**
	(2.941)*	**(2.371)**	**(2.379)**
SIZE	-0.030	-0.034	-0.038
	(-0.659)	(-0.750)	(-0.843)
BM	0.429	0.431	0.428
	(3.816)***	(3.839)***	(3.831)***
RET2-12	0.014	0.014	0.014
	(6.290)***	(6.261)***	(6.210)***
Panel B: Exclusion of small caps			
Intercept	1.206	1.231	1.248
	(3.094)***	(3.179)***	(3.233)***
DELTATURN A	**0.135**	**0.114**	**0.104**
	(1.870)*	**(1.708)***	**(1.791)***
SIZE	-0.037	-0.040	-0.041
	(-0.658)	(-0.700)	(-0.733)
BM	0.475	0.476	0.477
	(3.796)***	(3.807)***	(3.809)***
RET2-12	0.015	0.015	0.015
	(6.520)***	(6.511)***	(6.486)***

This table reports coefficient estimates of Pooled OLS regressions when excluding stocks with low market capitalizations (return series from March 1997 to August 2008). In *Panel A (B)*, all stocks with firm market capitalization below CHF 50 (200) million have been elminated in each cross-section. The dependent variable is a stock's return in a given month. The independent variables are defined as follows: DELTATURN A is the percentage change in last month's turnover versus the average turnover in the preceding *J = 3, 6, 12* months. SIZE is the logarithm of a company's market capitalization at the beginning of the previous month. BM is the logarithm of the ratio of book value of equity to market capitalization at the beginning of the previous month. RET2-12 is the stock's cumulative return over the 11 months ending at the beginning of the previous month. ***/**/* Denotes statistical significance at the 1%/5%/10% level. T-statistics (in parentheses) are calculated using Newey-West (1987) adjusted, heteroskedasticity and serial correlation robust standard errors.

In the next robustness check, the stability of the base regression estimates is tested over time. Results reported in Table 4.23 show a systematic, significantly positive relationship between abnormal volume and expected returns in both sub-periods (March 1997 to November 2002 and December 2002 to August 2008).

For completeness, we again compare regression results in the second sub-period using either free-float adjusted or non-free-float adjusted share turnover. However, we expect only marginal differences between the two analyses, because abnormal volume is independent of volume levels (which are altered as part of this test). The results (not reported in a table for conciseness) confirm our intuition.[151]

In the next analysis, we repeat regressions in the second sub-period while excluding all stocks with free-float factors below 30% and 60% (see Table 4.24). We find that the relationship between abnormal volume and expected returns is stronger for stocks with low free-floats. Nevertheless, the coefficients on abnormal volume remain positive across all reference periods. In addition, these coefficient estimates lose their statistical significance only for the reference period of $J = 6$ months.

Finally, we compare regressions using either Pooled OLS or fixed effects estimation procedure. Table 4.25 reports results of this test conducted over the entire return series from March 1997 to August 2008. While the coefficients on abnormal volume remain positive across all reference periods using fixed effects transformation (Panel B), they lose almost all statistical significance. Only the volume coefficient of the $J = 12$ months reference period remains statistically significant at the 10% level. The finding that $J = 12$ months is the most significant variable would be in line with intuition that abnormal volume should best be measured when compared to a longer-term reference period.[152] Note, however, that we cannot say with certainty which estimation procedure is better suited in our setting. As mentioned above, 3.3.1.1.1, Pooled OLS is a more appropriate estimation procedure than fixed effects transformation if the linear model without unobserved effects is correctly specified or if there exists an unobserved effect which is not

[151] The abnormal volume coefficients and corresponding t-statistics (in parentheses) for $J = 3, 6, 12$ are 0.237 (3.402), 0.184 (2.069), 0.300 (4.126) using non-free-float adjusted share turnover and 0.241 (3.519), 0.188 (2.163), 0.291 (4.094) using free-float adjusted share turnover.

[152] Recall that at $J = 12$ the abnormal volume variable measures the percentage change of last month's share turnover versus the average monthly share turnover in the preceding *12* months.

correlated with any regressor, i.e., $E(x'c) = 0$. Again, we hope that results of portfolio-based tests help to shed more light on this point.

Table 4.23: FM Regression Estimates in Different Sub-Periods (Abnormal Turnover)

	Reference period *J*		
Variable	3	6	12
Panel A: Return series 03/1997-11/2002			
Intercept	0.246	0.283	0.325
	(0.507)	(0.582)	(0.669)
DELTATURN A	**0.151**	**0.162**	**0.145**
	(2.322)**	**(2.159)****	**(2.116)****
SIZE	0.011	0.006	0.001
	(0.144)	(0.084)	(0.013)
BM	0.470	0.470	0.463
	(2.792)***	(2.787)***	(2.752)***
RET2-12	0.018	0.018	0.018
	(6.851)***	(6.850)***	(6.381)***
Panel B: Return series 12/2002-08/2008			
Intercept	2.236	2.307	2.309
	(6.226)***	(6.514)***	(6.547)***
DELTATURN A	**0.241**	**0.188**	**0.291**
	(3.519)***	**(2.163)****	**(4.094)*****
SIZE	-0.095	-0.102	-0.103
	(-1.784)***	(-1.946)*	(-1.972)**
BM	0.405	0.404	0.402
	(2.852)***	(2.851)***	(2.846)***
RET2-12	0.004	0.004	0.004
	(1.773)*	(1.716)*	(1.672)*

This table reports coefficient estimates of Pooled OLS regressions over two sub-periods. The first return series from March 1997 to November 2002 is reported in *Panel A. T*he second return series from December 2002 to August 2008 is reported in *Panel B*. The dependent variable is a stock's return in a given month. The independent variables are defined as follows: DELTATURN A is the percentage change of last month's turnover versus the average turnover in the preceding $J = 3, 6, 12$ months. SIZE is the logarithm of a company's market capitalization at the beginning of the previous month. BM is the logarithm of the ratio of book value of equity to market capitalization at the beginning of the previous month. RET2-12 is the stock's cumulative return over the 11 months ending at the beginning of the previous month. ***/**/* Denotes statistical significance at the 1%/5%/10% level. T-statistics (in parentheses) are calculated using Newey-West (1987) adjusted, heteroskedasticity and serial correlation robust standard errors.

Table 4.24: FM Regression Estimates, Excluding Different Free-Float Groups, (Abnormal Turnover)

	Reference period *J*		
Variable	3	6	12
Panel A: Exclusion of stocks with free-float below 30%			
Intercept	2.300 (5.605)***	2.381 (5.765)***	2.375 (5.836)***
DELTATURN A	**0.248 (2.551)****	**0.168 (1.563)**	**0.294 (2.624)*****
SIZE	-0.103 (-1.715)*	-0.112 (-1.850)*	-0.112 (-1.866)*
BM	0.403 (2.696)***	0.403 (2.691)***	0.401 (2.673)***
RET2-12	0.004 (1.500)	0.004 (1.421)	0.004 (1.402)
Panel B: Exclusion of stocks with free-float below 60%			
Intercept	2.060 (4.410)***	2.145 (4.582)***	2.129 (4.657)***
DELTATURN A	**0.286 (1.729)***	**0.153 (0.847)**	**0.341 (2.328)****
SIZE	-0.077 (-1.181)	-0.086 (-1.302)	-0.086 (-1.321)
BM	0.288 (1.746)*	0.291 (1.768)*	0.284 (1.729)*
RET2-12	0.002 (0.535)	0.001 (0.468)	0.001 (0.451)

This table reports coefficient estimates of Pooled OLS regressions when excluding stocks with low free-floats (only second sub-period from December 2002 to August 2008). In *Panel A (B)*, all stocks with a free-float factor below 30% (60%) have been elminated in each cross-section. The dependent variable is a stock's return in a given month. The independent variables are defined as follows: DELTATURN A is the percentage change of last month's turnover versus the average turnover in the preceding $J = 3, 6, 12$ months. SIZE is the logarithm of a company's market capitalization at the beginning of the previous month. BM is the logarithm of the ratio of book value of equity to market capitalization at the beginning of the previous month. RET2-12 is the stock's cumulative return over the 11 months ending at the beginning of the previous month. ***/**/* Denotes statistical significance at the 1%/5%/10% level. T-statistics (in parentheses) are calculated using Newey-West (1987) adjusted, heteroskedasticity and serial correlation robust standard errors.

Table 4.25: FM Regression Estimates, Using Different Empirical Methods (Abnormal Turnover)

	Reference period *J*		
Variable	3	6	12
Panel A: Pooled OLS method			
Intercept	1.189 (4.068)***	1.232 (4.265)***	1.265 (4.403)***
DELTATURN A	**0.175** **(3.192)*****	**0.167** **(2.806)*****	**0.174** **(2.649)*****
SIZE	-0.036 (-0.810)	-0.041 (-0.924)	-0.046 (-1.028)
BM	0.454 (4.008)***	0.453 (4.009)***	0.448 (3.976)***
RET2-12	0.014 (6.494)***	0.014 (6.479)***	0.014 (6.427)***
Panel B: Fixed effects method			
Intercept	1.145 (4.190)***	1.165 (4.302)***	1.174 (4.349)***
DELTATURN A	**0.078** **(1.579)**	**0.072** **(1.425)**	**0.095** **(1.680)***
SIZE	-0.035 (-0.840)	-0.037 (-0.897)	-0.039 (-0.937)
BM	0.274 (2.632)***	0.274 (2.631)***	0.272 (2.617)***
RET2-12	0.011 (5.266)***	0.011 (5.262)***	0.011 (5.257)***

This table compares coefficient estimates of Fama-MacBeth regressions using two different econometric methods (return series from March 1997 to August 2008). In *Panel A*, coefficients were estimated by applying the Pooled OLS method. This is the estimation procedure applied in all previous analyses. In *Panel B*, coefficients were estimated by using the fixed effects transformation methodology. The dependent variable is a stock's return in a given month. The independent variables are defined as follows: DELTATURN A is the percentage change of last month's turnover versus the average turnover in the preceding *J = 3, 6, 12* months. SIZE is the logarithm of a company's market capitalization at the beginning of the previous month. BM is the logarithm of the ratio of book value of equity to market capitalization at the beginning of the previous month. RET2-12 is the stock's cumulative return over the 11 months ending at the beginning of the previous month. ***/**/* Denotes statistical significance at the 1%/5%/10% level. T-statistics (in parentheses) are calculated using Newey-West (1987) adjusted, heteroskedasticity and serial correlation robust standard errors.

4.1.2.3 Volume Growth

The third volume measure investigated is volume growth, defined as the average monthly percentage change in volume. In the base regressions, we find a negative but mostly insignificant relationship between volume growth and expected returns. In this section, we investigate the sensitivity of this result to some key assumptions by repeating the same robustness checks performed for volume level and abnormal volume.

Table 4.26 reports average coefficient estimates of FM regressions of stock returns on share turnover growth. Panel A repeats the base results and Panel B reports results of regressions including a one-month lag between turnover growth variables and returns. The inclusion of a one-month lag does not alter the basic conclusions, namely the existence of a negative but non-systematic relationship between volume growth and expected returns.

The surprising results of the outlier analysis are reported in Table 4.27. Once we exclude the most extreme 1% of volume variables from both tails per cross-section (Panel A), the relationship between turnover growth and expected returns becomes mostly positive. This positive relationship between short-term volume growth ($J = 1, 3$ months) and expected returns is even strongly significant once outliers are disregarded. Thus, base results seem to be caused by outliers. The implications of this finding for the profitability of volume based portfolios strategies is analyzed below, 4.2.3.

The size analysis yields similar results. When limiting the regressions to stocks with market capitalizations of at least CHF 200 million, the coefficient estimates on the volume growth variables become mostly positive (see Table 4.28, Panel B). The relationship between last month's volume growth ($J = 1$ month) and expected returns even becomes significantly positive. It thus seems that the negative base results are mainly caused by small stocks with extreme (positive or negative) turnover growth.

Table 4.26: FM Regression Estimates, Including 1-Month Lag in Volume Variable (Turnover Growth)

	Formation period *J*			
Variable	1	3	6	12
Panel A: No lag in volume variable				
Intercept	1.315 (4.567)***	1.338 (4.608)***	1.383 (4.676)***	1.390 (4.702)***
DELTATURN B	**0.000** **(0.043)**	**-0.010** **(-1.052)**	**-0.031** **(-2.136)****	**-0.036** **(-0.971)**
SIZE	-0.049 (-1.095)	-0.051 (-1.150)	-0.057 (-1.246)	-0.057 (-1.270)***
BM	0.453 (4.001)***	0.452 (3.992)***	0.450 (3.973)***	0.451 (3.980)***
RET2-12	0.013 (6.355)***	0.013 (6.343)***	0.013 (6.347)***	0.013 (6.370)***
Panel B: 1-month lag in volume variable				
Intercept	1.319 (4.577)***	1.363 (4.668)***	1.356 (4.528)***	1.415 (4.367)***
DELTATURN B	**-0.000** **(-0.101)**	**-0.020** **(-2.308)****	**-0.018** **(-0.734)**	**-0.043** **(-1.111)**
SIZE	-0.049 (-1.110)	-0.055 (-1.212)	-0.054 (-1.168)	-0.059 (-1.314)
BM	0.452 (3.392)***	0.450 (3.975)***	0.451 (3.967)***	0.450 (3.970)***
RET2-12	0.013 (6.356)***	0.013 (6.345)***	0.013 (6.360)***	0.013 (6.380)***

This table compares coefficient estimates of Pooled OLS regressions with and without the inclusion of a one-month lead-lag interval between the volume variable and returns (return series from March 1997 to August 2008). The dependent variable is a stock's return in a given month. In *Panel A*, DELTATURN B is the average monthly percentage change in turnover in the last *J = 1, 3, 6, 12* months. In *Panel B*, DELTATURN B is the average monthly percentage change in turnover in the *J = 1, 3, 6, 12 months ending in the second to last month.* Definition of the independent control variables: SIZE is the logarithm of a company's market capitalization at the beginning of the previous month. BM is the logarithm of the ratio of book value of equity to market capitalization at the beginning of the previous month. RET2-12 is the stock's cumulative return over the 11 months ending at the beginning of the previous month. ***/**/* Denotes statistical significance at the 1%/5%/10% level. T-statistics (in parentheses) are calculated using Newey-West (1987) adjusted, heteroskedasticity and serial correlation robust standard errors.

Table 4.27: FM Regression Estimates, Excluding Different Levels of Outliers (Turnover Growth)

	Formation period *J*			
Variable	1	3	6	12
Panel A: Exclusion of outliers at 2% level				
Intercept	1.093 (3.653)***	1.116 (3.520)***	1.398 (4.321)***	1.487 (4.474)***
DELTATURN B	**0.317** **(5.344)*****	**0.249** **(3.305)*****	**0.022** **(0.226)**	**-0.172** **(-1.577)**
SIZE	-0.028 (-0.608)	-0.033 (-0.683)	-0.065 (-1.353)	-0.064 (-1.322)
BM	0.458 (3.800)***	0.454 (3.976)***	0.415 (3.618)***	0.452 (4.071)***
RET2-12	0.014 (6.593)***	0.014 (6.694)***	0.014 (6.594)***	0.014 (6.588)***
Panel B: Exclusion of outliers at 10% level				
Intercept	1.074 (3.294)***	0.816 (2.343)**	1.290 (3.523)***	1.707 (4.413)***
DELTATURN B	**0.756** **(7.196)*****	**0.704** **(3.869)*****	**0.292** **(1.455)**	**-0.317** **(-1.580)**
SIZE	-0.031 (-0.612)	-0.002 (-0.049)	-0.061 (-1.148)	-0.089 (-1.611)
BM	0.484 (3.999)***	0.459 (3.892)***	0.435 (3.778)***	0.469 (3.981)***
RET2-12	0.015 (7.161)***	0.015 (6.826)***	0.015 (6.985)***	0.015 (6.730)***

This table shows the robustness of the coefficient estimates of Pooled OLS regressions to outliers (return series from March 1997 to August 2008). In *Panel A (B)*, the 1% (5%) highest and 1% (5%) lowest DELTATURN B observations have been eliminated per cross-section. The independent variables are defined as follows: DELTATURN B is the average monthly pecentage change in turnover in the last $J = 1, 3, 6, 12$ months. SIZE is the logarithm of a company's market capitalization at the beginning of the previous month. BM is the logarithm of the ratio of book value of equity to market capitalization at the beginning of the previous month. RET2-12 is the stock's cumulative return over the 11 months ending at the beginning of the previous month. ***/**/* Denotes statistical significance at the 1%/5%/10% level. T-statistics (in parentheses) are calculated using Newey-West (1987) adjusted, heteroskedasticity and serial correlation robust standard errors.

Table 4.28: FM Regression Estimates, Excluding Different Size Groups (Turnover Growth)

	Formation period *J*			
Variable	1	3	6	12
Panel A: Exclusion of micro caps				
Intercept	1.215	1.237	1.276	1.442
	(4.074)***	(4.126)***	(4.229)***	(4.580)***
DELTATURN B	**0.016**	**0.002**	**-0.025**	**-0.144**
	(0.649)	**(0.063)**	**(-0.820)**	**(-2.798)*****
SIZE	-0.037	-0.039	-0.043	-0.060
	(-0.809)	(-0.859)	(-0.943)	(-1.282)
BM	0.434	0.433	0.433	0.433
	(3.871)***	(3.867)***	(3.861)***	(3.863)***
RET2-12	0.014	0.014	0.014	0.014
	(6.166)***	(6.149)***	(6.143)***	(6.215)***
Panel B: Exclusion of small caps				
Intercept	1.194	1.201	1.209	1.303
	(3.070)***	(3.049)***	(3.047)***	(3.231)***
DELTATURN B	**0.076**	**0.067**	**0.058**	**-0.036**
	(2.334)**	**(1.478)**	**(0.960)**	**(-0.421)**
SIZE	-0.035	-0.036	-0.037	-0.045
	(-0.624)	(-0.627)	(-0.636)	(-0.776)
BM	0.479	0.479	0.480	0.482
	(3.813)***	(3.824)***	(3.834)***	(3.847)***
RET2-12	0.015	0.015	0.015	0.015
	(6.491)***	(6.469)***	(6.462)***	(6.470)***

This table reports coefficient estimates of Pooled OLS regressions when excluding stocks with low market capitalizations (return series from March 1997 to August 2008). In *Panel A (B)*, all stocks with firm market capitalization below CHF 50 (200) million have been elminated in each cross-section. The dependent variable is a stock's return in a given month. The independent variables are defined as follows: DELTATURN B is the average monthly percentage change in turnover in the last $J = 1, 3, 6, 12$ months. SIZE is the logarithm of a company's market capitalization at the beginning of the previous month. BM is the logarithm of the ratio of book value of equity to market capitalization at the beginning of the previous month. RET2-12 is the stock's cumulative return over the 11 months ending at the beginning of the previous month. ***/**/* Denotes statistical significance at the 1%/5%/10% level. T-statistics (in parentheses) are calculated using Newey-West (1987) adjusted, heteroskedasticity and serial correlation robust standard errors.

Next, we again divide the sample into two sub-periods. Results reported in Table 4.29 show that there is no systematically significant effect in either of the sub-periods. In the first return series from March 1997 to November 2002 (Panel A), coefficient estimates of turnover growth are positive but non-significant in two formation periods *(J = 1, 12)* and negative in the other two formation periods (significant at the 10% level for the *J = 6* months formation period). In the second return series from December 2002 to August 2008 (Panel B), all four coefficient estimates of turnover growth have a negative sign, but only once at a significant level *(J = 12)*. It is difficult to induce any systematic differences between the two sub-periods from these results. Unfortunately we also cannot compare our results to WATKINS (2007), whose analyzed sample period ends in 1999.

For completeness, we again compare regression results in the second sub-period using either free-float adjusted or non-free-float adjusted share turnover. As in the respective abnormal volume test we do not expect large differences between the two analyses, because volume growth is independent from volume levels. The results (not reported in a table) confirm this.[153]

As a further robustness check, we repeat regressions in the more recent sub-period while excluding all stocks with free-floats below 30% respectively 60% (see Table 4.30). These adjustments only marginally affect results. While the significance levels increase for short-term volume growth (*J = 1* month), they slightly decrease for other formation periods.

Next, we repeat the base analysis applying an alternative estimation method, namely fixed effects transformation. Coefficient estimates reported in Table 4.31 show that results are qualitatively the same in both econometric models.

[153] The volume growth coefficients and corresponding t-statistics (in parentheses) for *J = 1, 3, 6, 12* are -0.004 (-0.275), -0.016 (-1.028), -0.030 (-1.264), -0.088 (-2.442) using non-free-float adjusted share turnover and -0.004 (-0.269), -0.016 (-1.022), -0.028 (-1.148), -0.085 (-2.265) using free-float adjusted share turnover.

Table 4.29: FM Regression Estimates in Different Sub-Periods (Turnover Growth)

	Formation period J			
Variable	1	3	6	12
Panel A: Return series 03/1997-11/2002				
Intercept	0.344	0.364	0.422	0.310
	(0.710)	(0.744)	(0.842)	(0.628)
DELTATURN B	**0.005**	**-0.003**	**-0.028**	**0.022**
	(0.752)	**(-0.240)**	**(-1.663)***	**(0.389)**
SIZE	0.002	0.000	-0.006	0.006
	(0.032)	(0.003)	(-0.080)	(0.081)
BM	0.470	0.469	0.468	0.471
	(2.788)***	(2.780)***	(2.766)***	(2.788)***
RET2-12	0.018	0.018	0.018	0.018
	(6.801)***	(6.792)***	(6.812)***	(6.736)***
Panel B: Return series 12/2002-08/2008				
Intercept	2.414	2.439	2.462	2.572
	(6.795)***	(6.888)***	(6.906)***	(7.014)***
DELTATURN B	**-0.004**	**-0.016**	**-0.028**	**-0.085**
	(-0.269)	**(-1.022)**	**(-1.148)**	**(-2.265)****
SIZE	-0.113	-0.116	-0.119	-0.132
	(-2.145)**	(-2.206)**	(-2.244)**	(-2.444)**
BM	0.404	0.403	0.402	0.398
	(2.841)***	(2.837)***	(2.825)***	(2.797)***
RET2-12	0.004	0.004	0.004	0.004
	(1.595)	(1.581)	(1.574)	(1.562)

This table reports coefficient estimates of Pooled OLS regressions over two sub-periods. The first return series from March 1997 to November 2002 is reported in *Panel A.* The second return series from December 2002 to August 2008 is reported in *Panel B*. The dependent variable is a stock's return in a given month. The independent variables are defined as follows: DELTATURN B is the average monthly percentage change in turnover in the last J = *1, 3, 6, 12* months. SIZE is the logarithm of a company's market capitalization at the beginning of the previous month. BM is the logarithm of the ratio of book value of equity to market capitalization at the beginning of the previous month. RET2-12 is the stock's cumulative return over the 11 months ending at the beginning of the previous month. ***/**/* Denotes statistical significance at the 1%/5%/10% level. T-statistics (in parentheses) are calculated using Newey-West (1987) adjusted, heteroskedasticity and serial correlation robust standard errors.

Table 4.30: FM Regression Estimates, Excluding Different Free-Float Groups (Turnover Growth)

	Formation period *J*			
Variable	1	3	6	12
Panel A: Exclusion of stocks with free-float below 30%				
Intercept	2.499	2.508	2.518	2.616
	(6.046)***	(5.992)***	(5.997)***	(6.117)***
DELTATURN B	**-0.017**	**-0.020**	**-0.027**	**-0.080**
	(-1.964)**	**(-0.975)**	**(-0.942)**	**(-2.271)****
SIZE	-0.125	-0.126	-0.127	-0.139
	(-2.054)**	(-2.055)**	(-2.068)**	(-2.226)**
BM	0.403	0.403	0.402	0.399
	(2.693)***	(2.693)***	(2.687)***	(2.663)**
RET2-12	0.003	0.003	0.003	0.003
	(1.337)	(1.330)	(1.330)	(1.318)
Panel B: Exclusion of stocks with free-float below 60%				
Intercept	2.241	2.223	2.239	2.311
	(4.832)***	(4.701)***	(4.718)***	(4.806)***
DELTATURN B	**-0.026**	**-0.013**	**-0.024**	**-0.077**
	(-2.587)***	**(-0.372)**	**(-0.590)**	**(-1.575)**
SIZE	-0.095	-0.093	-0.095	-0.103
	(-1.444)	(-1.398)	(-1.415)	(-1.523)
BM	0.294	0.294	0.294	0.291
	(1.786)*	(1.789)*	(1.786)*	(1.770)*
RET2-12	0.001	0.001	0.001	0.001
	(0.414)	(0.416)	(0.408)	(0.395)

This table reports coefficient estimates of Pooled OLS regressions when excluding stocks with low free-floats (only second sub-period from December 2002 to August 2008). In *Panel A (B)*, all stocks with a free-float factor below 30% (60%) have been elminated in each cross-section. The dependent variable is a stock's return in a given month. The independent variables are defined as follows: DELTATURN B is the average monthly percentage change in turnover in the last *J* = *1, 3, 6, 12* months. SIZE is the logarithm of a company's market capitalization at the beginning of the previous month. BM is the logarithm of the ratio of book value of equity to market capitalization at the beginning of the previous month. RET2-12 is the stock's cumulative return over the 11 months ending at the beginning of the previous month. ***/**/* Denotes statistical significance at the 1%/5%/10% level. T-statistics (in parentheses) are calculated using Newey-West (1987) adjusted, heteroskedasticity and serial correlation robust standard errors.

Table 4.31: FM Regression Estimates, Using Different Empirical Methods (Turnover Growth)

	Formation period J			
Variable	1	3	6	12
Panel A: Pooled OLS method				
Intercept	1.315	1.338	1.383	1.390
	(4.567)***	(4.608)***	(4.676)***	(4.702)***
DELTATURN B	**0.000**	**-0.010**	**-0.031**	**-0.036**
	(0.043)	**(-1.052)**	**(-2.136)****	**(-0.971)**
SIZE	-0.049	-0.051	-0.057	-0.057
	(-1.095)	(-1.150)	(-1.246)	(-1.270)***
BM	0.453	0.452	0.450	0.451
	(4.001)***	(3.992)***	(3.973)***	(3.980)***
RET2-12	0.013	0.013	0.013	0.013
	(6.355)***	(6.343)***	(6.347)***	(6.370)***
Panel B: Fixed effects method				
Intercept	1.216	1.239	1.281	1.246
	(4.503)***	(4.552)***	(4.623)***	(4.455)***
DELTATURN B	**-0.008**	**-0.018**	**-0.038**	**-0.023**
	(-0.826)	**(-1.619)**	**(-2.421)****	**(-0.563)**
SIZE	-0.042	-0.045	-0.050	-0.046
	(-1.021)	(-1.079)	(-1.178)	(-1.081)
BM	0.273	0.272	0.271	0.272
	(2.618)***	(2.610)***	(2.591)***	(2.605)***
RET2-12	0.011	0.011	0.011	0.011
	(5.212)***	(5.213)***	(5.221)***	(5.232)***

This table compares coefficient estimates of Fama-MacBeth regressions using two different econometric methods (return series from March 1997 to August 2008). In *Panel A*, coefficients were estimated by applying the Pooled OLS method. This is the estimation procedure applied in all previous analyses. In *Panel B*, coefficients were estimated by using fixed effects transformation methodology. The dependent variable is a stock's return in a given month. The independent variables are defined as follows: DELTATURN B is the average monthly percentage change in turnover in the last J = *1, 3, 6, 12* months. SIZE is the logarithm of a company's market capitalization at the beginning of the previous month. BM is the logarithm of the ratio of book value of equity to market capitalization at the beginning of the previous month. RET2-12 is the stock's cumulative return over the 11 months ending at the beginning of the previous month. ***/**/* Denotes statistical significance at the 1%/5%/10% level. T-statistics (in parentheses) are calculated using Newey-West (1987) adjusted, heteroskedasticity and serial correlation robust standard errors.

Table 4.32: FM Regression Estimates over Longer Return Horizons (Turnover Growth)

	Formation period *J*			
Holding period K	1 month	3 months	6 months	12 months
Panel A: Turnover growth (DELTATURN B) coefficient				
1 month	0.000	-0.009	**-0.026**	-0.018
	(0.036)	(-0.959)	**(-1.890)***	(-0.475)
3 months	-0.012	-0.043	-0.068	-0.114
	(-0.466)	(-0.925)	(-1.013)	(-1.091)
6 months	-0.023	-0.068	-0.087	-0.313
	(-0.368)	(-0.617)	(-0.552)	(-1.292)
12 months	-0.047	-0.166	-0.388	-0.941
	(-0.275)	(-0.554)	(-0.910)	(-1.448)
Panel B: Turnover growth (DELTATURN B) coefficient, controlled for Size, Book-to-market, and Momentum				
1 month	0.000	-0.010	**-0.031**	-0.036
	(0.043)	(-1.052)	**(-2.136)****	(-0.971)
3 months	-0.013	-0.050	-0.089	**-0.188**
	(-0.518)	(-1.089)	(-1.322)	**(-1.771)***
6 months	-0.031	-0.097	-0.152	**-0.507**
	(-0.488)	(-0.874)	(-0.967)	**(-2.068)****
12 months	-0.074	-0.254	-0.575	**-1.402**
	(-0.437)	(-0.849)	(-1.343)	**(-2.127)****

This table reports coefficient estimates of DELTATURN B (average monthly percentage change in turnover in the last $J = 1, 3, 6, 12$ months) in Pooled OLS regressions over a return series from March 1997 to August 2008. The dependent variable is a stock's return over $K = 1, 3, 6, 12$ months. In *Panel A*, DELTATURN B is the only independent variable. In *Panel B*, we additionally include SIZE, BM and RET2-12 as control variables. ***/**/* Denotes statistical significance at the 1%/5%/10% level. For the $K = 1$ month return horizon, t-statistics (in parentheses) are calculated using Newey-West (1987) adjusted, heteroskedasticity and serial correlation robust standard errors. For the $K > 1$ month return horizon, reported t-statistics are calculated using the Hjalmarsson (2008) adjustment methodology, i.e., by dividing the standard t-statistic by the square root of the forecasting (return) horizon K.

As a final robustness check, we analyze the results over longer return horizons. Table 4.32, Panel A, reports volume growth coefficient estimates of FM regressions of stock returns on volume growth alone, over different formation *and* return horizons. Results show that the basic finding of a negative but insignificant relationship between volume growth and expected returns is also valid over longer-term return horizons. In fact, all coefficient estimates for multi-month holding periods (i.e., $K > 1$ month) are negative, but none at statistically significant levels. Panel B reports coefficient estimates of volume growth once we additionally control for size, book-to-market ratio, and momentum. For short- to intermediate-term formation periods ($J = 1, 3, 6$ months), above conclusion is still true. The average volume growth over the last 12 months ($J = 12$), however, seems to be significantly negatively related to expected returns for the next three to 12 months ($K = 3, 6, 12$). We analyze in the portfolio-based tests whether this result is important (below, 4.2.3).

4.1.2.4 Variability in Volume

The fourth and final base result that needs further investigation is the apparently negative relationship between variability in volume and expected returns. Results of the first four robustness checks, namely the inclusion of a one-month lag in variability in volume, the exclusion of small stocks, the exclusion of outliers, and the analysis in different sub-periods, are all reported in Table 4.33.

The first analysis is the introduction of a one-month lead-lag interval between the variability in volume variables used as independent regressors and the stock returns representing the dependent variable in our regressions. Coefficient estimates reported in Panel A show that this change does not largely affect results.

The same is true when excluding stocks with a market capitalization below CHF 50 million respectively CHF 200 million. Results reported in Table 4.33, Panel B, show that the negative relationship between variability in volume and expected returns is not limited to stocks of small size.

As a further robustness check, we exclude extreme values of coefficient of variation in turnover. The basic conclusions are again unaffected as reported in Table 4.33, Panel C. The negative relationship between variability in volume and expected returns does not result from outliers.

Table 4.33: FM Regression Estimates, Robustness Checks, Part 1 (Coefficient of Variation in Turnover)

	Panel A: One-month lag in volume		Panel B: Exlusion of size groups	
Variable	No lag	1-month lag	No micro caps	No small caps
Intercept	1.655	1.778	1.598	1.670
	(5.606)***	(6.022)***	(5.244)***	(4.170)***
CVTURN	**-0.693**	**-0.943**	**-0.628**	**-0.639**
	(-4.082)***	**(-5.328)*****	**(-3.855)*****	**(-3.837)*****
SIZE	-0.173	-0.217	-0.158	-0.167
	(-3.330)***	(-4.177)***	(-2.959)***	(-2.532)**
BM	0.438	0.431	0.424	0.473
	(3.892)***	(3.844)***	(3.791)***	(2.760)***
RET2-12	0.014	0.014	0.014	0.015
	(6.434)***	(6.522)***	(6.167)***	(6.453)***
	Panel C: Exclusion of outliers		Panel D: Different sub-periods	
Variable	At 2%-level	At 10%-level	03/1997-11/2002	12/2002-08/2008
Intercept	1.711	1.719	0.461	2.638
	(5.655)***	(5.297)***	(0.927)	(7.194)***
CVTURN	**-0.664**	**-0.748**	**-0.223**	**-0.503**
	(-3.805)***	**(-3.773)*****	**(-0.849)**	**(-2.336)****
SIZE	-0.180	-0.193	-0.033	-0.209
	(-3.397)***	(-3.334)***	(-0.391)	(-3.203)***
BM	0.400	0.393	0.468	0.393
	(3.541)***	(3.618)***	(2.774)***	(2.777)***
RET2-12	0.014	0.014	0.018	0.004
	(6.342)***	(6.471)***	(6.839)***	(1.665)*

This table compares coefficient estimates of Pooled OLS regressions performing various robustness checks (return series from March 1997 to August 2008). In the first column of *Panel A*, CVTURN is the logarithm of the coefficient of variation in share turnover, calculated *over the past 12 months*. In the second column, CVTURN is calculated *over the past 12 months ending in the second to last month*. In *Panel B*, stocks with low market capitalizations were excluded in each cross-section (micro / small caps are stocks with firm market capitalization below CHF 50 / 200 million. In the first (second) column of *Panel C*, we exclude the 1% (5%) highest and 1% (5%) lowest CVTURN observations per cross-section. And in *Panel D*, we separately report regression results for two sub-periods. The dependent variable is a stock's return in a given month.
Definition of the independent control variables (the same across all panels): SIZE is the logarithm of a company's market capitalization at the beginning of the previous month. BM is the logarithm of the ratio of book value of equity to market capitalization at the beginning of the previous month. RET2-12 is the stock's cumulative return over the 11 months ending at the beginning of the previous month. ***/**/* Denotes statistical significance at the 1%/5%/10% level. T-statistics (in parentheses) are calculated using Newey-West (1987) adjusted, heteroskedasticity and serial correlation robust standard errors.

Next, the sample is divided into the two return series from March 1997 to November 2002 respectively December 2002 to August 2008 (Table 4.33, Panel D). Interestingly, the variability in volume coefficient is only significantly negative in the second sub-period, while it is negative but insignificant in the first sub-period. One possible explanation for this result could be that a negative 'variability in volume'-return effect is a relatively recent empirical phenomenon. However, existing literature from the US stock markets contradicts this. In fact, CHORDIA ET AL. (2001) respectively KEENE/ PETERSON (2007) find a statistically significant negative relationship between variability in volume and expected returns in sample periods from 1966 to 1995 respectively from 1963 to 2002. A second possibility for the differences in the two sub-periods could be the presence of varying underlying market regimes displaying different 'variability in volume'-return dynamics. This point is further examined in chapter 5. Finally, the more significant relationship between variability in volume and expected returns could be due to the improvement of the quality of our data over time as indicated by the substantial reduction of stocks with missing data (see Table 3.1 above).

In above discussion regarding the time-instability of the 'volume level'-return relationship (4.1.2.1) we additionally mention that only the analysis in the second sub-period is conducted using free-float adjusted turnover. Therefore, as a further robustness check, we again investigate the influence of free-float adjustment on the relationship between the coefficient in variation in turnover and expected returns in the second sub-period. The results, which are not reported in a table, show that free-float adjustment does indeed increase the significance of results. In fact, coefficient estimates decrease from -0.468 to -0.503 with corresponding t-statistics decreasing from -2.020 to -2.336. However, these differences only explain a small part of the deviations in results in the two sub-periods as reported in Table 4.33, Panel D.

Results of the next two robustness checks, the *exclusion of small free-float stocks* and the *comparison of different empirical methods*, are reported in Table 4.34. In the free-float test, we again repeat the base regressions in the more recent sub-period while excluding all stocks with a free-float below 30% and 60%. As shown in Table 4.34, Panel A, this exclusion does hardly affect results.

Table 4.34: FM Regression Estimates, Robustness Checks, Part 2 (Coefficient of Variation in Turnover)

	Panel A: Exclusion of free-float		Panel B: Different empirical methods	
Variable	Free-float <30%	Free-float <60%	Pooled OLS	Fixed effects
Intercept	2.720	2.451	1.655	1.276
	(6.242)***	(5.025)***	(5.606)***	(4.602)***
CVTURN	**-0.567**	**-0.617**	**-0.693**	**-0.164**
	(-2.335)**	**(-2.124)****	**(-4.082)*****	**(-1.017)**
SIZE	-0.229	-0.207	-0.173	-0.069
	(-2.861)***	(-2.296)**	(-3.330)***	(-1.428)
BM	0.389	0.283	0.438	0.270
	(2.602)***	(1.724)*	(3.892)***	(2.600)***
RET2-12	0.004	0.001	0.014	0.011
	(1.418)	(0.439)	(6.434)***	(5.267)***

This table compares coefficient estimates of regressions performing two additional robustness checks. In *Panel A*, we exclude stocks with low free-floats (only second sub-period from December 2002 to August 2008). In the first (second) column, all stocks with a free-float factor below 30% (60%) have been eliminated in each cross-section. In *Panel B*, results of two different econometric methods are compared (full return series from March 1997 to August 2008). In the first column, coefficients were estimated by applying the Pooled OLS method. This is the estimation procedure used in all previous analyses (including Panel A of this table). In the second column, coefficients were estimated by using the fixed effects transformation methodology.
The dependent variable is a stock's return in a given month. Definition of the independent control variables (the same across all panels): SIZE is the logarithm of a company's market capitalization at the beginning of the previous month. BM is the logarithm of the ratio of book value of equity to market capitalization at the beginning of the previous month. RET2-12 is the stock's cumulative return over the 11 months ending at the beginning of the previous month. ***/**/* Denotes statistical significance at the 1%/5%/10% level. T-statistics (in parentheses) are calculated using Newey-West (1987) adjusted, heteroskedasticity and serial correlation robust standard errors.

So far, the variability in volume effect has proven to be quite robust across all sensitivity tests, with the exception of the insignificant results in the first sub-period. But when we estimate the relationship between the coefficient of variation in turnover and expected returns using the fixed effects method (over the entire return series), the effect completely loses its significance (see Table 4.34, Panel B). In other words, under the assumption that an unobserved cross-sectionally constant effect correlates with one of the regressors, the de-meaning of both dependent and independent variables in the regressions eliminates the significance of the observed 'variability in volume' effect. Results of portfolio-based tests reported below (4.2.4) help to clarify this point.

Because of the large differences depending on the chosen estimation procedure, we report results over longer return horizons for both the Pooled OLS and the fixed effects method (see Table 4.35).

Table 4.35: FM Regression Estimates over Longer Return Horizons (Coefficient of Variation in Turnover)

	Panel A: Pooled OLS		Panel B: Fixed effects	
Holding period K	Volume only	Controlled	Volume only	Controlled
1 month	-0.153 (-1.052)	**-0.693** **(-4.082)*****	0.126 (0.944)	-0.164 (-1.017)
3 months	-0.529 (-1.234)	**-2.525** **(-4.591)*****	0.372 (0.949)	-0.741 (-1.450)
6 months	-0.758 (-0.771)	**-5.450** **(-4.327)*****	1.364 (1.526)	-1.152 (-0.989)
12 months	-1.273 (-0.477)	**-11.598** **(-3.391)*****	3.394 (1.351)	-2.192 (-0.668)

This table reports coefficient estimates of CVTURN (logarithm of the coefficient of variation in share turnover, calculated over the past 12 months) in regressions over a return series from March 1997 to August 2008. In *Panel A*, coefficients were estimated by applying the Pooled OLS method. In *Panel B*, coefficients were estimated by using the fixed effects transformation methodology. In both panels, CVTURN is the only independent variable in the first column, while in the second column we additionally include SIZE, BM, and RET2-12 as control variables. ***/**/* Denotes statistical significance at the 1%/5%/10% level. For the $K = 1$ month return horizon, t-statistics (in parentheses) are calculated using Newey-West (1987) adjusted, heteroskedasticity and serial correlation robust standard errors. For the $K > 1$ month return horizon, reported t-statistics are calculated using the Hjalmarsson (2008) adjustment methodology, i.e., by dividing the standard t-statistic by the square root of the forecasting (return) horizon K.

Recall from the base results using Pooled OLS that the negative relationship between variability in volume and expected returns only becomes significant once we control for size, book-to-market ratio, and momentum. The same is true for longer return horizons (see Table 4.35, Panel A). Coefficient estimates of FM regressions of stock returns on variability in volume alone are negative but insignificant over all return horizons studied ($K = 1, 3, 6, 12$ months). Once we additionally control for size, book-to-market ratio, and momentum, however, the coefficient estimates of variability in volume become strongly significant over all these return horizons. The picture looks very different when applying fixed effects transformation (Table 4.35, Panel B). On the one hand, coefficient estimates of regressions of stock returns on variability in volume alone become positive (but insignificant) across all return horizons. On the other hand, once we control for previously documented cross-sectional effects, the coefficients of variability in volume become negative but at systematically insignificant levels.

These results leave us with two doubts. First, the existence of a negative 'variability in volume' effect as reported for US stocks is unclear in the cross-section of Swiss stocks. And second, even if such an effect exists, it would be difficult to exploit it via portfolio strategies, since it at best becomes apparent (i.e., significant) once we additionally control for size, book-to-market ratio, and momentum.

4.1.3 Summary of Regression Analysis

Before moving to the portfolio-based tests we provide a short summary of the results of the various regression analyses, divided into the four volume-return relations investigated.

1. Relationship between volume level and expected returns. We find a positive relationship between short-term measures of volume level and expected stock returns. In other words, stocks with a higher trading volume subsequently have higher returns. This effect is strongest for the very short-term volume measures (i.e., a stock's average volume in the last month) and exists across different empirical estimation procedures. In the robustness checks, we show that the positive 'volume level'-return relation does not result from outliers and is stronger but not limited to stocks with low free-float factors and among small companies. In addition, the effect became more significant in recent times. Finally, the effect seems to exist across various return horizons investigated, meaning that high volume level in a given month has a positive effect on stock returns for the next one to 12 months. The existence of a positive relationship between volume level and expected returns would be surprising given results of most previous studies in other stock markets.

2. Relationship between abnormal volume and expected returns. We also find a positive relationship between abnormal volume and expected returns. This means that stocks with a high trading volume in a given month compared to average trading volume in the preceding three to 12 months have higher subsequent returns. This effect seems relatively short-lived, i.e., it mainly exists in the return month immediately following abnormally high volume. Further robustness checks show that the effect is again not driven by outliers and stronger but not limited to stocks with low free-float factors and among small companies. In addition, the regression analysis suggests that the positive abnormal volume effect is relatively stable across the full 1997 to 2008 sample period. One point that needs further analysis is the fact that the positive effect is either strongly significant or only marginally significant depending on the chosen empirical estimation procedure. The existence of a positive abnormal volume effect in the Swiss stock market would not be surprising given existing literature concerning high-volume return premium and the investor visibility hypothesis.

3. Relationship between volume growth and expected returns. The relationship between volume growth and expected returns is not very clear. In the base regressions, we find this relationship to be negative but at mostly statistically insignificant levels. A first set of sensitivity analyses only marginally affects this finding: there is no clear difference between results in the two sub-periods investigated, across different econometric models, and between stocks with different free-float factors. However, once we exclude the most extreme volume growth values from our analysis, we find that the relationship between turnover growth and expected returns becomes rather positive, even partially at significant levels. This finding would be more consistent with related work by WATKINS (2007). The portfolio-based tests give us more clarity regarding this volume-return relationship.

4. Relationship between variability in volume and expected returns. Also the fourth volume-return relation needs further investigation. The base regressions identify a significantly negative relationship between variability in volume and expected returns, but only once we include additional variables known to affect the cross-section of stock returns, namely company size, book-to-market ratio, and past returns. Some robustness checks confirm the existence of a negative 'variability in volume' effect in the Swiss stock market, which would be in line with previous US evidence: the negative relationship between variability in volume and expected returns is not limited to stocks of small size or stocks with low free-float factors and does not result from outliers. However, results of two other sensitivity analyses cast some doubt on the stability, or even existence, of a 'variability in volume' effect. First, the negative effect seems only significant in the second sub-period since December 2002. And second, once we apply a different empirical method, namely the fixed effects transformation, the effect completely loses its statistical significance. Again, results of the portfolio-based tests provide clarification regarding the existence of this volume-return relationship.

As a final remark, note that our tests suggest that the relationships between the four different volume measures and expected returns are mostly independent from one another.

4.2 Base Portfolio Strategies

In this section, we present results of the portfolio-based empirical tests designed to provide additional evidence on the role of different measures of trading volume in the cross-sectional variation of Swiss stock returns. We again split the discussion into the four types of measures analyzed, namely *volume level*, *abnormal volume*, *volume growth*, and *variability in volume*. For each volume-return relation investigated we first perform one-way sorts based on a single trading volume measure. In a second step, we implement two-way sorts of both a control variable and a volume measure to ensure that potentially discovered volume-effects are not simply the result of another, previously discovered return determinant. We again divide the discussion into one-month and multi-month holding periods. The methodology applied is described in detail above (3.3.1.2). However, for ease of understanding, we repeat the most important aspects of the chosen approach at the relevant positions in the text.

Some comments about the variables used: as noted previously, the base regression results are qualitatively similar but stronger using share turnover instead of Swiss franc volume, especially when investigating potential volume level effects. The predominant reason for this result is the lower correlation of share turnover with company size. Therefore, we only use share turnover[154] based volume measures going forward. Second, we only use coefficient of variation in turnover as the measure of variability in volume due to the high correlation between the standard deviation of volume and the volume level that contaminates results (see above, 4.1.1.4).

One word about the formation periods investigated: in the regression analysis, we use up to four different formation / reference periods for the volume measures (e.g., TURN is defined as the average monthly share turnover in the stock in the last $J = 1, 3, 6, 12$

[154] Number of shares traded in a stock divided by number of shares outstanding of that stock.

months). We generally analyze the same formation periods in the portfolio-based tests. For conciseness, however, we report results of a maximum of two formation periods in the tables. The discussion of test results using the remaining formation horizons is integrated into the text where appropriate.

4.2.1 Volume Level

In the regression analysis, we find a positive relationship between short-term measures of volume level and expected returns in the Swiss stock market. This finding is surprising given the results of most previous studies in US and other developed (non-European) stock markets who largely find a negative relationship between volume level and returns. However, as we will show in this section, *statistical significance of the positive 'volume level-return' relation completely disappears in a portfolio-based setting.*

In Table 4.36, we report average monthly returns to equal-weighted portfolios formed on the basis of share turnover in the last $J = 1, 12$ months. These portfolios are rebalanced monthly (i.e., holding period $K = 1$). We report results of the $J = 1$ month formation period, because the positive relationship between volume level and expected returns identified in the regression analysis is strongest using short-term volume measures. Additionally, we present results using a long-term volume measure, namely average volume in the last 12 months ($J = 12$). Panel A reports average monthly returns of quintile portfolios, V1 being the portfolio containing the stocks with the highest 20% past share turnover. Let us start with the discussion of the short-term formation period ($J = 1$). Based on the regression results, we suspect the portfolio returns to increase in volume. While this is true for the portfolios V5 to V2 (from 0.61 to 1.32% average monthly returns), the stocks with the highest turnover, V1, have relatively low average returns of only 1.06%. In addition, the zero-cost arbitrage strategy (V1-V5) consisting of long positions in high volume stocks and short positions of equal size in low volume stocks does not generate statistically significant positive returns. The above findings are even more pronounced for the $J = 12$ months formation period. Again, returns to the V5 to V2 portfolios are increasing in size. However, the V1 portfolio containing the highest volume stocks is even the portfolio with the lowest average monthly returns of only 0.68%. As a result, the returns to the zero-cost arbitrage strategies become negative (but not statistically significant from zero). Results for formation periods $J = 3, 6$, which are not reported in a table, are qualitatively the same, except that the V3 portfolio contains the stocks with the highest returns. Table 4.36, Panel B, reports average monthly returns to decile portfolios. Again, the zero-cost arbitrage strategies do not yield statistically significant returns.

Particularly the $J = 1$ month results are surprising given the rather strong positive relationship between short-term volume level and expected returns implied by the regression analysis. Recall, however, results of the outlier analysis reported in Table 4.12. In fact, the exclusion of the highest / lowest volume observations increases the significance levels of the (positive) turnover coefficients in the regressions. Results reported in Table 4.36 suggest that this is driven by the highest volume stocks (which are included in V1), having a below average performance. Another reason for the difference between results of regressions and portfolio-based tests could be the inadequacy of the estimation procedure used. Recall from 3.3.1.1.1 that fixed effects transformation removes only any potentially disturbing, *cross-sectionally* constant unobserved effect. However, there also exists the possibility of the data exhibiting an unobserved, *time-constant* effect. Were this true in our setting, it would bias downwards the standard errors in a Fama-MacBeth regression context, and would thereby wrongly inflate the corresponding t-statistics – as shown in PETERSEN (2009).

The descriptive statistics reported in Table 4.36 reveal some additional insights:[155] It seems that high volume stocks:

- Are generally large, which is not surprising given the previously reported correlation between turnover and size of 0.385;
- Have a low book-to-market ratio; and
- Have systematically higher past returns, which is again not surprising given the discussion of previous literature on contemporaneous volume-return relations (presented in section 2.3).

[155] These are reported for the $J = 1$ month portfolios. Results are practically identical for $J = 12$ months portfolios.

Table 4.36: Monthly Returns to Portfolios Sorted on Share Turnover

	Formation period *J*		Descriptive statistics *(J = 1)*			
Portfolio	1	12	TURN	SIZE	BM	RET2-12
Panel A: Equal-weighted quintile portfolios, sorted on share turnover						
V1	1.06	0.68	14.14	10'228	0.70	22.80
V2	1.32	1.32	5.68	10'816	0.72	21.39
V3	1.23	1.29	2.95	2'129	0.89	17.94
V4	1.04	1.12	1.43	744	1.05	14.07
V5	0.61	0.86	0.45	610	1.83	9.67
V1-V5	0.45 (0.937)	-0.18 (-0.328)				
Panel B: Equal-weighted decile portfolios, sorted on share turnover						
V1	1.03	0.52	18.78	8'335	0.74	23.26
V10	0.46	0.72	0.25	484	1.96	8.62
V1-V10	0.57 (0.940)	-0.20 (-0.329)				

This table reports average monthly returns (time series from March 1997 to August 2008) of equal-weighted portfolios formed each month on the basis of average monthly share turnover in a stock in the last *J = 1, 12* months. The portfolios are rebalanced monthly. V1 is the portfolio containing the stocks with the highest 20 % (Panel A) respectively 10% (Panel B) past share turnover. V1 to V10 are portfolios containing long stock positions, while V1-V5 and V1-V10 are zero-cost arbitrage strategies consisting of long positions in high volume and short positions of equal size in low volume stocks. The descriptive statistics (share turnover, firm market capitalization, firm book-to-market ratio, past twelve months' stock return with the exception of the immediate last month) report averages for stocks within the respective portfolios. ***/**/* Denotes statistical significance at the 1%/5%/10% level. T-statistics (in parentheses) are calculated using Newey-West (1987) adjusted, heteroskedasticity and serial correlation robust standard errors.

These systematic differences between volume portfolios potentially dilute results, which is why we control for them via two-way sorted portfolios. For ease of understanding, we briefly repeat and illustrate the approach applied in these two-way sorts: first, we sort stocks into three portfolios based on the examined control variable (e.g., large stocks, medium-sized stocks, and small stocks, if the control variable is company size). Then, within each control quantile (e.g., large stocks), we sort stocks based on their average monthly share turnover into three volume portfolios (large stocks with high volume, large stocks with medium volume, large stocks with low volume). The equal-weighted portfolios are rebalanced monthly. Finally, we average the returns of each volume portfolio over the corresponding control quantiles per month (e.g., large stocks with high volume, medium-sized stocks with high volume, small stocks with high volume). Thereby we control for differences in the specific control variable. The time-series average monthly returns of these averaged portfolios are reported in Table 4.37 for all the different control variables investigated. Note that additionally to firm market capitalization, firm book-to-market ratio, and past stock returns, we also control for industry belonging. The results are similar to the one-way sorted portfolios. Returns neither systematically increase nor decrease in volume, and the medium turnover portfolio (V2) mostly generates the highest average returns. In addition, no zero-cost arbitrage strategy yields statistically significant returns. Finally, results of portfolios sorted on the basis of the other formation periods investigated ($J = 3, 6$, not reported in a table) yield qualitatively identical results.

Going back to the descriptive statistics of one-way sorted portfolios reported in Table 4.36, there is one additionally interesting point. It seems that within large stocks (portfolios V1 and V2) there is a negative relationship between turnover and expected returns, while this relationship is positive for small stocks (V4 and V5). We test this assumption in the 'two-way sort' setting by separately analyzing returns to volume stocks within each size quantile. Returns reported in Table 4.38 confirm that the relationship between turnover and expected returns is rather negative for large stocks and positive for medium-sized and small stocks but not at statistically significant levels[156]. This finding, which is in line with the size robustness check in the regression analysis (see Table 4.13), is surprising given previous results by AGGARWAL/SUN (2003). In fact, these authors find the negative relationship between the volume level and expected returns in the US stock markets to be most pronounced for small stocks, not large stocks. We abstain from reporting similar details on the other control variables (i.e., book-to-market ratio, past returns, industry affiliation). Note, however, that not one single zero-cost arbitrage strategy investigated yields statistically significant returns, not even at the 10% level.

[156] The same is again true for the other formation periods ($J = 3$ and $J = 6$, not reported in the table).

Table 4.37: Returns to Turnover Portfolios Averaged over 3 Quantiles of the Control Variable

	Control variable			
Volume portfolio	SIZE	BM	RET2-12	Industry Group
Panel A: Formation period J = 1				
V1	1.22	1.17	1.01	1.13
V2	1.11	1.24	1.32	1.28
V3	0.83	0.75	0.83	0.81
V1-V3	0.39	0.43	0.18	0.32
	(0.924)	(1.140)	(0.563)	(1.010)
Panel B: Formation period J = 12				
V1	1.06	0.89	0.88	0.96
V2	1.11	1.20	1.27	1.29
V3	1.00	1.07	1.01	0.98
V1-V3	0.07	-0.18	-0.14	-0.02
	(0.150)	(-0.458)	(-0.383)	(-0.060)

Each month, we sort stocks into three terciles based on the examined control variable (firm market capitalization, firm book-to-market ratio, past twelve months' stock return with exception of the immediate last month) respectively into four industry groups (Manufacturing, Technology & Health, Finance, Consumer). Then, within each control quantile, we sort stocks based on their average monthly share turnover in the last $J = 1, 12$ months into three volume portfolios. The portfolios are rebalanced monthly and are equal-weighted. We then average the returns of each volume tercile portfolio over the corresponding control quantiles per month and calculate time-series average monthly returns (03/1997-08/2008), which are reported in this table. V1, V2, V3 are portfolios containing long stock positions (V1 stocks having the highest past share turnover), while V1-V3 are zero-cost arbitrage strategies. ***/**/* Denotes statistical significance at the 1%/5%/10% level. T-statistics (in parentheses) are calculated using Newey-West (1987) adjusted, heteroskedasticity and serial correlation robust standard errors.

Table 4.38: Returns to Turnover Portfolios Averaged over 3 Size Quantiles

	Size portfolio			
Volume portfolio	Large firms	Medium firms	Small firms	Averaged
Panel A: Formation period J = 1				
V1	0.66	1.50	1.51	1.22
V2	1.00	1.05	1.27	1.11
V3	1.11	0.79	0.60	0.83
V1-V3	-0.45	0.71	0.90	0.39
	(-1.254)	(1.380)	(1.543)	(0.924)
Panel B: Formation period J = 12				
V1	0.62	1.32	1.25	1.06
V2	0.99	1.10	1.24	1.11
V3	1.17	0.92	0.89	1.00
V1-V3	-0.55	0.39	0.36	0.07
	(-1.411)	(0.773)	(0.571)	(0.150)

Each month, we sort stocks into three quantiles based on firm market capitalization. Then, within each size quantile, we sort stocks based on their average monthly share turnover in the last $J = 1, 12$ months into three volume portfolios. The portfolios are rebalanced monthly and are equal-weighted. The figures reported in this table are time-series average monthly portfolio returns (03/1997-08/2008). The column labeled 'Averaged' reports the time-series average of monthly average returns of each volume portfolio over all size quantiles. V1, V2, V3 are portfolios containing long stock positions (V1 stocks having the highest past share turnover), while V1-V3 are zero-cost arbitrage strategies. ***/**/* Denotes statistical significance at the 1%/5%/10% level. T-statistics (in parentheses) are calculated using Newey-West (1987) adjusted, heteroskedasticity and serial correlation robust standard errors.

As a final analysis on the relationship between volume level and expected returns we investigate monthly returns to one-way sorted turnover portfolios over multi-month holding periods. In the regression analysis (Table 4.18), we find that short-term turnover is significantly positively related to expected returns over all horizons investigated (*K = 1, 3, 6, 12* months). Table 4.39 shows that this is not the case for any holding period in a portfolio-setting. In fact, over most formation periods the medium-volume portfolio (V3) generates the highest average returns. In addition, we see that returns to zero-cost arbitrage strategies (that are long in high volume stocks and short in low volume stocks) even decrease in the holding period.[157] We abstain from separately showing multi-month holding period returns for two-way sorted portfolios. Note, however, that we obtain no statistically significant results for any time horizon or control variable investigated.[158]

Some concluding remarks: the regression results indicate a positive relationship between volume and expected returns in the cross-section of Swiss stocks. This assumption does not hold in a portfolio-based setting. In fact, results presented in this section suggest no systematic relationship between volume level and expected returns in the Swiss stock market. This finding contradicts results in US and other developed (non-European) stock markets, who mostly find a significant negative relationship. However, there exists no generally accepted view about the cause of this negative relationship (see literature review, 2.1.1.2 and 2.1.1.3). In addition, ROUWENHORST (1999) finds little evidence of a difference between average returns of high and low share turnover portfolios in a study of 20 emerging stock markets (including three European stock markets: Greece, Portugal, and Turkey), which is consistent with our Swiss results. In that sense, our analysis provides additional evidence of the controversial (if any) role of share turnover (more generally 'volume level') in the cross-section of stock returns, particularly in international markets.

---

[157] Again, qualitatively identical results are obtained for the other formation periods *(J = 3, 6)*.

[158] Recall from Table 4.18, Panel B (above, 4.1.2.1), that significance levels of turnover coefficients increase in the holding period for longer-term formation horizons in a regression setting (when controlled for size, book-to-market, and momentum). The portfolio-based results presented here suggest, as suspected earlier, that these significant long-horizon regression results are driven by some remaining serial correlation, which could not entirely be eliminated by the HJALMARSSON (2008) adjustment procedure.

Table 4.39: Returns to Portfolios Sorted on Turnover, Multi-Month Holding Periods

	Formation period $J = 1$; Varying holding periods K			Formation period $J = 12$; Varying holding periods K		
Portfolio	K = 3	K = 6	K = 12	K = 3	K = 6	K = 12
Panel A: Equal-weighted quintile portfolios, sorted on share turnover						
V1	0.92	0.89	0.86	0.70	0.72	0.69
V2	1.27	1.21	1.19	1.24	1.20	1.16
V3	1.32	1.32	1.22	1.30	1.26	1.19
V4	1.05	1.06	1.06	1.11	1.17	1.23
V5	0.70	0.82	0.92	0.91	0.95	0.99
V1-V5	0.22	0.08	-0.06	-0.21	-0.23	-0.30
	(0.466)	(0.168)	(-0.120)	(-0.415)	(-0.455)	(-0.582)
Panel B: Equal-weighted decile portfolios, sorted on share turnover						
V1	0.77	0.78	0.82	0.42	0.56	0.59
V10	0.53	0.66	0.82	0.80	0.91	0.95
V1-V10	0.24	0.12	-0.01	-0.38	-0.35	-0.36
	(0.422)	(0.223)	(-0.012)	(-0.633)	(-0.589)	(-0.672)

This table reports average monthly returns (time series 03/1997-08/2008) of equal-weighted portfolios formed on the basis of share turnover. Each month, we sort stocks into quantiles on the basis of average monthly share turnover in a stock in the last $J = 1, 12$ months and hold the resulting portfolios for $K = 3, 6, 12$ months. The monthly return for a K-month holding period is calculated as the equal-weighted average of returns from strategies initiated at the beginning of this month and past $K-1$ months. V1 is the portfolio containing the stocks with the highest 20% (Panel A) respectively 10% (Panel B) past share turnover. V1 to V10 are portfolios containing long stock positions, while V1-V5 and V1-V10 are zero-cost arbitrage strategies consisting of long positions in high volume and short positions of equal size in low volume stocks. ***/**/* Denotes statistical significance at the 1%/5%/10% level. T-statistics (in parentheses) are calculated using Newey-West (1987) adjusted, heteroskedasticity and serial correlation robust standard errors.

4.2.2 Abnormal Volume

Results of the regression analysis suggest a positive relationship between abnormal volume and expected returns in the cross-section of Swiss stocks. This outcome is not surprising when compared to the related literature on the existence of a 'high volume return premium' and the 'investor visibility hypothesis'. The strength of this abnormal volume effect, however, remains unclear considering differences depending on the chosen empirical estimation method. Results discussed in this section provide more clarity. In fact, we show that the *positive abnormal volume effect is very strong in a portfolio-based setting* and stable when controlling for various other cross-sectional effects.

Table 4.40 reports average monthly returns to equal-weighted portfolios formed on the basis of abnormal share turnover in a stock, which is defined as the percentage change of last month's turnover versus the average turnover in the preceding $J = 3, 12$ months. These portfolios are rebalanced monthly. We tabulate results of the $J = 12$ months reference period, because we intuitively expect abnormal volume to be best measured when compared to a long-term reference period. Additionally, we show a shorter reference period of $J = 3$ months, which is more in line with previous related literature, e.g., GERVAIS ET AL. (2001). Results using the other reference period investigated in the regression analysis, $J = 6$ months, are again integrated into the text.

Discussion of results: In short, results in Table 4.40 reveal a strong and consistent cross-sectional relation between abnormal volume and expected returns, which is larger for the long-term reference period ($J = 12$). Returns to quintile portfolios (reported in Panel A) systematically increase in abnormal volume. Considering for example the $J = 12$ reference period, we find that average monthly returns increase from 0.54% for the V5 portfolio (containing stocks with the lowest 20% abnormal turnover) to 1.60% for the V1 portfolio (highest 20 percent). As a result, zero-cost arbitrage strategies consisting of long positions in high-volume stocks and short positions of equal-size in low-volume stocks yield large and strongly significant positive returns across different reference periods. Considering again the $J = 12$ months portfolios, this average monthly return difference is 1.06% for quintile portfolios (Panel A) and as high as 1.58% for decile portfolios (Panel B). The size of this return difference is promising regarding the economic significance of the discovered abnormal volume premium. In addition, our results are larger than those by KANIEL ET AL. (2007) in a related empirical investigation in the

Swiss stock market using an alternative volume measure, namely volume shocks (see above, 3.5, for a detailed account of methodological differences between the two studies). These authors find return differences of 0.65 and 1.28% for 20% and 10% cut-offs respectively. Finally, note that above conclusions are equally true for the $J = 6$ months reference period, which are not reported in a table (e.g., average monthly returns to zero-cost arbitrage strategies are 0.93 and 1.32% for quintile and decile portfolios, both statistically significant at the 1% level).

Let us turn to the descriptive statistics in Table 4.40.[159] Recall that previous literature as well as our regression results suggests that small companies generally outperform large companies, high book-to-market firms outperform low book-to-market firms, and past one-year winners outperform past one-year losers. Our outperforming high abnormal volume stocks (V1 portfolios), however, are on average larger, have lower book-to-market ratio, and lower past returns than the underperforming low abnormal volume stocks (V5). Thus, we do not expect these previously discovered cross-sectional effects to cause the positive abnormal volume premium. To be sure, however, we again investigate returns of portfolios built on a two-way sort of a control variable and abnormal volume.

Table 4.41 displays average monthly returns to volume tercile portfolios, averaged over three quantiles of each control variable. For an illustration consider 1.39%. This figure represents the average return of high abnormal volume stocks within large firms, high abnormal volume stocks within medium-sized companies, and high abnormal volume stocks within small companies. The reported results confirm that the discovered abnormal volume premium is independent of size, book-to-market, and momentum effects, as well as of industry affiliation. Portfolio returns increase in abnormal volume across all control variables and reference periods, and the arbitrage profits are consistently significant at the 1% level (the same is true for $J = 6$, which is not reported in a table).

[159] These statistics are reported for the $J = 12$ months reference period, but conclusions are equally true for other reference periods.

Table 4.40: Monthly Returns to Portfolios Sorted on Abnormal Turnover

	Reference period *J*		Descriptive statistics *(J = 12)*			
Portfolio	3	12	DELTA A	SIZE	BM	RET2-12
Panel A: Equal-weighted quintile portfolios, sorted on abnormal turnover						
V1	1.49	1.60	1.69	3'985	1.03	14.74
V2	1.21	1.10	0.21	8'568	0.88	16.50
V3	1.01	1.05	-0.13	7'776	0.84	18.08
V4	1.00	0.99	-0.37	3'450	1.03	18.21
V5	0.58	0.54	-0.67	755	1.41	18.32
V1-V5	**0.91**	**1.06**				
	(3.849)***	**(3.759)*****				
Panel B: Equal-weighted decile portfolios, sorted on abnormal turnover						
V1	1.75	1.85	2.68	2'294	1.18	13.05
V10	0.65	0.27	-0.77	521	1.39	17.58
V1-V10	**1.10**	**1.58**				
	(3.526)***	**(4.389)*****				

This table reports average monthly returns (time series from March 1997 to August 2008) of equal-weighted portfolios formed each month on the basis of abnormal share turnover in a stock (percentage change of last month's turnover versus the average turnover in the preceding *J = 3, 12* months). The portfolios are rebalanced monthly. V1 is the portfolio containing the stocks with the highest 20% (Panel A) respectively 10% (Panel B) abnormal turnover. V1 to V10 are portfolios containing long stock positions, while V1-V5 and V1-V10 are zero-cost arbitrage strategies consisting of long positions in high volume and short positions of equal size in low volume stocks. The descriptive statistics (abnormal turnover, firm market capitalization, firm book-to-market ratio, past twelve months' stock return with the exception of the immediate last month) report averages for stocks within the respective portfolios. ***/**/* Denotes statistical significance at the 1%/5%/10% level. T-statistics (in parentheses) are calculated using Newey-West (1987) adjusted, heteroskedasticity and serial correlation robust standard errors.

Table 4.41: Returns to Abnormal Turnover Portfolios Averaged over 3 Quantiles of the Control Variable

	Control variable			
Volume portfolio	SIZE	BM	RET2-12	Industry Group
Panel A: Reference period J = 3				
V1	1.39	1.42	1.44	1.47
V2	0.97	0.98	0.95	0.91
V3	0.81	0.76	0.77	0.84
V1-V3	**0.58**	**0.67**	**0.67**	**0.63**
	(3.426)*	**(3.929)***	**(3.644)***	**(3.027)***
Panel B: Reference period J = 12				
V1	1.50	1.46	1.46	1.33
V2	0.92	0.96	0.96	1.08
V3	0.74	0.73	0.74	0.81
V1-V3	**0.76**	**0.73**	**0.72**	**0.52**
	(4.010)*	**(4.135)***	**(3.897)***	**(2.623)***

Each month, we sort stocks into three terciles based on the examined control variable (firm market capitalization, firm book-to-market ratio, past twelve months' stock return with exception of the immediate last month) respectively into four industry groups (Manufacturing, Technology & Health, Finance, Consumer). Then, within each control quantile, we sort stocks based on their abnormal share turnover (percentage change of last month's turnover versus the average turnover in the preceding $J = 3, 12$ months) into three volume portfolios. The portfolios are rebalanced monthly and are equal-weighted. We then average the returns of each volume tercile portfolio over the corresponding control quantiles per month and calculate time-series average monthly returns (03/1997-08/2008), which are reported in this table. V1, V2, V3 are portfolios containing long stock positions (V1 stocks having the highest abnormal turnover), while V1-V3 are zero-cost arbitrage strategies. ***/**/* Denotes statistical significance at the 1%/5%/10% level. T-statistics (in parentheses) are calculated using Newey-West (1987) adjusted, heteroskedasticity and serial correlation robust standard errors.

In a next step, still in a 'two-way sort setting', we separately investigate returns to abnormal volume portfolios within each control variable quantile (Table 4.42 to Table 4.45). Our primary objective is to gain further insights into the nature of the discovered abnormal volume premium, especially regarding the investor visibility hypothesis as a potential explanation of empirical results.

We start by analyzing returns to abnormal volume stocks within each size quantile. Results for volume tercile portfolios over different reference periods are displayed in Table 4.42, Panels A and B. The table's main finding is that the strength of the abnormal volume effect strongly decreases in size.[160] This is consistent with related research on 'volume shocks' by GERVAIS ET AL. (2001), AGGARWAL/SUN (2003), and KANIEL ET AL. (2007), as well as with the results of our own size robustness check in a regression context presented above (Table 4.22). The finding is also in line with the investor visibility hypothesis, because, as KANIEL ET AL. (2007) put it, 'smaller firms are the stocks we would expect to be more affected by increased visibility'.

As a further indication regarding economic significance of results, we additionally analyze the size of the identified abnormal volume premium. Recall that we so far implement two-way sorts by constructing nine portfolios, namely three volume quantiles within each of three control variable quantiles. This procedure ensures having well-diversified portfolios containing at least 10 stocks at each point in time, which is important for the analysis of the general volume-return dynamics. To increase the probability of identifying economically significant portfolio returns, we now increase the number of portfolios to 30 (10 volume portfolios within the three size quantiles).[161] Results for the $J = 12$ months reference period are reported in Table 4.42, Panel C, and show that the monthly return difference between high and low abnormal volume stocks is as high as 2.54% for small firms.[162] This is substantial, especially given the average monthly returns to the SPI index of only 0.67% in the respective time-series.

---

[160] This finding is identical for the $J = 6$ months portfolios.

[161] We acknowledge that the resulting portfolios are not well diversified at all times – in certain months at the beginning of the time-series the portfolios contain less than the five stocks recommended by VAIHEKOSKI (2004). But the primary objective of this analysis is to identify the most profitable portfolios. Other authors pursuing the same goal in a similar context only use one stock per portfolio, e.g., REY/SCHMID (2007).

[162] We restrict this analysis to $J = 12$ months portfolios, since both intuition and our results so far suggest the abnormal volume premium to be strongest in this setting.

Table 4.42: Returns to Abnormal Turnover Portfolios Averaged over 3 Size Quantiles

	Size portfolio			
Volume portfolio	Large firms	Medium firms	Small firms	Averaged
Panel A: Reference period $J = 3$, tercile portfolios				
V1	1.05	1.29	1.83	1.39
V2	0.84	1.17	0.89	0.97
V3	0.89	0.87	0.66	0.81
V1-V3	0.16	**0.42**	**1.17**	**0.58**
	(0.639)	**(1.795)***	**(3.569)*****	**(3.426)*****
Panel B: Reference period $J = 12$, tercile portfolios				
V1	1.17	1.43	1.90	1.50
V2	0.76	1.10	0.91	0.92
V3	0.85	0.79	0.57	0.74
V1-V3	0.32	**0.64**	**1.32**	**0.76**
	(1.197)	**(2.691)*****	**(4.215)*****	**(4.010)*****
Panel C: Reference period $J = 12$, decile portfolios				
V1	1.35	1.32	2.43	1.70
V10	0.69	0.37	-0.11	0.32
V1-V10	0.66	**0.95**	**2.54**	**1.38**
	(1.303)	**(2.267)****	**(3.668)*****	**(3.848)*****

Each month, we sort stocks into three quantiles based on firm market capitalization. Then, within each size quantile, we sort stocks based on their abnormal share turnover (percentage change of last month's turnover versus the average turnover in the preceding $J = 3, 12$ months) into three (Panels A and B) respectively ten (Panel C) volume portfolios. The portfolios are rebalanced monthly and are equal-weighted. The figures reported in this table are time-series average monthly portfolio returns (03/1997 - 08/2008). The column labeled 'Averaged' reports the time-series average of monthly average returns of each volume portfolio over all size quantiles. V1, V2, V3, V10 are portfolios containing long stock positions (V1 stocks having the highest abnormal turnover), while V1-V3 and V1-V10 are zero-cost arbitrage strategies. ***/**/* Denotes statistical significance at the 1%/5%/10% level. T-statistics (in parentheses) are calculated using Newey-West (1987) adjusted, heteroskedasticity and serial correlation robust standard errors.

In a next analysis, we investigate returns to abnormal volume stocks within separate book-to-market quantiles. Results displayed in Table 4.43 suggest that the size of the abnormal volume effect does not vary largely across different levels of book-to-market ratios (except within the less diversified decile portfolios, Panel C).[163] If anything, the abnormal volume premium is slightly stronger for stocks with low book-to-market ratios. This is surprising given that stocks with low book-to-market ratios are also called 'glamour stocks', which implies an existing interest by investors. In that sense, we would rather expect a stronger effect of increased visibility (induced by abnormal volume) on value stocks. LERMAN ET AL. (2008), in a related context, do find a marginally stronger effect on value stocks, but much less pronounced than the discovered difference in size quantiles. These authors conclude that the book-to-market ratio seems a much noisier proxy for visibility than size, which is consistent with our findings.

Next, Table 4.44 shows that the strength of the abnormal volume effect decreases in stocks' past returns. In other words, the abnormal volume effect is particularly strong for past losers. This matches results in GERVAIS ET AL. (2001) and reinforces the plausibility of the visibility hypothesis, because it is comprehensible that investors (and analysts) rather lose interest in low performing stocks than in high performing stocks. In that sense, increased visibility induced by abnormal volume in a stock is likely to have a stronger effect on these low performing stocks.

[163] The same is again true for the $J = 6$ months reference period.

Table 4.43: Returns to Abnormal Turnover Portfolios Averaged over 3 Book-to-Market Quantiles

	Book-to-market portfolio			
Volume portfolio	High BM	Medium BM	Low BM	Averaged
Panel A: Reference period J = 3, tercile portfolios				
V1	1.57	1.25	1.46	1.42
V2	0.86	1.04	1.03	0.98
V3	0.96	0.71	0.59	0.76
V1-V3	**0.61** **(1.996)****	**0.54** **(2.466)****	**0.86** **(3.148)*****	**0.67** **(3.929)*****
Panel B: Reference period J = 12, tercile portfolios				
V1	1.54	1.45	1.40	1.46
V2	0.96	0.85	1.08	0.96
V3	0.90	0.69	0.61	0.73
V1-V3	**0.64** **(2.346)****	**0.76** **(2.675)*****	**0.79** **(2.726)*****	**0.73** **(4.135)*****
Panel C: Reference period J = 12, decile portfolios				
V1	1.53	1.89	1.65	1.69
V10	0.24	0.77	-0.20	0.27
V1-V10	**1.29** **(2.412)****	**1.12** **(2.353)****	**1.84** **(3.511)*****	**1.42** **(4.296)*****

Each month, we sort stocks into three quantiles based on firm book-to-market ratio. Then, within each book-to-market quantile, we sort stocks based on their abnormal share turnover (percentage change of last month's turnover versus the average turnover in the preceding $J = 3, 12$ months) into three (Panels A and B) respectively ten (Panel C) volume portfolios. The portfolios are rebalanced monthly and are equal-weighted. The figures reported in this table are time-series average monthly portfolio returns (03/1997-08/2008). The column labeled 'Averaged' reports the time-series average of monthly average returns of each volume portfolio over all book-to-market quantiles. V1, V2, V3, V10 are portfolios containing long stock positions (V1 stocks having the highest abnormal turnover), while V1-V3 and V1-V10 are zero-cost arbitrage strategies. ***/**/* Denotes statistical significance at the 1%/5%/10% level. T-statistics (in parentheses) are calculated using Newey-West (1987) adjusted, heteroskedasticity and serial correlation robust standard errors.

Table 4.44: Returns to Abnormal Turnover Portfolios Averaged over 3 Past Return Quantiles

	Past return (RET2-12) portfolio			
Volume portfolio	Past winners	Medium	Past losers	Averaged
Panel A: Reference period J = 3, tercile portfolios				
V1	1.96	1.26	1.11	1.44
V2	1.69	0.77	0.40	0.95
V3	1.51	0.70	0.09	0.77
V1-V3	0.44	**0.56**	**1.02**	**0.67**
	(1.469)	**(2.738)*** **	**(3.260)*** **	**(3.644)*** **
Panel B: Reference period J = 12, tercile portfolios				
V1	1.98	1.24	1.16	1.46
V2	1.67	1.06	0.16	0.96
V3	1.52	0.42	0.28	0.74
V1-V3	**0.45**	**0.82**	**0.88**	**0.72**
	**(1.720)* **	**(3.459)*** **	**(3.063)*** **	**(3.897)*** **
Panel C: Reference period J = 12, decile portfolios				
V1	2.03	1.59	1.72	1.78
V10	0.84	0.33	0.16	0.44
V1-V10	**1.19**	**1.25**	**1.55**	**1.33**
	(2.770)* **	**(2.465)** **	**(2.798)*** **	**(3.949)*** **

Each month, we sort stocks into three quantiles based on past twelve months' stock return. Then, within each past return quantile, we sort stocks based on their abnormal share turnover (percentage change of last month's turnover versus the average turnover in the preceding J = *3, 12* months) into three (Panels A and B) respectively ten (Panel C) volume portfolios. The portfolios are rebalanced monthly and are equal-weighted. The figures reported in this table are time-series average monthly portfolio returns (03/1997-08/2008). The column labeled 'Averaged' reports the time-series average of monthly average returns of each volume portfolio over all past return quantiles. V1, V2, V3, V10 are portfolios containing long stock positions (V1 stocks having the highest abnormal turnover), while V1-V3 and V1-V10 are zero-cost arbitrage strategies. ***/**/* Denotes statistical significance at the 1%/5%/10% level. T-statistics (in parentheses) are calculated using Newey-West (1987) adjusted, heteroskedasticity and serial correlation robust standard errors.

Finally, we analyze the strength of the abnormal volume effect within different industries. As previously noted the abnormal volume premium is strongly significant when controlling for industry affiliation by averaging over different industry groups (see the identical results reported in Table 4.41 and in the column 'Averaged' in Table 4.45). This result implies that stocks with high abnormal volume in a given time period do not systematically belong to the same industry. Within industries, however, the strength of the abnormal volume effect varies considerably, and is stronger for Finance and Consumer stocks (see Table 4.45).[164] How can we relate this result to the investor visibility hypothesis? Intuitively, it makes sense that stocks in some industries naturally enjoy more attention by (potential) investors. We would expect these stocks to be less affected by increased visibility, along the same line of reasoning that explains why large stocks or past winner stocks should be less affected. This has already been recognized by MILLER (1977). But why should stocks in the Finance and Consumer industries be less closely followed than Manufacturing or Technology & Health companies, which would explain the stronger importance of volume-induced visibility in these industries? This is a difficult question to answer directly, because the four individual industry groups are not homogeneous themselves. There are probably even large differences between the 'base attention level' given to stocks within one specific industry group. As an illustration, MILLER (1977) hypothesizes that within the category of consumer goods companies, those selling to higher income consumers (e.g., makers of luxury goods) should be better known to those individuals with funds to invest than those selling to lower-income classes. The problem in our data of the Swiss stock market is that there are not enough stocks per individual homogenous industry cluster to conduct a meaningful analysis. We therefore propose, as a topic for further research, to implement such an analysis in the US stock markets.

[164] The results are again identical for the $J = 6$ months reference period.

Table 4.45: Returns to Abnormal Turnover Portfolios Averaged over 4 Industry Quantiles

Volume portfolio	Industry portfolio				
	Manuf	Tech&Health	Finance	Consumer	Averaged
Panel A: Reference period J = 3, tercile portfolios					
V1	1.38	1.86	1.21	1.42	1.47
V2	1.00	0.65	0.96	1.05	0.91
V3	1.02	0.97	0.78	0.60	0.84
V1-V3	0.36	0.90	**0.42**	**0.83**	**0.63**
	(1.473)	(1.466)	**(1.862)***	**(3.435)*****	**(3.027)*****
Panel B: Reference period J = 12, tercile portfolios					
V1	1.23	1.49	1.33	1.29	1.33
V2	1.22	1.01	1.01	1.09	1.08
V3	0.95	0.99	0.60	0.71	0.81
V1-V3	0.29	0.50	**0.73**	**0.58**	**0.52**
	(1.030)	(0.860)	**(3.045)*****	**(2.098)****	**(2.623)*****
Panel C: Reference period J = 12, decile portfolios					
V1	1.96	2.19	1.60	1.62	1.84
V10	1.09	-0.10	0.40	0.18	0.39
V1-V10	0.87	**2.29**	**1.21**	**1.44**	**1.45**
	(1.639)	**(2.183)****	**(2.585)****	**(3.106)*****	**(3.776)*****

Each month, we sort stocks into four quantiles based on industry affiliation (according to the sector classification provided by Factset). Then, within each industry quantile, we sort stocks based on their abnormal share turnover (percentage change of last month's turnover versus the average turnover in the preceding *J = 3, 12* months) into three (Panels A and B) respectively ten (Panel C) volume portfolios. The portfolios are rebalanced monthly and are equal-weighted. The figures reported in this table are time-series average monthly portfolio returns (03/1997-08/2008). The column labeled 'Averaged' reports the time-series average of monthly average returns of each volume portfolio over all industry groups. V1, V2, V3, V10 are portfolios containing long stock positions (V1 stocks having the highest abnormal turnover), while V1-V3 and V1-V10 are zero-cost arbitrage strategies. ***/**/* Denotes statistical significance at the 1%/5%/10% level. T-statistics (in parentheses) are calculated using Newey-West (1987) adjusted, heteroskedasticity and serial correlation robust standard errors.

When constructing volume decile portfolios within each industry (Table 4.45, Panel C) we obtain another interesting result, namely the return difference between high and low abnormal volume stocks of 2.29% in the Technology & Health industry. This return difference is very high, especially considering that the abnormal volume effect is not statistically significant using tercile volume portfolios as displayed in Panels A and B. However, this unusual result is driven by the fact that Technology & Health portfolios are not well-diversified. An additional analysis shows that this industry contains very few stocks at the beginning of the time-series, e.g., only 17 in February 1997. Building decile portfolios in such a setting implies that some portfolios only contain one stock. If that single stock has very low or high subsequent returns, this largely affects results, which is exactly what happened in our data set.

We additionally investigate monthly returns to abnormal volume portfolios over multi-month holding periods. The regression analysis implies that the positive abnormal volume effect is largely driven by the immediate return month following abnormal volume (see Table 4.19). The portfolio-based results confirm this. Table 4.46 reports returns to one-way sorted abnormal volume portfolios held for $K = 3, 6, 12$ months. The average monthly returns to zero-cost arbitrage strategies are smaller than the respective figures for the one-month holding period reported in Table 4.40. However, unlike suggested by the regression results, the positive effect persists at statistically significant levels for up to 12 months (particularly for $J = 12$).[165] Two remarks about this result: first, our abnormal volume effect seems longer-lived than the related 'high volume return premium' investigated by GERVAIS ET AL. (2001) and AGGARWAL/SUN (2003). And second, given that monthly rebalancing ($K = 1$) might entail prohibitive transaction costs, the relative persistence of the abnormal volume effect could increase its practical significance. For example, the average monthly V1-V10 returns of 0.74% over the next twelve months following abnormal volume in the $J = 12$ months setting should more than make up for transaction costs.

[165] This is true across different reference periods, including $J = 6$, which is not explicitly reported in Table 4.46.

Table 4.46: Returns to Portfolios Sorted on Abnormal Turnover, Multi-Month Holding Periods

	Reference period $J = 3$; Varying holding periods K			Reference period $J = 12$; Varying holding periods K		
Portfolio	K = 3	K = 6	K = 12	K = 3	K = 6	K = 12
Panel A: Equal-weighted quintile portfolios, sorted on abnormal turnover						
V1	1.31	1.24	1.27	1.36	1.29	1.34
V2	1.15	1.11	1.03	1.26	1.17	1.04
V3	1.01	0.94	0.96	1.01	1.10	1.09
V4	1.04	1.03	1.04	0.97	0.93	0.94
V5	0.75	0.98	0.96	0.66	0.80	0.86
V1-V5	**0.56**	**0.26**	**0.31**	**0.70**	**0.49**	**0.47**
	(3.485)***	**(3.066)*****	**(4.342)*****	**(3.695)*****	**(3.323)*****	**(3.422)*****
Panel B: Equal-weighted decile portfolios, sorted on abnormal turnover						
V1	1.48	1.32	1.35	1.37	1.28	1.45
V10	0.74	0.99	0.95	0.44	0.60	0.71
V1-V10	**0.74**	**0.33**	**0.39**	**0.93**	**0.67**	**0.74**
	(3.556)***	**(2.358)****	**(3.686)*****	**(3.758)*****	**(3.401)*****	**(3.987)*****

This table reports average monthly returns (time series 03/1997-08/2008) of equal-weighted portfolios formed on the basis of abnormal turnover. Each month, we sort stocks into quantiles on the basis of abnormal share turnover in a stock (percentage change of last month's turnover versus the average turnover in the preceding $J = 3, 12$ months) and hold the resulting portfolios for $K = 3, 6, 12$ months. The monthly return for a K-month holding period is calculated as the equal-weighted average of returns from strategies initiated at the beginning of this month and past K-1 months. V1 is the portfolio containing the stocks with the highest 20% (Panel A) respectively 10% (Panel B) abnormal turnover. V1 to V10 are portfolios containing long stock positions, while V1-V5 and V1-V10 are zero-cost arbitrage strategies consisting of long positions in high volume and short positions of equal size in low volume stocks. ***/**/* Denotes statistical significance at the 1%/5%/10% level. T-statistics (in parentheses) are calculated using Newey-West (1987) adjusted, heteroskedasticity and serial correlation robust standard errors.

As a final manifestation of the stability of the discovered abnormal volume effect, Table 4.47 also displays results of two-way sorted portfolios over longer return horizons. For conciseness, the table only reports returns of zero-cost arbitrage strategies of volume portfolios (V1-V3), averaged over all quantiles of the control variables respectively industry groups. The results show that the return difference between portfolios containing high and low abnormal volume stocks is positive at statistically significant levels across all reference periods, control variables, *and* holding periods.

Table 4.47: Returns to Abnormal Turnover Portfolios Averaged over 3 Quantiles of the Control Variable, Multi-Month Holding Periods

	Reference period $J = 3$; Varying holding periods K			Reference period $J = 12$; Varying holding periods K		
Control variable	K = 3	K = 6	K = 12	K = 3	K = 6	K = 12
Monthly returns to zero-cost arbitrage portfolio (V1-V3), averaged over 3 quantiles of the control variable						
SIZE	0.34	0.17	0.19	0.55	0.42	0.42
	(2.889)***	(2.890)***	(4.268)***	(4.233)***	(4.338)***	(4.442)***
BM	0.40	0.20	0.20	0.52	0.36	0.34
	(3.417)***	(3.190)***	(3.931)***	(4.368)***	(4.009)***	(3.530)***
RET2-12	0.40	0.18	0.16	0.53	0.37	0.30
	(3.346)***	(2.854)***	(2.626)**	(4.143)***	(3.640)***	(2.990)***
Monthly returns to zero-cost arbitrage portfolio (V1-V3), averaged over 4 industry groups						
Industry Group	0.34	0.14	0.16	0.42	0.30	0.28
	(2.553)**	(1.980)**	(3.062)***	(3.080)***	(2.647)***	(2.972)***

Each month, we sort stocks into three quantiles based on the examined control variable respectively into four industry groups. Then, within each control quantile, we sort stocks based on their abnormal share turnover (percentage change of last month's turnover versus the average turnover in the preceding $J = 3, 12$ months). Next, we build zero-cost arbitrage strategies consisting of long positions in stocks in the highest volume tercile (V1) and short positions of equal size in the lowest volume tercile (V3). We hold these equal-weighted strategies for $K = 3, 6, 12$ months. The monthly return for a K-month holding period is calculated as the equal-weighted average of returns from strategies initiated at the beginning of this month and past $K-1$ months. The reported numbers represent the time-series average monthly returns (03/1997-08/2008) of average monthly holding period returns of each volume strategy (V1-V3) over the corresponding control quantiles. ***/**/* Denotes statistical significance at the 1%/5%/10% level. T-statistics (in parentheses) are calculated using Newey-West (1987) adjusted, heteroskedasticity and serial correlation robust standard errors.

We conclude this section by summarizing its findings. Most importantly, the portfolio-based tests confirm the existence of a systematically positive abnormal volume premium in the cross-section of Swiss stocks, as indicated by the regression analysis. This effect is very stable when controlling for various other cross-sectional effects and is particularly strong for small stocks and past losers. Additionally, and in contrast to regression results, the portfolio-based tests suggest that the high abnormal volume premium is not exclusively a short-term effect but persists over a one-year holding period. Most of above results are consistent with the investor visibility hypothesis.

4.2.3 Volume Growth

The relationship between volume growth and expected returns in the Swiss stock market is not very clear from regression results. While we generally identify a negative but mostly insignificant effect, this relationship becomes rather positive once we exclude the most extreme volume growth observations. The latter finding is more consistent with related literature in the US stock markets by WATKINS (2007).[166] Results of the portfolio-based tests presented in this section confirm the existence of a positive relationship between volume growth and expected returns in the cross-section of Swiss stocks. This effect, however, is not systematically significant.

We again start by presenting average monthly returns to equal-weighted portfolios that are formed on the basis of past volume growth and rebalanced monthly ($K = 1$). Note that results in Table 4.48 are reported for two formation periods, $J = 3$ and $J = 12$ months. $J = 12$ is chosen in order to be consistent with the only comparable study known to us by WATKINS (2007).[167] Regarding a shorter-term formation period, we prefer average turnover growth in the past three months ($J = 3$) to last month's turnover growth ($J = 1$). The reason is that definitions of turnover growth and abnormal volume are identical for $J = 1$, which might create a mixture of two potential volume-return effects.[168] We do not face this problem at $J = 3$ months.

166 This author disregards the top and bottom 5% of observations throughout his (portfolio-based) analysis.

167 WATKINS (2007) finds that stocks with high-mean turnover growth in the *past 12 months* experience higher subsequent returns.

168 However, we abstain from analyzing the $J = 1$ reference period for abnormal volume. The reason is that the strength of the abnormal volume effect increases in J.

Table 4.48: Returns to Portfolios Sorted on Turnover Growth

	Formation period *J*		Descriptive statistics *(J = 12)*			
Portfolio	3	12	DELTA B	SIZE	BM	RET2-12
Panel A: Equal-weighted quintile portfolios, sorted on turnover growth						
V1	1.32	1.20	2.09	398	1.66	18.15
V2	1.30	1.36	0.49	743	1.19	19.12
V3	0.76	1.15	0.27	1'585	0.91	18.86
V4	1.15	0.91	0.15	4'311	0.79	15.97
V5	0.74	0.66	0.04	17'474	0.64	13.75
V1-V5	**0.57** **(2.444)****	**0.54** **(1.757)***				
Panel B: Equal-weighted decile portfolios, sorted on turnover growth						
V1	1.11	1.13	3.31	272	1.82	17.77
V10	0.73	0.50	0.01	23'478	0.65	12.44
V1-V10	0.38 (1.369)	**0.63** **(1.708)***				

This table reports average monthly returns (time series from March 1997 to August 2008) of equal-weighted portfolios formed each month on the basis of average turnover growth in a stock in the last *J* = *3, 12* months. The portfolios are rebalanced monthly. V1 is the portfolio containing the stocks with the highest 20% (Panel A) respectively 10% (Panel B) past turnover growth. V1 to V10 are portfolios containing long stock positions, while V1-V5 and V1-V10 are zero-cost arbitrage strategies consisting of long positions in high volume and short positions of equal size in low volume stocks. The descriptive statistics (turnover growth, firm market capitalization, firm book-to-market ratio, past twelve months' stock return with the exception of the immediate last month) report averages for stocks within the respective portfolios. ***/**/* Denotes statistical significance at the 1%/5%/10% level. T-statistics (in parentheses) are calculated using Newey-West (1987) adjusted, heteroskedasticity and serial correlation robust standard errors.

Table 4.48, Panel A, reports average monthly returns to quintile portfolios; V1 is again the portfolio containing stocks with the highest 20% past volume growth. The table shows that portfolio returns generally increase in volume growth but not systematically. In the $J = 3$ case, for example, the V3 portfolio has very low returns. And in the $J = 12$ portfolios, V2 earns the highest monthly returns, although V1 stocks have significantly larger turnover growth. Analyzing the return differences between portfolios containing high and low volume growth stocks, we find them to be statistically significant for quintile portfolios (i.e., V1-V5 in Panel A) but not consistently for decile portfolios (V1-V10 in Panel B). As a further illustration of the fact that the relationship is not systematic consider $J = 3$ decile portfolios. Results, which are not reported in a table, show that the highest average monthly returns were earned in the V2 portfolio and the lowest returns in V6 (not V10!). Note that above findings are qualitatively the same for the other formation periods analyzed, i.e., $J = 1, 6$. A first discussion point following these results is the difference to the regression analysis. However, as noted in the introduction, this is driven by extreme volume growth observations (at the 1% level) that substantially influence regression results (see Table 4.27). This outlier issue is less severe in portfolio-based settings, because each stock contributes equally to overall returns.

Next, consider the descriptive statistics in Table 4.48.[169] Interestingly, the generally better performing high volume growth stocks are on average much smaller, have a higher book-to-market ratio, and higher past one-year returns than the worse performing low volume growth stocks. The positive relationship between volume growth and expected returns could thus simply proxy for size, book-to-market, or momentum effects. We control for these possibilities via two-way sorted portfolios. Table 4.49 reports average monthly returns to volume growth tercile portfolios averaged over three quantiles of each control variable respectively over different industry groups. The results further reinforce the conclusion that the generally positive relationship between volume growth and expected returns is not a systematic one.[170] It seems that particularly the negative correlation between turnover growth and size influences results. Once we control for size, the positive return difference between high and low turnover portfolios seizes to be statistically significant. In a next step, we therefore investigate the relationship between volume growth and expected returns separately for each size group.

[169] These are reported for the $J = 12$ months portfolios.

[170] The $J = 1$ results, on the other hand, are consistently significant across all control variables / industry groups, at least at the 10% level. However, this could also be a small 'abnormal volume effect'.

Table 4.49: Returns to Turnover Growth Portfolios Averaged over 3 Quantiles of the Control Variable

	Control variable			
Volume portfolio	SIZE	BM	RET2-12	Industry Group
Panel A: Formation period J = 3				
V1	1.23	1.27	1.35	1.38
V2	0.96	0.98	0.98	0.78
V3	0.97	0.92	0.83	1.07
V1-V3	0.26	**0.35**	**0.52**	0.31
	(1.349)	**(1.812)***	**(2.718)*****	(1.563)
Panel B: Formation period J = 12				
V1	1.21	1.29	1.25	1.28
V2	1.07	1.07	1.16	1.19
V3	0.88	0.80	0.75	0.75
V1-V3	0.32	**0.50**	**0.50**	**0.52**
	(1.451)	**(1.960)***	**(2.260)****	**(2.456)****

Each month, we sort stocks into three terciles based on the examined control variable (firm market capitalization, firm book-to-market ratio, past twelve months' stock return with exception of the immediate last month) respectively into four industry groups (Manufacturing, Technology & Health, Finance, Consumer). Then, within each control quantile, we sort stocks based on their average turnover growth in the last $J = 3, 12$ months into three volume portfolios. The portfolios are rebalanced monthly and are equal-weighted. We then average the returns of each volume tercile portfolio over the corresponding control quantiles per month and calculate time-series average monthly returns (03/1997-08/2008), which are reported in this table. V1, V2, V3 are portfolios containing long stock positions (V1 stocks having the highest past turnover growth), while V1-V3 are zero-cost arbitrage strategies. ***/**/* Denotes statistical significance at the 1%/5%/10% level. T-statistics (in parentheses) are calculated using Newey-West (1987) adjusted, heteroskedasticity and serial correlation robust standard errors.

Results in Table 4.50 find that the return difference between high and low volume growth portfolios is only significantly positive for medium-sized companies. But even within these medium-sized companies the portfolio returns do not always systematically increase in volume growth. Finally, within large stocks, the relationship is even negative for some formation periods but not at significant levels. All these results are qualitatively the same for formation periods of $J = 1$ and $J = 12$ months.[171]

Table 4.50: Returns to Turnover Growth Portfolios Averaged over 3 Size Quantiles

	Size portfolio			
Volume portfolio	Large firms	Medium firms	Small firms	Averaged
Panel A: Formation period J = 3				
V1	0.92	1.33	1.44	1.23
V2	0.82	1.09	0.98	0.96
V3	1.05	0.90	0.97	0.97
V1-V3	-0.13	**0.43**	0.47	0.26
	(-0.486)	**(1.707)***	(1.602)	(1.349)
Panel B: Formation period J = 12				
V1	1.11	1.30	1.21	1.21
V2	0.84	1.33	1.04	1.07
V3	0.82	0.69	1.13	0.88
V1-V3	0.29	**0.60**	0.07	0.32
	(1.021)	**(2.483)****	(0.167)	(1.451)

Each month, we sort stocks into three quantiles based on firm market capitalization. Then, within each size quantile, we sort stocks based on their average monthly turnover growth in the last $J = 3, 12$ months into three volume portfolios. The portfolios are rebalanced monthly and are equal-weighted. The figures reported in this table are time-series average monthly portfolio returns (03/1997-08/2008). The column labeled 'Averaged' reports the time-series average of monthly average returns of each volume portfolio over all size quantiles. V1, V2, V3 are portfolios containing long stock positions (V1 stocks having the highest past turnover growth), while V1-V3 are zero-cost arbitrage strategies. ***/**/* Denotes statistical significance at the 1%/5%/10% level. T-statistics (in parentheses) are calculated using Newey-West (1987) adjusted, heteroskedasticity and serial correlation robust standard errors.

[171] Again being slightly more significant for $J = 1$. For large stocks, however, the return difference is 0.00%.

As a final analysis, we report monthly returns to one-way sorted volume growth portfolios over multi-month holding periods. This is of particular interest, since WATKINS (2007) finds the positive effect of volume growth on expected returns to be long-lived in US markets. The results reported in Table 4.51, however, are not as strong.

Table 4.51: Returns to Portfolios Sorted on Turnover Growth, Multi-Month Holding Periods

	Formation period $J = 3$; Varying holding periods K			Formation period $J = 12$; Varying holding periods K		
Portfolio	K = 3	K = 6	K = 12	K = 3	K = 6	K = 12
Panel A: Equal-weighted quintile portfolios, sorted on turnover growth						
V1	1.17	1.21	1.27	1.20	1.20	1.13
V2	1.37	1.30	1.18	1.27	1.31	1.26
V3	0.91	0.91	0.96	1.20	1.18	1.23
V4	0.92	0.89	0.89	0.89	0.93	0.91
V5	0.89	0.98	0.97	0.69	0.68	0.72
V1-V5	0.27	0.23	**0.31**	**0.51**	**0.52**	0.41
	(1.500)	(1.557)	**(2.316)****	**(1.758)***	**(1.797)***	(1.435)
Panel B: Equal-weighted decile portfolios, sorted on turnover growth						
V1	0.92	1.03	1.18	1.13	1.13	1.00
V10	0.90	1.02	0.98	0.58	0.61	0.71
V1-V10	0.02	0.00	0.20	0.55	0.52	0.28
	(0.095)	(0.011)	(1.271)	(1.544)	(1.441)	(0.886)

This table reports average monthly returns (time series 03/1997-08/2008) of equal-weighted portfolios formed on the basis of turnover growth. Each month, we sort stocks into quantiles on the basis of average monthly turnover growth in a stock in the last $J = 3, 12$ months and hold the resulting portfolios for $K = 3, 6, 12$ months. The monthly return for a K-month holding period is calculated as the equal-weighted average of returns from strategies initiated at the beginning of this month and past K-1 months. V1 is the portfolio containing the stocks with the highest 20% (Panel A) respectively 10% (Panel B) past turnover growth. V1 to V10 are portfolios containing long stock positions, while V1-V5 and V1-V10 are zero-cost arbitrage strategies consisting of long positions in high volume and short positions of equal size in low volume stocks. ***/**/* Denotes statistical significance at the 1%/5%/10% level. T-statistics (in parentheses) are calculated using Newey-West (1987) adjusted, heteroskedasticity and serial correlation robust standard errors.

We again find a mostly positive but non-systematic relationship between volume growth and expected returns, which becomes neither stronger nor weaker with increasing holding periods.[172] The conclusions for returns to two-way sorted portfolios are identical, which is why we do not separately report them in a table. As a final remark, recall the long-horizon results in a regression context (Table 4.32). The respective analysis at $J = 12$ finds a negative relationship between volume growth and expected returns, which becomes significant for multi-month return horizons. However, it is again possible that this result is driven by some remaining serial correlation that cannot entirely be eliminated by the HJALMARSSON (2008) adjustment procedure (see above, 3.3.1.1.3).

In sum, the results of portfolio-based tests indicate a rather positive but non-systematic relationship between volume growth and expected returns. This result is relatively consistent with the respective Fama-MacBeth regressions (without outliers). Our finding, however, is not in line with WATKINS (2007) who reports a systematically positive and long-lived volume growth effect, which he interprets as long-horizon confirmation of the 'high volume return premium'. Our results, on the other hand, suggest that volume growth and abnormal volume are two independent measures with different dynamics. While abnormal volume is systematically positively related to expected returns, also over longer return horizons (see 4.2.2), this is not the case for volume growth. Note, however, that a direct comparison between these studies is not possible due to some methodological differences. WATKINS (2007) uses a slightly different measure of volume growth (market and firm-adjusted excess trading volume growth), an older time-series (1963-1999), and analyzes the relationship in the US stock markets. In addition, GERVAIS ET AL. (2001) analyze the existence of the addressed 'high volume return premium' using volume shocks, not abnormal volume, which is again not identical (recall the discussion in 3.5).

[172] The same is true for the remaining formation periods not included in the table ($J = 1, 6$). The results are again slightly more significant for $J = 1$, which indicates the presence of a minor 'abnormal volume effect'.

4.2.4 Variability in Volume

Regression results are somewhat mixed regarding the role of variability in volume in the cross-section of Swiss stock returns. In the base regressions, we find a negative relationship between variability in volume and expected returns, which is significant once we control for size, book-to-market, and momentum variables. This would be consistent with previous US evidence. However, once we apply the fixed effects transformation methodology, the effect completely loses its statistical significance in a regression context. This last result, namely the lack of a significant relationship between variability in volume and expected returns in the cross-section of Swiss stocks, is consistent with results of the portfolio-based tests presented below.

Table 4.52 displays average monthly returns to equal-weighted portfolios formed on the basis of stocks' coefficient of variation in turnover, which is calculated over the past 12 months. Panel A, reporting returns to quintile portfolios, finds no systematically positive or negative relationship between variability in volume and expected returns. In fact, it is the portfolio containing stocks with a medium level of coefficient of variation in turnover (V3) that yields the highest average returns of 1.23%. This finding of a *non-systematic (respectively insignificant) relationship in a one-way sort setting* is consistent with the respective regression analysis on coefficient of variation in turnover alone (see Table 4.7 in 4.1.1.4).

Considering the descriptive statistics in Table 4.52, we find that high variability in volume portfolios (V1, V2) on average contain relatively small stocks with a high book-to-market ratio, while low variability in volume stocks (V5) are very large and have low book-to-market ratios. This finding is even more pronounced when considering decile portfolios as reported in Panel B. These systematic differences between variability in volume portfolios potentially influence results. More concretely, they could 'artificially' inflate returns of V1 portfolios and lower returns of V5 portfolios, independent of a potentially existing relationship between variability in volume and expected returns. Note that this is exactly what happens in the regression analysis, which is the reason why these results only become significant once controlled for company size or book-to-market ratio. We again control for this by constructing two-way sorted portfolios.

Table 4.52: Returns to Portfolios Sorted on Coefficient of Variation in Turnover

		Descriptive statistics			
Portfolio	Returns	CVTURN	SIZE	BM	RET2-12
Panel A: Equal-weighted quintile portfolios, sorted on coefficient of variation in turnover					
V1	1.03	1.12	474	1.32	18.46
V2	1.15	0.72	615	1.59	15.27
V3	1.23	0.56	1'117	0.98	18.76
V4	1.05	0.43	2'068	0.77	17.23
V5	0.81	0.28	20'241	0.53	16.15
V1-V5	0.22 (0.863)				
Panel B: Equal-weighted decile portfolios, sorted on coefficient of variation in turnover					
V1	0.93	1.33	452	1.23	18.27
V10	0.88	0.23	34'449	0.46	15.51
V1-V10	0.05 (0.148)				

This table reports average monthly returns (time series from March 1997 to August 2008) of equal-weighted portfolios formed each month on the basis of the coefficient of variation in share turnover (calculated over the past 12 months). The portfolios are rebalanced monthly. V1 is the portfolio containing the stocks with the highest 20% (Panel A) respectively 10% (Panel B) past coefficient of variation in turnover. V1 to V10 are portfolios containing long stock positions, while V1-V5 and V1-V10 are zero-cost arbitrage strategies consisting of long positions in high volume and short positions of equal size in low volume stocks. The descriptive statistics (coefficient of variation in turnover, firm market capitalization, firm book-to-market ratio, past twelve months' stock return with the exception of the immediate last month) report averages for stocks within the respective portfolios. ***/**/* Denotes statistical significance at the 1%/5%/10% level. T-statistics (in parentheses) are calculated using Newey-West (1987) adjusted, heteroskedasticity and serial correlation robust standard errors.

Results in Table 4.53 show that even when controlling for size and book-to-market ratio (as well as past returns and industry affiliation), the relationship between variability in volume and expected returns remains nonexistent in a portfolio context. On the one hand, stocks with a medium level of variability in volume mostly remain the best-performing over the one-month holding period. On the other hand, the return difference between high volume and low volume portfolios is marginal, non-systematic, and non-significant.

Table 4.53: Returns to Coefficient of Variation in Turnover Portfolios Averaged over 3 Quantiles of the Control Variable

	Control variable			
Volume portfolio	SIZE	BM	RET2-12	Industry Group
V1	1.04	1.06	1.05	1.08
V2	1.04	1.20	1.17	1.17
V3	1.08	0.90	0.95	0.97
V1-V3	-0.04	0.16	0.09	0.11
	(-0.187)	(0.737)	(0.438)	(0.491)

Each month, we sort stocks into three terciles based on the examined control variable (firm market capitalization, firm book-to-market ratio, past twelve months' stock return with exception of the immediate last month) respectively into four industry groups (Manufacturing, Technology & Health, Finance, Consumer). Then, within each control quantile, we sort stocks based on their coefficient of variation in share turnover (calculated over the past 12 months) into three volume portfolios. The portfolios are rebalanced monthly and are equal-weighted. We then average the returns of each volume tercile portfolio over the corresponding control quantiles per month and calculate time-series average monthly returns (03/1997-08/2008), which are reported in this table. V1, V2, V3 are portfolios containing long stock positions (V1 stocks having the highest past coefficient of variation in turnover), while V1-V3 are zero-cost arbitrage strategies. ***/**/* Denotes statistical significance at the 1%/5%/10% level. T-statistics (in parentheses) are calculated using Newey-West (1987) adjusted, heteroskedasticity and serial correlation robust standard errors.

Also within individual size quantiles, there are no systematic return differences between different variability in volume portfolios (Table 4.54). While the return difference between high volume and low volume stocks is rather positive for large and medium-sized stocks, and negative for small stocks, this is not even close to being at statistically significant levels. We obtain the same unsystematic and insignificant results for different variability in volume portfolios within other control variable quantiles, which is why these results are not separately reported.

Table 4.54: Returns to Coefficient of Variation in Turnover Portfolios Averaged over 3 Size Quantiles

	Size portfolio			
Volume portfolio	Large firms	Medium firms	Small firms	Averaged
V1	0.97	1.13	1.02	1.04
V2	0.90	1.16	1.07	1.04
V3	0.90	1.03	1.30	1.08
V1-V3	0.07 (0.290)	0.09 (0.435)	-0.27 (-0.708)	-0.04 (-0.187)

Each month, we sort stocks into three quantiles based on firm market capitalization. Then, within each size quantile, we sort stocks based on their coefficient of variation in share turnover (calculated over the past 12 months) into three volume portfolios. The portfolios are rebalanced monthly and are equal-weighted. The figures reported in this table are time-series average monthly portfolio returns (03/1997 - 08/2008). The column labeled 'Averaged' reports the time-series average of monthly average returns of each volume portfolio over all size quantiles. V1, V2, V3 are portfolios containing long stock positions (V1 stocks having the highest past coefficient of variation in turnover), while V1-V3 are zero-cost arbitrage strategies. ***/**/* Denotes statistical significance at the 1%/5%/10% level. T-statistics (in parentheses) are calculated using Newey-West (1987) adjusted, heteroskedasticity and serial correlation robust standard errors.

Finally, we analyze portfolio returns over multi-month holding periods. The results reported in Table 4.55 confirm previous findings of a non-systematic relationship, also over longer return horizons. This is also true for two-way sorted portfolios, which is why we abstain from separately reporting these results in a table.

To summarize, the portfolio-based tests reveal neither a systematic nor a significant relationship between variability in volume and expected returns in the cross-section of Swiss stocks, even after interfering variables (company size and book-to-market ratio) have been controlled for. This seems to confirm the existence of a bias in the base regression analysis as indicated by the strong return differences between Pooled OLS and fixed effects estimation procedures. Our results are contrary to existing evidence of a systematically negative cross-sectional relationship between variability of trading volume and expected returns in US stock markets. Note, however, that to our knowledge there exists no model that can consistently explain this negative relationship. In fact, CHORDIA ET AL. (2001) are surprised by their own finding, intuitively expecting a rather positive relationship. And also the subsequent attempt to match their empirical evidence with the clientele effect hypothesis does not fully succeed (see above, section 2.1.3).

Table 4.55: Returns to Portfolios Sorted on Coefficient of Variation in Turnover, Multi-Month Holding Periods

	Varying holding periods K			
Portfolio	K = 1	K = 3	K = 6	K = 12
Panel A: Equal-weighted quintile portfolios, sorted on coefficient of variation in turnover				
V1	1.03	0.99	1.04	1.00
V2	1.15	1.20	1.29	1.31
V3	1.23	1.20	1.18	1.22
V4	1.05	1.07	1.03	1.02
V5	0.81	0.80	0.76	0.72
V1-V5	0.22	0.20	0.28	0.28
	(0.863)	(0.810)	(1.117)	(1.171)
Panel B: Equal-weighted decile portfolios, sorted on coefficient of variation in turnover				
V1	0.93	0.91	0.91	0.85
V10	0.88	0.82	0.77	0.72
V1-V10	0.05	0.09	0.14	0.13
	(0.148)	(0.292)	(0.427)	(0.452)

This table reports average monthly returns (time series 03/1997-08/2008) of equal-weighted portfolios formed on the basis of coefficient of variation in turnover. Each month, we sort stocks into quintiles (A) / deciles (B) on the basis of coefficient of variation in share turnover (calculated over the past 12 months) and hold the resulting portfolios for $K = 1, 3, 6, 12$ months. The monthly return for a K–month holding period is calculated as the equal-weighted average of returns from strategies initiated at the beginning of this month and past $K\text{-}1$ months. V1 is the portfolio containing the stocks with the highest 20% (Panel A) respectively 10% (Panel B) past coefficient of variation in turnover. V1 to V10 are portfolios containing long stock positions, while V1-V5 and V1-V10 are zero-cost arbitrage strategies consisting of long positions in high volume and short positions of equal size in low volume stocks. ***/**/* Denotes statistical significance at the 1%/5%/10% level. T-statistics (in parentheses) are calculated using Newey-West (1987) adjusted, heteroskedasticity and serial correlation robust standard errors.

4.3 Chapter Summary

This chapter presented results of regression and portfolio-based tests, designed to answer the first research question whether different measures of trading volume play an important role in the cross-sectional variation of expected returns in the Swiss stock market. These results yield two main conclusions:

1. There exists a positive relationship between abnormal volume and expected returns:

We find that stocks with high trading volume in a given month compared to their average trading volume in the preceding three to 12 months experience systematically higher subsequent returns. This effect is strongest in the month immediately following abnormal volume. However, portfolios containing high abnormal volume stocks continue to significantly outperform portfolios of low abnormal volume stocks for at least the next 12 months. The positive volume-return effect is very stable when controlling for various other cross-sectional effects and is particularly strong for small stocks and past losers. These results are in line with related literature on the existence of a high volume return premium. Most of our findings are also consistent with the *investor visibility hypothesis* that abnormal volume increases a stock's visibility, thereby leading to higher subsequent demand and price for that stock.

2. There is no systematic relationship between other volume measures and expected returns:

Volume level: the regression results indicate the existence of a positive relationship between volume level and expected returns. The portfolio-based tests, however, find no systematic relationship at statistically significant levels. This finding is consistent with results in 20 emerging stock markets (including three European markets) but not with the negative relationship identified in US and other developed (non-European) stock markets. Given the previously inconclusive results and the fact that there exists no generally accepted view as to the nature of a potentially negative volume level effect, our results provide additional evidence of the controversial (if any) role of volume level in the cross-section of stock returns.

Volume growth: the relationship between volume growth and expected returns is also found to be non-systematic. While the relationship is slightly negative in base regressions, it becomes positive once extreme volume growth observations are excluded. Portfolio-based tests confirm the existence of a rather positive but non-systematic relationship between volume growth and expected returns. It is difficult to compare these results with previous literature, because no study known to us applies the exact same methodology.

Variability in volume: the variability in volume, finally, seems not to play a role in the cross-section of Swiss stock returns either. Depending on the chosen estimation procedure the relationship between variability in volume and expected returns is either negative or nonexistent in the regression analysis. Portfolio-based tests strongly confirm the lack of a significant relationship between variability in volume and expected returns. These findings are contrary to evidence of a systematically negative relationship in the cross-section of US stocks. To our knowledge, however, no model is able to consistently explain the nature of a potentially negative relationship.

5 Results: Time-Stability of Portfolio Returns

In the last chapter, we identified a systematically positive relationship between abnormal volume and expected returns in the cross-section of Swiss stocks. In a next step, we investigate the *robustness of portfolio returns across time and different market regimes*, which is our research question [2]. This set of analyses commences the testing of the practicability of abnormal volume based portfolio strategies, which continues in chapter 6 (investigation of the economic significance of portfolio returns). The *focus of this chapter is abnormal volume*, because it is the only measure investigated shown to systematically and significantly relate to the cross-section of Swiss stock returns. However, we also briefly analyze the time-stability of the other volume measures, namely *volume level*, *volume growth*, and *variability in volume*. The reason is that there exists the possibility that these other volume-return relations are only systematically significant in specific states of the market, which would be an interesting finding by itself. The methodology applied is described in detail above, 3.3.2. Nevertheless, we repeat the most important aspects as deemed necessary.

5.1 Abnormal Volume

The analysis of the time-stability of the abnormal volume effect is divided into three parts, the dependence of results on few months with extreme returns, the dependence of results on returns of specific calendar months, and the analysis of portfolio returns across different market regimes. Before reporting test results, there are two methodological remarks regarding reference period and portfolios investigated:

Reference period investigated: the analysis so far shows that the positive relationship between abnormal volume and expected returns is systematically significant across different reference periods investigated. However, the portfolio returns are increasing in the reference period and consistently the highest when measuring abnormal volume compared to a long-term reference period of $J = 12$ months. We therefore restrict the analysis going forward to the $J = 12$ months reference period.

Portfolios investigated: first, we again analyze quintile and decile portfolios based on one-way sorts on abnormal share turnover. Regarding two-way sorts, recall two important findings in 4.2.2. First, we showed that the abnormal volume effect does not proxy for previously discovered return determinants such as company size, book-to-market ratio, momentum, or industry affiliation. And second, we discovered particularly profitable portfolio strategies within specific control variable quantiles, which is interesting regarding the practical implementation of volume based portfolio strategies. We thus also discuss the time-stability of abnormal volume deciles within the smallest one-third of firms per month (see Table 4.42, Panel C), within the one-third of firms with the lowest book-to-market ratio (see Table 4.43, Panel C), and within those one-third of stocks with the lowest past one-year returns (see Table 4.44, Panel C). Due to the diversification issue within industry groups, which by construction does not exist for other control variables, we abstain from individually testing abnormal volume decile portfolios within specific industry groups regarding practicability.

5.1.1 Dependence on Few Months with Extreme Returns

In this first analysis, we investigate whether the highly significant positive abnormal volume effect is driven by only a few of the 138 return months in the sample (from March 1997 to August 2008). Table 5.1 reports average monthly returns to zero-cost arbitrage strategies based on one-way sorted portfolios, i.e., the time-series of the difference in monthly returns between the portfolio containing high volume stocks (V1) and the portfolio containing low volume stocks (V5, V10). We limit the analysis to zero-cost arbitrage strategies, because this allows us to conduct standard tests of statistical significance of the abnormal volume effect. The column labeled '$p = 0$' displays average monthly returns over the complete time-series, which is identical to the results presented in the last chapter (Table 4.40 and Table 4.46). In the remaining four columns, the highest $p = 1, 2, 3, 5$ monthly returns of a given strategy are excluded from the time-series.

Panel A reports strategy returns over the $K = 1$ month holding period. The returns decrease monotonically in p by construction, but remain significant at the 1% level for both quintile and decile strategies, even when excluding the 5 highest monthly returns. Additionally, recall above result that the positive return difference between high and low abnormal volume portfolios remains strongly significant over multi-month holding periods of $K = 3, 6, 12$ months (Table 4.45). As a further robustness check, we thus test the sensitivity of results to extreme monthly returns for the longest holding period, $K = 12$. Results reported in Table 5.1, Panel B, show that the positive return difference between high and low abnormal volume portfolios also remains strongly significant upon exclusion of the $p = 5$ highest 12-month holding period returns.

Table 5.1: Returns to Abnormal Turnover Portfolios after Excluding Highest Monthly Values

	Complete time-series	Exclusion of p highest monthly returns			
Portfolio	$p = 0$	$p = 1$	$p = 2$	$p = 3$	$p = 5$
Panel A: Monthly returns to long-short strategies, reference period J = 12, holding period K = 1					
V1-V5	1.06	0.98	0.91	0.86	0.77
	(3.759)***	(3.534)***	(3.434)***	(3.442)***	(3.328)***
V1-V10	1.58	1.50	1.42	1.36	1.23
	(4.389)***	(4.358)***	(4.303)***	(4.070)***	(3.968)***
Panel B: Monthly returns to long-short strategies, reference period J = 12, holding period K = 12					
V1-V5	0.47	0.43	0.40	0.37	0.33
	(3.422)***	(3.444)***	(3.280)***	(3.237)***	(3.129)***
V1-V10	0.74	0.68	0.62	0.58	0.52
	(4.389)***	(4.142)***	(4.114)***	(3.858)***	(3.622)***

This table reports average monthly returns of equal-weighted portfolios formed monthly on the basis of stocks' abnormal share turnover (percentage change of last month's turnover versus the average turnover in the preceding $J = 12$ months) and held for $K = 1$ (Panel A) or $K = 12$ months (Panel B). V1-V5 (V1-V10) is the zero-cost arbitrage strategy consisting of long positions in stocks with the highest 20% (10%) abnormal turnover in a given month and short positions of equal size in stocks with the lowest 20% (10%) abnormal turnover. In each column, the highest p monthly returns of a given strategy are excluded from the time-series (03/1997 - 08/2008). ***/**/* Denotes statistical significance at the 1%/5%/10% level. T-statistics (in parentheses) are calculated using Newey-West (1987) adjusted, heteroskedasticity and serial correlation robust standard errors.

The dependence of results on few months with extreme returns is potentially stronger for the specifically investigated two-way sorted portfolios. The rationale is that each of these portfolios only contains 1/30 of stocks in each cross-section, which adversely affects diversification.[173] Results reported in Table 5.2 confirm our intuition. In fact, the statistical significance of some of the investigated strategies drops from the 1% level to the 5% level once we exclude the $p = 3$ highest monthly returns from the time-series.

[173] We construct 30 portfolios, i.e., 10 abnormal volume portfolios within one of the 3 control variable quantiles. In one-way sorted quintile (decile) portfolios, on the other hand, we construct only 5 (10) portfolios.

Nevertheless, the statistical significance of the positive return difference between high and low abnormal volume portfolios remains strong (i.e., at least a the 5% level) across all strategies and investigated holding periods. Based on these results, we conclude that the positive abnormal volume effect is not driven by extreme performance in only a few months.

Table 5.2: Returns to Two-Way Sorted Abnormal Turnover Portfolios after Excluding Highest Monthly Values

	Complete time-series	Exclusion of *p* highest monthly returns			
V1-V10 Portfolio	p = 0	p = 1	p = 2	p = 3	p = 5
Panel A: Monthly returns to V1-V10 strategies, reference period J = 12, holding period K = 1					
Small firms	2.54	2.37	2.20	2.04	1.74
	(3.668)***	(3.717)***	(3.603)***	(3.386)***	(3.192)***
Low BM firms	1.84	1.72	1.61	1.50	1.33
	(3.511)***	(3.370)***	(3.293)***	(3.174)***	(3.084)***
Past losers	1.55	1.38	1.23	1.10	0.85
	(2.798)***	(2.859)***	(2.759)***	(2.540)**	(2.203)**
Panel B: Monthly returns to V1-V10 strategies, reference period J = 12, holding period K = 12					
Small firms	0.86	0.75	0.69	0.64	0.54
	(3.104)***	(3.084)***	(3.134)***	(2.897)***	(2.532)**
Low BM firms	0.89	0.81	0.73	0.66	0.55
	(3.525)***	(3.336)***	(2.969)***	(3.003)***	(2.448)**
Past losers	0.83	0.76	0.71	0.67	0.58
	(3.108)***	(2.816)***	(2.837)***	(2.602)**	(2.200)**

This table reports average monthly returns of equal-weighted portfolios formed monthly on the basis of stocks' abnormal share turnover (percentage change of last month's turnover versus the average turnover in the preceding $J = 12$ months) within specific control variable tercile portfolios (smallest 1/3 of firms, 1/3 of firms with the lowest book-to-market ratio, 1/3 of stocks with the lowest past one-year returns). The portfolios are held for $K = 1$ (Panel A) or $K = 12$ months (Panel B). V1-V10 is the zero-cost arbitrage strategy consisting of long positions in stocks with the highest 10% abnormal turnover in a given month and short positions of equal size in stocks with the lowest 10% abnormal turnover. In each column, the highest p monthly returns of a given strategy are excluded from the time-series (03/1997 - 08/2008). ***/**/* Denotes statistical significance at the 1%/5%/10% level. T-statistics (in parentheses) are calculated using Newey-West (1987) adjusted, heteroskedasticity and serial correlation robust standard errors.

5.1.2 Dependence on Returns of Single Calendar Months

As a next test, we investigate the portfolio returns in different calendar months. The objectives of this analysis are two-fold. On the one hand, it is another test of the general stability of the abnormal volume effect. On the other hand, it is a further robustness check to ensure that abnormal volume is not just a proxy for a previously documented effect in the cross-section of stock returns. More precisely, we want to make sure that the abnormal volume premium is not driven by the well-know January or December seasonality.[174] We start with this second objective.

In Table 5.3, we once more report average monthly returns to one-way sorted abnormal turnover portfolios. The row labeled 'Complete' displays average returns over the entire time-series, which is again identical to the results presented in the previous chapter (Table 4.40 and Table 4.46). In the other rows, we either exclude the portfolio returns in January ('Excl. January') or in December and January ('Excl. December & January') from the time-series. Panel A reports strategy returns over the $K = 1$ month holding period. It is apparent from these results that the abnormal volume effect is not driven by the returns in December and January. The return difference between portfolios containing high (V1) and low (V5, V10) abnormal volume stocks is even a bit higher once we exclude December and January returns. As a robustness check, we again repeat the analysis for the $K = 12$ months holding period. Results in Panel B confirm that the abnormal volume effect is not driven by the return months of December and January. Contrary to the above, the return difference between high and low volume portfolios remains quite stable across the different time-series (i.e., with or without December and January). Again, we also conduct the analysis for the three investigated two-way sorted abnormal volume portfolios. Results reported in Table 5.4 show that the positive return difference between high and low abnormal volume portfolios is systematically significant at the 1% level across different control variables, holding periods, and return months (i.e., with or without December and January). All these results imply that the abnormal volume effect is not caused by extreme positive returns in the months of December and January.

[174] See e.g., KEIM (1983) and CHEN/SINGAL (2003) for background on the January respectively December seasonality.

Table 5.3: Returns to Abnormal Turnover Portfolios, Excluding December and January

	Quintile portfolios			Decile portfolios		
Time-series	V1	V5	V1-V5	V1	V10	V1-V10
Panel A: Reference period J = 12, holding period K = 1						
Complete	1.60	0.54	1.06 (3.759)***	1.85	0.27	1.58 (4.389)***
Excl. January	1.60	0.48	1.12 (3.937)***	1.85	0.18	1.67 (4.660)***
Excl. December & January	1.60	0.32	1.28 (4.022)***	1.82	0.01	1.82 (4.674)***
Panel B: Reference period J = 12, holding period K = 12						
Complete	1.34	0.86	0.47 (3.422)***	1.45	0.71	0.74 (3.987)***
Excl. January	1.25	0.79	0.46 (3.552)***	1.34	0.65	0.69 (4.305)***
Excl. December & January	1.19	0.69	0.49 (3.832)***	1.26	0.56	0.70 (4.491)***

This table reports average monthly returns of equal-weighted portfolios formed monthly on the basis of stocks' abnormal share turnover (percentage change of last month's turnover versus the average turnover in the preceding $J = 12$ months) and held for $K = 1$ (Panel A) or $K = 12$ months (Panel B). V1 is the portfolio containing the stocks with the highest 20% (quintiles) or 10% (deciles) abnormal turnover in a given month. V1, V5, V10 are portfolios containing long stock positions, while V1-V5 and V1-V10 are zero-cost arbitrage strategies. 'Complete' reports average monthly returns over the entire time-series (03/1997 - 08/2008), while in 'Excl. January' and 'Excl. December & January' the returns in the respective calendar months are removed from the time-series. ***/**/* Denotes statistical significance at the 1%/5%/10% level. T-statistics (in parentheses) are calculated using Newey-West (1987) adjusted, heteroskedasticity and serial correlation robust standard errors.

Table 5.4: Returns to Two-Way Sorted Abnormal Turnover Portfolios, Excluding December and January

	Reference period $J = 12$; Holding period $K = 1$			Reference period $J = 12$; Holding period $K = 12$		
Time-series	V1	V10	V1-V10	V1	V10	V1-V10
Panel A: Small companies						
Complete	2.43	-0.11	2.54 (3.668)***	1.50	0.64	0.86 (3.104)***
Excl. January	2.39	-0.23	2.63 (4.080)***	1.32	0.51	0.81 (3.356)***
Excl. December & January	2.40	-0.52	2.92 (4.095)***	1.25	0.44	0.82 (3.271)***
Panel B: Low BM companies						
Complete	1.65	-0.20	1.84 (3.511)***	1.22	0.33	0.89 (3.525)***
Excl. January	1.72	-0.28	2.00 (3.798)***	1.13	0.24	0.89 (3.974)***
Excl. December & January	1.55	-0.61	2.16 (3.939)***	0.99	0.15	0.85 (3.859)***
Panel C: Past loser stocks						
Complete	1.72	0.16	1.55 (2.798)***	1.38	0.55	0.83 (3.108)***
Excl. January	1.79	0.15	1.63 (3.131)***	1.31	0.53	0.78 (2.872)***
Excl. December & January	1.84	-0.11	1.95 (3.308)***	1.36	0.48	0.88 (2.833)***

This table reports average monthly returns of equal-weighted portfolios formed monthly on the basis of stocks' abnormal share turnover (percentage change of last month's turnover versus the average turnover in the preceding $J = 12$ months) within specific control variable tercile portfolios (smallest 1/3 of firms, 1/3 of firms with the lowest book-to-market ratio, 1/3 of stocks with the lowest past one-year returns). The portfolios are held for $K = 1, 12$ months. V1 (V10) is the portfolio containing the stocks with the highest (lowest) 10% abnormal turnover in a given month. V1 and V10 are portfolios containing long stock positions, while V1-V10 are zero-cost arbitrage strategies. 'Complete' reports average monthly returns over the entire time-series (03/1997 - 08/2008), while in 'Excl. January' and 'Excl. December & January' the returns in the respective calendar months are removed from the time-series. ***/**/* Denotes statistical significance at the 1%/5%/10% level. T-statistics (in parentheses) are calculated using Newey-West (1987) adjusted, heteroskedasticity and serial correlation robust standard errors.

As a second set of tests in this section, we separately analyze the performance of abnormal volume strategies per individual calendar month. In Table 5.5, we report results for the one-way sorted portfolios. For conciseness, we only report the time-series of the monthly return difference between high volume portfolios and low volume portfolios, i.e., V1-V5 and V1-V10. Note that we abstain from tests of statistical significance in this analysis, because we only have a maximum of 12 return observations per calendar month.

Table 5.5: Returns to Abnormal Turnover Portfolios in Different Return Months

	Panel A: Reference period $J = 12$; Holding Period $K = 1$		Panel B: Reference period $J = 12$; Holding Period $K = 12$	
Return month	Quintiles (V1-V5)	Deciles (V1-V10)	Quintiles (V1-V5)	Deciles (V1-V10)
January	**0.41**	**0.50**	**0.61**	**1.32**
February	**0.68**	**3.09**	**0.67**	**1.08**
March	**1.13**	**2.21**	**0.22**	**0.43**
April	**1.93**	**2.34**	**0.77**	**1.18**
May	**0.23**	-0.27	-0.32	-0.07
June	**1.20**	**2.31**	**0.39**	**0.77**
July	**1.35**	**1.71**	**0.74**	**0.90**
August	**1.29**	**1.46**	**0.34**	**0.79**
September	**1.10**	**0.86**	**0.25**	-0.03
October	**2.45**	**2.56**	**0.92**	**0.91**
November	**1.45**	**2.00**	**1.02**	**1.01**
December	-0.56	**0.20**	**0.14**	**0.62**
Average	**1.06**	**1.58**	**0.47**	**0.74**

This table reports average monthly returns, per calendar month, of equal-weighted portfolios formed monthly on the basis of stocks' abnormal share turnover (percentage change of last month's turnover versus the average turnover in the preceding $J = 12$ months) and held for $K = 1$ (Panel A) or $K = 12$ months (Panel B). V1-V5 (V1-V10) is the zero-cost arbitrage strategy consisting of long positions in stocks with the highest 20% (10%) abnormal turnover in a given month and short positions of equal size in stocks with the lowest 20% (10%) abnormal turnover.

The main result of Table 5.5 is that across the different strategies (quintiles, deciles) and holding periods ($K = 1, 12$), the high abnormal volume portfolios outperform the low abnormal volume portfolios in at least 10 of the 12 calendar months. We consider this evidence as further proof of the stability of the abnormal volume effect. Additionally, and in spite of the results displayed in Table 5.3, all January return differences are positive as well as most of the December returns. Finally, while there are naturally differences between returns in single calendar months, we do not detect any striking and systematic seasonality or pattern in the data displayed in Table 5.5. As a last analysis in this section, we report the performance of the three specifically investigated two-way sorted abnormal volume strategies per individual calendar month (Table 5.6).

Table 5.6: Returns to Two-Way Sorted Abnormal Turnover Portfolios in Different Return Months

	Panel A: Reference period $J = 12$; Holding Period $K = 1$			Panel B: Reference period $J = 12$; Holding Period $K = 12$		
Return month	Small (V1-V10)	Low BM (V1-V10)	Losers (V1-V10)	Small (V1-V10)	Low BM (V1-V10)	Losers (V1-V10)
January	**1.51**	**0.09**	**0.60**	**1.47**	**0.91**	**1.39**
February	**6.78**	**2.23**	**0.94**	**0.72**	**1.14**	**0.46**
March	**4.19**	**0.24**	**1.06**	**1.36**	**1.01**	**1.23**
April	**4.22**	**4.55**	**2.01**	**1.82**	**2.06**	**1.00**
May	-0.74	**1.14**	-1.29	**0.21**	-0.52	**0.24**
June	**3.36**	**1.19**	**3.31**	**0.71**	-0.47	**0.78**
July	**0.95**	**4.84**	**2.24**	**1.16**	**1.74**	**0.33**
August	**2.88**	**1.06**	**1.24**	**0.69**	**0.42**	**0.58**
September	**2.65**	**1.53**	**0.08**	**1.23**	-0.03	**0.28**
October	**2.26**	**0.85**	**4.65**	**0.44**	**2.34**	**1.91**
November	**2.85**	**4.01**	**5.55**	-0.30	**0.87**	**2.05**
December	-0.41	**0.22**	-1.73	**0.72**	**1.34**	-0.22
Average	**2.54**	**1.84**	**1.55**	**0.86**	**0.89**	**0.83**

This table reports average monthly returns, per calendar month, of equal-weighted portfolios formed monthly on the basis of stocks' abnormal share turnover (percentage change of last month's turnover versus the average turnover in the preceding $J = 12$ months) within specific control variable tercile portfolios (smallest 1/3 of firms, 1/3 of firms with the lowest book-to-market ratio, 1/3 of stocks with the lowest past one-year returns). The portfolios are held for $K = 1$ (Panel A) or $K = 12$ months (Panel B). V1-V10 is the zero-cost arbitrage strategy consisting of long positions in stocks with the highest 10% abnormal turnover in a given month and short positions of equal size in stocks with the lowest 10% abnormal turnover.

The general finding of a stable abnormal volume effect is confirmed by these results. In fact, across the three strategies and the two holding periods, the high abnormal volume portfolios outperform the low abnormal volume portfolios in 9 to 12 out of the 12 calendar months.

5.1.3 Portfolio Returns across Market Regimes

Having shown that the discovered positive abnormal volume effect is not driven by only a few extreme return months and is independent of the December and January seasonality, we now investigate the performance of portfolio strategies across different market regimes. The definitions of the analyzed market regimes, namely *sub-periods*, *market phases*, *market volatility*, and *market volume*, are described in detail above, 3.3.2.3.

We only conduct this market regime analysis for the $K = 1$ month holding period. This has several reasons. First, results of previously presented tests suggest that the dynamics of the abnormal volume effect are driven by the first holding period month (see for example the respective robustness check in the regression analysis, Table 4.19, or the average monthly portfolio returns in multi-month holding periods, Table 4.46, which generally decrease in the holding period K). We therefore do not expect the finding to strongly diverge across different holding period lengths. In addition, there is a small potential bias at $K > 1$. As noted in 3.3.3.1, we cannot invest in all K investment cohorts in the first and in the last $K-1$ months of the time-series due to data availability. This creates a potential bias regarding the underlying market regimes influencing the strategy returns in these months. In the practical setting in chapter 6, however, we are able to eliminate this problem as described in 3.3.3.1. Thus, in 6.1.4 we perform a robustness check of the validity of the $K = 1$ results in the multi-month holding period setting.

5.1.3.1 Sub-Periods

Based on the relevant regression results reported in Table 4.23, we do not expect a large difference between returns in the two analyzed sub-periods. Additionally, KANIEL ET AL. (2007), in unreported tests, do not find any clustering of returns in certain time periods. These authors conclude that the magnitude of their high-volume return premium is not affected by different macroeconomic events. Results of our own portfolio-based tests reported in Table 5.7, however, show a very different picture. In the first return series from March 1997 to November 2002, the return difference between high and low abnormal turnover portfolios is substantial (1.65 and 2.23% on average per month for quintile respectively decile portfolios). This return difference is still positive in the more recent return series (0.48 respectively 0.93%), but at almost statistically insignificant levels. The specifically analyzed two-way sorted abnormal volume strategies show the same pattern, namely a substantially higher and generally more significant return difference between high and low abnormal volume portfolios in the first sub-period.[175] These individual two-way sorted results are reported in the appendix, Table A1, for the interested reader.

Table 5.7: Returns to Abnormal Turnover Portfolios in Different Sub-Periods

	Quintile portfolios				Deciles
Time-series	V1	V3	V5	V1-V5	V1-V10
Full (03/1997 - 08/2008)	1.60	1.05	0.54	1.06 (3.759)***	1.58 (4.389)***
Sub-Period 1 (03/1997 - 11/2002)	1.43	0.50	-0.22	1.65 (4.091)***	2.23 (4.565)***
Sub-Period 2 (12/2002 - 08/2008)	1.77	1.60	1.30	0.48 (1.398)	0.93 (1.914)*

This table reports average monthly portfolio returns in 2 sub-sets of the complete return time-series (03/1997 - 08/2008). The equal-weighted portfolios are formed monthly on the basis of stocks' abnormal share turnover (percentage change of last month's turnover versus the average turnover in the preceding $J = 12$ months) and are rebalanced monthly ($K = 1$). V1 is the portfolio containing the stocks with the highest 20% (quintiles) or 10% (deciles) abnormal turnover in a given month. V1, V3, V5 are portfolios containing long stock positions, while V1-V5 and V1-V10 are zero-cost arbitrage strategies. ***/**/* Denotes statistical significance at the 1%/5%/10% level. T-statistics (in parentheses) are calculated using Newey-West (1987) adjusted, heteroskedasticity and serial correlation robust standard errors.

[175] The relatively low significance level for past losers in both sub-periods seems to be driven by heteroskedasticity. If we use standard t-statistics (instead of Newey-West adjusted t-statistics), the average monthly return difference of 1.85% in the first sub-period becomes significant at the 5% level.

We see mainly two potential explanations for these surprising empirical results: the first possibility is that the previously discovered *abnormal volume premium* was merely a market inefficiency (i.e., profit opportunity) and *disappeared in more recent times.* SCHWERT (2002), for example, finds that the size effect, the dividend yield effect, the value effect, and the weekend effect seem to have weakened or disappeared after the papers that discovered them were published. He concludes that 'even if anomalies existed in the sample period in which they were first identified, the activities of practitioners who implement strategies to take advantage of anomalous behavior can cause the anomalies to disappear (as research findings cause the market to become more efficient)'. We find some support for this hypothesis in our case. In fact, the first paper to address 'volume shocks' (namely GERVAIS ET AL. (2001)), which is related to our abnormal volume measure, was published in the Journal of Finance in 2001, not long before the beginning of our second and less significant sub-period.

The second possibility is that the *strength of the abnormal volume premium varies across market regimes*, while the underlying regimes differ in our two sub-periods. Figure 3.6 (in 3.3.2.3.3) provides some supporting evidence for the difference in underlying regimes in the two sub-periods. There is a pronounced phase of low market volatility in the second half of the time-series, but no such phase exists in the first half. Results reported in the next two sections, namely stock market phases and market volatility, give further support for this second potential explanation.

5.1.3.2 Market Phases

Table 5.8 reports average monthly portfolio returns in different stock market phases as defined in 3.3.2.3.2. First, consider the differences between bull and bear markets (first two rows). By construction, portfolio returns are on average positive in bull market phases and negative in bear market phases (see portfolios V1, V3, and V5). Regarding the abnormal volume premium, we see that the return difference between high and low volume portfolios (i.e., V1-V5, V1-V10) is both positive and strongly significant in both states of the market. But the absolute value of the return difference seems slightly higher in bear markets, e.g., 2.00 versus 1.37% for decile portfolios.

Table 5.8: Returns to Abnormal Turnover Portfolios in Different Market Phases

	Quintile portfolios				Deciles
Time-series	V1	V3	V5	V1-V5	V1-V10
Bull markets	2.91	2.53	1.89	1.02 (2.812)***	1.37 (2.998)***
Bear markets	-1.01	-1.90	-2.16	1.14 (2.608)**	2.00 (3.784)***
Up market states	1.91	1.80	1.19	0.72 (2.371)**	0.97 (2.800)***
Down market states	**0.88**	**-0.73**	**-0.99**	**1.87** **(3.653)*** **	**3.02** **(4.653)*** **
Positive market return months	3.52	3.26	2.29	1.23 (3.800)***	1.68 (3.846)***
Negative market return months	-1.78	-2.85	-2.54	0.76 (1.765)*	1.41 (2.463)**

This table reports average monthly portfolio returns in different sub-sets of the complete return time-series (03/1997 - 08/2008), as defined in section 3.3.2.3.2. The equal-weighted portfolios are formed monthly on the basis of stocks' abnormal share turnover ($J = 12$ months) and are rebalanced monthly ($K = 1$). V1 is the portfolio containing the stocks with the highest 20% (quintiles) or 10% (deciles) abnormal turnover in a given month. V1, V3, V5 are portfolios containing long stock positions, while V1-V5 and V1-V10 are zero-cost arbitrage strategies. ***/**/* Denotes statistical significance at the 1%/5%/10% level. T-statistics (in parentheses) are calculated using Newey-West (1987) adjusted, heteroskedasticity and serial correlation robust standard errors.

In a second step, we divide the time-series into up and down market states of the SPI (rows three and four in Table 5.8). Recall from above that the market is defined as being in an 'Up' ('Down') state, if the lagged one-year market return is positive (negative) at the time of the investment decision. Discussion of results: while the abnormal volume premium is significantly positive in both states of the market, it is more than double the size in down market states, namely 1.87 versus 0.72% for quintile portfolios and 3.02 versus 0.97% for deciles. In addition, the V1 quintile portfolio, containing the stocks with the highest 20% abnormal turnover, is the only portfolio with a positive average return in down market states.[176] Finally, note that the number of months in a down mar-

[176] V2 and V4 (not explicitly reported in the table) have average monthly returns of -0.62 respectively -0.88%.

ket state is 24 in the first sub-period, but only 17 in the second sub-period, which could be one reason causing the different results in the two time-series.

As a next step, we evaluate potential explanations for the finding that the abnormal volume premium seems particularly strong in down market states.

One obvious explanation for the strong performance of high abnormal volume stocks in down markets could be that these stocks have lower market betas. But two observations are in conflict with this hypothesis. First, rows five and six in Table 5.8 display the performance of abnormal volume strategies in months with positive and negative market returns. If the high abnormal volume stocks had indeed lower betas, the positive return difference between high and low abnormal volume portfolios should be stronger and more significant in months with negative market returns. But this is not the case. In fact, the abnormal volume premium is both stronger (e.g., 1.23 versus 0.76% for quintile portfolios) and more significant (t-statistics of 3.800 versus 1.765) in positive market return months. This even suggests that high abnormal volume stocks have higher market betas, which we will confirm in the risk-based analysis in 6.1.2. A second reason why sensitivities to market returns cannot explain results is that the return difference between high and low abnormal volume portfolios is positive, at consistently significant levels, in all six market phases investigated in Table 5.8.

An additional explanation for the results could be that stocks in different industries perform differently across market cycles. If high abnormal volume portfolios (predominantly) contained stocks in industries with a better 'down market protection', such portfolios would perform strongly in these states of the market. However, recall that we control for industry affiliation above, Table 4.41. Nevertheless, as a further robustness check, we repeat the industry analysis specifically in down markets. Results reported in Table 5.9 confirm that the strong down market performance of abnormal volume strategies is not driven by industry affiliation. When averaging abnormal volume portfolio returns over different industry groups, the monthly average return difference between high and low volume portfolios is 1.16%, statistically significant at the 1% level. And even if the return difference is not statistically significant within all industry portfolios, it is still quite strongly positive throughout (at least 0.81% per month). These results suggest that the strong abnormal volume effect observed in down market states is not simply a proxy for the fact that stocks in certain industry groups provide 'downturn protection'.

Table 5.9: Returns to Abnormal Turnover Portfolios in Down Market States, Averaged over 4 Industry Groups

	Industry portfolio				
Volume portfolio	Manu-facturing	Tech&Health	Finance	Consumer	Averaged
Down market states					
V1	-0.02	-0.02	0.23	0.47	0.17
V3	-0.83	-1.33	-0.61	-1.21	-1.00
V1-V3	0.81	1.31	0.84	1.68	**1.16**
	(1.237)	(1.086)	(1.888)*	(3.213)***	**(2.926)***

This table reports average monthly portfolio returns in down market states, as defined in 3.3.2.3.2. The equal-weighted portfolios are formed monthly on the basis of stocks' abnormal share turnover ($J = 12$ months) within specific industry groups. The portfolios are rebalanced monthly ($K = 1$). V1-V3 is the zero-cost arbitrage strategy consisting of long positions in stocks with the highest 1/3 abnormal turnover in a given month and short positions of equal size in stocks with the lowest 1/3 abnormal turnover. The column labeled 'Averaged' reports the time-series average of monthly average returns of each volume portfolio over all industry portfolios. ***/**/* Denotes statistical significance at the 1%/5%/10% level. T-statistics (in parentheses) are calculated using Newey-West (1987) adjusted, heteroskedasticity and serial correlation robust standard errors.

Finally, we address the question how the presence of a stronger and more significant abnormal volume premium in down markets could relate to the investor visibility hypothesis. We do not know of any existing research explicitly studying the stability of the investor visibility hypothesis over time. Intuitively, however, we do see a connection as outlined below. First, recall that the effect of increased visibility on demand (induced by abnormal volume) is not the same for all stocks. For example, evidence by GERVAIS ET AL. (2001), KANIEL ET AL. (2007), and our own results, suggest that the visibility effect is stronger for small stocks, because large stocks are more likely to be visible to potential investors anyway. In line with the fact that the effect of increased visibility is not the same across stocks, we see the possibility that the strength of this effect is not the same across time. GERVAIS ET AL. (2001) state that past losers are more likely to have fallen out of the investors' radar (due to their relatively poor past performance), which causes these stocks to be more affected by increased visibility induced by abnormal volume. Along the same line of reasoning, one can argue that due to the average stock market's poor recent performance, the included stocks have on average fallen out of investors' radar. Our hypothesis is that in such an environment (i.e., a 'down market'), the effect of increased visibility in a stock is likely to be stronger on average than in 'up markets', just as it is generally stronger for past loser stocks than for past winner stocks. While our data supports this hypothesis, it is again important to note that it is just that, a hypothesis, which needs to be analyzed more in-depth. This, however, is not in scope of this research project.

Next, we briefly discuss a favorable side-effect of the fact that the abnormal volume premium is stronger in down markets. Recall that up and down market states are defined ex-ante, i.e., at the beginning of month *t* when an investment decision is taken. This allows us to define dynamic portfolio strategies, for example strategies that are long in the market (e.g., SPI) in up states and long-short in abnormal volume portfolios in down states. We test the feasibility of such strategies as an outlook in the next chapter (section 6.1.4).

As a final remark, note again results of abnormal volume decile strategies (V1-V10) within specific control variable quantiles. While the three individual strategies do not exhibit identical dynamics across different market phases, the main findings are the same, i.e., a stronger return difference between high and low abnormal turnover portfolios in bear markets and a significantly higher return difference in down market states. For the interested reader, these results are again presented in the appendix, Table A2.

5.1.3.3 Market Volatility

In the last section, we identify a first potential regime-related cause for the stronger abnormal volume effect in the first sub-period, namely the difference in up and down markets. We now show that volatility regimes seem to play an even more important role in explaining why results in the recent sub-period are significantly less strong.

Table 5.10, Panel A, reports average monthly portfolio returns in different market volatility regimes as defined in 3.3.2.3.3. There are three main findings. First, the return difference between high and low abnormal turnover portfolios is strongest in high volatility phases (as high as 2.04 and 3.38% for quintile and decile portfolios respectively). Second, this return difference is also strongly significant at the 1% level in normal volatility phases, which implies that the discovered abnormal volume premium over the full time-series is not exclusively driven by results in high volatility regimes. And third, although still being slightly positive, the abnormal volume premium is mostly non-existent in low volatility phases. Interestingly, there are no low volatility months in the first sub-period, but 38 out of 65 months in the second sub-period. We thus have the strong hypothesis that the low performance in low volatility regimes is the main driver behind the weaker abnormal volume premium in the more recent sub-period.

Next, we evaluate potential explanations for the fact that the abnormal volume effect seems to be particularly strong in high volatility phases. First, it is possible that high abnormal volume stocks have higher sensitivities to innovations in aggregate volatility. But ANG ET AL. (2006) find that stocks with large, positive sensitivities to volatility risk have low, not high average returns. One reason provided by economic theory is that increasing volatility represents a deterioration in investment opportunities, while risk-averse agents favor stocks that hedge against this risk (e.g., CAMPBELL (1993, 1996), CHEN (2002)). Another reason provided by BAKSHI/KAPADIA (2003) is that assets with high sensitivities to market volatility risk provide hedges against market downside risk.[177] The higher demand for these stocks by risk-averse investors increases their price and lowers their average return. If, however, the higher sensitivities of high abnormal volume stocks to innovations in aggregate volatility were to explain their particularly strong performance in high volatility regimes, this abnormal volume premium would need to be negative on average. Our results, on the other hand, indicate a positive return difference between high and low abnormal volume stocks both in high volatility regimes and on average.

[177] As noted by ANG ET AL. (2006), periods of high volatility tend to coincide with downward market movements.

Table 5.10: Returns to Abnormal Turnover Portfolios in Different Volatility Regimes

	Quintile portfolios				Deciles
Time-series	V1	V3	V5	V1-V5	V1-V10
Panel A: Real volatility regimes					
Low volatility	2.31	2.25	2.13	0.17 (0.409)	0.42 (1.018)
Normal volatility	1.82	1.65	0.95	0.87 (2.825)***	1.32 (3.255)***
High volatility	**0.39**	**-1.46**	**-2.05**	**2.04** **(4.324)*****	**3.38** **(4.796)*****
Panel B: Forecasted volatility regimes					
Low volatility	2.38	2.49	2.57	-0.18 (-0.507)	-0.24 (-0.853)
Normal volatility	1.21	0.73	0.21	1.00 (3.057)***	1.46 (3.494)***
High volatility	**2.01**	**0.66**	**-0.31**	**2.32** **(4.208)*****	**3.48** **(4.827)*****

This table reports average monthly portfolio returns in different sub-sets of the complete return time-series (03/1997 - 08/2008), as defined in section 3.3.2.3.3. The equal-weighted portfolios are formed monthly on the basis of stocks' abnormal share turnover ($J = 12$ months) and are rebalanced monthly ($K = 1$). V1 is the portfolio containing the stocks with the highest 20% (quintiles) or 10% (deciles) abnormal turnover in a given month. V1, V3, V5 are portfolios containing long stock positions, while V1-V5 and V1-V10 are zero-cost arbitrage strategies. ***/**/* Denotes statistical significance at the 1%/5%/10% level. T-statistics (in parentheses) are calculated using Newey-West (1987) adjusted, heteroskedasticity and serial correlation robust standard errors.

Another potential explanation for the results could be that stocks in different industries perform differently across volatility regimes (which is similar to the respective explanation explored regarding down markets). If high abnormal volume portfolios contained stocks in industries with a better 'volatility protection', these portfolios would naturally perform strongly in high volatility regimes. As noted in the discussion on down market performance, this result would be surprising, because Table 4.41 already controlled for industry affiliation. Nevertheless, this industry analysis is repeated specifically in high volatility regimes. Results in Table 5.11 show that the abnormal volume effect remains strongly significant when averaging over industry groups in high volatility phases, i.e., the average monthly return difference is 1.27% with a t-statistic of 2.734. In other words, the strong abnormal volume effect in high volatility regimes is not simply a proxy for the fact that stocks in specific industries provide a 'volatility protection'.

Table 5.11: Returns to Abnormal Turnover Portfolios in High Volatility Phases, Averaged over 4 Industry Groups

	Industry portfolio				
Volume portfolio	Manu-facturing	Tech&Health	Finance	Consumer	Averaged
Real volatility regimes - high volatility					
V1	-1.07	0.22	-0.15	-0.41	-0.35
V3	-2.15	-1.44	-1.08	-1.80	-1.62
V1-V3	1.08	1.66	0.94	1.39	**1.27**
	(2.208)**	(1.077)	(1.569)	(2.531)**	**(2.734)*** **

This table reports average monthly portfolio returns in high market volatility phases, as defined in 3.3.2.3.3. The equal-weighted portfolios are formed monthly on the basis of stocks' abnormal share turnover ($J = 12$ months) within specific industry groups. The portfolios are rebalanced monthly ($K = 1$). V1-V3 is the zero-cost arbitrage strategy consisting of long positions in stocks with the highest 1/3 abnormal turnover in a given month and short positions of equal size in stocks with the lowest 1/3 abnormal turnover. The column labeled 'Averaged' reports the time-series average of monthly average returns of each volume portfolio over all industry groups. ***/**/* Denotes statistical significance at the 1%/5%/10% level. T-statistics (in parentheses) are calculated using Newey-West (1987) adjusted, heteroskedasticity and serial correlation robust standard errors.

Finally, we again examine how the particularly strong abnormal volume premium could relate to the investor visibility hypothesis. Recall its basic presumption that abnormal volume increases a stock's visibility, which subsequently increases demand through the higher number of potential buyers, and thus price. In times of increased uncertainty, which is undoubtedly the case if the market volatility is high, investors are probably more insecure regarding investment opportunities. It is therefore possible that the influence of a signaling of a potential investment opportunity through abnormal volume is stronger in such an environment. Additionally, BARBER/ODEAN (2008) find that the buying behavior of individual investors is more heavily influenced by attention than the buying behavior of professional investors.[178] Finally, we hypothesize that individual investors are probably more affected by sentiments such as uncertainty than institutional investors. In sum, we see three potential influence factors, namely the possibly higher significance of increased visibility in uncertain times, the stronger significance of attention / visibility for individual investors' buying behavior, and the fact that individual investors are potentially more sensitive to uncertainty in the market. A combination of these three factors might help to explain the particularly strong abnormal volume premium discovered in high volatility regimes. Note again that this is just a hypothesis, which needs to be analyzed more in-depth. But this is not in scope of this research project.

Next, consider Table 5.10, Panel B. These results represent average monthly portfolio returns using the volatility forecasting model presented in 3.3.2.3.3. Recall that this forecasting model is built on the basis of a one-month lag, meaning that a month's real volatility regime is expected to continue in the following month. Interestingly, the results are very similar to those attained using true volatility regimes (Panel A), particularly the highly significant abnormal volume effect in high forecasted volatility phases.[179] This has two implications. First, it provides some support for above intuition regarding the investor visibility hypothesis. Due to the one-month lag, the forecasted regime represents the volatility at the point when the investment decision is taken, which is when the investor faces uncertainty. The fact that results are as strong in this setting, although the model correctly forecasts the true volatility regime in just over 70% of return months, further supports above visibility explanation. A second implication is a consequence of the fact that forecasted volatility regimes are known ex-ante. This allows us to define dynamic portfolio strategies, e.g., long positions in the market in low respectively normal forecasted volatility regimes and long-short abnormal volume investments in times of high forecasted volatility. We test the feasibility of such a strategy below, 6.1.4.

[178] Besides other measures, these authors use a form of abnormal volume in their empirical tests.

[179] The return difference between high and low abnormal turnover portfolios is even slightly negative in low forecasted volatility phases, but this could be driven by chance (the difference is not even closely statistically significant).

As a final remark, note that the abnormal volume premium is again by far the strongest in the high volatility and high forecasted volatility regimes in the analysis within specific control variable quantiles, i.e., small companies, low book-to-market companies, and past loser stocks. We included these results in the appendix for the interested reader (Table A3).

5.1.3.4 Market Volume

As a fourth regime definition, we analyze the returns to abnormal turnover portfolios in times of different aggregate market volumes.[180] Table 5.12 reports returns to one-way sorted portfolios.

Table 5.12: Returns to Abnormal Turnover Portfolios in Different Volume Regimes

	Quintile portfolios				Deciles
Time-series	V1	V3	V5	V1-V5	V1-V10
Normal Swiss franc volume	1.93	1.23	0.74	1.19 (3.829)***	1.67 (4.111)***
High Swiss franc volume	-0.59	-0.20	-0.71	0.12 (0.230)	0.98 (1.537)
Normal market turnover	1.78	0.86	0.26	1.53 (4.599)***	2.06 (4.573)***
High market turnover	1.18	1.47	1.21	-0.03 (-0.085)	0.48 (1.085)

This table reports average monthly portfolio returns in different sub-sets of the complete return time-series (03/1997 - 08/2008), as defined in section 3.3.2.3.4. The equal-weighted portfolios are formed monthly on the basis of stocks' abnormal share turnover ($J = 12$ months) and are rebalanced monthly ($K = 1$). V1 is the portfolio containing the stocks with the highest 20% (quintiles) or 10% (deciles) abnormal turnover in a given month. V1, V3, V5 are portfolios containing long stock positions, while V1-V5 and V1-V10 are zero-cost arbitrage strategies. ***/**/* Denotes statistical significance at the 1%/5%/10% level. T-statistics (in parentheses) are calculated using Newey-West (1987) adjusted, heteroskedasticity and serial correlation robust standard errors.

[180] See 3.3.2.3.4 for a detailed definition of volume regimes.

Interestingly, both the results in regimes defined by total Swiss franc trading volume and by average market turnover suggest that the abnormal volume premium is strongly significant in normal volume phases but insignificant in high volume phases. The fact that the high volume regimes are situated exclusively at the end of the time-series, however, also offers two alternative explanations. First, the results could be further support for the hypothesis that the abnormal volume premium disappeared in more recent times. And second, the result could be caused by previously discussed regime dynamics. For example, of the 43 months in the high market turnover time-series, 30 were in the low volatility regime.

The differences between results in various volume regimes are not as strong within specific control variable quantiles, particularly using total Swiss franc trading volume as regime defining variable.[181] But when using average market turnover, these differences become more pronounced (see appendix, Table A4). Given that the Swiss franc volume time-series contains 32% low volatility months, while this number is 70% for market turnover, this provides further support that the volume results are mostly driven by the weak performance in low volatility regimes. In 6.1.4 below, we provide some further evidence in favor of this explanation.

5.2 Other Volume Measures

The remainder of this chapter is dedicated to the time-stability of the other volume measures, namely *volume level*, *volume growth*, and *variability in volume*. Because the base analysis shows no systematic relationship between these measures and expected returns, we follow an approach that is slightly adapted from the previously presented abnormal volume tests. Namely, we abstain from the analysis of the dependence of portfolio returns on few months with extreme returns or single calendar months but focus on the stability across different market regimes. Within this set of analyses, returns to portfolio strategies are again tested across all definitions of market regimes presented in 3.3.2.3, namely *sub-periods*, *market phases*, *market volatility*, and *market volume*. For conciseness, however, only those test results are reported that diverge from the expected outcome of no systematic volume-return relationship.

[181] This is particularly true for past loser stocks.

We again conduct the market regime analysis only for the $K = 1$ month holding period, due to the small potential bias at $K > 1$ (see the discussion in 5.1.3). In 6.2 below, we perform a small robustness check of the $K = 1$ results in the multi-month holding period.

5.2.1 Volume Level

In the base portfolio strategies presented in 4.2.1 we report results for the $J = 1$ and $J = 12$ months formation periods. While the strongest returns are generated in medium volume portfolios in both these formation periods, we also find minor differences between them. Namely, the return difference between high and low volume portfolios (V1-V5, V1-V10) decreases in the formation period, being slightly positive for $J = 1$ and marginally negative for $J = 12$, but not even close to statistically significant levels. For consistency reasons, we conduct below regime analysis for the same two formation periods. Starting with a portfolio formation based on last month's share turnover ($J = 1$) we find interesting results for the *regime definition based on market phases* (reported in Table 5.13). While the return difference between high and low turnover stocks is non-significant over the entire time-series from March 1997 to August 2008 (first row), it is significantly positive in bull market phases and significantly negative in bear markets. In other words, high (low) volume stocks significantly outperform low (high) volume stocks in bull (bear) market phases.

In a next step, we explore the possibility that the results are driven by potential differences of the volume portfolios regarding firm size, book-to-market ratio, past stock returns, and industry affiliation. Using the identical approach followed in the base strategies we control for these potential differences respectively disturbances via two-way sorted portfolios. Our unreported test results reveal that the discovered relations remain significant.

An obvious explanation for the strong deviation in the volume-return relationship across bull and bear markets could be that there are differences in market betas between high and low turnover stocks. More concretely, the results suggest that high volume stocks have significantly higher sensitivities to market returns, i.e., market betas. If this were true, the return difference between high and low volume portfolios should be significantly positive in months with positive market returns and significantly negative in months with negative market returns. Results reported in Table 5.13 confirm this. In the next chapter, we provide additional evidence for this beta-explanation by regressing monthly excess returns of turnover based portfolio strategies on the time-series of monthly excess returns on the market portfolio, as described in 3.3.3.2.

Table 5.13: Returns to Turnover Portfolios in Different Market Phases (J = 1 Month)

	Quintile portfolios				Deciles
Time-series	V1	V3	V5	V1-V5	V1-V10
Formation period J = 1, holding period K = 1					
Full (03/1997 - 08/2008)	1.06	1.23	0.61	0.45 (0.937)	0.57 (0.940)
Bull markets	2.94	2.69	1.55	**1.39** **(2.724)*****	**1.87** **(2.810)*****
Bear markets	-2.69	-1.69	-1.26	**-1.43** **(-1.819)***	**-2.04** **(-2.532)****
Positive market return months	4.16	3.21	1.58	**2.58** **(4.892)*****	**3.02** **(3.983)*****
Negative market return months	-4.39	-2.25	-1.09	**-3.30** **(-4.112)*****	**-3.75** **(-4.114)*****
Up market states	1.69	1.79	1.28	0.41 (0.895)	0.60 (1.026)
Down market states	-0.42	-0.09	-0.97	0.55 (0.629)	0.50 (0.361)

This table reports average monthly portfolio returns in different sub-sets of the complete return time-series (03/1997 - 08/2008), as defined in section 3.3.2.3.2. The equal-weighted portfolios are formed monthly on the basis of stocks' monthly share turnover in the last $J = 1$ month and are rebalanced monthly ($K = 1$). V1 is the portfolio containing the stocks with the highest 20% (quintiles) or 10% (deciles) share turnover in a given month. V1, V3, V5 are portfolios containing long stock positions, while V1-V5 and V1-V10 are zero-cost arbitrage strategies. ***/**/* Denotes statistical significance at the 1%/5%/10% level. T-statistics (in parentheses) are calculated using Newey-West (1987) adjusted, heteroskedasticity and serial correlation robust standard errors.

Finally, the last two rows in Table 5.13 report portfolio returns in up and down market states. These results show no systematic return difference between the two market regimes. This has important implications, because only these up and down market states are known ex-ante (when an investment decision is taken). Since this is not true for bull

/ bear markets respectively positive / negative market return months, above insights cannot be transformed to dynamic portfolio strategies.

All the above (results and related discussion) is equally true for the $J = 12$ months formation period, as shown in Table 5.14.

Table 5.14: Returns to Turnover Portfolios in Different Market Phases (J = 12 Months)

	Quintile portfolios				Deciles
Time-series	V1	V3	V5	V1-V5	V1-V10
Formation period J = 12, holding period K = 1					
Full (03/1997 - 08/2008)	0.68	1.29	0.86	-0.18 (0.937)	-0.20 (-0.329)
Bull markets	2.66	2.72	1.54	**1.12** **(2.161)****	**1.21** **(2.053)****
Bear markets	-3.26	-1.58	-0.51	**-2.76** **(-3.196)*****	**-3.01** **(-2.935)*****
Positive market return months	4.09	3.15	1.63	**2.46** **(4.298)*****	**2.68** **(3.954)*****
Negative market return months	-5.31	-1.98	-0.50	**-4.81** **(-5.272)*****	**-5.27** **(-5.178)*****
Up market states	1.29	1.98	1.28	0.01 (0.030)	-0.01 (-0.027)
Down market states	-0.76	-0.34	-0.13	-0.62 (-0.473)	-0.64 (-0.433)

This table reports average monthly portfolio returns in different sub-sets of the complete return time-series (03/1997 - 08/2008), as defined in section 3.3.2.3.2. The equal-weighted portfolios are formed monthly on the basis of stocks' average share turnover in the last $J = 12$ months and are rebalanced monthly ($K = 1$). V1 is the portfolio containing the stocks with the highest 20% (quintiles) or 10% (deciles) share turnover in a given month. V1, V3, V5 are portfolios containing long stock positions, while V1-V5 and V1-V10 are zero-cost arbitrage strategies. ***/**/* Denotes statistical significance at the 1%/5%/10% level. T-statistics (in parentheses) are calculated using Newey-West (1987) adjusted, heteroskedasticity and serial correlation robust standard errors.

5.2.2 Volume Growth

In the base portfolio strategies presented in 4.2.3 above, the conclusion of a positive but non-systematic relationship between volume growth and expected returns is equally true for both formation periods reported, namely $J = 3$ and $J = 12$ months. Nevertheless, we conduct the regime analyses for both these formation periods to ensure comparability of results. We again find interesting results for the *regime definitions based on market phases*. First, Table 5.15 reports results for the $J = 3$ months formation period.

Table 5.15: Returns to Turnover Growth Portfolios in Different Market Phases (J = 3 Months)

	Quintile portfolios				Deciles
Time-series	V1	V3	V5	V1-V5	V1-V10
Formation period J = 3, holding period K = 1					
Full (03/1997 - 08/2008)	1.32	0.76	0.74	**0.57**	0.38
				(2.444)**	(1.369)
Bull markets	2.51	2.32	2.18	0.33	0.17
				(1.243)	(0.550)
Bear markets	-1.07	-2.38	-2.13	**1.06**	0.79
				(2.518)**	(1.495)
Up market states	1.82	1.49	1.45	0.38	0.10
				(1.603)	(0.336)
Down market states	0.12	-0.97	-0.92	**1.04**	**1.03**
				(1.995)*	**(1.755)***
Positive market return months	2.86	2.99	2.89	-0.03	-0.29
				(-0.126)	(-1.183)
Negative market return months	-1.40	-3.18	-3.04	**1.64**	**1.54**
				(5.200)***	**(3.274)*****

This table reports average monthly portfolio returns in different sub-sets of the complete return time-series (03/1997 - 08/2008), as defined in section 3.3.2.3.2. The equal-weighted portfolios are formed monthly on the basis of stocks' average turnover growth in the last $J = 3$ months and are rebalanced monthly ($K = 1$). V1 is the portfolio containing the stocks with the highest 20% (quintiles) or 10% (deciles) turnover growth in a given month. V1, V3, V5 are portfolios containing long stock positions, while V1-V5 and V1-V10 are zero-cost arbitrage strategies. ***/**/* Denotes statistical significance at the 1%/5%/10% level. T-statistics (in parentheses) are calculated using Newey-West (1987) adjusted, heteroskedasticity and serial correlation robust standard errors.

The result in the last row reveals that the rather positive relationship between volume growth and expected returns seems to be primarily caused by the significantly positive return difference between high and low volume portfolios in months with negative market returns. This finding is even more pronounced in the $J = 12$ months formation period reported in Table 5.16.

Table 5.16: Returns to Turnover Growth Portfolios in Different Market Phases (J = 12 Months)

	Quintile portfolios				Deciles
Time-series	V1	V3	V5	V1-V5	V1-V10
Formation period J = 12, holding period K = 1					
Full (03/1997 - 08/2008)	1.20	1.15	0.66	**0.54** **(1.755)***	**0.63** **(1.708)***
Bull markets	2.32	2.73	2.19	0.13 (0.435)	0.04 (0.105)
Bear markets	-1.05	-2.02	-2.40	**1.35** **(2.045)****	**1.79** **(2.861)*****
Up market states	1.74	1.88	1.37	0.36 (1.352)	0.32 (0.866)
Down market states	-0.07	-0.60	-1.03	0.96 (1.214)	1.36 (1.636)
Positive market return months	2.43	3.39	3.44	**-1.01** **(-4.452)*****	**-1.77** **(-4.686)*****
Negative market return months	-0.97	-2.80	-4.23	**3.26** **(6.596)*****	**3.80** **(6.163)*****

This table reports average monthly portfolio returns in different sub-sets of the complete return time-series (03/1997 - 08/2008), as defined in section 3.3.2.3.2. The equal-weighted portfolios are formed monthly on the basis of stocks' average turnover growth in the last $J = 12$ months and are rebalanced monthly ($K = 1$). V1 is the portfolio containing the stocks with the highest 20% (quintiles) or 10% (deciles) turnover growth in a given month. V1, V3, V5 are portfolios containing long stock positions, while V1-V5 and V1-V10 are zero-cost arbitrage strategies. ***/**/* Denotes statistical significance at the 1%/5%/10% level. T-statistics (in parentheses) are calculated using Newey-West (1987) adjusted, heteroskedasticity and serial correlation robust standard errors.

In the $J = 12$ months setting, the return difference between high and low volume growth portfolios is not only significantly positive in negative market return months, but also significantly negative in positive market return months. These results again suggest a beta-based explanation. More concretely, it seems that high turnover growth stocks have lower market betas than low turnover growth stocks. In the next chapter, we confirm this hypothesis by regressing monthly excess returns of volume growth based portfolio strategies on the time-series of monthly excess returns on the market portfolio.

Table 5.17: Returns to Turnover Growth Portfolios in Different Market Phases, Averaged over 3 Size Quantiles

	Panel A: Formation period $J = 3$; Holding period $K = 1$			Panel B: Formation period $J = 12$; Holding period $K = 1$		
Time-series	V1	V3	V1-V3	V1	V3	V1-V3
Full (03/1997 - 08/2008)	1.23	0.97	0.26 (1.349)	1.21	1.07	0.32 (1.451)
Bull markets	2.58	2.37	0.21 (0.980)	2.57	2.41	0.16 (0.677)
Bear markets	-1.47	-1.83	0.36 (0.924)	-1.52	-2.17	0.65 (1.386)
Up market states	1.79	1.60	0.19 (1.026)	1.79	1.55	0.24 (1.304)
Down market states	-0.10	-0.52	0.42 (0.924)	-0.17	-0.70	0.52 (0.863)
Positive market months	3.08	3.07	0.01 (0.077)	2.86	3.30	**-0.46** **(-2.142)****
Negative market months	-2.02	-2.71	**0.68** **(2.165)****	-1.70	-3.37	**1.67** **(4.114)*****

This table reports average monthly portfolio returns in different sub-sets of the complete return time-series (03/1997 - 08/2008), as defined in section 3.3.2.3.2. Portfolio construction: each month, we sort stocks into three terciles based on firm market capitalization. Then, within each size quantile, we sort stocks based on their average turnover growth in the last $J = 3$ (Panel A) or $J = 12$ months (Panel B) into three volume portfolios. The portfolios are rebalanced monthly ($K = 1$) and are equal-weighted. To calculate the 'averaged return' in a given month we average the monthly returns of each volume tercile portfolio over the 3 size quantiles. V1 is the portfolio containing the stocks with the highest 1/3 turnover growth in a given month. V1, V3 are portfolios containing long stock positions, while V1-V3 is a zero-cost arbitrage strategy. ***/**/* Denotes statistical significance at the 1%/5%/10% level. T-statistics (in parentheses) are calculated using Newey-West (1987) adjusted, heteroskedasticity and serial correlation robust standard errors.

As a final remark, note that results in Table 5.15 and Table 5.16 show a significantly positive return difference between high and low volume growth portfolios in bear markets and partially also in down markets. However, recall from the base portfolios that the negative correlation between turnover growth and size influences one-way sorted results. Once we control for size (see Table 4.49 in 4.2.3 above), the positive return difference between high and low turnover growth portfolios seizes to be statistically significant. We thus repeat this size analysis in different market phases for both formation periods investigated *(J = 3, 12)*. Table 5.17 shows that the significant one-way results in bear and down markets vanish once we control for size. Only the prior results in positive and negative market months remain statistically significant.[182] As a consequence, we abstain from individually analyzing portfolio performance in bear and down markets going forward.

5.2.3 Variability in Volume

As a last volume measure, we analyze variability in volume, which has also shown no systematic relation with expected returns in the base strategies. The only finding worth mentioning in the context of the time-stability analysis is again the relationship between variability in volume and expected returns in positive and negative market return months. Results reported in Table 5.18 indicate a significantly negative return difference between high and low coefficient of variation in turnover portfolios in months with positive market returns.

At the same time, this return difference is significantly positive in negative market return months.[183] Similar to the volume growth story this suggests that stocks with a high variability in volume have significantly lower market betas than stocks with a low variability in volume. This hypothesis is again confirmed in the next chapter in regressions of monthly excess returns of volume growth based portfolio strategies on the time-series of monthly excess returns on the market portfolio.

[182] Unreported results show that these results in positive and negative market return months remain statistically significant when controlling for book-to-market ratio, momentum, or industry affiliation.

[183] Unreported test results reveal that the discovered relation remains strongly significant when controlling for firm size, book-to-market ratio, momentum, and industry affiliation via two-way sorted portfolios.

Table 5.18: Returns to Coefficient of Variation in Turnover Portfolios in Different Market Phases

	Quintile portfolios				Deciles
Time-series	V1	V3	V5	V1-V5	V1-V10
Holding period K = 1					
Full (03/1997 - 08/2008)	1.03	1.23	0.81	0.22 (0.863)	0.05 (0.148)
Positive market return months	2.31	3.42	3.46	**-1.15 (-4.593)*****	**-1.61 (-4.284)*****
Negative market return months	-1.22	-2.63	-3.84	**2.62 (5.958)*****	**2.97 (4.840)*****

This table reports average monthly portfolio returns in different sub-sets of the complete return time-series (03/1997 - 08/2008), as defined in section 3.3.2.3.2. The equal-weighted portfolios are formed monthly on the basis of stocks' coefficient of variation in share turnover (calculated over the past 12 months) and are rebalanced monthly ($K = 1$). V1 is the portfolio containing the stocks with the highest 20% (quintiles) or 10% (deciles) coefficient of variation in turnover in a given month. V1, V3, V5 are portfolios containing long stock positions, while V1-V5 and V1-V10 are zero-cost arbitrage strategies. ***/**/* Denotes statistical significance at the 1%/5%/10% level. T-statistics (in parentheses) are calculated using Newey-West (1987) adjusted, heteroskedasticity and serial correlation robust standard errors.

5.3 Chapter Summary

This chapter reported results of tests designed to answer research question [2] whether *the portfolio returns are robust across time and different market regimes*. Because abnormal volume is the only measure investigated with a systematic and significant relationship to expected Swiss stock returns, the bulk of the presented analyses focused on this measure.

1. Time-stability of abnormal volume premium:

We find that the positive relationship between abnormal volume and expected returns is not driven by only a few months with extreme returns and is independent of the December and January seasonality. Further analysis, however, reveals that the abnormal volume premium is much stronger in the first sub-period from March 1997 to November 2002. We explore two potential explanations for the finding that the abnormal volume premium is almost non-existent in the second sub-period from December 2002 to August 2008. While it could be that the discovered abnormal volume premium was merely a market inefficiency and disappeared in more recent times, our hypothesis is that the main driver is the weak strategy performance in low volatility regimes. In fact, no return month in the first sub-period is in a phase of low volatility but more than 50 percent of all months in the more recent sub-period. Additionally, we find particularly strong abnormal volume premiums in down market states and high volatility regimes. We do not find any obvious explanations for this evidence but show possibilities to relate the findings to the investor visibility hypothesis. Further evidence regarding the drivers behind the almost insignificant abnormal volume premium in the second sub-period is collected in the next chapter, namely by expanding the return series to December 2008. If the abnormal volume premium is strong in this very volatile, down market environment (particularly September to December 2008), this would support our hypothesis that the volume-return relation still exists, but is driven by volatility and market phase regimes. If not, the finding would provide further support for the 'market inefficiency' explanation.

2. Time-stability of the relationship between other volume measures and expected returns:

Portfolio strategies were again analyzed across all definitions of market regimes (subperiods, market phases, market volatility, and market volume), but only those test results were reported that diverged from the expected outcome of no systematic volume-return relationship, namely:

Volume level: the return difference between high and low turnover stocks is significantly positive (negative) in bull (bear) market phases. At the same time, this return difference is significantly positive (negative) in months with positive (negative) market returns. These results suggest that high volume stocks have significantly higher market betas.

Volume growth: the return difference between high and low turnover growth stocks is significantly positive in months with negative market returns and, depending on the analyzed formation period, significantly negative in months with positive market returns. This implies that high volume growth stocks have significantly lower market betas.

Variability in volume: again, we find a significantly negative (positive) return difference between high and low coefficient of variation in turnover portfolios in months with positive (negative) market returns, which indicates that stocks with a high variability in volume have significantly lower market betas.

The next chapter provides additional evidence confirming above relations between these volume measures and market beta.

6 Results: Economic Significance of Volume-Return Relations

In chapter 4, we identify a systematically positive relationship between abnormal volume and expected returns in the cross-section of Swiss stocks. In chapter 5, we investigate the stability of the discovered volume-return relation across various market regimes and find quite substantial differences, particularly between different phases of market volatility. As a last empirical analysis, we test *whether the discovered relationship between abnormal volume and expected returns is economically significant*, which is research question [3]. The focus of this chapter is again *abnormal volume*, because it is the only measure investigated shown to systematically relate to the cross-section of Swiss stock returns. Additionally, we briefly analyze the other volume measures as well (*volume level, volume growth,* and *variability in volume*), particularly regarding the presumed strong relationship between these volume measures and market beta identified in the last chapter. The methodology applied is described in detail above, 3.3.3, but we repeat the most important aspects at the relevant places in the text.

6.1 Abnormal Volume

The analysis of the economic significance of abnormal volume portfolio returns is divided into four parts. In a first step, we repeat selected base strategies from chapter 4 in a setting that is more realistic from an investor's perspective *(6.1.1 Portfolio Returns in a Practical Setting)*. Note that all analyses in this chapter are based on these 'practical strategies'. Next, we calculate risk-adjusted portfolio returns and compare performance and risk attributes of different portfolio strategies *(6.1.2 Risk-Based Analysis)*. In the third part, we test whether investors would have actually earned money in the past by implementing abnormal volume based portfolio strategies in the Swiss stock market *(6.1.3 Investability)*. This section particularly entails the inclusion of transaction costs. And finally, we analyze the performance of abnormal volume strategies in selected market phases *(6.1.4 Performance in Selected Market States)*. This includes an outlook on dynamic portfolio strategies implemented based on insights from last chapter's results and a stress test regarding portfolio performance in 2008.

The analysis is again limited to the $J = 12$ months reference period for the same reasons mentioned in 5.1. In other words, *abnormal volume is consistently defined as the percentage change of last month's turnover versus the average turnover in the preceding J = 12 months.*

6.1.1 Portfolio Returns in a Practical Setting

We start with the repetition of selected base strategies in a more practical setting to ensure that the returns obtained so far are realistic from an investor's perspective. The methodological differences between base and practical strategies are described in detail in 3.3.3.1, but we briefly repeat the most important changes regarding data and return calculation. *Data*: the biggest practical difference is the elimination of the first 11 months from the return series. In other words, the return series in the practical setting starts in February 1998 instead of March 1997. *Return calculation:* both within portfolios and across *(K)* investment cohorts, the return calculation accounts for a stock's / portfolio's performance in previous holding period months. It is important to note that this last point only concerns the multi-month holding period setting (i.e., $K > 1$ month).

Table 6.1 reports average monthly returns to equal-weighted *practical* abnormal turnover portfolios over different holding periods *K*. The results confirm the existence of a systematically significant positive relationship between abnormal volume and expected returns in the cross-section of Swiss stocks. This relationship is again strongest in the first holding period month (i.e., $K = 1$ strategies have the highest monthly average returns) but remains statistically significant across all multi-month holding periods investigated $(K = 3, 6, 12)$. Additionally, a comparison of the absolute value of the return difference between the highest and the lowest abnormal volume portfolio shows that this difference is quite similar for base and practical strategies. V1-V5 quintile results displayed in Panel A are 1.09, 0.73, 0.52 and 0.51% for $K = 1, 3, 6, 12$ months, compared to 1.06 (Table 4.40), 0.70, 0.49 and 0.47% (Table 4.46) in base strategies. Results are similar for V1-V10 decile strategies, namely 1.59, 0.94, 0.57, and 0.69% for practical strategies (Table 6.1, Panel B) and 1.58 (Table 4.40), 0.93, 0.67, and 0.74% (Table 4.46) for base strategies.

Table 6.1: Returns to Abnormal Turnover Portfolios in a Practical Setting

	Holding period K			
Volume portfolio	K = 1	K = 3	K = 6	K = 12
Panel A: Equal-weighted quintile portfolios, reference period J = 12				
V1	1.50	1.23	1.22	1.32
V2	1.07	1.21	1.12	1.07
V3	0.87	0.91	1.02	1.01
V4	0.96	0.97	0.97	1.04
V5	0.40	0.50	0.70	0.82
V1-V5	**1.09**	**0.73**	**0.52**	**0.51**
	(3.586)***	**(3.597)*****	**(3.434)*****	**(2.857)*****
V1-SPI	**1.06**	**0.80**	**0.79**	**0.89**
	(3.262)***	**(2.756)*****	**(3.045)*****	**(2.911)*****
V1-EW	**0.54**	**0.27**	**0.27**	**0.36**
	(2.533)**	**(2.112)****	**(3.104)*****	**(2.984)*****
Panel B: Equal-weighted decile portfolios, reference period J = 12				
V1	1.72	1.23	1.16	1.36
V5	0.89	0.92	0.98	1.01
V10	0.14	0.29	0.59	0.67
V1-V10	**1.59**	**0.94**	**0.57**	**0.69**
	(4.220)***	**(3.542)*****	**(2.849)*****	**(3.025)*****
V1-SPI	**1.29**	**0.80**	**0.73**	**0.93**
	(3.382)***	**(2.512)****	**(2.707)*****	**(2.862)*****
V1-EW	**0.77**	0.27	0.20	**0.40**
	(2.942)***	(1.577)	(1.605)	**(2.594)****

This table reports average monthly returns (time-series from February 1998 to August 2008) of equal-weighted portfolios formed monthly on the basis of abnormal share turnover in a stock (percentage change of last month's turnover versus the average turnover in the preceding *J = 12* months). Methodological differences between the more practical setting applied here and the base strategies analyzed in the last chapters are described in 3.3.3.1. V1 is the portfolio containing the stocks with the highest 20% (Panel A) respectively 10% (Panel B) abnormal turnover. V1 to V10 are portfolios containing long stock positions, while V1-V5 and V1-V10 are zero-cost arbitrage strategies. V1-SPI and V1-EW are average return differences between V1 and two benchmarks, the Swiss Performance Index and a hypothetical, equal-weighted index constructed from the stocks included in the database. ***/**/* Denotes statistical significance at the 1%/5%/10% level. T-statistics (in parentheses) are calculated using Newey-West (1987) adjusted, heteroskedasticity and serial correlation robust standard errors.

The implementation of these systematically profitable zero-cost arbitrage strategies (V1-V5, V1-V10) includes taking both long and short stock positions. As a second possibility, we also test the returns to portfolio strategies that only contain long positions in high abnormal volume stocks (V1). To analyze whether such strategies are able to systematically outperform relevant benchmarks, we additionally investigate the time-series of the return difference between the highest abnormal volume portfolio (V1) and two benchmark indices for statistical significance. The first benchmark is the value-weighted Swiss Performance Index (SPI). Across this project report we show that small stocks strongly outperform large stocks in our concrete sample. Results reported in Table 6.1 (V1-SPI) are not surprising from this perspective. The equal-weighted[184] V1 strategies significantly outperform the SPI across all holding periods analyzed. To ensure consistency we additionally compare the V1 time-series with a hypothetical, *equal-weighted* index constructed from the stocks included in our database (labeled 'EW' going forward). The resulting V1-EW return difference is strongest for holding periods of $K = 1$ and $K = 12$ months, which is obvious given that the V1 portfolio returns are the highest in these two holding period lengths. The positive average return difference between V1 and EW even loses its statistical significance for $K = 3$ and $K = 6$ months. In sum, results in Table 6.1 show that long-only investments in high abnormal volume portfolios generally outperform the two investigated benchmark returns, but that portfolios over the $K = 1$ and $K = 12$ holding periods obtain the more systematic and significant outperformance. Additionally, $K = 12$ is naturally the most promising multi-month holding period due to the relatively low level of transaction costs associated with the implementation of this strategy. Thus, for conciseness, we only report results of analyses for the $K = 1$ and $K = 12$ months holding periods going forward.

As a final remark regarding Table 6.1, recall from 3.3.3.1 that the monthly portfolio return across the K parallel investment cohorts (in multi-month holding periods[185]) is calculated as the percentage change in total NAV (Net Asset Value), which is the sum of the K individual cohorts' NAVs. Of course, the NAVs of the individual cohorts change over time based on the performance of the included stocks. To ensure that the resulting changes in the weights given to different cohorts do not largely affect results, we addi-

[184] This means that we initially allocate equal CHF amounts to each stock in a portfolio.

[185] For the $K = 1$ month holding period this calculation is not necessary, because we only invest in one cohort each month.

tionally conduct a robustness check with rebalancing of NAVs across the K cohorts at the end of January each year. Results (not reported in a table) show that the differences between the two methods – with or without yearly rebalancing – are very marginal, i.e., no more than 0.04% for any zero-cost arbitrage strategy analyzed in Table 6.1.

In a next step, we again control for other cross-sectional effects via two-way sorted portfolios. First, we use the same control variables tested in the base strategies, namely firm market capitalization, firm book-to-market ratio, past twelve-months' stock return with exception of the immediate last month, and industry affiliation. Results reported in Table 6.2 again show systematically positive and significant return differences between high and low abnormal volume portfolios across all these control variables.[186] However, the abnormal volume premium seems reduced when controlling for industry belonging. How could this relate to the investor visibility hypothesis? Intuitively, it could be caused by spillover effects. Namely, a high abnormal volume of a stock in a given industry could raise awareness (i.e., visibility) and thus investor interest in other stocks in that industry. As a result, the relationship between abnormal volume of a given stock and subsequent returns in the same stock could be less direct when restricting the analysis to one industry.[187] But again, this is just a hypothesis that needs further in-depth analysis (not in scope of this research project).

[186] The average return differences reported in Table 6.2 are again very similar in the unreported robustness check with yearly rebalancing of NAVs across investment cohorts (differences of no more than 0.01%).

[187] We are aware that such a spillover effect in principle would also exist over the entire sample. However, its strength is likely to be strongly diminished.

Table 6.2: Returns to Abnormal Turnover Portfolios Averaged over 3 Quantiles of the Control Variable, Practical Setting

	Control variable				
Volume portfolio	SIZE	BM	RET2-12	Liquidity	Industry Group
Panel A: Reference period J = 12, holding period K = 1					
V1	1.40	1.35	1.36	1.34	1.25
V2	0.86	0.86	0.88	0.98	0.99
V3	0.62	0.67	0.65	0.56	0.71
V1-V3	**0.79**	**0.68**	**0.71**	**0.79**	**0.53**
	(3.772)***	**(3.740)*****	**(3.654)*****	**(3.776)*****	**(2.509)****
Panel B: Reference period J = 12, holding period K = 12					
V1	1.25	1.21	1.20	1.24	1.17
V2	1.04	1.04	1.00	1.08	1.06
V3	0.83	0.87	0.88	0.81	0.95
V1-V3	**0.42**	**0.34**	**0.33**	**0.43**	**0.22**
	(3.251)***	**(2.767)*****	**(2.492)****	**(3.399)*****	**(1.974)***

Each month, we sort stocks into three terciles based on the examined control variable respectively into four industry groups. Then, within each control quantile, we sort stocks based on their abnormal share turnover *(J = 12)* into three volume portfolios. The portfolios are rebalanced every *K = 1, 12* months and are equal-weighted. We then average the returns of each volume tercile portfolio over the corresponding control quantiles per month and calculate time-series average monthly returns (02/1998-08/2008), which are reported in this table. Methodological differences between the more practical setting applied here and the base strategies analyzed in the last chapters are described in 3.3.3.1. V1, V2, V3 are portfolios containing long stock positions (V1 stocks having the highest abnormal turnover), while V1-V3 are zero-cost arbitrage strategies. ***/**/* Denotes statistical significance at the 1%/5%/10% level. T-statistics (in parentheses) are calculated using Newey-West (1987) adjusted, heteroskedasticity and serial correlation robust standard errors.

Additionally, recall the discussion on the relationship between liquidity and expected returns in the literature review (2.1.1.2). Previous research mostly finds a significantly negative relationship between liquidity and expected returns. To ensure that the abnormal volume premium does not proxy for a potential liquidity effect in the Swiss stock market, we thus additionally include a liquidity measure in the two-way sorted tests. GERVAIS ET AL. (2001), in their related investigation of the 'high-volume return premium', use a stock's bid-ask spread[188] as a liquidity measure and find that returns to their volume based strategies are unexplained by these spreads. Because data on trading volume is easier to obtain than spreads, we use a different measure, namely AMIHUD'S (2002) 'illiquidity' ratio. This measure is defined as the daily absolute price change per dollar of trading volume in a stock, averaged over the last year.[189] Results reported in Table 6.2 (Control variable 'Liquidity') show that the abnormal volume premium is independent of a potential liquidity effect. The portfolio returns monotonically increase in abnormal turnover (from V3 to V1) and the return difference is statistically significant at the 1% level when averaging over the three liquidity quantiles.

GERVAIS ET AL. (2001) investigate two additional potential explanations for their 'high-volume return premium', namely *return autocorrelations* and *firm announcements*. We do not explicitly account for these possibilities. Nevertheless, we do not want to withhold these authors' results from the discussion.

Short-term return autocorrelations: GERVAIS ET AL. (2001) find that their high-volume return premium is not a by-product of the effect that trading volume might have on short-term return autocorrelations, because the effect is as prevalent for stocks that experience little or no price change at the time of their abnormally high volume (see 2.2.2.1 above for an overview of this literature, particularly Table 2.7). Additional evidence from our analysis: we show that the positive abnormal volume premium is not very short-term in nature. The effect exists over a longer formation period, namely one month, and is statistically significant in a portfolio-setting for at least 12 months. The effect of volume on return autocorrelations discussed in 2.2.2.1, however, is much more short-term. CONRAD ET AL. (1994), for example, find that their profits disappear after three weeks. Additionally, the *evidence regarding the influence of volume on short-term return autocorrelations is even contradicting*, as outlined in Table 2.7. The visibility hypothesis, on the other hand, seems a comprehensible explanation for the abnormal volume premium according to our tests.

---

188 The measure introduced by AMIHUD/MENDELSON (1986), see 2.1.1.2.

189 As described in 2.1.1.2, AMIHUD (2002) finds that illiquid stocks have significantly higher expected returns.

Firm announcements: GERVAIS ET AL. (2001) also test the possibility that their volume-price relation is driven by firm announcements. They implement this test by removing from each trading interval the stocks that had a dividend or an earnings announcement either the day before, the day of, or the day after the formation period (recall that these authors use one-day formation periods, while we use one-month formation periods). GERVAIS ET AL. (2001) report little or no effect from removing firm announcements from the sample and conclude that it is thus unlikely that their high-volume return premium is driven by firm announcements. We do not explicitly repeat this test in our analysis. However, we do not see an obvious reason why firm announcements should severely influence our one-month formation periods but not GERVAIS ET AL.'S (2001) daily formation periods (where we intuitively expect a much stronger influence of a specific event, such as a firm announcement, on trading volume). Nevertheless, it seams feasible that firm announcements (important: among other factors) can increase a stock's trading volume and thus its visibility.

Results of the separate investigation of returns to abnormal volume portfolios within each control quantile (not reported in a table) confirm that the abnormal volume premium is particularly strong for small firms, low book-to-market firms, and firms with low past one-year returns.[190] We thus continue to analyze abnormal volume deciles within these control variable quantiles with the objective of identifying particularly profitable (and thus marketable) portfolio strategies. Table 6.3 reports average monthly returns to these strategies in a practical setting. Again, we separately analyze results for zero-cost arbitrage strategies (V1-V10) and long-only positions in high abnormal volume stocks (V1).

[190] For the book-to-market ratio, this is only true in 3 x 10 portfolios (i.e., abnormal volume deciles within book-to-market terciles). In the more diversified 3 x 3 portfolios, however, the highest abnormal volume premium seems attainable for firms with a medium book-to-market ratio.

Table 6.3: Returns to Two-Way Sorted Abnormal Turnover Portfolios in Practical Setting

	Reference period $J = 12$; Holding period $K = 1$			Reference period $J = 12$; Holding period $K = 12$		
Portfolio	Small	Low BM	Losers	Small	Low BM	Losers
V1	2.36	1.43	1.47	1.56	1.12	1.14
V5	0.36	0.40	0.06	1.47	0.75	0.96
V10	-0.20	-0.55	0.03	0.57	0.28	0.48
V1-V10	**2.56**	**1.99**	**1.44**	**0.99**	**0.84**	**0.66**
	(3.431)* **	**(3.533)*** **	**(2.394)** **	**(2.742)*** **	**(3.609)*** **	**(2.667)*** **
V1-SPI	**1.93**	**1.00**	**1.04**	**1.13**	**0.69**	**0.71**
	(3.140)* **	**(1.857)* **	**(2.073)** **	**(2.417)** **	**(1.867)* **	**(1.991)** **
V1-EW	**1.40**	0.47	0.51	**0.60**	0.16	0.18
	(2.707)* **	(1.021)	(1.104)	**(1.864)* **	(0.702)	(0.935)

This table reports average monthly returns (time-series from 02/1998-08/2008) of equal-weighted portfolios formed monthly on the basis of stocks' abnormal share turnover ($J = 12$) within specific control variable tercile portfolios. The portfolios are held for $K = 1, 12$ months. Methodological differences between the more practical setting applied here and the base strategies analyzed in the last chapters are described in 3.3.3.1. V1 is the portfolio containing the stocks with the highest 10% abnormal turnover. V1 to V10 are portfolios containing long stock positions, while V1-V10 is a zero-cost arbitrage strategy. V1-SPI and V1-EW are average return differences between V1 and the Swiss Performance Index respectively a hypothetical, equal-weighted index constructed from the stocks included in the database. ***/**/* Denotes statistical significance at the 1%/5%/10% level. T-statistics (in parentheses) are calculated using Newey-West (1987) adjusted, heteroskedasticity and serial correlation robust standard errors.

Zero-cost arbitrage strategies (V1-V10): the abnormal volume premium is strongly significant across all three strategies and two holding periods. Regarding the absolute value of the return differences we can directly compare the $K = 1$ practical returns of 2.56, 1.99, and 1.44% (for small firms, low book-to-market firms, and past losers) to the base strategy results. These are quite comparable, namely 2.54, 1.84, and 1.55% (see Table 4.42 to Table 4.44).

Long-only positions in high abnormal volume stocks (V1): all V1 portfolios again significantly outperform the SPI (V1-SPI) across all three individual strategies and different holding periods investigated. When compared to the equal-weighted index (V1-EW), however, only the high abnormal volume portfolio within small firms ('Small') remains statistically significant. On the other hand, the result that long-only positions of high abnormal volume stocks within low book-to-market firms ('Low BM') and past loser stocks ('Losers') do not significantly outperform the relevant benchmark is not surprising. The reason is that both previous research and our own analysis show that *high* book-to-market firms and past *winners* generally have higher expected returns. By restricting the abnormal volume strategies to the generally lower performing low book-to-market and past loser stocks, we thus automatically reduce long-only returns. As a consequence of this (expected) result, we abstain from separately analyzing the long-only performance of 'Low BM' and 'Losers' strategies going forward.

To conclude this section, we graphically illustrate the performance of different practical abnormal volume strategies discussed above (Table 6.1 and Table 6.3). In Figure 6.1, we separately plot the development of abnormal turnover decile arbitrage strategies for the two holding periods investigated ($K = 1$ and $K = 12$), indexed to 100 at the beginning of the time-series. The graphs nicely illustrate previous findings, namely:

- On average, high abnormal turnover stocks strongly outperform low abnormal turnover stocks;
- This outperformance is stronger for the one-month holding period;
- The relationship between abnormal volume and expected returns is not very stable across time. Examples are the weak strategy performance in the low volatility regime from 2004 to 2007 (particularly evident for $K = 1$ decile strategies within small stocks that even have a negative performance) and the strong performance in high volatility regimes in 2002/03 and at the end of the time-series. We come back to the time-stability of portfolio returns in 6.1.4.

Figure 6.1: NAVs of Abnormal Turnover Arbitrage Strategies (V1-V10)

(a) Holding Period K = 1

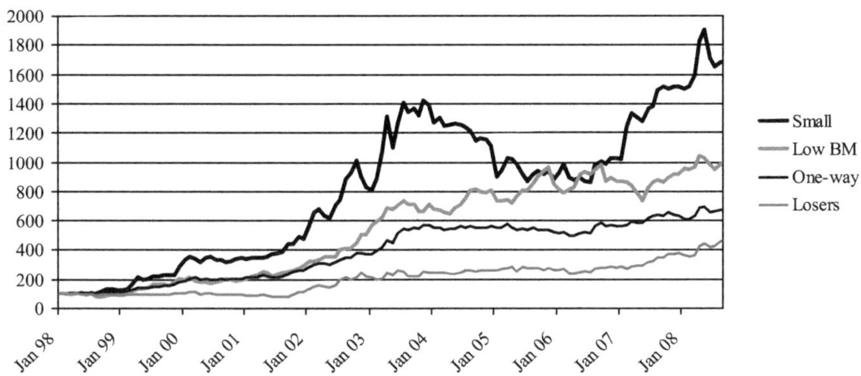

(b) Holding Period K = 12

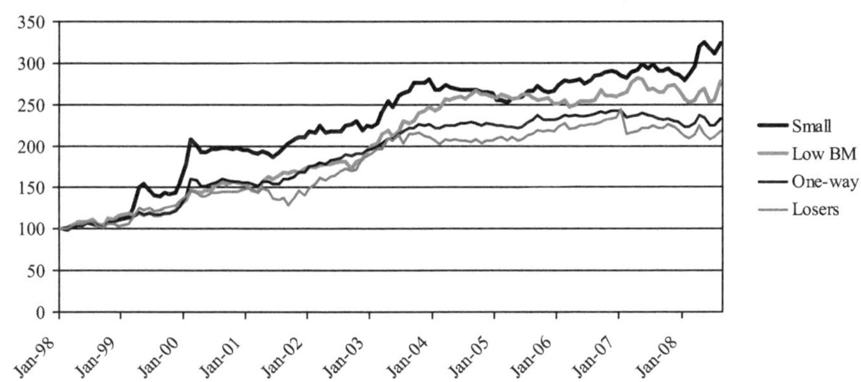

There is one important additional point in Figure 6.1 (b). It seems as though the abnormal volume premium over the 12-month holding period is mainly caused by a few months in 1999 and 2000. We thus repeat the respective robustness check from 5.1.1 and exclude the $p = 5$ highest monthly returns from the $K = 12$ months time-series. This reduces the monthly average one-way decile (V1-V10) premium from 0.69 to 0.40%. But the reduced time-series is still significantly positive at the 1% level (t-statistic

2.790). Additionally, Figure 6.1 (b) suggests that the influence of extreme return months in 1999 and 2000 is particularly strong for decile-sorted strategies within small stocks ('Small'). The exclusion of the $p = 5$ highest monthly returns confirms this – the monthly average abnormal volume premium decreases from 0.99 to 0.46%. Again, however, the reduced time-series of the abnormal volume premium is still significantly positive (at the 5% level; t-statistic 2.243). We conclude that the abnormal volume effect in the 12-month holding period is not solely driven by outliers, although few extreme return months at the beginning of the time-series seem to strongly influence the size of the premium.

Finally, Figure 6.2 displays the development of long-only high abnormal turnover decile portfolios, compared to the two benchmark indices. Both $K = 1$ month strategies significantly outperform the benchmarks over the time-series. The $K = 12$ months outperformance, on the other hand, again seems strongly driven by a few months in 1999 and 2000. When excluding the five highest monthly observations from the time-series, the average monthly return to the one-way sorted abnormal volume decile portfolio is reduced from 1.36 to 0.90%. The average return difference between V1 and the equal-weighted index (V1-EW) is even reduced from 0.40 to 0.21%. But this return difference remains significant at the 5% level (t-statistic of 2.011). The influence of the five highest return months on the 'Small' long-only strategy is even more pronounced. The average monthly return of the reduced time-series is 0.91% (from 1.56% over the entire time-series) and the resulting average V1-EW return difference is reduced from 0.60 to 0.17%, now at statistically insignificant levels (t-statistic of 0.863). These results cast some doubt on the profitable implementation of long-only abnormal volume strategies over multi-month holding periods.

Figure 6.2: NAVs of Long-Only Abnormal Turnover Portfolios (Deciles)

(a) Holding Period K = 1

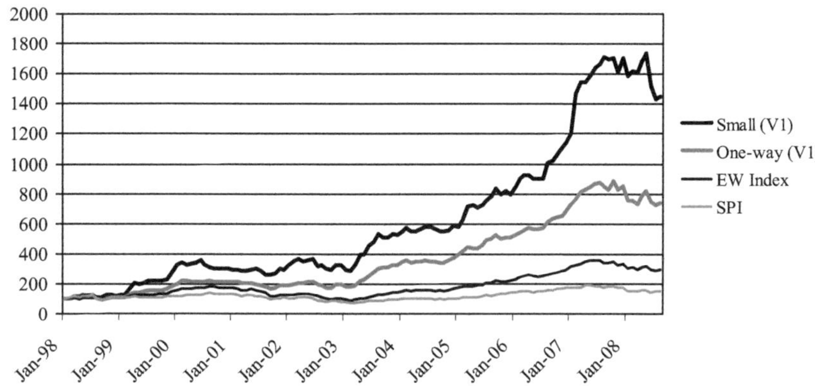

(b) Holding Period K = 12

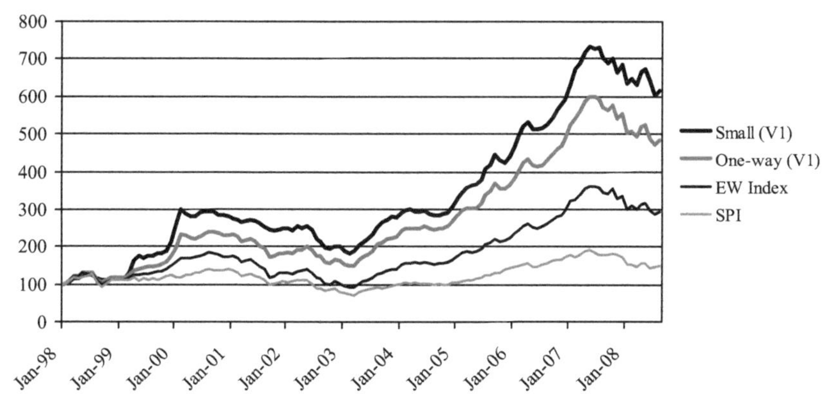

6.1.2 Risk-Based Analysis

6.1.2.1 Risk-Adjusted Portfolio Returns

In the last section, we show that the base strategies' main findings generally remain valid in a more practical setting. As a further test of economic significance we analyze risk-adjusted portfolio returns. As detailed in 3.3.3.2, we execute this analysis by regressing monthly excess returns to our (practical) abnormal volume based portfolio strategies on the time-series of several risk factor premiums in the Swiss stock market. The resulting regression intercept coefficients ('Alphas') are then interpretable as the risk-adjusted returns of the portfolios relative to the analyzed risk model. We include the following three standard risk factor models in our analysis:

- The *Capital Asset Pricing Model (CAPM)* by SHARPE (1964), LINTNER (1965) and MOSSIN (1966), which only accounts for market risk (RMRF);
- The *Fama-French three-factor model* by FAMA/FRENCH (1993), which additionally accounts for the size effect (SMB) and the value effect (HML);
- The *Carhart four-factor model* by CARHART (1995, 1997), which additionally accounts for momentum (UMD).

The estimated risk-adjusted returns to one-way sorted portfolios are reported in Table 6.4. We start by discussing the two main findings of results of quintile portfolios (Panel A).

Table 6.4: Time-Series Regression Alphas of Abnormal Turnover Portfolios

	Reference period $J = 12$; Holding period $K = 1$			Reference period $J = 12$; Holding period $K = 12$		
Portfolio	CAPM Alpha	FF3 Alpha	Carhart Alpha	CAPM Alpha	FF3 Alpha	Carhart Alpha
Panel A: Equal-weighted quintile portfolios						
V1	1.13	0.64	0.69	0.97	0.47	0.39
	(3.417)***	(2.742)***	(2.765)***	(2.946)***	(3.327)***	(2.713)***
V2	0.69	0.31	0.30	0.70	0.29	0.22
	(2.333)**	(1.741)*	(1.578)	(2.604)**	(2.495)**	(1.922)*
V3	0.48	0.10	0.06	0.64	0.22	0.15
	(1.927)*	(0.619)	(0.359)	(2.407)**	(1.703)*	(1.090)
V4	0.59	0.11	0.12	0.67	0.22	0.19
	(1.883)*	(0.614)	(0.681)	(2.315)**	(1.552)	(1.227)
V5	0.07	-0.39	-0.34	0.50	0.06	0.06
	(0.242)	(-2.296)**	(-1.966)*	(1.686)*	(0.417)	(0.372)
V1-V5	**1.05**	**1.03**	**1.02**	**0.47**	**0.41**	**0.33**
	(3.317)***	**(3.454)*****	**(3.450)*****	**(2.586)****	**(2.918)*****	**(2.547)****
Wald	31.35***	16.90***	15.38***	42.38***	15.16***	8.94
Panel B: Equal-weighted decile portfolios						
V1	1.37	0.86	0.95	1.03	0.49	0.42
	(3.615)***	(3.096)***	(3.168)***	(2.906)***	(3.228)***	(2.613)**
V10	-0.18	-0.64	-0.57	0.37	-0.02	0.00
	(-0.582)	(-2.824)***	(-2.439)**	(1.241)	(-0.158)	(-0.021)
V1-V10	**1.55**	**1.50**	**1.52**	**0.65**	**0.52**	**0.43**
	(3.956)***	**(3.851)*****	**(3.734)*****	**(2.776)*****	**(2.759)*****	**(2.531)****

This table reports estimated intercept coefficients of regressions of monthly excess returns of the practical abnormal turnover portfolios (reported in 6.1.1) on the time-series of monthly excess returns on the market portfolio RMRF (CAPM), on the time-series of Swiss factor premiums RMRF, SMB, HML (Fama-French factors, i.e., FF3), and on the four Swiss factor premiums RMRF, SMB, HML, UMD (Carhart factors). The methodology applied is described in detail in 3.3.3.2. 'Wald' denotes a Wald test for the restriction that all alphas are zero. ***/**/* Denotes statistical significance at the 1%/5%/10% level. T-statistics (in parentheses) are calculated using Newey-West (1987) adjusted, heteroskedasticity and serial correlation robust standard errors.

First, the risk-adjusted returns to portfolios containing the highest 20% abnormal volume stocks (V1) are strongly significantly positive across all three risk models and both holding periods. And second, the return difference between high and low abnormal volume portfolios (V1-V5) remains statistically significantly positive when accounting for various risk factors in the cross-section of Swiss stocks. The absolute value of this return difference is similar to the raw returns for one-month *(K = 1)* holding period strategies and slightly lower for 12-month *(K = 12)* holding period strategies. More concretely, raw returns displayed in Table 6.1 are 1.09 *(K = 1)* and 0.51% *(K = 12)*, while the respective risk-adjusted returns using the Carhart model (Table 6.4) are 1.02 and 0.33%. An additional Wald test for the restriction that all alphas are zero is rejected at the 1% level across all models and holding periods (including the unreported *K = 3* and *K = 6* months holding period lengths) with the exception of the Carhart model for the *K = 12* months holding period (p-value of 0.112).[191] Results of abnormal decile portfolios, reported in Panel B, confirm the existence of strongly significant risk-adjusted returns to both long-only (V1) and long-short (V1-V10) portfolios.

In a next step, we separately report individual regressions of abnormal turnover arbitrage strategies (Table 6.5). For conciseness, we only show results of decile strategies because their higher absolute returns make them more attractive regarding practical implementation – the focal point of this chapter. But the two main findings are very similar for quintile portfolios (not reported in a table). First, the standard risk factors incorporated in the various regressions can only explain a very small part of stock return variations. In fact, the adjusted R^2 figures are only between 2 to 4% in the one-month holding period displayed in Panel A and between 8 to 17% in the 12-month holding period (Panel B). As a second finding, recall from 5.1.3.2 above that the abnormal volume premium is stronger in positive market return months, which suggests that high abnormal volume stocks have higher market betas. Results in Table 6.5 confirm this, because the coefficient estimate on the market factor, RMRF, is positive across all risk models. However, the difference between market betas of high and low abnormal volume stocks is only significantly positive for the *K = 12* months holding period displayed in Panel B.

---

[191] But more importantly, the risk-adjusted portfolio returns of the V1 and V1-V5 portfolios are strongly significant.

Table 6.5: Time-Series Regression Coefficients of Abnormal Turnover Arbitrage Strategies

Risk model	Alpha	RMRF	SMB	HML	UMD	R2-adj
Panel A: Equal-weighted decile portfolios (V1-V10), reference period J = 12, holding period K = 1						
CAPM	1.55	0.15				0.02
	(3.956)***	(1.458)				
FF3	1.50	0.16	0.07	-0.26		0.04
	(3.851)***	(1.353)	(0.391)	(-1.710)*		
Carhart	1.52	0.15	0.07	-0.26	-0.02	0.03
	(3.734)***	(1.285)	(0.388)	(-1.723)*	(-0.189)	
Panel B: Equal-weighted decile portfolios (V1-V10), reference period J = 12, holding period K = 12						
CAPM	0.65	0.14				0.08
	(2.776)***	(2.731)***				
FF3	0.52	0.20	0.25	-0.11		0.16
	(2.759)***	(3.711)***	(1.359)	(-1.306)		
Carhart	0.43	0.23	0.24	-0.11	0.09	0.17
	(2.531)**	(5.062)***	(1.388)	(-1.221)	(2.508)**	

This table reports estimated coefficients of regressions of monthly returns of the practical abnormal turnover decile arbitrage strategies (V1-V10, reported in 6.1.1) on the time-series of monthly excess returns on the market portfolio RMRF (CAPM), on the time-series of Swiss factor premiums RMRF, SMB, HML (Fama-French factors, i.e., FF3), and on the four Swiss factor premiums RMRF, SMB, HML, UMD (Carhart factors). The methodology applied is described in detail in 3.3.3.2. ***/**/* Denotes statistical significance at the 1%/5%/10% level. T-statistics (in parentheses) are calculated using Newey-West (1987) adjusted, heteroskedasticity and serial correlation robust standard errors.

In sum, the results in Table 6.4 and Table 6.5 show two important facts:

- The positive abnormal volume premium in the Swiss stock market cannot be explained by previously documented market, size, value, and momentum risk factors. This raises the question whether high abnormal volume proxies for an additional risk factor not considered here. This, however, is not in the scope of this empirical investigation and is proposed as a topic for further research.

- The analysis confirms that the premium is mainly driven by the first month following abnormal volume (i.e., one-month holding period). Despite this result, we continue to analyze the $K = 12$ months holding period due to the potentially prohibitive transaction costs caused by monthly rebalancing.

Next, we estimate risk-adjusted returns to abnormal volume decile portfolios within specific control variable quantiles (smallest firms, firms with low book-to-market ratios, loser stocks). V1-V10 results reported in Table 6.6 show that the strategy returns remain significantly positive. Again, we also analyze individual regressions for each of the three strategies. The results are included in the appendix for the interested reader (Table A5, Table A6, and Table A7).

Table 6.6: Time-Series Regression Alphas of Two-Way Sorted Abnormal Turnover Portfolios

	Panel A: Reference period $J = 12$; Holding period $K = 1$			Panel B: Reference period $J = 12$; Holding period $K = 12$		
Portfolio	CAPM Alpha	FF3 Alpha	Carhart Alpha	CAPM Alpha	FF3 Alpha	Carhart Alpha
Small	2.58	2.56	2.75	0.97	0.96	0.97
	(3.654)***	(3.716)***	(3.733)***	(2.750)***	(2.954)***	(2.838)***
Low BM	1.96	1.97	1.96	0.79	0.76	0.68
	(3.341)***	(3.352)***	(3.074)***	(3.312)***	(3.383)***	(3.161)***
Losers	1.38	1.36		0.60	0.52	
	(2.125)**	(2.048)**		(2.288)**	(2.011)**	

This table reports estimated intercept coefficients of regressions of monthly returns of the practical abnormal turnover decile arbitrage strategies (V1-V10) within specific control variable tercile portfolios (reported in 6.1.1) on the time-series of monthly excess returns on the market portfolio RMRF (CAPM), on the time-series of Swiss factor premiums RMRF, SMB, HML (Fama-French factors, i.e., FF3), and on the four Swiss factor premiums RMRF, SMB, HML, UMD (Carhart factors). The methodology applied is described in detail in 3.3.3.2. Remarks regarding factors: no SMB ('Small Minus Big') factor used in 'Small' portfolio, because it contains only small firms. No HML ('High Minus Low') factor used in 'Low BM' portfolio, because it only comprises of firms with low book-to-market ratios. No Carhart regression containing UMD ('Up Minus Down') estimated for 'Losers' portfolio, because it only contains stocks with weak past performance.

***/**/* Denotes statistical significance at the 1%/5%/10% level. T-statistics (in parentheses) are calculated using Newey-West (1987) adjusted, heteroskedasticity and serial correlation robust standard errors.

6.1.2.2 Risk and Performance Analysis

A second risk-based analysis is the comparison of risk and performance attributes of abnormal volume based portfolio strategies with two reference indices (the Swiss Performance Index SPI and 'EW', an equal-weighted index constructed from the stocks included in the database). Results of this risk and performance analysis for one-way sorted portfolios are reported in Table 6.7. Results are again displayed for decile strategies, because the focus of this analysis is to investigate particularly profitable abnormal volume strategies.

Let us start the discussion with the zero-cost arbitrage portfolios (V1-V10). The $K = 1$ month strategy displayed in Panel A has many attractive properties. First, it has high returns (annualized average returns of 19.72%[192]) but not at the cost of a particularly high volatility. The annualized standard deviation of 13.09% is lower than the respective figures for the reference indices (16.49 respectively 16.28% for SPI and EW). This results in a Sharpe ratio of 1.39, compared to 0.14 and 0.56 for the benchmarks. An additionally positive result is the drawdown analysis, showing that the strategy's NAV never consecutively dropped by more than 13.7% (from a local maximum to a local minimum), compared to almost 50% for the reference indices. Finally, the correlation with reference index returns is quite low, which is not surprising given that V1-V10 is a long-short strategy. As expected from previous results, the properties of the $K = 12$ months V1-V10 arbitrage strategy displayed in Table 6.7, Panel B, are similar but at a much smaller scale. The average annualized return, for example, is 8.24%, which is much higher than the SPI (3.91%) but smaller than the EW returns (10.74%). However, the abnormal volume strategy's volatility is also much smaller, resulting in a higher Sharpe ratio of 0.88 (compared to 0.14 and 0.56 for SPI and EW respectively). Finally, to emphasize the positive risk attributes of the $K = 12$ strategy, its maximum drawdown is only 8.1% over the entire time-series.

[192] Recall from 3.3.3.1 that we take arithmetic averages of all monthly returns to calculate mean returns over the entire time-series. As a robustness check, we also calculate geometric average annualized returns to the six strategies displayed in Table 6.7. These returns are only marginally lower, namely 18.84, 18.00, 14.88, 7.92, 3.84 and 10.20%.

Turning the discussion to the long-only high abnormal volume strategies (V1 in Table 6.7) we find that their returns naturally correlate more strongly with the reference indices. At the same time, both the $K = 1$ and the $K = 12$ months holding period strategies have significantly higher returns but similar volatilities, which results in substantially higher Sharpe ratios (1.05 and 0.91 for $K = 1$ and $K = 12$ versus 0.14 and 0.56 for SPI and EW). Additionally, the long-only abnormal volume strategies both have a smaller maximum drawdown in the sample period.

Table 6.7: Risk and Performance Analysis of Abnormal Turnover Decile Portfolios

	Panel A: $J = 12; K = 1$		Panel B: $J = 12; K = 12$		Panel C: Reference indices	
	V1	V1-V10	V1	V1-V10	SPI	EW
Average return (ann.)	20.73%	19.72%	16.04%	8.24%	3.91%	10.74%
Standard deviation (ann.)	18.19%	13.09%	15.93%	7.59%	16.49%	16.28%
Sharpe ratio	1.05	1.39	0.91	0.88	0.14	0.56
Correlation (SPI)	0.68	0.16	0.69	0.30	1.00	0.83
Correlation (EW)	0.88	0.19	0.93	0.41	0.83	1.00
% positive months	68%	65%	65%	61%	62%	66%
Maximum drawdown	-25.7%	-13.7%	-37.2%	-8.1%	-49.1%	-49.7%
Months in drawdown	18	13	30	14	31	31
Months of recovery	20	5	11	>7	33	23
Average monthly return	1.72%	1.59%	1.36%	0.69%	0.43%	0.96%
Median monthly return	1.35%	1.07%	1.29%	0.44%	1.30%	1.57%
Maximum monthly return	17.72%	12.54%	16.79%	15.08%	12.24%	11.74%
Minimum monthly return	-17.71%	-8.86%	-13.82%	-4.57%	-16.92%	-14.54%

This table reports performance and risk attributes of selected practical abnormal turnover decile portfolios (reported in 6.1.1) and two benchmarks, the Swiss Performance Index (SPI) and a hypothetical, equal-weighted index constructed from the stocks included in the database (EW). V1 is the portfolio containing the stocks with the highest 10% abnormal turnover, while V1-V10 is a zero-cost arbitrage strategy (i.e., time-series of return difference between V1 and V10 portfolios).

All these results emphasize the attractiveness of the different abnormal volume based portfolio strategies (important: before taking into account transaction costs). We conclude this section by analyzing performance and risk attributes of abnormal volume decile portfolios within small firms, firms with low book-to-market ratios, and loser stocks. Results for arbitrage strategies (V1-V10) are displayed in Table 6.8 for the $K = 1$ month holding period. For comparison, we also report results of the more diversified one-way sorted decile strategy from Table 6.7 (labeled 'One-way').

Table 6.8: Risk and Performance Analysis of Two-Way Sorted Abnormal Turnover Arbitrage Strategies

	V1-V10; Reference period: $J = 12$; Holding period $K = 1$				Reference indices	
	Small	Low BM	Losers	One-way	SPI	EW
Average return (ann.)	30.53%	24.11%	15.35%	19.72%	3.91%	10.74%
Standard deviation (ann.)	26.88%	19.95%	23.66%	13.09%	16.49%	16.28%
Sharpe ratio	1.14	1.21	0.65	1.39	0.14	0.56
Correlation (SPI)	-0.04	0.06	0.16	0.16	1.00	0.83
Correlation (EW)	-0.01	0.05	0.11	0.19	0.83	1.00
% positive months	54%	60%	49%	65%	62%	66%
Maximum drawdown	-39.0%	-25.1%	-29.1%	-13.7%	-49.1%	-49.7%
Months in drawdown	31	8	16	13	31	31
Months of recovery	14	11	4	5	33	23
Average monthly return	2.56%	1.98%	1.44%	1.59%	0.43%	0.96%
Median monthly return	1.41%	1.88%	0.44%	1.07%	1.30%	1.57%
Maximum monthly return	25.94%	19.33%	24.94%	12.54%	12.24%	11.74%
Minimum monthly return	-18.84%	-17.04%	-15.66%	-8.86%	-16.92%	-14.54%

This table reports performance and risk attributes of practical abnormal turnover decile arbitrage strategies (V1-V10) within specific control variable tercile portfolios (smallest 1/3 of firms, 1/3 of firms with lowest book-to-market ratio, 1/3 of stocks with the lowest past one-year returns), as reported in 6.1.1. All the analyzed strategies are rebalanced monthly $(K = 1)$. These numbers are compared with the one-way sorted abnormal turnover decile arbitrage strategy (One-way) and two benchmarks, the Swiss Performance Index (SPI) and a hypothetical, equal-weighted index constructed from the stocks included in the database (EW).

Regarding the positive attributes of these 'special' strategies Table 6.8 shows that 'Small' and 'Low BM' have higher average returns and are less correlated with the reference indices than the one-way sorted decile strategy (this is only partially true for 'Losers'). On the other hand, the returns to the 'Small', 'BM', and 'Losers' strategies are considerably more volatile than the one-way sorted strategy, which results in lower Sharpe ratios. One potential explanation for the increased volatility could be the fact that the strategies are less diversified, because they contain only 1/30 of the entire cross-section per month while decile portfolios contain 1/10. In other words, single stock returns have a stronger influence on portfolio returns. An additionally negative property of these 'special' strategies is that they have a much higher maximum drawdown of between minus 25.1 and minus 39.0%, compared to the one-way sorted strategy's maximum drawdown of minus 13.7%. For completeness, the appendix also contains the same analysis for the $K = 12$ months holding period (Table A8) and a risk and performance analysis of the long-only abnormal volume strategy (V1) within small stocks (Table A9). To conclude, recall that the prime objective of individually testing these (less-diversified) 'special' strategies within specific control variable quantiles was to increase the probability of identifying economically significant portfolio returns. But the analysis in this section suggests that these strategies are not significantly more attractive than the better diversified one-way sorted abnormal volume strategy. This is particularly true for the 'Losers' strategy, which even seems to perform weaker regarding most analyzed properties.

6.1.3 Investability

6.1.3.1 Inclusion of Transaction Costs

Previously presented results show that portfolio strategies formed on the basis of past abnormal volume have attractive return and risk attributes. So far, however, we ignore the influence of transaction costs on results, which is of course crucial regarding practical implementation. Details regarding the calculation of transaction costs are described in 3.3.3.3. Table 6.9 reports portfolio returns after the *inclusion of different levels of transaction costs*. The analysis is again restricted to decile strategies, because our focus is the *practicability* of abnormal volume strategies.

Table 6.9: Inclusion of Transaction Costs to Abnormal Turnover Decile Portfolios

	Transaction cost level (one-way costs)				
Volume portfolio	0.0%	0.3%	0.5%	1.0%	1.5%
Panel A: Equal-weighted decile portfolios, reference period J = 12, holding period K = 1					
Long (V1)	1.72	1.28	0.99	0.25	-0.47
Short (V10)	0.14	0.52	0.77	1.41	2.05
Long-Short (V1-V10)	**1.59**	**0.76**	0.21	-1.16	-2.53
	(4.220)***	**(2.025)****	(0.568)	(-3.033)***	(-6.558)***
Long-SPI	**1.29**	**0.85**	0.56	-0.18	-0.90
	(3.382)***	**(2.219)****	(1.448)	(-0.462)	(-2.344)**
Long-EW	**0.77**	0.32	0.03	-0.71	-1.43
	(2.942)***	(1.234)	(0.103)	(-2.658)***	(-5.451)***
Panel B: Equal-weighted decile portfolios, reference period J = 12, holding period K = 12					
Long (V1)	1.36	1.31	1.28	1.20	1.12
Short (V10)	0.67	0.71	0.74	0.81	0.88
Long-Short (V1-V10)	**0.69**	**0.60**	**0.54**	**0.39**	0.24
	(3.025)***	**(2.635)*****	**(2.375)****	**(1.722)***	(1.067)
Long-SPI	**0.93**	**0.88**	**0.85**	**0.77**	**0.69**
	(2.862)***	**(2.720)*****	**(2.625)*****	**(2.387)****	**(2.149)****
Long-EW	**0.40**	**0.35**	**0.32**	0.24	0.16
	(2.594)**	**(2.290)****	**(2.087)****	(1.581)	(1.074)

This table reports average monthly returns of selected practical abnormal turnover decile portfolios (reported in 6.1.1) after the inclusion of transaction costs. The calculation assumes the same level of transaction costs for long and short investments. The included one-way (i.e., buying or selling) transaction costs of 0.3%, 0.5%, 1%, 1.5% correspond to round-trip costs of 0.6%, 1%, 2%, 3%. The calculation of transaction costs is described in detail in 3.3.3.3. SPI is the Swiss Performance Index and EW is a hypothetical, equal-weighted index constructed from the stocks included in the database. ***/**/* Denotes statistical significance at the 1%/5%/10% level. T-statistics (in parentheses) are calculated using Newey-West (1987) adjusted, heteroskedasticity and serial correlation robust standard errors.

We first discuss results for the one-month holding period *($K = 1$)*, which are displayed in Panel A. Intuitively, we expect a strong influence of transaction costs on these strategies for the following reasons. First and foremost, a strategy requiring monthly rebalancing is trading-intensive and thus costly. Second, we do not expect a high level of persistence within portfolios. Persistence in this context means that a stock with abnormally high turnover in a given month continues to have abnormally high turnover in the following month. As a result, the stock might remain in the same abnormal volume portfolio (e.g., V1) from one month to the other, which reduces transaction costs.

We expect a particularly strong influence on arbitrage strategies, because transaction costs affect both long and short positions in this setting. We therefore start with these long-short (V1-V10) strategies. First, we include a one-way transaction cost of 30 basis points (bps), which is the level reported by DOMOWITZ ET AL. (2001) for institutional traders in Swiss stocks. This reduces average monthly arbitrage profits by half, from 1.59 to 0.76% (note that the profit is still significantly positive at the 5% level). It is difficult to compare these results with KANIEL ET AL'S (2007) 0.68% in a related study on the high-volume return premium for Swiss stocks (see 3.5). While these authors use the same transaction cost level, they do not explicitly calculate the influence of transaction costs via equations (3.11) to (3.14). Rather, they simply deduct 0.60% from the raw arbitrage profits of 1.28%. In our opinion, this approach underestimates the true level of transaction costs, because it either ignores the fact that transaction costs are being incurred both for buying and selling, or that they affect both long and short positions. In other words, such a 'brute force' analysis should entail a reduction of 1.20% (4 x 0.30%). Going back to Table 6.9: when increasing the transaction cost level to 50 bps, the average arbitrage profits remain positive (0.21%), but at statistically insignificant levels. Finally, at a one-way transaction cost level above 50 bps, the arbitrage profits are driven to zero. Although our results only provide an indication, it thus seems that transaction costs might be prohibitive for the theoretically appealing $K = 1$ arbitrage strategy, particularly for private investors. Next, we analyze the performance of the long-only high abnormal volume portfolio (V1 in Table 6.9). For simplicity, we assume that no transaction costs are being incurred for the buy and hold index investments in the SPI and the equal-weighted index (EW). The findings are similar to the arbitrage strategies. While the long position itself remains positive even upon inclusion of a one-way transaction cost of 100 basis points, the strategy ceases to outperform the benchmarks at cost levels around 50 bps. In sum, our results confirm that the $K = 1$ strategies are difficult to practically implement due to a high level of rebalancing and a relatively low persistence of portfolio affiliation in consecutive holding periods.

We now turn to the $K = 12$ months strategies (reported in Table 6.9, Panel B) that are only rebalanced annually, which implies a much lower level of transaction costs. These long-short (V1-V10) profits remain positive across all levels of transaction costs investigated, at statistically significant levels up to a one-way cost of 100 basis points. But a monthly average return of 0.39% (at the 100 bps cost level) is much smaller than the initial 0.69% and it is unclear whether this represents an attractive investment opportunity (particularly when additionally considering the discussion of Figure 6.1 (b) that a few extreme return months at the beginning of the time-series strongly influence the size of this premium). Finally, the long-only abnormal volume strategy continues to outperform both reference indices across all horizons investigated, mostly at statistically significant levels. Again, however, recall the discussion of Figure 6.2 (b) above (6.1.1) that a few return months strongly influence the size of this premium, even more than for arbitrage strategies.

In a next step, Table 6.10 shows the influence of transaction costs on abnormal volume arbitrage profits within small firms ('Small'), low book-to-market firms ('Low BM') and loser stocks ('Losers'). The results of these two-way sorted portfolios are qualitatively similar to the one-way sorted returns. On the one hand, transaction costs strongly influence strategies that require monthly rebalancing (Panel A). On the other hand, results remain persistently significant across most levels of transaction costs for strategies that are only rebalanced annually (Panel B). For the interested reader, Table A10 in the appendix separately analyzes the performance of long-only abnormal volume strategies within small companies upon the inclusion of different levels of transaction costs.

Table 6.10: Inclusion of Transaction Costs to Two-Way Sorted Abnormal Turnover Arbitrage Strategies

	Transaction cost level (one-way costs)				
Volume portfolio	0.0%	0.3%	0.5%	1.0%	1.5%
Panel A: Equal-weighted decile portfolios (V1-V10), reference period J = 12, holding period K = 1					
One-way, Long-Short	**1.59**	**0.76**	0.21	-1.16	-2.53
	(4.220)***	**(2.025)****	(0.568)	(-3.033)***	(-6.558)***
Small, Long-Short	**2.56**	**1.68**	1.09	-0.37	-1.84
	(3.431)***	**(2.236)****	(1.499)	(-0.485)	(-2.365)**
Low BM, Long-Short	**1.99**	**1.16**	0.61	-0.76	-2.13
	(3.533)***	**(2.050)****	(1.074)	(-1.320)	(-3.638)***
Losers, Long-Short	**1.44**	0.53	-0.07	-1.57	-3.08
	(2.394)**	(0.881)	(-0.112)	(-2.534)**	(-4.862)***
Panel B: Equal-weighted decile portfolios (V1-V10), reference period J = 12, holding period K = 12					
One-way, Long-Short	**0.69**	**0.60**	**0.54**	**0.39**	0.24
	(3.025)***	**(2.635)*****	**(2.375)****	**(1.722)***	(1.067)
Small, Long-Short	**0.99**	**0.89**	**0.83**	**0.67**	0.51
	(2.742)***	**(2.484)****	**(2.312)****	**(1.878)***	(1.442)
Low BM, Long-Short	**0.84**	**0.75**	**0.69**	**0.54**	**0.39**
	(3.609)***	**(3.219)*****	**(2.959)*****	**(2.309)****	**(1.659)***
Losers, Long-Short	**0.66**	**0.56**	**0.50**	0.33	0.17
	(2.667)***	**(2.273)****	**(2.010)****	(1.351)	(0.690)

This table reports average monthly returns to selected practical abnormal turnover decile arbitrage strategies (V1-V10) within specific control variable tercile portfolios ('Small', 'Low BM', 'Losers'; as reported in 6.1.1) after the inclusion of transaction costs. For comparison, the table also includes one-way sorted abnormal turnover decile arbitrage strategies ('One-way'). The calculation assumes the same level of transaction costs for long and short investments. The included one-way (i.e., buying or selling) transaction costs correspond to round-trip costs of 0.6%, 1%, 2%, 3%. The calculation of transaction costs is described in detail in 3.3.3.3. ***/**/* Denotes statistical significance at the 1%/5%/10% level. T-statistics (in parentheses) are calculated using Newey-West (1987) adjusted, heteroskedasticity and serial correlation robust standard errors.

Some final remarks regarding transaction costs: the main objective of this analysis was to get a feeling for the influence of transaction costs on abnormal volume strategy returns. In very general terms our results suggest the following:

- As expected, the inclusion of transaction costs has a strong influence on $K = 1$ month strategy returns, which makes them unfeasible for any one-way cost level above 50 basis points. Most probably this result implies that the abnormal volume premium is not profitably marketable via one-month holding period strategies, at least for most types of traders.

- Returns to the 12-month $(K = 12)$ holding period strategies, on the other hand, remain more stable across different levels of transaction costs investigated. But the question whether the concrete return levels are attractive for a particular investor (profile) is not in scope of this analysis.

6.1.3.2 Scalability Tests

In a next step, we report results of two additional robustness checks addressing the question of *scalability*, which is particularly important for institutional investors. First, recall that we generally analyze equal-weighted portfolios. As an alternative, we consider the construction of value-weighted portfolios with initial CHF allocation to each stock in a portfolio depending on the weight of its market capitalization in relation to the total market capitalization of all stocks in the respective portfolio. Table 6.11 compares the returns of these two portfolio construction methods.[193] The results reveal that most abnormal volume profits remain statistically significant in a value-weighted setting. However, a general conclusion as to which of the two methods is more attractive is difficult, because it seems to depend on the specific strategy or holding period considered. At first, the significant value-weighted returns are surprising given results in Table 4.42 that the abnormal volume premium is not statistically significant for large firms. At the same time, descriptive statistics in Table 4.40 reveal that the abnormal volume strategies

[193] The table again reports *decile* portfolio returns, because the focus is on particularly profitable portfolio strategies.

generally do not invest in the very large stocks. Additionally, there is a methodological difference regarding the measure of market capitalization used.[194]

Table 6.11: Abnormal Turnover Decile Portfolios in Practical Setting, Value-Weighted

	Equal-weighted portfolios; Varying holding periods K		Value-weighted portfolios; Varying holding periods K	
Volume portfolio	K = 1	K = 12	K = 1	K = 12
Panel A: One-way sorts, reference period J = 12				
Long (V1)	1.72	1.36	1.80	0.97
Short (V10)	0.14	0.67	-0.13	0.35
Long-Short (V1-V10)	**1.59**	**0.69**	**1.93**	**0.62**
	(4.220)* **	**(3.025)*** **	**(3.001)*** **	**(2.184)** **
Panel B: Two-way sorts, reference period J = 12				
Small, Long-Short (V1-V10)	**2.56**	**0.99**	**3.04**	**1.12**
	(3.431)* **	**(2.742)*** **	**(3.876)*** **	**(2.996)*** **
Low BM, Long-Short (V1-V10)	**1.99**	**0.84**	**1.56**	**0.97**
	(3.533)* **	**(3.609)*** **	**(2.397)** **	**(3.323)*** **
Losers, Long-Short (V1-V10)	**1.44**	**0.66**	1.06	**0.98**
	(2.394) **	**(2.667)*** **	(1.037)	**(1.873)***

This table compares average returns of *equal-weighted* practical abnormal turnover decile portfolios (as reported in 6.1.1) with average returns of *value-weighted* practical abnormal turnover portfolios. Details on value-weighted return calculation are described in 3.3.3.3. V1 and V10 are portfolios containing long stock positions, while V1-V10 are zero-cost arbitrage strategies. ***/**/* Denotes statistical significance at the 1%/5%/10% level. T-statistics (in parentheses) are calculated using Newey-West (1987) adjusted, heteroskedasticity and serial correlation robust standard errors.

[194] Recall from 3.2 that we only include those stocks in our analysis that represent a company's main share class. But for the calculation of market capitalizations we integrate multiple classes into the main share class. The reason is that, up to this point, we use market capitalizations mainly to investigate respectively control for a potential *'company size'* effect. In the scalability test, however, it is important to use free-float adjusted *market capitalizations of the individual (main share class) stock*, because this defines the maximum level of potential investments in the respective stock. These different definitions of market capitalization could influence results.

As a second scalability test, we exclude the smallest firms from the analysis. Regarding the $K = 1$ month holding period strategy, the related robustness checks in a regression (Table 4.22) and a portfolio-based context (Table 4.42) suggest that this should decrease strategy returns.[195] Results reported in Table 6.12, Panel A, confirm this. The 12-month holding period returns, on the other hand, remain at comparable levels when disregarding all stocks with a market capitalization below CHF 100 million (Table 6.12, Panel B). We do not repeat this analysis for the two-way sorted decile strategies ('Small', 'Low BM', 'Losers'), because the exclusion of the smallest stocks leads to some situations with empty portfolios.

Table 6.12: Abnormal Turnover Decile Portfolios in Practical Setting, Exclusion of Micro Cap Stocks

Volume portfolio	Panel A: No market cap lower limit	Panel B: Market cap lower limit CHF 50 million	Panel C: Market cap lower limit CHF 100 million
Panel A: Equal-weighted decile portfolios, reference period $J = 12$, holding period $K = 1$			
Long (V1)	1.72	1.64	1.34
Short (V10)	0.14	0.25	0.17
Long-Short (V1-V10)	**1.59** **(4.220)*** **	**1.39** **(3.582)*** **	**1.17** **(2.744)*** **
Panel B: Equal-weighted decile portfolios, reference period $J = 12$, holding period $K = 12$			
Long (V1)	1.36	1.40	1.25
Short (V10)	0.67	0.63	0.57
Long-Short (V1-V10)	**0.69** **(3.025)*** **	**0.77** **(2.899)*** **	**0.68** **(2.689)*** **

This table compares average returns of equal-weighted practical abnormal turnover decile portfolios (Panel A; as reported in 6.1.1) with average returns of the same portfolios but excluding stocks with a market capitalization below CHF 50 million (Panel B) and CHF 100 million (Panel C). V1 and V10 are portfolios containing long stock positions, while V1-V10 are zero-cost arbitrage strategies. ***/**/* Denotes statistical significance at the 1%/5%/10% level. T-statistics (in parentheses) are calculated using Newey-West (1987) adjusted, heteroskedasticity and serial correlation robust standard errors.

[195] However, we face the same methodological discrepancies discussed in the value-weighted analysis.

6.1.3.3 More Realistic Calculation of Long-Short Profits in Multi-Month Setting

The results so far suggest that abnormal volume arbitrage strategies with annual rebalancing *(K = 12)* might be attractive for some investors, even after considering transaction costs. We thus perform one additional analysis, namely the *more realistic calculation of profits of long-short strategies in a multi-month holding period* setting. Details of this calculation are described in 3.3.3.3. The main idea is the following: so far, monthly returns to zero-cost arbitrage strategies are calculated as the time-series of the monthly return difference between the long portfolio and the short portfolio. In a multi-month holding period setting (i.e., $K > 1$), however, LIU/STRONG (2008) note that the long and short sides increase or decrease with changes in the market values of the long and short portfolios. In this particular test, we account for this fact via equation (3.17). Results in Table 6.13 seem to confirm LIU/STRONG (2008) who state that the simple return difference generally underestimates the true profits if the phenomenon under examination (in our case the abnormal volume premium) holds. In fact, the first column shows that the 'more realistic' arbitrage profits are much higher for all strategies considered except the 'Losers' strategy (which, as previous analysis in this chapter suggests, does not seem particularly attractive from a practicability point of view anyway). For example, returns to the more diversified one-way sorted decile strategy ('One-Way') increase by more than 50%, while the abnormal volume decile strategy within small companies even doubles (from average monthly returns of 0.99% to 1.99%). But at the same time, the statistical significance of these strategies decreases.

A detailed investigation of the large differences in the 'Small' strategy reveals that these are mainly caused by an individual stock investment: at the beginning of March 1999, the stock 'Distefora' (market capitalization of CHF 68 million) is included among only five stocks in the high abnormal turnover portfolio (V1). In the following year, this stock has five extreme return months. First, its returns in March and April 1999 are 168 and 123% respectively. The consequences for the remaining 10 holding period months (until rebalancing) are the following:

- The V1 portfolio return is almost entirely driven by this one stock return;
- At the same time, the long-short V1-V10 portfolio return is almost exclusively driven by the long (V1) position;
- And finally, almost the entire monthly return across the $K = 12$ cohorts is driven by the one investment cohort that includes 'Distefora' in the V1 portfolio.

In this situation, the extreme subsequent 'Distefora' returns of 50, 55, and 50% in December 1999 as well as in January and February 2000 strongly influence overall results. In fact, excluding these five portfolio returns from the overall time-series reduces the average 'realistic' arbitrage profit to the 'Small' strategy from 1.99 to below 1% per month. Note that these five strategy months also influence results in the 'simple' practical calculation as illustrated above, 6.1.1, in Figure 6.1 (b) (and Figure 6.2 (b) for the long-only V1 position). However, the effect is accentuated in the context of the 'more realistic calculation of arbitrage profits' because of the increasing weight given to the long position in equation (3.17).

To conclude, our takeaways from the results in Table 6.13 and the subsequent discussion are the following: first, results seem to confirm that the *real long-short profits are generally higher in reality than suggested by simply taking the return difference* between long and short positions. This is generally positive regarding practical implementation. But at the same time, the extreme differences in Table 6.13 probably result from our concrete dataset. In that sense, the *high returns in Panel B should be handled with care*. Building on that, we feel that an *investment in the individually analyzed two-way sorted abnormal volume strategies* ('Small', 'Low BM', 'Losers') is *questionable from a diversification respectively risk point of view*, despite the attractive average returns suggested by our data. The reason is that these strategies only contain 1/30 of stocks per cross-section (in our case this can be as low as four stocks per portfolio). As a consequence, returns to single stocks within the portfolio can significantly influence results, in both positive (see 'Small' strategy) and negative directions.

Table 6.13: More Realistic Long-Short Calculation of Abnormal Turnover Decile Strategies

	Transaction cost level (one-way costs)				
Volume portfolio	0.0%	0.3%	0.5%	1.0%	1.5%
Panel A: 'Simple' long short (V1-V10), reference period J = 12, holding period K = 12					
One-Way	**0.69**	**0.60**	**0.54**	**0.39**	0.24
	(3.025)***	**(2.635)*****	**(2.375)****	**(1.722)***	(1.067)
Small companies	**0.99**	**0.89**	**0.83**	**0.67**	0.51
	(2.742)***	**(2.484)****	**(2.312)****	**(1.878)***	(1.442)
Low BM companies	**0.84**	**0.75**	**0.69**	**0.54**	**0.39**
	(3.609)***	**(3.219)*****	**(2.959)*****	**(2.309)****	**(1.659)***
Loser stocks	**0.66**	**0.56**	**0.50**	0.33	0.17
	(2.667)***	**(2.273)****	**(2.010)****	(1.351)	(0.690)
Panel B: 'More realistic' long short (V1-V10), reference period J = 12, holding period K = 12					
One-Way	**1.09**	**0.99**	**0.92**	0.76	0.59
	(2.234)**	**(2.045)****	**(1.916)***	(1.587)	(1.247)
Small companies	**1.99**	1.88	1.68	1.62	1.17
	(1.777)*	(1.615)	(1.614)	(1.487)	(1.171)
Low BM companies	**1.56**	**1.46**	**1.39**	**1.23**	**1.06**
	(3.415)***	**(3.197)*****	**(3.050)*****	**(2.680)*****	**(2.308)****
Loser stocks	**0.90**	**0.80**	**0.73**	0.51	0.38
	(2.050)**	**(1.818)***	**(1.662)***	(1.180)	(0.868)

This table compares average returns of equal-weighted practical abnormal turnover decile arbitrage strategies (V1-V10; Panel A) with average returns using a more realistic calculation method for long-short profits (Panel B). Details on this calculation method are described in 3.3.3.3. Returns are only reported for the $K = 12$ months holding period, because results of the two calculation methods are identical for $K = 1$ month. ***/**/* Denotes statistical significance at the 1%/5%/10% level. T-statistics (in parentheses) are calculated using Newey-West (1987) adjusted, heteroskedasticity and serial correlation robust standard errors.

6.1.4 Performance in Selected Market States

A final set of tests on the basis of the practical abnormal volume portfolios is the analysis of the strategy performance in selected market states. This investigation is divided into three parts, namely a *robustness check of the time-stability of portfolio returns*, the *feasibility of simple dynamic portfolio strategies building on these insights*, and a *stress test of our results in 2008*. Based on the last section's findings we abstain from specifically investigating two-way sorted abnormal volume strategies but focus on the more diversified one-way sorts. At the same time, we are aware that these two-way sorts would significantly increase returns to the dynamic strategies presented below. But our goal is to provide a general outlook on a potentially attractive implementation of insights gained throughout our research and not to present the most profitable strategy attainable in our concrete data set (which would be data mining).

6.1.4.1 Robustness Check of Time-Stability of Portfolio Returns

We start by performing a general robustness check of the stability of portfolio returns across different market regimes. For conciseness, we only report return differences (between high and low abnormal volume portfolios). First, we analyze the time-stability of the $K = 1$ strategies, which is directly comparable to base strategy results discussed in chapter 5. These results are reported in Table 6.14 (Panel A) and Table 6.15 (Panel A). The main findings regarding time-stability are identical in the base and the practical setting, namely:

- A significantly higher abnormal volume premium in the first sub-period;
- A particularly strong abnormal volume effect in down markets and high (forecasted) volatility regimes;
- Low abnormal volume premiums in the low volatility and high volume regimes, which both only existed in the more recent sub-period.

Table 6.14: Abnormal Turnover Portfolios in Practical Setting, Performance across Market Regimes (Part 1)

	Panel A: Reference period $J = 12$; Holding period $K = 1$		Panel B: Reference period $J = 12$; Holding period $K = 12$	
Volume portfolio	V1-V5	V1-V10	V1-V5	V1-V10
Full (02/1998 - 08/2008)	1.09	1.59	0.51	0.69
	(3.586)***	(4.220)***	(2.857)***	(3.025)***
Subperiod 1 (02/1998 - 11/2002)	1.85	2.39	0.89	1.16
	(4.020)***	(4.458)***	(2.742)***	(2.750)***
Subperiod 2 (12/2002 - 08/2008)	0.46	0.91	0.18	0.30
	(1.366)	(1.934)*	(1.362)	(1.690)*
Bull markets	1.06	1.40	0.62	0.82
	(2.617)**	(2.831)***	(2.498)**	(2.512)**
Bear markets	1.15	1.91	0.30	0.47
	(2.569)**	(3.625)***	(1.482)	(1.833)*
Up market states	0.73	0.95	0.41	0.50
	(2.154)**	(2.550)**	(1.687)*	(1.601)
Down market states	**1.86**	**2.92**	**0.70**	**1.09**
	(3.586)***	**(4.591)*****	**(3.998)*****	**(5.203)*****
Positive market return months	1.25	1.65	0.84	1.04
	(3.515)***	(3.326)***	(3.857)***	(4.005)***
Negative market return months	0.83	1.49	-0.05	0.12
	(1.903)*	(2.615)**	(-0.220)	(0.349)

This table reports average monthly returns to selected practical abnormal turnover arbitrage strategies (reported in 6.1.1) in different sub-sets of the complete return time-series (02/1998 - 08/2008), as defined in 3.3.2. V1-V5 (V1-V10) are zero-cost arbitrage strategies consisting of long positions in stocks with the highest 20% (10%) abnormal turnover and short positions of equal size in stock with the lowest 20% (10%) abnormal turnover. ***/**/* Denotes statistical significance at the 1%/5%/10% level. T-statistics (in parentheses) are calculated using Newey-West (1987) adjusted, heteroskedasticity and serial correlation robust standard errors.

Table 6.15: Abnormal Turnover Portfolios in Practical Setting, Performance across Market Regimes (Part 2)

	Panel A: Reference period $J = 12$; Holding period $K = 1$		Panel B: Reference period $J = 12$; Holding period $K = 12$	
Volume portfolio	V1-V5	V1-V10	V1-V5	V1-V10
Low volatility	0.18 (0.429)	0.42 (1.014)	0.08 (0.569)	0.13 (0.827)
Normal volatility	0.91 (2.488)**	1.42 (3.035)***	0.69 (2.016)**	0.95 (2.076)**
High volatility	2.42 (4.201)***	3.16 (4.434)***	0.67 (2.771)***	0.90 (3.148)***
Low forecasted volatility	-0.11 (-0.281)	-0.16 (-0.549)	0.09 (0.681)	0.21 (1.109)
Normal forecasted volatility	0.96 (2.701)***	1.40 (3.068)***	0.47 (1.647)	0.59 (1.579)
High forecasted volatility	**2.52** **(4.407)*****	**3.64** **(5.506)*****	**0.96** **(6.145)*****	**1.39** **(6.900)*****
Normal Swiss franc volume	1.24 (3.652)***	1.68 (3.931)***	0.63 (3.252)***	0.85 (3.375)***
High Swiss franc volume	0.12 (0.230)	0.98 (1.540)	-0.36 (-1.605)	-0.39 (-1.173)
Normal market turnover	1.63 (4.446)***	2.13 (4.438)***	0.75 (3.164)***	1.00 (3.226)***
High market turnover	-0.03 (-0.091)	0.48 (1.085)	-0.04 (-0.287)	0.02 (0.076)

This table reports average monthly returns to selected practical abnormal turnover arbitrage strategies (reported in 6.1.1) in different sub-sets of the complete return time-series (02/1998 - 08/2008), as defined in 3.3.2. V1-V5 (V1-V10) are zero-cost arbitrage strategies consisting of long positions in stocks with the highest 20% (10%) abnormal turnover and short positions of equal size in stock with the lowest 20% (10%) abnormal turnover. ***/**/* Denotes statistical significance at the 1%/5%/10% level. T-statistics (in parentheses) are calculated using Newey-West (1987) adjusted, heteroskedasticity and serial correlation robust standard errors.

Recall that we do not analyze the time-stability of multi-month holding period strategies in chapter 5. We therefore perform an additional robustness check of the validity of the $K = 1$ results. The corresponding 12-month holding period returns across market regimes are displayed in Table 6.14, Panel B, and Table 6.15, Panel B. We report the simple return difference (instead of the 'more realistic long-short calculation), because we feel that this method is better suited to show the general dynamics of the strategy. Results reveal some differences to the one-month holding period. This is not surprising, because we show throughout the empirical tests that the dynamics of the abnormal volume effect are mostly driven by the first return month. At the same time, the main findings remain identical, namely a much stronger abnormal volume premium in the first sub-period, in down markets, in high (forecasted) volatility phases, and in the normal volume regimes.

As mentioned above, the high abnormal volume premiums in down markets and high forecasted volatility regimes are particularly interesting, because these two states of the market are known to investors at the time when an investment decision is taken. Before discussing dynamic strategies building on these insights, we want to ensure that the abnormal volume premiums in these specific market regimes remain strong when accounting for previously documented market, size, value, and momentum risk factors. Table 6.16 reports intercept coefficient estimates ('Alphas') of regressions of excess returns to abnormal volume based portfolios strategies on the time-series of these Carhart risk factor premiums in down market states respectively high forecasted volatility regimes. The results reveal that the risk-adjusted abnormal volume premiums remain strongly significant in these market phases, at approximately the same levels as the raw returns.

Table 6.16: Abnormal Turnover Portfolios in Practical Setting, Selected Risk-Adjusted Returns

	Carhart Alphas Reference period *J* = *12;* Holding period *K* = *1*		Carhart Alphas Reference period *J* = *12;* Holding period *K* = *12*	
Volume portfolio	V1-V5	V1-V10	V1-V5	V1-V10
Down market states	1.97	3.24	0.78	1.19
	(3.936)***	(4.587)***	(4.652)***	(5.081)***
High forecasted volatility	2.43	3.65	0.90	1.37
	(4.901)***	(5.242)***	(4.820)***	(5.691)***

This table reports estimated intercept coefficients of regressions of monthly excess returns of practical abnormal turnover arbitrage strategies in selected market regimes (defined in 3.3.2) on the four Swiss factor premiums RMRF, SMB, HML, and UMD (i.e., Carhart factors, described in 3.3.3.2). ***/**/* Denotes statistical significance at the 1%/5%/10% level. T-statistics (in parentheses) are calculated using Newey-West (1987) adjusted, heteroskedasticity and serial correlation robust standard errors.

6.1.4.2 Outlook: Dynamic Portfolio Strategies

In a next step, we present simple dynamic portfolio strategies on the basis of down market and high forecasted volatility regimes. We first discuss *dynamic down market strategies*. Because the abnormal volume premium is particularly strong in down markets, we invest in the V1-V10 arbitrage strategy in this regime.[196] In up markets, however, we take a buy and hold position in the hypothetical equal-weighted index constructed from the stocks in the database, EW. The performance and risk attributes of this *dynamic down market strategy (V1-V10)* are reported in the first column of Table 6.17. This strategy is compared with three benchmarks: the first benchmark, *base strategy (V1-V10)*, is the practical abnormal turnover arbitrage strategy across both up and down markets. The second benchmark, *base strategy (EW)*, is the buy and hold investment in the equal-weighted index across the entire time-series. Finally, there is the possibility that the outperformance of our dynamic strategy is solely caused by the fact that it is not invested in the index in down markets, and not by the superior performance of the ab-

[196] We only analyze the $K = 1$ month holding period strategy, because the abnormal volume effect is more pronounced in this setting.

normal volume arbitrage strategy itself. We control for this via the third benchmark, labeled *dynamic down market strategy (EW)*. This strategy invests in the equal-weighted index in up markets and in the risk-free rate in down markets.

Table 6.17: Evaluation of Dynamic Down Market Strategy (Reference Index: EW)

	Dynamic down market strategies		Base strategies	
	V1-V10	EW	V1-V10	EW
Average return (ann.)	26.36%	14.39%	19.72%	10.74%
Standard deviation (ann.)	13.99%	11.26%	13.09%	16.28%
Sharpe ratio	1.77	1.14	1.39	0.56
Correlation (EW)	0.60	0.71	0.19	1.00
% positive months	72%	81%	65%	66%
Maximum drawdown	-22.5%	-22.5%	-13.7%	-49.7%
Months in drawdown	2	2	13	31
Months of recovery	9	15	5	23
Average monthly return	2.05%	1.18%	1.59%	0.96%
Median monthly return	1.79%	0.32%	1.07%	1.57%
Maximum monthly return	12.54%	11.74%	12.54%	11.74%
Minimum monthly return	-14.43%	-14.43%	-8.86%	-14.54%

This table compares performance and risk attributes of four different strategies. *Dynamic down market strategy (V1-V10)* is a strategy that is long in EW in up markets and long-short in the practical abnormal turnover decile arbitrage strategy in down markets (up and down markets are defined in 3.3.2.3.2). *Dynamic down market strategy (EW)* is a strategy long in EW in up markets and long in the risk-free rate in down markets. *Base strategy (V1-V10)* is the pratical abnormal turnover decile arbitrage strategy across the complete return time-series (02/1998 - 08/2008) and *base strategy (EW)* is the return time-series of a hypothetical, equal-weighted index constructed from the stocks in the database. The V1-V10 strategies are rebalanced monthly *(K = 1)*.

Based on the results in Table 6.17, the dynamic *down market strategy (V1-V10)* seems promising. Most importantly, its average returns are by far the highest, while the volatility is in line with the benchmarks. This results in a significantly higher Sharpe ratio of 1.77, which is for example three times the size of a 'static' buy and hold investment in the equal-weighted index. Additionally, the comparison with the *dynamic down market strategy (EW)* shows that this outperformance is not solely caused by the fact that we are not invested in the index in down markets. Finally, a profitable implementation is more likely for the *dynamic down market strategy (V1-V10)* than for the *base abnormal volume arbitrage strategy* due to the lower level of transaction costs. To understand this, recall that the dynamic strategy invests in the less trading intensive buy and hold strategy in up markets, which are relatively persistent phases (see Figure 3.5), while the static strategy invests in the trading-intensive $K = 1$ strategy across the entire time-series. In Figure 6.3, we graphically show the development of an initial CHF 100 investment in the four strategies.

Figure 6.3: NAVs of Dynamic Down Market Strategy and Benchmarks (EW-Based)

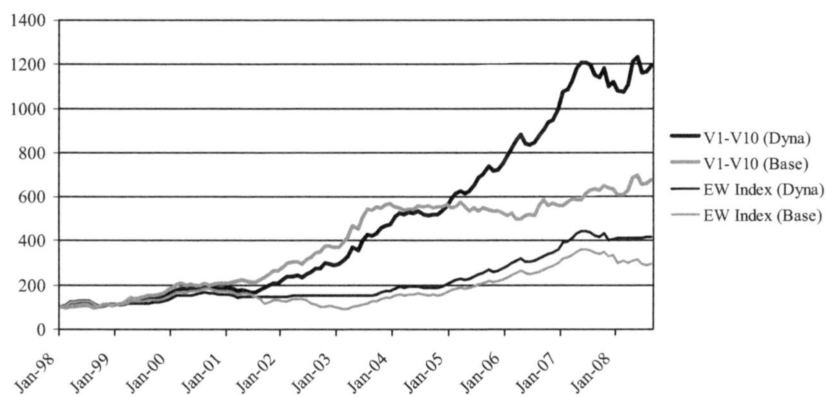

It becomes clearly visible that the *dynamic down market strategy (V1-V10)* profits both from the abnormal volume effect in down markets and the high long-only index returns in up markets. Because an investment in the 'hypothetical' equal-weighted index is not readily available, however, we repeat the dynamic down market strategies using buy and hold positions in the Swiss Performance Index as an alternative investment in up markets. The results reported in Table A11 and Figure A1 in the appendix reveal similar dynamics but at a smaller scale, which is as expected since the SPI strongly underperforms the equal-weighted index in our time-series.

As an alternative to the dynamic down market strategy, we evaluate the performance of a *dynamic volatility strategy (V1-V10)*, thereby trying to profit from the fact that the abnormal volume premium is particularly pronounced in high forecasted volatility regimes. More concretely, this strategy invests in the V1-V10 abnormal volume arbitrage strategy in months with high forecasted volatility and in the EW index in the remaining months. Results of the dynamic volatility strategy and the three corresponding benchmarks are reported in Figure 6.4 and Table 6.18.

Figure 6.4: NAVs of Dynamic High Forecasted Volatility Strategy and Benchmarks (EW-Based)

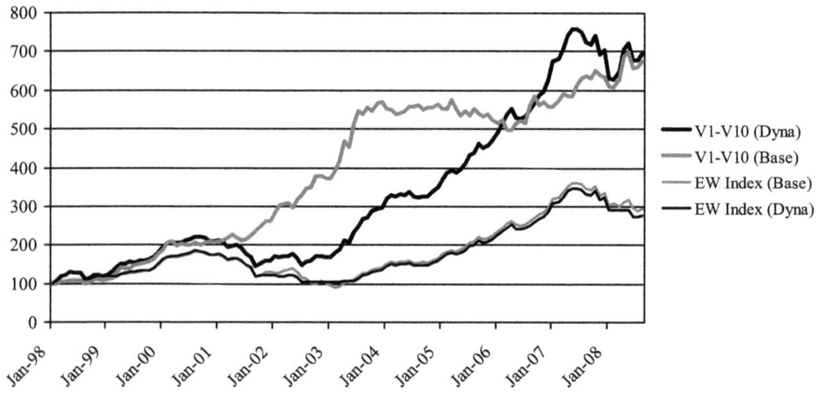

Its performance and risk attributes are slightly less promising than the dynamic down market strategy, but this could also be caused by our concrete dataset.[197] Again, we repeat the analysis using the SPI as an alternative buy and hold investment (in phases with low or normal forecasted market volatility). The results are included in the appendix for the interested reader (Table A12, Figure A2).

[197] For example, 41 of the total of 127 return months are in down markets, but only 28 months are in the high forecasted volatility regime.

Table 6.18: Evaluation of Dynamic High Forecasted Volatility Strategy (Reference Index: EW)

	Dynamic volatility strategies		Base strategies	
	V1-V10	EW	V1-V10	EW
Average return (ann.)	20.15%	10.08%	19.72%	10.74%
Standard deviation (ann.)	15.83%	13.99%	13.09%	16.28%
Sharpe ratio	1.17	0.61	1.39	0.56
Correlation (EW)	0.79	0.85	0.19	1.00
% positive months	71%	76%	65%	66%
Maximum drawdown	-35.0%	-43.5%	-13.7%	-49.7%
Months in drawdown	13	24	13	31
Months of recovery	21	34	5	23
Average monthly return	1.64%	0.88%	1.59%	0.96%
Median monthly return	1.77%	0.60%	1.07%	1.57%
Maximum monthly return	12.54%	11.74%	12.54%	11.74%
Minimum monthly return	-14.54%	-14.54%	-8.86%	-14.54%

This table compares performance and risk attributes of four different strategies. *Dynamic volatility strategy (V1-V10)* is a strategy that is long in EW in low / normal forecasted volatility regimes and long-short in the practical abnormal turnover decile arbitrage strategy in high forecasted volatility regimes (volatility regimes are defined in 3.3.2.3.3). *Dynamic volatility strategy (EW)* is a strategy long in EW in low / normal forecasted volatility regimes and long in the risk-free rate in high forecasted volatility regimes. *Base strategy (V1-V10)* is the pratical abnormal turnover decile arbitrage strategy across the complete return time-series (02/1998 - 08/2008) and *base strategy (EW)* is the return time-series of a hypothetical, equal-weighted index constructed from the stocks in the database. The V1-V10 strategies are rebalanced monthly $(K = 1)$.

Finally, we test the hypothesis that a profitable implementation is more likely for the dynamic abnormal volume strategies due to the lower level of transaction costs. For the purpose of this illustration we take the simplified view that transaction costs are only being incurred when the strategy invests in the abnormal volume strategy (i.e., in down markets or high forecasted volatility regimes). For buy and hold investments in the respective indices, however, we assume no transaction costs. As a consequence, the reported average dynamic strategy returns are slightly overstated. However, this bias is probably not very grave, because Figure 3.5 and Figure 3.7 (above, in 3.3.2.3.2 respectively in 3.3.2.3.3) show that phases of buy and hold investments (i.e., up markets respectively low / normal forecasted volatility regimes) are relatively persistent. Results for EW-based strategies, reported in Table 6.19, show that once transaction costs are included in the analysis, average returns to the dynamic strategies are dramatically higher than the simple abnormal volume arbitrage strategy ('Base Strategy', first row). The absolute size of these returns even suggests the existence of economically significant profits. However, the objective of this analysis was to give an outlook on a potentially attractive implementation of insights gained from the abnormal volume premium, despite the possibly prohibitive transaction costs involved with simple $K = 1$ month arbitrage strategies. In that sense, the exact size of the reported dynamic profits is secondary. Finally, transaction cost-adjusted SPI-strategies are included in the appendix, Table A13. The main findings remain identical.

Table 6.19: Inclusion of Transaction Costs to Dynamic Strategies (EW-Based)

	Transaction cost level (one-way costs)				
Strategy	0.0%	0.3%	0.5%	1.0%	1.5%
Base Strategy, $K = 1$ (V1-V10)	1.59	0.76	0.21	-1.16	-2.53
Dyna down market (V1-V10)	**2.05**	**1.79**	**1.62**	**1.20**	**0.77**
Dyna down market (EW)	1.18				
Dyna high vola forecast (V1-V10)	**1.64**	**1.46**	**1.35**	**1.05**	**0.76**
Dyna high vola forecast (EW)	0.88				
EW	0.96				

This table reports average monthly returns of different EW-based dynamic strategies after the inclusion of transaction costs (the calculation of transaction costs is described in detail in 3.3.3.3). These returns are compared to the practical abnormal turnover decile arbitrage strategy with monthly rebalancing ('Base Strategy') and to the return time-series of a hypothetical, equal-weighted index constructed from the stocks in the database (EW).

6.1.4.3 Stress-Test: 2008 Results

As a final test in this section, we expand the time-series to December 2008 and individually analyze the 2008 performance of abnormal volume based portfolio strategies. This serves two purposes. First, we hope to get more clarity on the drivers behind the significantly lower abnormal volume premium in more recent times. And second, it is a stress test of results in a particularly challenging market environment.

We start with the first objective. Recall from Chapter 5 that we explore two possibilities for the significantly lower abnormal volume premium in the more recent sub-period from December 2002 to August 2008. A first explanation could be that the previously discovered abnormal volume premium was only a market inefficiency and disappeared in more recent times. If this were true, we would expect a very low abnormal volume premium in 2008. The alternative explanation is that the premium is much stronger in down market phases and particularly in high volatility regimes. Because almost 60% of return months in the second sub-period are in low volatility phases, this could explain the weak strategy performance in more recent times. Since 2008 was essentially a down market (Figure 3.5) with high volatility (Figure 3.6), a strong abnormal volume premium would support the hypothesis that this volume-return relation still exists but is driven by volatility and market phase regimes. We focus on the $K = 1$ month holding period, because all our previous tests show that the dynamics of the abnormal volume effect are mostly driven by the first return month. Results reported in Table 6.20, Panel A, show that the abnormal volume premium is very high in 2008. The average monthly return difference between high and low abnormal volume portfolios (1.67 and 2.03% for quintile and decile portfolios) is even substantially higher than the overall average across the full sample period (1.09 and 1.59% respectively).

Additionally, the abnormal volume premium is even more pronounced in the fourth quarter of 2008, a particularly volatile, down market environment (4.22 and 4.39% for quintile and decile portfolios). These results thus provide further evidence that the abnormal volume premium is strongly influenced by volatility and market phase regimes, and that it still exists today.

Table 6.20: 2008 Performance of Abnormal Turnover Portfolios in Practical Setting (K = 1 Month)

	Quintile portfolios			Decile portfolios		
Return period	V1	V5	V1-V5	V1	V10	V1-V10
Panel A: 2008 performance (reference period J = 12, holding period K = 1)						
Full (02/1998 - 08/2008)	1.50	0.40	**1.09**	1.72	0.14	**1.59**
01/2008-12/2008	-2.98	-4.65	**1.67**	-2.87	-4.90	**2.03**
09/2008-12/2008	-5.55	-9.77	**4.22**	-5.39	-9.78	**4.39**
Panel B: Individual Q4 2008 months (reference period J = 12, holding period K = 1)						
September 2008	-2.93	-6.85	3.93	-1.54	-4.49	2.95
October 2008	**-12.97**	**-20.03**	**7.06**	**-10.77**	**-20.00**	**9.23**
November 2008	-3.86	-7.22	3.36	-4.04	-7.65	3.60
December 2008	-2.44	-4.97	2.53	-5.21	-6.98	1.77

This table compares average monthly returns of selected practical abnormal turnover portfolios over the time-series from February 1998 to August 2008 (reported in 6.1.1) with average monthly returns of the same strategies in 2008 (January to December), in Q4 2008 (September to December), and in individual months of Q4 2008. V1 is the portfolio containing the stocks with the highest 20% (quintiles) respectively 10% (deciles) abnormal turnover. V1, V5, V10 are portfolios containing long stock positions, while V1-V5 and V1-V10 are zero-cost arbitrage strategies.

The Q4 2008 results also address the second objective of this exercise, namely the stress test of previous results. Table 6.20, Panel B, reports abnormal volume portfolio returns in individual months from September to December 2008. October returns are of particular interest, because this was in many aspects an extreme month in the stock markets, also in Switzerland. The results show that the abnormal volume premium is particularly positive in October 2008, namely 7.06 and 9.23% for quintile and decile portfolios respectively. In that sense, the abnormal volume effect passes this small stress test. As a further remark, recall the discussion regarding market volume regimes in 5.1.3.4: while we discover that the abnormal volume premium is insignificant in high volume phases, we hypothesize that this result is mostly driven by the weak performance in low volatility regimes. The results reported in Table 6.20 provide support for this hypothesis, because the entire year 2008 was characterized by high market volume but strong abnormal volume premiums.[198]

Finally, we repeat the 2008 tests for the $K = 12$ months holding period. The results reported in Table 6.21 are not as clear.

Table 6.21: 2008 Performance of Abnormal Turnover Portfolios in Practical Setting (K = 12 Months)

	Quintile portfolios			Decile portfolios		
Return period	V1	V5	V1-V5	V1	V10	V1-V10
Panel A: 2008 performance (reference period J = 12, holding period K = 12)						
Full (02/1998 - 08/2008)	1.32	0.82	**0.51**	1.36	0.67	**0.69**
01/2008-12/2008	-3.40	-3.76	**0.36**	-3.32	-3.70	**0.38**
09/2008-12/2008	-7.04	-7.95	**0.90**	-6.82	-7.52	**0.70**
Panel B: Individual Q4 2008 months (reference period J = 12, holding period K = 12)						
September 2008	-5.92	-6.26	0.34	-5.71	-4.89	-0.82
October 2008	**-15.54**	**-16.37**	**0.83**	**-14.59**	**-15.35**	**0.76**
November 2008	-5.31	-5.40	0.09	-5.76	-6.00	0.24
December 2008	-1.40	-3.76	2.35	-1.22	-3.83	2.61

This table compares average monthly returns of selected practical abnormal turnover portfolios over the time-series from February 1998 to August 2008 (reported in 6.1.1) with average monthly returns of the same strategies in 2008 (January to December), in Q4 2008 (September to December), and in individual months of Q4 2008. V1 is the portfolio containing the stocks with the highest 20% (quintiles) respectively 10% (deciles) abnormal turnover. V1, V5, V10 are portfolios containing long stock positions, while V1-V5 and V1-V10 are zero-cost arbitrage strategies.

198 To show this, we expand the time-series for both total Swiss franc volume of trading and average market share turnover to the end of 2008. Figure A3 and Figure A4 are included in the appendix for the interested reader.

On the one hand, the abnormal volume premium is below average in 2008. In the fourth quarter and particularly in October 2008, however, this premium is above the long-term average. In our view, these results might provide important insights (respectively some doubts) regarding the practical implementation of 12-month holding period strategies. Their importance regarding the existence of the abnormal volume premium itself, however, is limited. The reason is that all analyses throughout this project show that the dynamics of the abnormal volume premium are driven by the first return month, which is better analyzed in above $K = 1$ month setting.

6.2 Other Volume Measures

In the second part of this chapter we briefly examine the other volume measures (*volume level, volume growth*, and *variability in volume*), particularly regarding their presumed relationship with market beta identified in the last chapter.

6.2.1 Volume Level

Results of the base portfolio strategies reported in chapter 4 suggest no systematic relationship between volume level and expected returns at statistically significant levels. In chapter 5, however, we identify systematic volume-return relations in selected market states. The return difference between high and low turnover stocks is significantly positive (negative) in bull (bear) market phases. At the same time, this return difference is significantly positive (negative) in months with positive (negative) market returns.

In a first step, we repeat these base strategy tests in a more practical setting. The methodological differences between base and practical strategies are described in detail in 3.3.3.1. In the previous chapter, we report test results for two different formation periods, namely the monthly average share turnover in the last $J = 1$ and $J = 12$ months. To be consistent, we calculate returns to practical strategies for the same formation periods. For conciseness, however, we only discuss the $J = 1$ strategies in detail. Results of the $J = 12$ months strategies, which are qualitatively the same, are reported in the appendix for the interested reader (Table A14). As an additional remark, recall that we do not analyze the time-stability of multi-month holding period strategies in chapter 5 for reasons outlined in the introduction of 5.1.3. In this section, however, we also report results for

12-month holding period returns, thereby performing a robustness check of the validity of the $K = 1$ results. Table 6.22 reports average monthly returns to practical turnover based portfolio strategies over $K = 1$ (Panel A) and $K = 12$ months (Panel B) holding periods.

Table 6.22: Returns to Turnover Portfolios in Practical Setting (J = 1 Month)

	Quintile portfolios				Deciles
Time-series	V1	V3	V5	V1-V5	V1-V10
Panel A: Raw returns (formation period J = 1, holding period K = 1)					
Full (02/1998 - 08/2008)	0.92	1.13	0.52	0.40	0.44
Bull markets	2.96	2.73	1.53	**1.43****	**1.89****
Bear markets	-2.68	-1.68	-1.26	**-1.42***	**-2.11*****
Positive market return months	4.06	3.17	1.50	**2.57*****	**2.87*****
Negative market return months	-4.26	-2.22	-1.09	**-3.18*****	**-3.55*****
Panel B: Raw returns (formation period J = 1, holding period K = 12)					
Full (02/1998 - 08/2008)	0.89	1.24	0.83	0.06	0.09
Bull markets	2.97	2.95	1.72	**1.25****	**1.53****
Bear markets	-2.77	-1.77	-0.75	**-2.02*****	**-2.46*****
Positive market return months	3.96	3.20	1.74	**2.22*****	**2.46*****
Negative market return months	-4.15	-1.99	-0.67	**-3.48*****	**-3.83*****

This table reports average monthly portfolio returns in different sub-sets of the complete return time-series (02/1998 - 08/2008) as defined in 3.3.2.3.2. The equal-weighted portfolios are formed monthly on the basis of stocks' monthly share turnover in the last $J = 1$ month and are rebalanced every $K = 1$ (Panel A) or $K = 12$ (Panel B) months. V1 is the portfolio containing the stocks with the highest 20% (quintiles) or 10% (deciles) share turnover in a given month. V1, V3, V5 are portfolios containing long stock positions, while V1-V5 and V1-V10 are zero-cost arbitrage strategies. ***/**/* Denotes statistical significance at the 1%/5%/10% level (t-statistics are calculated using Newey-West (1987) adjusted, heteroskedasticity and serial correlation robust standard errors).

Results of Table 6.22, in both holding periods, confirm previous findings, namely:

- There is no systematic relationship between volume level and expected returns across the full time-series;
- However, we find a significantly positive relationship in bull markets and months with positive market returns;
- In bear markets and months with negative market returns, on the other hand, the relationship between volume level and expected returns is negative.

Our hypothesis from 5.2.1 is that the main driver behind these results is that high volume stocks have significantly higher sensitivities to market returns, i.e., market betas. To test this, we regress monthly excess returns to the practical turnover quintile arbitrage strategies (V1-V5, reported in Table 6.22) on the time-series of Carhart risk factors in the Swiss stock market.[199]

Results displayed in Table 6.23 confirm our hypothesis: first, risk-adjusted portfolio returns (i.e., regression intercepts or 'Alphas') seize to be at statistically significant levels. Second, portfolio returns in bull and bear markets even change their sign (from a positive relation in bull markets to a positive relation in bear markets and vice versa) but not at statistically significant levels. Additionally, risk-adjusted returns in both positive and negative return months become negative, but only in one case at a (marginally) significant level. And most importantly, the difference in market betas between high and low volume portfolios (RMRF) is high in absolute values and strongly significantly positive across all market regimes and both holding periods investigated.

[199] Results for decile arbitrage strategies are very similar. We abstain from separately reporting them for simplicity.

Table 6.23: Time-Series Regression Coefficients of Turnover Arbitrage Strategies (J = 1 Month)

Time-series	Alpha	RMRF	SMB	HML	UMD	R2-adj
Panel A: Carhart regression coefficients (V1-V5), formation period J = 1, holding period K = 1						
Full time-series	0.11	**0.91*****	0.43*	0.11	-0.18***	0.56
Bull markets	-0.46	**0.98*****	0.62**	0.07	-0.24	0.52
Bear markets	0.94	**1.04*****	0.30	0.17	-0.12	0.54
Positive market	-0.39	**1.05*****	0.27	0.10	-0.42***	0.36
Negative market	-0.48	**0.95*****	0.67**	-0.05	0.04	0.56
Panel B: Carhart regression coefficients (V1-V5), formation period J = 1, holding period K = 12						
Full time-series	-0.26	**0.87*****	0.46**	0.15	-0.14	0.64
Bull markets	-0.45	**0.85*****	0.62**	0.10	-0.13	0.49
Bear markets	0.15	**0.99*****	0.28**	0.18	-0.07	0.75
Positive market	-0.16	**0.86*****	0.39**	0.10	-0.27**	0.57
Negative market	-1.02*	**0.84*****	0.59*	1.18	-0.03	0.56

This table reports estimated coefficients of regressions of monthly excess returns of the practical turnover quintile arbitrage strategies (V1-V5), in different sub-sets of the complete time-series (02/1998 - 08/2008) as defined in 3.3.2.3.2, on the time-series of Swiss factor premiums RMRF, SMB, HML, UMD (Carhart factors). The methodology applied is described in detail in 3.3.3.2. ***/**/* Denotes statistical significance at the 1%/5%/10% level (t-statistics are calculated using Newey-West (1987) adjusted, heteroskedasticity and serial correlation robust standard errors).

There are further interesting findings regarding the sensitivities to other risk factors besides market risk:[200] The (slightly) significantly positive coefficient estimate on the 'Small Minus Big' (SMB) factor suggests that high turnover stocks behave more like small stocks than low turnover stocks. This is surprising given results in Table 4.36 that high turnover stocks are on average significantly larger than low turnover stocks. But it is in line with LEE/SWAMINATHAN (2000). These authors do not provide an explana-

[200] We only discuss these sensitivities in the full return time-series, i.e., the first row in both panels.

tion for this finding. Additionally, LEE/SWAMINATHAN (2000) find that high volume stocks have a much more negative loading on the 'High Minus Low' (HML) factor in US markets, which implies that these stocks behave more like glamour stocks, i.e., stocks with low book-to-market ratios. We expect the same relationship, because the descriptive statistics of our base strategies (Table 4.36) show that high volume stocks have much lower book-to-market ratios in our sample. But results in Table 6.23 find that this is not the case in the Swiss stock market. In fact, the coefficient on the HML factor is even slightly positive, but not at significant levels. Finally, the significantly negative coefficient estimate on the momentum (UMD) factor suggests that high volume stocks behave more like past losers than low volume stocks. This is again counterintuitive, because the descriptive statistics in Table Table 4.36 show that high volume stocks have much higher past returns than low volume stocks.

As a final remark, note that all these results are very similar for the $J = 12$ months formation periods (reported in the appendix, Table A14 and Table A15, for the interested reader).

6.2.2 Volume Growth

The base portfolio strategies (chapter 4) suggest a positive but not systematically significant relationship between volume growth and expected returns. In chapter 5, on the other hand, we identify systematic volume-return relations in selected market states. The return difference between high and low turnover growth portfolios appears significantly positive in months with negative market returns and negative in months with positive market returns.

In a first step, we again repeat above analyses in a more practical setting (described in 3.3.3.1). To be consistent with previous tests we analyze portfolio returns for the $J = 3$ and $J = 12$ months formation periods. However, because state-dependent return differences in chapter 5 are particularly strong when using average turnover growth over the past *12 months*, we only report these results. But the main findings of the $J = 3$ months formation period, displayed in Table A16 in the appendix, are very similar. Additionally, we also show results for 12-month holding period strategies as a robustness check of the validity of the $K = 1$ month results. Table 6.24 reports average monthly returns to practical turnover growth based portfolio strategies over $K = 1$ (Panel A) and $K = 12$ months (Panel B) holding periods.

Table 6.24: Returns to Turnover Growth Portfolios in Practical Setting (J = 12 Months)

	Quintile portfolios				Deciles
Time-series	V1	V3	V5	V1-V5	V1-V10
Panel A: Raw returns (formation period $J = 12$, holding period $K = 1$)					
Full (02/1998 - 08/2008)	1.12	1.09	0.52	**0.60***	**0.69***
Positive market return months	2.38	3.37	3.34	**-0.96*****	**-1.13*****
Negative market return months	-0.95	-2.66	-4.12	**3.17*****	**3.69*****
Panel B: Raw returns (formation period $J = 12$, holding period $K = 12$)					
Full (02/1998 - 08/2008)	1.09	1.23	0.61	0.47	0.36
Positive market return months	2.24	3.37	3.15	**-0.90*****	**-1.28*****
Negative market return months	-0.81	-2.27	-3.55	**2.74*****	**3.07*****

This table reports average monthly portfolio returns in different sub-sets of the complete return time-series (02/1998 - 08/2008) as defined in 3.3.2.3.2. The equal-weighted portfolios are formed monthly on the basis of stocks' average turnover growth in the last $J = 12$ months and are rebalanced every $K = 1$ (Panel A) or $K = 12$ (Panel B) months. V1 is the portfolio containing the stocks with the highest 20% (quintiles) or 10% (deciles) turnover growth in a given month. V1, V3, V5 are portfolios containing long stock positions, while V1-V5 and V1-V10 are zero-cost arbitrage strategies. ***/**/* Denotes statistical significance at the 1%/5%/10% level (t-statistics are calculated using Newey-West (1987) adjusted, heteroskedasticity and serial correlation robust standard errors).

These results confirm previous findings, namely:

- A slightly positive but non-systematic relationship between volume growth and expected returns over the full time-series;
- A significantly negative relationship in months with positive market returns and a particularly significant positive relationship in months with negative market returns.

Regarding this second point, our hypothesis is that the root-cause of this result is that high volume growth stocks have lower market betas. We test this via regressions of practical quintile portfolio returns on the time-series of Carhart risk factors in the Swiss stock market.[201] Results displayed in Table 6.25 confirm our hypothesis.

Table 6.25: Time-Series Regression Coefficients of Turnover Growth Arbitrage Strategies (J =12 Months)

Time-series	Alpha	RMRF	SMB	HML	UMD	R2-adj
Panel A: Carhart regression coefficients (V1-V5), formation period J = 12, holding period K = 1						
Full time-series	**0.51****	**-0.46*****	0.23	0.04	0.11*	0.50
Positive market	0.39	**-0.41****	0.13	-0.04	0.05	0.14
Negative market	0.49	**-0.40*****	0.37**	0.15	0.16**	0.48
Panel B: Carhart regression coefficients (V1-V5), formation period J = 12, holding period K = 12						
Full time-series	0.28	**-0.38*****	0.30***	0.07	0.18***	0.59
Positive market	0.42	**-0.44*****	0.22**	-0.02	0.21***	0.34
Negative market	0.32	**-0.32*****	0.43***	0.25*	0.14***	0.51

This table reports estimated coefficients of regressions of monthly excess returns of the practical turnover growth quintile arbitrage strategies (V1-V5), in different sub-sets of the complete time-series (02/1998 - 08/2008) as defined in 3.3.2.3.2, on the time-series of Swiss factor premiums RMRF, SMB, HML, UMD (Carhart factors). The methodology applied is described in detail in 3.3.3.2. ***/**/* Denotes statistical significance at the 1%/5%/10% level (t-statistics are calculated using Newey-West (1987) adjusted, heteroskedasticity and serial correlation robust standard errors).

The difference in market betas between high and low volume growth portfolios (coefficient estimate of RMRF) is strongly significantly negative across all market regimes and both holding periods investigated. Additionally, the slightly positive risk-adjusted returns (i.e., regression intercepts or 'Alphas') in months with positive market returns show that the negative raw returns in this market regime are strongly driven by the lower market betas of high volume growth stocks. Interestingly, risk-adjusted strategy returns

[201] We do not explicitly report results of decile arbitrage strategies. However, these results are qualitatively identical.

('Alphas') remain significantly positive over the full time-series for the one-month holding period (first row in Panel A). However, this again does not seem systematic – risk-adjusted returns are insignificant in both positive and negative market return months. Additionally, the size of the raw portfolio returns in Table 6.24 implies that this insight could not be profitably implemented anyway.

The results are similar for the $J = 3$ months formation periods (reported in the appendix, Table A17, for the interested reader). The risk-adjusted strategy returns over the entire time-series are even slightly more significant, but it seems again that the raw returns (in the appendix, Table A16) are not profitably marketable once we include transaction costs.

6.2.3 Variability in Volume

As a final test, we discuss practical strategies formed on the basis of coefficient of variation in turnover. Results of the base portfolio strategies reported in Chapter 4 find no relationship between variability in volume and expected returns. When analyzing the portfolio performance in different market regimes (5.2.3), however, we find a significantly negative (positive) return difference between high and low coefficient of variation in turnover portfolios in months with positive (negative) market returns.

The results are similar when repeating the base portfolio strategies in a more practical setting. Table 6.26 reports average monthly returns to practical coefficient of variation in turnover based portfolio strategies, for one-month ($K = 1$, Panel A) and 12-month ($K = 12$, Panel B) holding periods:

- Over the entire time-series ('Full'), the return difference between high and low volume portfolios is positive but insignificant. In fact, portfolios with a medium level of variability in volume earn the highest average returns.

- In months with positive (negative) market returns, however, we find a significantly negative (positive) relationship between variability in volume and expected returns.

Table 6.26: Returns to Coefficient of Variation in Turnover Portfolios in Practical Setting

	Quintile portfolios				Deciles
Time-series	V1	V3	V5	V1-V5	V1-V10
Panel A: Raw returns (holding period K = 1)					
Full (02/1998 - 08/2008)	0.92	1.20	0.63	0.29	0.17
Positive market return months	2.22	3.44	3.33	**-1.11*****	**-1.50*****
Negative market return months	-1.22	-2.30	-3.81	**2.59*****	**2.92*****
Panel B: Raw returns (holding period K = 12)					
Full (02/1998 - 08/2008)	0.93	1.25	0.62	0.30	0.09
Positive market return months	2.24	3.29	3.22	**-0.98*****	**-1.51*****
Negative market return months	-1.24	-2.11	-3.65	**2.41*****	**2.74*****

This table reports average monthly portfolio returns in different sub-sets of the complete return time-series (02/1998 - 08/2008) as defined in 3.3.2.3.2. The equal-weighted portfolios are formed monthly on the basis of stocks' coefficient of variation in share turnover (calculated over the past 12 months) and are rebalanced every $K = 1$ (Panel A) or $K = 12$ (Panel B) months. V1 is the portfolio containing the stocks with the highest 20% (quintiles) or 10% (deciles) turnover growth in a given month. V1, V3, V5 are portfolios containing long stock positions, while V1-V5 and V1-V10 are zero-cost arbitrage strategies. ***/**/* Denotes statistical significance at the 1%/5%/10% level (t-statistics are calculated using Newey-West (1987) adjusted, heteroskedasticity and serial correlation robust standard errors).

In a second step, we again regress practical quintile portfolio returns (V1-V5) on the time-series of Carhart risk factors in the Swiss stock market.[202] Results in Table 6.27 confirm the hypothesis from Chapter 5 that different levels of market betas between high and low variability in volume stocks explain the differences depending on the state of the market. Once we control for previously discovered risk factors in the cross-section of Swiss stock returns, all risk-adjusted strategy returns (i.e., regression 'Alphas') seize to be statistically significant. Additionally, the loading on the market factor (RMRF) is strongly negative across the investigated market regimes and both holding

[202] Results for decile strategies are qualitatively identical (not reported for simplicity).

periods. As a final remark, note the strongly positive loading on the size factor (SMB) suggesting that stocks with a high variability in volume behave like small stocks. This confirms our intuition based on the descriptive statistics of base portfolio strategies in Table 4.52, which shows that firms with a high (low) variability in volume are significantly smaller (larger).

Table 6.27: Time-Series Regression Coefficients of Coefficient of Variation in Turnover Arbitrage Strategies

Time-series	Alpha	RMRF	SMB	HML	UMD	R2-adj
Panel A: Carhart regression coefficients (V1-V5), holding period K = 1						
Full time-series	0.10	**-0.33*****	0.40***	0.21*	0.11**	0.52
Positive market	-0.16	**-0.28*****	0.41***	0.19	0.17*	0.27
Negative market	0.48	**-0.31*****	0.37**	0.26*	0.06	0.36
Panel B: Carhart regression coefficients (V1-V5), holding period K = 12						
Full time-series	0.07	**-0.29*****	0.44***	0.16**	0.11***	0.58
Positive market	0.07	**-0.31*****	0.42***	0.12	0.15***	0.38
Negative market	0.37	**-0.24*****	0.47**	0.25	0.07*	0.40

This table reports estimated coefficients of regressions of monthly excess returns of the practical coefficient of variation in turnover quintile arbitrage strategies (V1-V5), in different sub-sets of the complete time-series (02/1998 - 08/2008) as defined in 3.3.2.3.2, on the time-series of Swiss factor premiums RMRF, SMB, HML, UMD (Carhart factors). The methodology applied is described in detail in 3.3.3.2. ***/**/* Denotes statistical significance at the 1%/5%/10% level (t-statistics are calculated using Newey-West (1987) adjusted, heteroskedasticity and serial correlation robust standard errors).

6.3 Chapter Summary

This last empirical chapter reported results of tests to answer research question [3] *whether the discovered volume-return relations are economically significant*. The presented analyses mainly focused on abnormal volume, because it is the only measure investigated with a systematic and significant relationship to expected returns in the Swiss stock market.

1. Economic significance of abnormal volume based portfolio strategies

The results presented in this chapter do not allow clear conclusions regarding the economic significance of abnormal volume based portfolio strategies:

From a risk perspective, the relationship between abnormal volume and expected returns is economically significant, as tested via time-series regressions of portfolio returns on several risk factor premiums in the Swiss stock market. These tests reveal that the positive abnormal volume premium cannot be explained by previously documented market, size, value, and momentum risk factors.

From an investor's perspective, however, the results are mixed. The analysis of portfolio returns in a practical setting, the evaluation of risk and performance attributes of abnormal volume based portfolio strategies, and a stress test in 2008 consistently suggest the one-month $(K = 1)$ holding period setting to be (the most) attractive. But once we include transaction costs into our analysis, the results imply that the abnormal volume premium is most probably not profitably marketable via one-month holding period strategies, at least for most types of investors.

As an outlook, however, we present simple dynamic portfolio strategies allowing to implement insights gained from the abnormal volume premium (particularly regarding time-stability), despite the possibly prohibitive transaction costs involved with simple one-month holding period strategies. These strategies invest in the abnormal volume arbitrage portfolio in ex-ante known down markets (respectively high forecasted volatility regimes) and in a buy and hold index in up markets (respectively low / medium forecasted volatility regimes). The obtained results are promising, even after the inclusion of transaction costs.

Finally, the generally less profitable 12-month $(K = 12)$ holding period strategies are attractive due to their lower level of incurred transaction costs. Despite the continuing positive and significant returns of the 12-month strategies upon the inclusion of these costs, however, at least three important questions remain. First, it is unclear whether the absolute level of strategy returns represents an attractive investment opportunity. Of course this depends on an individual investor (profile). Second, the size of the $K = 12$ profits could be driven by our concrete dataset, namely the very strong performance of one stock at the beginning of the time-series investigated. And third, results in 2008 cast some doubt on the profitable implementation of 12-month strategies going forward. Only a repetition of our tests in other markets and a continuous monitoring of portfolio returns in the future can provide more clarity on the last two points.

2. Relationship between other volume measures and market beta

Selected tests regarding the other volume measures confirm results and assumptions from previous chapters.

Volume level: the analysis of portfolio returns in a practical setting finds no systematic relationship between volume level and expected returns over the complete time-series. In specific market states, on the other hand, we again identify significant return differences between high and low volume portfolios. However, these results are solely caused by the fact that high volume stocks have significantly higher market betas. Once this is controlled for, no volume-return relations remain significant.

Volume growth: portfolio returns in a practical setting confirm a slightly positive but non-systematic (and not profitably marketable) relationship between volume growth and expected returns. When restricting the analysis to months with negative (positive) market returns, this relationship is again systematically positive (negative). But once we control for the fact that high volume growth stocks have significantly lower market betas, these relationships become insignificant.

Variability in volume: the findings are very similar for portfolios based on variability in volume. First, there is no systematic relationship between variability in volume and expected returns over the full time-series. Second, we find a significantly positive (negative) relationship between variability in volume and expected returns in months with negative (positive) market returns. And finally, once we control for the fact that high variability in volume stocks have significantly lower market betas, these regime-dependent relationships become completely insignificant.

7 Summary and Conclusions

The main objective of this research project was to investigate the relationship between trading volume and expected returns in the cross-section of Swiss stocks, with a particular emphasis on the practicability of portfolio strategies formed on the basis of past trading volume. Four research questions guided us in the empirical tests designed to achieve this overall objective, namely:

[1] Do different measures of trading volume play an important role in the cross-sectional variation of expected returns in the Swiss stock market?

[2] How robust are the portfolio returns across time and different market regimes?

[3] Are the discovered volume-return relations economically significant?

[4] How sensitive are the results to changes in the experimental design?

We analyzed the role of four different volume measures in the cross-section of Swiss stock returns, namely *abnormal volume*, *volume level*, *volume growth*, and *variability in volume*. The subsequent summary of the main empirical findings is divided into these four volume measures. However, the bulk of the summary is dedicated to the *abnormal volume* measure, because it is the only measure investigated shown to systematically and significantly relate to the cross-section of Swiss stock returns.

1. The research project identified a systematic relationship between abnormal volume and expected returns in the cross-section of Swiss stocks

The abnormal volume measure analyzed in this research project is inspired by the 'high-volume return premium' discovered by GERVAIS ET AL. (2001). These authors show that stocks experiencing unusually high trading volume over a day (or a week) appreciate in the following month. They interpret the discovered high-volume return premium caused by short-term volume shocks as a consequence of increased visibility of a stock leading to increased subsequent demand and price for that stock. This *investor visibility hypothesis* goes back to MILLER (1977).

GERVAIS ET AL. (2001) define a stock as 'high volume' if its trading volume on a given day is among the top 5 out of the last 50 daily volumes. We transform this measure to allow for standard tests of the cross-sectional variation of returns (namely Fama-MacBeth regressions and portfolio-based tests using quantile-sorts) and to easily control for previously discovered cross-sectional effects. The resulting *'abnormal volume'* measure is defined as follows: *'The percentage change of last month's trading volume in a stock versus the average monthly trading volume in that stock in the preceding three to twelve months'*. We use share turnover, defined as the number of shares traded in a given stock divided by the number of shares outstanding of that stock, as the underlying trading volume variable in most tests. The reason is that share turnover is less correlated with firm size than Swiss franc volume, which is calculated by multiplying the number of shares traded in a given stock by the corresponding transaction price. A robustness check using Swiss franc volume reveals qualitatively the same findings.

This leads us to the discussion of the main results: at the outset of our tests, we expected our findings to be in line with the results by GERVAIS ET AL. (2001) and the investor visibility hypothesis by MILLER (1977). We thus hypothesized a positive relationship between abnormal volume and expected returns in the cross-section of Swiss stocks. Our analyses designed to answer research question [1] confirm this hypothesis (chapter 4).

> *Both regression and portfolio-based tests reveal a systematically and significantly positive relationship between abnormal volume and expected returns in the cross-section of Swiss stocks.*

In other words, we find that stocks with a high trading volume in a given month, compared to the stocks' average trading volume in the preceding three to twelve months, experience systematically higher subsequent returns.

> *We show that this effect is strongest in the month immediately following the abnormal volume.*

For example, the average monthly return difference between portfolios containing the highest and lowest 10% abnormal volume stocks is 1.58% over the one-month holding period.[203]

> *But subsequent analysis finds that portfolios containing high abnormal volume stocks continue to systematically outperform portfolios with low abnormal volume stocks for the next 12 months.*

Additional tests reveal that the significant role abnormal volume seems to play in the cross-sectional variation of expected returns in the Swiss stock market is very stable when controlling for various previously discovered cross-sectional effects (and when performing other robustness checks as part of research question [4]). These effects include company size, book-to-market ratio, momentum, liquidity, and industry affiliation. At the same time, the positive abnormal volume premium is particularly pronounced for small stocks and past losers, which is consistent with the investor visibility hypothesis. The rationale is that we expect smaller firms and low performing stocks to be less followed by investors and thus be more affected by increased visibility induced by abnormal volume.

In a next set of analyses, designed to answer research question [2], we test the *stability of abnormal volume portfolio returns across time and different market regimes* (chapter 5). We show that the positive relationship between abnormal volume and expected returns is not driven by a few months with extreme returns and is independent of the January and December seasonality.

> *Further analysis reveals that the positive abnormal volume premium became weaker in more recent times. Our hypothesis is that the strength of the abnormal volume effect varies across different market regimes, being particularly strong in down market states and high market volatility regimes. We thus suspect the weak strategy performance in low volatility regimes, which only existed in the second sub-period analyzed, to be the main driver behind the lower premium in recent times.*

---

[203] Using a reference period of $J = 12$ months.

A test of portfolio performance in 2008 provides further support for this hypothesis, because the abnormal volume premium was very strong in this volatile down market environment. At the same time, the 2008 results contradict a potential alternative explanation that the discovered effect was only a market inefficiency and disappeared in more recent times.

> *Concerning the strong abnormal volume effect in down markets and high volatility regimes, we show possibilities to relate them to the investor visibility hypothesis.*

Regarding *down markets*, our hypothesis is that due to the average stock market's poor recent performance (which defines the down market), the included stocks have on average fallen out of investors' radar. In such an environment, it is likely that the effect of abnormal volume on visibility in a stock is stronger than in up markets, just as it is generally stronger for past loser stocks than for past winner stocks. For *high volatility regimes*, on the other hand, we hypothesize that a combination of three factors might help to explain the particularly strong abnormal volume premium discovered in high volatility regimes. First, the influence of a signaling of a potential investment opportunity through abnormal volume is likely to be stronger in uncertain times (i.e., high market volatility). Second, individual investors are potentially more sensitive to uncertainty in the market. And finally, previous research finds a stronger significance of visibility events for individual investors' buying behavior.

As a third series of empirical tests, we analyze whether the discovered abnormal volume premium is *economically significant* (research question [3] discussed in chapter 6). From a risk perspective, we find this to be the case.

> *Time-series regressions of portfolio returns on several risk factors in the Swiss stock market reveal that the positive abnormal volume premium cannot be explained by previously documented market, size, value, and momentum risk factors.*

However, the main objective of the research project also entailed an '*emphasis on the practicability of portfolio strategies* formed on the basis of past trading volume'. Thus, we additionally tested the economic significance from an investor's perspective. These results are mixed.

Throughout our analysis, we find the one-month holding period setting to be (the most) attractive. But once we include transaction costs into our analysis, results imply that the abnormal volume premium is most probably not profitably marketable via these trading-intensive one-month holding period strategies (at least for most types of investors).

As an outlook, however, we also present simple dynamic portfolio strategies that allow us to implement insights from our analysis (particularly regarding the time-stability of abnormal volume strategies) despite these potentially prohibitive transaction costs.

These dynamic strategies only invest in the one-month abnormal volume strategy in the particularly profitable (and ex-ante known) down market phases respectively high forecasted volatility regimes.[204] In the remaining months, the strategies invest in a buy and hold index.

The obtained results of these dynamic portfolio strategies are very promising, even after the inclusion of transaction costs.

Finally, we also tested the practicability of the generally less profitable 12-month holding period strategies. Because such strategies are less trading-intensive, our results reveal the presence of continuing positive and significant returns after the inclusion of trading costs. But it is unclear whether the absolute level of these strategy returns represents an attractive investment opportunity.

[204] The forecasted volatility model assumes that this month's real volatility regime continues in the following month.

We see mainly three areas for future research, namely further analysis on the visibility hypothesis in the context of the discovered abnormal volume premium, potential risk-based explanations for the abnormal volume premium, and the profitability of multi-month holding period strategies.

Further analysis on the visibility hypothesis in the context of the discovered abnormal volume premium: our findings regarding the abnormal volume premium are mostly consistent with the investor visibility hypothesis. But some aspects require further investigation.

First, recall the discussion on the varying strength of the abnormal volume effect within different industries. Following MILLER (1977), we presume that there are probably large differences between the 'base attention level' given to stocks in various industries. This influences the strength of the visibility effect induced by abnormal volume. However, as previously mentioned, there are not enough stocks per individual homogenous industry group in our sample to conduct a meaningful analysis. We therefore propose to investigate the relation between industry affiliation and the strength of the abnormal volume (visibility) effect in the much larger US stock markets.

Second, we try to relate the finding that the abnormal volume premium is reduced when controlling for industry belonging to the visibility hypothesis. One possibility is the presence of spillover effects from abnormal volume of a stock in a given industry to investor interest (induced by increased awareness respectively visibility) in other stocks within that industry. As a result, the relationship between abnormal volume of a given stock and subsequent returns in that same stock could be less direct when restricting the analysis to one industry. It would be interesting to further analyze this hypothesis.

And third, the instability of the abnormal volume effect across different market regimes needs further research. We see the need for two specific analyses. On the one hand, we provide a visibility-based explanation for the fact that the abnormal volume premium is stronger in down markets and high volatility regimes. Further research could explore this presumed relationship more in-depth. On the other hand, our results suggest that the abnormal volume premium is not significantly positive in low volatility regimes. This seems to contradict the visibility hypothesis, even if the preceding analysis confirms that the effect of increased visibility on stock returns is stronger in high volatility phases. But one needs to bear in mind that this could be driven by our concrete dataset, because there is only one low volatility regime in our time-series. An additional investigation in a stock market with a longer time-series of available volume data and several low volatility phases could provide more clarity regarding this point.

Potential risk-based explanations for the abnormal volume premium: we find that the discovered positive abnormal volume premium in the Swiss stock market cannot be explained by previously documented market, size, value, and momentum risk factors. It would thus be interesting to explore whether additional economic risks could explain the premium for stocks with abnormally high recent volume, or in other words, whether abnormal volume proxies for an additional risk factor not considered in our analysis.

The profitability of multi-month holding period strategies: recall the discussion of the practicability of abnormal volume based strategies with annual (i.e., 12-month holding periods) rebalancing. Besides the uncertainty whether the absolute level of the strategy returns represents an attractive investment opportunity, there are two additional questions. On the one hand, we show that the size of the (12-month holding period) profits could be driven by our concrete dataset, namely the very strong performance of one stock with abnormally high volume at the beginning of the time-series. And on the other hand, strategy returns are below average in 2008 (a result that is in sharp contrast to the one-month holding period strategies), which casts some doubts on future profit potential. We thus propose a repetition of our multi-month holding period tests in other markets to clarify these questions. As a final remark, recall that we know of no other empirical study that investigates the role of abnormal volume in the cross-section of stock returns via the standard tests applied here. In that sense, a general repetition of our analysis in other stock markets would be interesting by itself.

2. The research project identified no systematic relationship between other volume measures and expected returns in the Swiss stock market

Volume Level: Regarding the second measure investigated, we ex-ante hypothesized a negative relationship between volume level and expected returns in the cross-section of Swiss stocks, based on considerable evidence in US and other (non-European) developed stock markets. In other words, we expected stocks that are heavily traded in the past to have lower subsequent returns. We define the volume level in our tests as the *'average monthly share turnover (or Swiss franc volume) in a stock in the last one to twelve months'*.

> *While the regression results even indicate the existence of a positive relationship between volume level and expected returns, the portfolio-based tests find no systematic relation at statistically significant levels.*

When investigating the time-stability of these results, we discover that the return difference between high and low volume stocks is significantly positive (negative) in bull (bear) markets and in months with positive (negative) market returns. Subsequent tests show that these results are caused by the fact that high volume stocks have significantly higher market betas. Once this is controlled for, no relations between volume level and expected returns remain statistically significant. Our findings that volume level plays no important role in the cross-sectional variation of expected returns in the Swiss stock market is consistent with results in 20 emerging stock markets, but not with the negative relationship identified in US and other developed (non-European) stock markets. Given these previously inconclusive results and the fact that there exists no generally accepted view as to the nature of a potentially negative volume level effect, our results thus provide additional evidence of the controversial (if any) role of volume level in the cross-section of stock returns. Nevertheless, recall that one frequent interpretation of a potentially negative relationship is that volume proxies for liquidity, with less liquid stocks generating higher expected returns. Our results imply two potential conclusions regarding such a liquidity effect. Either, volume level is generally not a good proxy for liquidity, as some researchers argue (see the discussion in Chapter 2). Or liquidity is not priced in the cross-section of Swiss stocks. To shed more light on this, we propose an investigation of the role of other liquidity measures (outlined in Chapter 2) in the cross-sectional variation of expected Swiss stock returns as a topic for further research. Such a measure could for example be AMIHUD'S (2002) 'illiquidity ratio' or PASTOR/ STAMBAUGH'S (2003) 'liquidity beta'.

Volume Growth: besides abnormal volume, we included another variable measuring *change in volume* in our tests. We label this measure 'volume growth' and define it as follows: *'The average monthly percentage change in a stock's trading volume in the last one to twelve months'.*[205] It was difficult to build an ex-ante opinion on the presumed direction (if any) of the relationship with expected returns, because we do not know of any other study using the exact same measure. But based on the results of one related study applying a similar measure of volume growth in the US stock markets we rather expected a positive relationship between volume growth and expected returns in the cross-section of Swiss stocks. However,

> *our results reveal a non-systematic relationship between volume growth and expected returns.*

The relationship is slightly negative in base regressions. But this is only driven by a few extreme volume growth observations. Once we exclude these outliers, the relationship becomes slightly positive. Portfolio-based tests confirm the presence of a rather positive but non-systematic relationship between volume growth and expected returns. Regarding the time-stability of these results, we find that the return difference between high and low volume growth stocks is significantly positive (negative) in months with negative (positive) market returns. Similar to the volume level results, however, we find that this is caused by different levels of market beta. Once we control for the fact that high volume growth stocks have significantly lower market betas, above relationships become insignificant. Our findings are not in line with the only comparable study known to us by WATKINS (2007), because this author finds a systematically positive and long-lived volume growth effect. However, WATKINS (2007) uses a slightly different measure of volume growth, namely market and firm-adjusted excess trading volume growth. In addition, the author uses and older time-series (1963 to 1999 versus our 1997 to 2008 data) and analyzes the relationship in the US stock markets. In that sense, a topic of fur-

[205] Again, we mainly use *share turnover* as the underlying trading volume measure. A robustness check using *Swiss franc volume* reveals the same findings.

ther research could be to repeat his identical methodology in the context of recent Swiss or other European stock market data.

Variability in volume: regarding the fourth measure investigated, variability in volume, we ex-ante hypothesized a negative relationship with expected returns based on according evidence from the US stock markets. In other words, we expected stocks with a high variability in volume to have lower subsequent returns. We show in our tests that the *coefficient of variation in volume*, defined as the *standard deviation of monthly trading volume over the past twelve months divided by the average level of monthly trading volume over the past twelve months*, is a more appropriate measure than simply using the standard deviation. The reason is that the coefficient of variation is a dimensionless quantity while the latter strongly correlates with the volume level.[206]

> *Overall, particularly the portfolio-based tests strongly contradict our ingoing hypothesis. These tests show no systematic relationship between variability in volume and expected returns.*

Regarding the time-stability, our analysis finds the same results as for volume growth, namely a significantly positive (negative) return difference between high and low variability in volume stocks in months with negative (positive) market returns. But this is again caused by the fact that stocks with a high variability in volume over the last year have significantly lower market betas. The presented findings contradict the evidence from US stock markets mentioned above. To our knowledge, however, no model is able to consistently explain the nature of a potentially negative relationship.

[206] Again, we mainly use *share turnover* as the underlying trading volume measure. A robustness check using *Swiss franc volume* reveals the same findings.

Appendix

Table A1: Returns to Two-Way Sorted Abnormal Turnover Portfolios in Different Sub-Periods

	Abnormal Turnover Portfolios (V1-V10)		
Time-series	Small companies	Low BM companies	Past loser stocks
Full	2.54 (3.668)***	1.84 (3.511)***	1.55 (2.798)***
Sub-Period 1 (03/1997 - 11/2002)	3.86 (4.109)***	2.58 (3.371)***	1.85 (1.911)*
Sub-Period 2 (12/2002 - 08/2008)	1.22 (1.352)	1.11 (1.691)*	1.25 (1.987)*

This table reports average monthly portfolio returns in 2 sub-sets of the complete return time-series (03/1997 - 08/2008). The equal-weighted portfolios are formed monthly on the basis of stocks' abnormal share turnover (percentage change of last month's turnover versus the average turnover in the preceding $J = 12$ months) within specific control variable tercile portfolios (smallest 1/3 of firms, 1/3 of firms with the lowest book-to-market ratio, 1/3 of stocks with the lowest past one-year returns). The portfolios are rebalanced monthly ($K = 1$). V1-V10 is the zero-cost arbitrage strategy consisting of long positions in stocks with the highest 10% abnormal turnover in a given month and short positions of equal size in stocks with the lowest 10% abnormal turnover. ***/**/* Denotes statistical significance at the 1%/5%/10% level. T-statistics (in parentheses) are calculated using Newey-West (1987) adjusted, heteroskedasticity and serial correlation robust standard errors.

Table A2: Returns to Two-Way Sorted Abnormal Turnover Portfolios in Different Market Phases

	Abnormal Turnover Portfolios (V1-V10)		
Time-series	Small companies	Low BM companies	Past loser stocks
Bull markets	2.20 (2.609)**	1.15 (1.620)	0.79 (1.797)*
Bear markets	3.22 (2.994)***	3.23 (5.038)***	3.07 (2.452)**
Up market states	1.53 (2.248)**	1.00 (1.737)*	0.64 (1.534)
Down market states	**4.91** **(3.612)*****	**3.87** **(4.468)*****	**3.71** **(2.604)****
Positive market return months	1.86 (2.586)**	1.41 (2.129)**	2.07 (2.746)***
Negative market return months	3.73 (3.764)***	2.61 (3.663)***	0.63 (0.607)

This table reports average monthly portfolio returns in different sub-sets of the complete return time-series (03/1997 - 08/2008), as defined in section 3.3.2.3.2. The equal-weighted portfolios are formed monthly on the basis of stocks' abnormal share turnover ($J = 12$ months) within specific control variable tercile portfolios (BM being a firm's book-to-market ratio). The portfolios are rebalanced monthly ($K = 1$). V1-V10 is the zero-cost arbitrage strategy consisting of long positions in stocks with the highest 10% abnormal turnover in a given month and short positions of equal size in stocks with the lowest 10% abnormal turnover. ***/**/* Denotes statistical significance at the 1%/5%/10% level. T-statistics (in parentheses) are calculated using Newey-West (1987) adjusted, heteroskedasticity and serial correlation robust standard errors.

Table A3: Returns to Two-Way Sorted Abnormal Turnover Portfolios in Different Volatility Regimes

	Abnormal Turnover Portfolios (V1-V10)		
Time-series	Small companies	Low BM companies	Past loser stocks
Panel A: Real volatility regimes			
Low volatility	0.41 (0.404)	0.49 (0.529)	1.05 (1.723)*
Normal volatility	2.13 (2.855)***	1.75 (2.794)***	0.20 (0.424)
High volatility	**5.72** **(3.462)*** **	**3.54** **(3.765)*** **	**4.73** **(2.922)*** **
Panel B: Forecasted volatility regimes			
Low volatility	-0.80 (-1.029)	-0.24 (-0.253)	0.93 (1.783)*
Normal volatility	2.71 (3.306)***	1.97 (3.682)***	0.63 (1.089)
High volatility	**4.97** **(3.249)*** **	**3.31** **(3.045)*** **	**4.61** **(3.033)*** **

This table reports average monthly portfolio returns in different sub-sets of the complete return time-series (03/1997 - 08/2008), as defined in section 3.3.2.3.3. The equal-weighted portfolios are formed monthly on the basis of stocks' abnormal share turnover (J = *12* months) within specific control variable tercile portfolios (BM being a firm's book-to-market ratio). The portfolios are rebalanced monthly (K = *1*). V1-V10 is the zero-cost arbitrage strategy consisting of long positions in stocks with the highest 10% abnormal turnover in a given month and short positions of equal size in stocks with the lowest 10% abnormal turnover. ***/**/* Denotes statistical significance at the 1%/5%/10% level. T-statistics (in parentheses) are calculated using Newey-West (1987) adjusted, heteroskedasticity and serial correlation robust standard errors.

Table A4: Returns to Two-Way Sorted Abnormal Turnover Portfolios in Different Volume Regimes

	Abnormal Turnover Portfolios (V1-V10)		
Time-series	Small companies	Low BM companies	Past loser stocks
Normal Swiss franc volume	2.52 (3.263)***	1.98 (3.370)***	1.37 (2.196)**
High Swiss franc volume	2.67 (1.702)	0.89 (0.857)	2.41 (2.721)**
Normal market turnover	3.04 (3.323)***	2.32 (3.580)***	1.59 (2.123)**
High market turnover	1.41 (1.572)	0.73 (0.925)	1.31 (1.960)*

This table reports average monthly portfolio returns in different sub-sets of the complete return time-series (03/1997 - 08/2008), as defined in section 3.3.2.3.4. The equal-weighted portfolios are formed monthly on the basis of stocks' abnormal share turnover ($J = 12$ months) within specific control variable tercile portfolios (BM being a firm's book-to-market ratio). The portfolios are rebalanced monthly ($K = 1$). V1-V10 is the zero-cost arbitrage strategy consisting of long positions in stocks with the highest 10% abnormal turnover in a given month and short positions of equal size in stocks with the lowest 10% abnormal turnover. ***/**/* Denotes statistical significance at the 1%/5%/10% level. T-statistics (in parentheses) are calculated using Newey-West (1987) adjusted, heteroskedasticity and serial correlation robust standard errors.

Table A5: Time-Series Regression Coefficients of Abnormal Turnover Arbitrage Strategies, Small Companies

Risk model	Alpha	RMRF	SMB	HML	UMD	R2-adj
Panel A: Equal-weighted decile portfolios (V1-V10), reference period J = 12, holding period K = 1						
CAPM	2.58	-0.07				0.00
	(3.654)***	(-0.420)				
FF2	2.56	-0.09		-0.61		0.02
	(3.716)***	(-0.553)		(-1.809)*		
Carhart	2.75	-0.16		-0.63	-0.20	0.02
	(3.733)***	(-1.057)		(-1.871)*	(-0.204)	
Panel B: Equal-weighted decile portfolios (V1-V10), reference period J = 12, holding period K = 12						
CAPM	0.97	0.06				0.00
	(2.750)***	(0.916)				
FF2	0.96	0.04		-0.36		0.04
	(2.954)***	(-0.355)		(-1.865)*		
Carhart	0.97	0.04		-0.36	-0.01	0.04
	(2.838)***	(0.667)		(-1.842)*	(-0.167)	

This table reports estimated coefficients of regressions of monthly excess returns of the practical abnormal turnover decile arbitrage strategies (V1-V10) within small companies (reported in 6.1.1) on the time-series of monthly excess returns on the market portfolio RMRF (CAPM), on the time-series of Swiss factor premiums RMRF, HML (Fama-French factors, i.e., FF2), and on the three Swiss factor premiums RMRF, HML, UMD (Carhart factors). The methodology applied is described in detail in 3.3.3.2. Remark regarding factors: no SMB ('Small Minus Big') factor used in FF2 / Carhart regressions because portfolio contains only small firms. ***/**/* Denotes statistical significance at the 1%/5%/10% level. T-statistics (in parentheses) are calculated using Newey-West (1987) adjusted, heteroskedasticity and serial correlation robust standard errors.

Table A6: Time-Series Regression Coefficients of Abnormal Turnover Arbitrage Strategies, Low Book-to-Market Companies

Risk model	Alpha	RMRF	SMB	HML	UMD	R2-adj
Panel A: Equal-weighted decile portfolios (V1-V10), reference period J = 12, holding period K = 1						
CAPM	1.96	0.09				0.00
	(3.341)***	(0.478)				
FF2	1.97	0.08	-0.02			0.00
	(3.352)***	(0.432)	(-0.075)			
Carhart	1.96	0.09	-0.02		0.01	0.00
	(3.074)***	(0.361)	(-0.075)		(0.044)	
Panel B: Equal-weighted decile portfolios (V1-V10), reference period J = 12, holding period K = 12						
CAPM	0.79	0.18				0.09
	(3.312)***	(2.929)***				
FF2	0.76	0.20	0.07			0.08
	(3.383)***	(2.964)***	(0.551)			
Carhart	0.68	0.22	0.07		0.08	0.09
	(3.161)***	(3.803)***	(0.560)		(1.361)	

This table reports estimated coefficients of regressions of monthly excess returns of the practical abnormal turnover decile arbitrage strategies (V1-V10) within low book-to-market companies (reported in 6.1.1) on the time-series of monthly excess returns on the market portfolio RMRF (CAPM), on the time-series of Swiss factor premiums RMRF, SMB (Fama-French factors, i.e., FF2), and on the three Swiss factor premiums RMRF, SMB, UMD (Carhart factors). The methodology applied is described in detail in 3.3.3.2. Remark regarding factors: no HML ('High Minus Low") factor used in FF2 / Carhart regressions because portfolio contains only firms with low book-to-market ratios. ***/**/* Denotes statistical significance at the 1%/5%/10% level. T-statistics (in parentheses) are calculated using Newey-West (1987) adjusted, heteroskedasticity and serial correlation robust standard errors.

Table A7: Time-Series Regression Coefficients of Abnormal Turnover Arbitrage Strategies, Loser Stocks

Risk model	Alpha	RMRF	SMB	HML	UMD	R2-adj
Panel A: Equal-weighted decile portfolios (V1-V10), reference period J = 12, holding period K = 1						
CAPM	1.38	0.22				0.01
	(2.125)**	(1.152)				
FF3	1.36	0.21	0.01	-0.54		0.03
	(2.048)**	(1.012)	(0.049)	(-1.833)*		
Panel B: Equal-weighted decile portfolios (V1-V10), reference period J = 12, holding period K = 12						
CAPM	0.60	0.22				0.11
	(2.288)**	(3.627)***				
FF3	0.52	0.26	0.14	0.01		0.11
	(2.011)**	(4.892)***	(1.187)	(0.065)		

This table reports estimated coefficients of regressions of monthly excess returns of the practical abnormal turnover decile arbitrage strategies (V1-V10) within stocks with the lowest past one-year returns (reported in 6.1.1) on the time-series of monthly excess returns on the market portfolio RMRF (CAPM), and on the time-series of Swiss factor premiums RMRF, SMB, HML (Fama-French factors, i.e., FF3). The methodology applied is described in detail in 3.3.3.2. ***/**/* Denotes statistical significance at the 1%/5%/10% level. T-statistics (in parentheses) are calculated using Newey-West (1987) adjusted, heteroskedasticity and serial correlation robust standard errors.

Table A8: Risk and Performance Analysis of Two-Way Sorted Abnormal Turnover Arbitrage Strategies (K = 12 Months)

	V1-V10; Reference period: $J = 12$; Holding period $K = 12$				Reference indices	
	Small	Low BM	Losers	One-way	SPI	EW
Average return (ann.)	11.67%	10.08%	7.59%	8.24%	3.91%	10.74%
Standard deviation (ann.)	11.67%	9.18%	10.50%	7.59%	16.49%	16.28%
Sharpe ratio	1.00	1.10	0.72	1.09	0.14	0.56
Correlation (SPI)	0.08	0.31	0.33	0.30	1.00	0.83
Correlation (EW)	0.25	0.29	0.43	0.41	0.83	1.00
% positive months	60%	63%	63%	61%	62%	66%
Maximum drawdown	-9.7%	-10.4%	-14.3%	-8.1%	-49.1%	-49.7%
Months in drawdown	15	10	13	14	31	31
Months of recovery	17	>6	>6	>7	33	23
Average monthly return	0.99%	0.84%	0.66%	0.69%	0.43%	0.96%
Median monthly return	0.29%	0.88%	0.80%	0.44%	1.30%	1.57%
Maximum monthly return	19.98%	8.90%	9.39%	15.08%	12.24%	11.74%
Minimum monthly return	-5.09%	-6.51%	-12.01%	-4.57%	-16.92%	-14.54%

This table reports performance and risk attributes of practical abnormal turnover decile arbitrage strategies (V1-V10) within specific control variable tercile portfolios (smallest 1/3 of firms, 1/3 of firms with lowest book-to-market ratio, 1/3 of stocks with the lowest past one-year returns), as reported in 6.1.1. All the analyzed strategies are rebalanced annually $(K = 12)$. The numbers are compared with the one-way sorted abnormal turnover decile arbitrage strategy (One-way) and two benchmarks, the Swiss Performance Index (SPI) and a hypothetical, equal-weighted index constructed from the stocks included in the database (EW).

Table A9: Risk and Performance Analysis of Long-Only Abnormal Turnover Decile Portfolios

	J = 12; K = 1		*J = 12; K = 12*		Reference indices	
	Small (V1)	One-way (V1)	Small (V1)	One-way (V1)	SPI	EW
Average return (ann.)	28.81%	20.73%	18.72%	16.04%	3.91%	10.74%
Standard deviation (ann.)	22.86%	18.19%	16.59%	15.93%	16.49%	16.28%
Sharpe ratio	1.26	1.14	1.13	1.01	0.24	0.66
Correlation (SPI)	0.34	0.68	0.44	0.69	1.00	0.83
Correlation (EW)	0.55	0.88	0.75	0.93	0.83	1.00
% positive months	60%	68%	61%	65%	62%	66%
Maximum drawdown	-27.5%	-25.7%	-39.5%	-37.2%	-49.1%	-49.7%
Months in drawdown	15	18	36	30	31	31
Months of recovery	6	20	22	11	33	23
Average monthly return	2.36%	1.72%	1.56%	1.36%	0.43%	0.96%
Median monthly return	1.63%	1.35%	1.18%	1.29%	1.30%	1.57%
Maximum monthly return	31.37%	17.72%	25.37%	16.79%	12.24%	11.74%
Minimum monthly return	-12.56%	-17.71%	-10.78%	-13.82%	-16.92%	-14.54%

This table reports performance and risk attributes of practical abnormal turnover decile portfolios within the smallest 1/3 of companies ('Small (V1)'), as reported in 6.1.1. The analyzed portfolios are rebalanced every *K = 1, 12* months. V1 is the portfolio containing the stocks with the highest 10% abnormal turnover. The numbers are compared with the respective one-way sorted abnormal turnover decile portfolios ('One-way') and two benchmarks, the Swiss Performance Index (SPI) and a hypothetical, equal-weighted index constructed from the stocks included in the database (EW).

Table A10: Inclusion of Transaction Costs to Abnormal Turnover Arbitrage Strategies, Small Companies

	Transaction cost level (one-way costs)				
Volume portfolio	0.0%	0.3%	0.5%	1.0%	1.5%
Panel A: Equal-weighted decile portfolios (V1-V10), reference period J = 12, holding period K = 1					
Small, long (V1)	2.36	1.89	1.58	0.81	0.04
Small, long-SPI	**1.93**	**1.46**	**1.15**	0.38	-0.39
	(3.140)*	**(2.379)**	**(1.872)***	(0.614)	(-0.632)
Small, long-EW	**1.40**	**0.93**	0.62	-0.15	-0.92
	(2.707)*	**(1.800)***	(1.199)	(-0.293)	(-1.764)*
Panel B: Equal-weighted decile portfolios (V1-V10), reference period J = 12, holding period K = 12					
Small, long (V1)	1.56	1.51	1.48	1.40	1.32
Small, long-SPI	**1.13**	**1.08**	**1.05**	**0.97**	**0.88**
	(2.417)	**(2.314)**	**(2.246)**	**(2.074)**	**(1.902)***
Small, long-EW	**0.60**	**0.55**	0.52	0.44	0.36
	(1.864)*	**(1.714)***	(1.614)	(1.363)	(1.111)

This table reports average monthly returns to practical abnormal turnover decile portfolios within the smallest 1/3 of companies (as reported in 6.1.1) after the inclusion of transaction costs. The included one-way (i.e., buying or selling) transaction costs correspond to round-trip costs of 0.6%, 1%, 2%, 3%. The calculation of transaction costs is described in detail in 3.3.3.3. SPI is the Swiss Performance Index and EW is a hypothetical, equal-weighted index constructed from the stocks included in the database. ***/**/* Denotes statistical significance at the 1%/5%/10% level. T-statistics (in parentheses) are calculated using Newey-West (1987) adjusted, heteroskedasticity and serial correlation robust standard errors.

Table A11: Evaluation of Dynamic Down Market Strategy (Reference Index: SPI)

	Dynamic down market strategies		Base strategies	
	V1-V10	SPI	V1-V10	SPI
Average return (ann.)	19.29%	7.18%	19.72%	3.91%
Standard deviation (ann.)	15.00%	12.09%	13.09%	16.49%
Sharpe ratio	1.18	0.46	1.39	0.14
Correlation (SPI)	0.67	0.74	0.16	1.00
% positive months	68%	76%	65%	62%
Maximum drawdown	-26.9%	-26.9%	-13.7%	-49.1%
Months in drawdown	2	2	13	31
Months of recovery	14	23	5	33
Average monthly return	1.57%	0.70%	1.59%	0.43%
Median monthly return	1.60%	0.31%	1.07%	1.30%
Maximum monthly return	12.54%	9.79%	12.54%	12.24%
Minimum monthly return	-16.92%	-16.92%	-8.86%	-16.92%

This table compares performance and risk attributes of four different strategies. *Dynamic down market strategy (V1-V10)* is a strategy that is long in the SPI in up markets and long-short in the practical abnormal turnover decile arbitrage strategy in down markets (up and down markets are defined in 3.3.2.3.2). *Dynamic down market strategy (SPI)* is a strategy long in the SPI in up markets and long in the risk-free rate in down markets. *Base strategy (V1-V10)* is the pratical abnormal turnover decile arbitrage strategy across the complete return time-series (02/1998 - 08/2008) and *base strategy (SPI)* is the return time-series of the Swiss Performance Index. The V1-V10 strategies are rebalanced monthly *(K = 1)*.

Figure A1: NAVs of Dynamic Down Market Strategy and Benchmarks (SPI-Based)

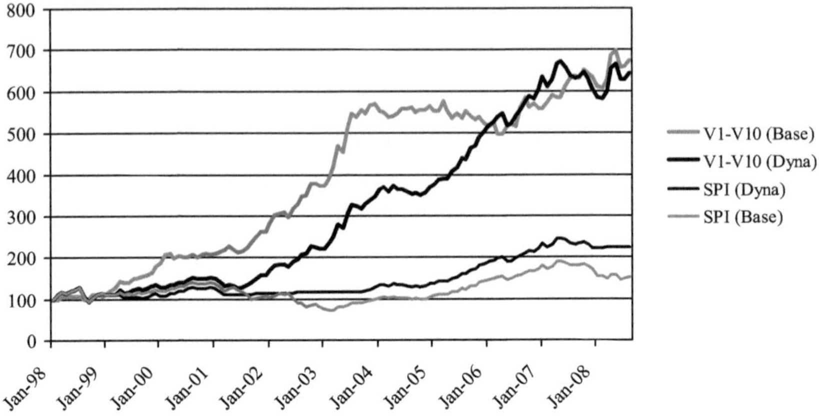

Table A12: Evaluation of Dynamic High Forecasted Volatility Strategy (Reference Index: SPI)

	Dynamic volatility strategies		Base strategies	
	V1-V10	SPI	V1-V10	SPI
Average return (ann.)	13.29%	3.79%	19.72%	3.91%
Standard deviation (ann.)	16.18%	14.10%	13.09%	16.49%
Sharpe ratio	0.72	0.16	1.39	0.14
Correlation (SPI)	0.79	0.85	0.16	1.00
% positive months	67%	72%	65%	62%
Maximum drawdown	-30.7%	-41.9%	-13.7%	-49.1%
Months in drawdown	23	23	13	31
Months of recovery	11	42	5	33
Average monthly return	1.15%	0.39%	1.59%	0.43%
Median monthly return	1.51%	0.32%	1.07%	1.30%
Maximum monthly return	12.54%	9.52%	12.54%	12.24%
Minimum monthly return	-16.92%	-16.92%	-8.86%	-16.92%

This table compares performance and risk attributes of four different strategies. *Dynamic volatility strategy (V1-V10)* is a strategy that is long in the SPI in low / normal forecasted volatility regimes and long-short in the practical abnormal turnover decile arbitrage strategy in high forecasted volatility regimes (volatility regimes are defined in 3.3.2.3.3). *Dynamic volatility strategy (SPI)* is a strategy long in the SPI in low / normal forecasted volatility regimes and long in the risk-free rate in high forecasted volatility regimes. *Base strategy (V1-V10)* is the pratical abnormal turnover decile arbitrage strategy across the complete return time-series (02/1998 - 08/2008) and *base strategy (SPI)* is the return time-series of the Swiss Performance Index. The V1-V10 strategies are rebalanced monthly $(K = 1)$.

Figure A2: NAVs of Dynamic High Forecasted Volatility Strategy and Benchmarks (SPI-Based)

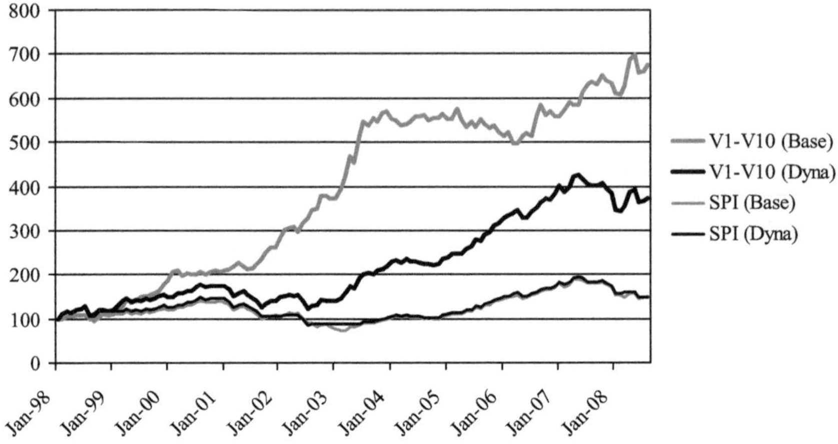

Table A13: Inclusion of Transaction Costs to Dynamic Strategies (SPI-Based)

	Transaction cost level (one-way costs)				
Strategy	0.0%	0.3%	0.5%	1.0%	1.5%
Base Strategy, $K = 1$ (V1-V10)	1.59	0.76	0.21	-1.16	-2.53
Dyna down market (V1-V10)	**1.57**	**1.31**	**1.14**	**0.72**	**0.29**
Dyna down market (SPI)	0.70				
Dyna high vola forecast (V1-V10)	**1.15**	**0.97**	**0.86**	**0.56**	**0.27**
Dyna high vola forecast (SPI)	0.39				
SPI	0.43				

This table reports average monthly returns of different SPI-based dynamic strategies after the inclusion of transaction costs (the calculation of transaction costs is described in detail in 3.3.3.3). These returns are compared to the practical abnormal turnover arbitrage strategy with monthly rebalancing ('Base Strategy') and to the return time-series of the Swiss Performance Index (SPI).

Figure A3: Market Trading Volume, De-Trended and Season-Adjusted (CHF Million), incl. 2008

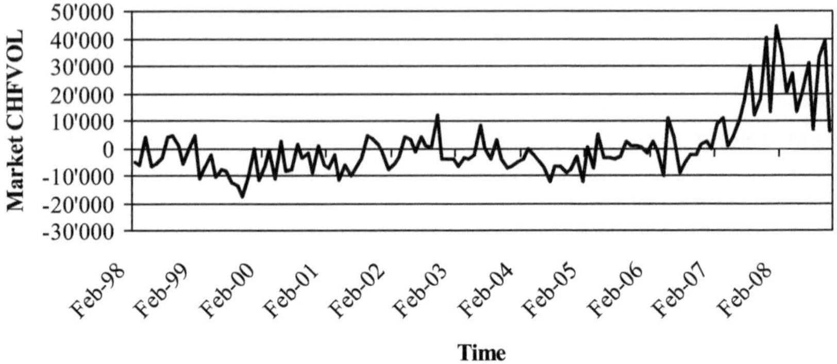

Figure A4: Average Market Turnover, Season-Adjusted (Percent), incl. 2008

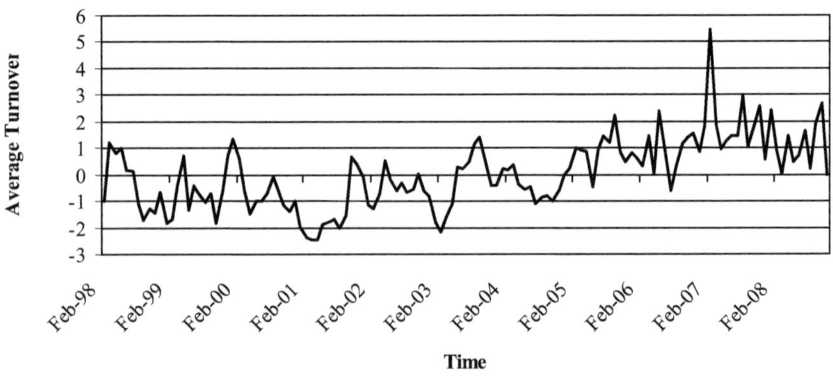

Table A14: Returns to Turnover Portfolios in Practical Setting (J = 12 Months)

	Quintile portfolios				Deciles
Time-series	V1	V3	V5	V1-V5	V1-V10
Panel A: Raw returns (formation period J = 12, holding period K = 1)					
Full (02/1998 - 08/2008)	0.51	1.26	0.77	-0.26	-0.39
Bull markets	2.66	2.84	1.48	**1.17****	1.08
Bear markets	-3.26	-1.53	-0.49	**-2.77*****	**-2.99*****
Positive market return months	3.99	3.19	1.54	**2.45*****	**2.51*****
Negative market return months	-5.21	-1.92	-0.50	**-4.71*****	**-4.897*****
Panel B: Raw returns (formation period J = 12, holding period K = 12)					
Full (02/1998 - 08/2008)	0.78	1.19	0.92	-0.14	-0.31
Bull markets	2.97	2.91	1.64	**1.33****	**1.17***
Bear markets	-3.08	-1.83	-0.35	**-2.72*****	**-2.91*****
Positive market return months	3.96	3.22	1.67	**2.29*****	**2.27*****
Negative market return months	-4.45	-2.15	-0.31	**-4.14*****	**-4.56*****

This table reports average monthly portfolio returns in different sub-sets of the complete return time-series (02/1998 - 08/2008) as defined in 3.3.2.3.2. The equal-weighted portfolios are formed monthly on the basis of stocks' average monthly share turnover in the last $J = 12$ months and are rebalanced every $K = 1$ (Panel A) or $K = 12$ (Panel B) months. V1 is the portfolio containing the stocks with the highest 20% (quintiles) or 10% (deciles) share turnover in a given month. V1, V3, V5 are portfolios containing long stock positions, while V1-V5 and V1-V10 are zero-cost arbitrage strategies. ***/**/* Denotes statistical significance at the 1%/5%/10% level (t-statistics are calculated using Newey-West (1987) adjusted, heteroskedasticity and serial correlation robust standard errors).

Table A15: Time-Series Regression Coefficients of Turnover Arbitrage Strategies (J = 12 Months)

Time-series	Alpha	RMRF	SMB	HML	UMD	R2-adj
Panel A: Carhart regression coefficients (V1-V5), formation period J = 12, holding period K = 1						
Full time-series	-0.50	**1.04*****	0.43**	0.29*	-0.26***	0.66
Bull markets	-0.77**	**1.04*****	0.57**	0.28*	-0.32**	0.60
Bear markets	0.02	**1.26*****	0.34*	0.33	-0.11	0.65
Positive market	-0.58	**1.10*****	0.44**	0.32	-0.44***	0.46
Negative market	-1.33**	**0.97*****	0.45	0.15	-0.09	0.53
Panel B: Carhart regression coefficients (V1-V5), formation period J = 12, holding period K = 12						
Full time-series	-0.40	**0.97*****	0.49**	0.19	-0.25**	0.64
Bull markets	-0.53	**0.95*****	0.66***	0.10	-0.24	0.48
Bear markets	-0.15	**1.08*****	0.26**	0.25	-0.16	0.74
Positive market	-0.44	**0.99*****	0.45***	0.11	-0.37**	0.38
Negative market	-0.87	**0.96*****	0.56*	0.26	-0.15	0.62

This table reports estimated coefficients of regressions of monthly excess returns of the practical turnover quintile arbitrage strategies (V1-V5), in different sub-sets of the complete time-series (02/1998 - 08/2008) as defined in 3.3.2.3.2, on the time-series of Swiss factor premiums RMRF, SMB, HML, UMD (Carhart factors). The methodology applied is described in detail in 3.3.3.2. ***/**/* Denotes statistical significance at the 1%/5%/10% level (t-statistics are calculated using Newey-West (1987) adjusted, heteroskedasticity and serial correlation robust standard errors).

Table A16: Returns to Turnover Growth Portfolios in Practical Setting (J = 3 Months)

	Quintile portfolios				Deciles
Time-series	V1	V3	V5	V1-V5	V1-V10
Panel A: Raw returns (formation period J = 3, holding period K = 1)					
Full (02/1998 - 08/2008)	1.20	0.70	0.62	**0.58****	0.40
Positive market return months	2.76	3.01	2.78	-0.03	-0.26
Negative market return months	-1.37	-3.09	-2.95	**1.58*****	**1.49*****
Panel B: Raw returns (formation period J = 3, holding period K = 12)					
Full (02/1998 - 08/2008)	1.26	0.91	1.01	**0.25***	0.10
Positive market return months	2.73	3.06	3.00	**-0.27***	**-0.51*****
Negative market return months	-1.15	-2.65	-2.27	**1.11*****	**1.11*****

This table reports average monthly portfolio returns in different sub-sets of the complete return time-series (02/1998 - 08/2008) as defined in 3.3.2.3.2. The equal-weighted portfolios are formed monthly on the basis of stocks' average monthly turnover growth in the last $J = 3$ months and are rebalanced every $K = 1$ (Panel A) or $K = 12$ (Panel B) months. V1 is the portfolio containing the stocks with the highest 20% (quintiles) or 10% (deciles) turnover growth in a given month. V1, V3, V5 are portfolios containing long stock positions, while V1-V5 and V1-V10 are zero-cost arbitrage strategies. ***/**/* Denotes statistical significance at the 1%/5%/10% level (t-statistics are calculated using Newey-West (1987) adjusted, heteroskedasticity and serial correlation robust standard errors).

Table A17: Time-Series Regression Coefficients of Turnover Growth Arbitrage Strategies (J = 3 Months)

Time-series	Alpha	RMRF	SMB	HML	UMD	R2-adj
Panel A: Carhart regression coefficients (V1-V5), formation period J = 3, holding period K = 1						
Full time-series	**0.71*** **	**-0.25*** **	-0.06	-0.09	-0.04	0.14
Positive market	**0.77***	**-0.28** **	-0.10	-0.02	-0.12	0.01
Negative market	0.68	**-0.20***	-0.20	0.11	0.02	0.04
Panel B: Carhart regression coefficients (V1-V5), formation period J = 3, holding period K = 12						
Full time-series	**0.21***	**-0.20*** **	0.10	0.00	0.05	0.48
Positive market	**0.51** **	**-0.26*** **	0.06	-0.01	0.08**	0.27
Negative market	-0.20	**-0.23*** **	0.17**	0.05	0.02	0.52

This table reports estimated coefficients of regressions of monthly excess returns of the practical turnover growth quintile arbitrage strategies (V1-V5), in different sub-sets of the complete time-series (02/1998 - 08/2008) as defined in 3.3.2.3.2, on the time-series of Swiss factor premiums RMRF, SMB, HML, UMD (Carhart factors). The methodology applied is described in detail in 3.3.3.2. ***/**/* Denotes statistical significance at the 1%/5%/10% level (t-statistics are calculated using Newey-West (1987) adjusted, heteroskedasticity and serial correlation robust standard errors).

References

AGGARWAL, RAJ, and MEGAN Y. SUN (2003), "Trading Volume Extremes and the Subsequent Price Behavior", Working paper, Kent State University.

AITKEN, MICHAEL, and R. WINN (1997), "What is this Thing Called Liquidity?", Working Paper, Securities Industry Research Centre of Asia-Pacific Sydney, Australia.

AMIHUD, YAKOV (2002), "Illiquidity and Stock Returns: Cross-Section and Time-Series Effects", *Journal of Financial Markets,* 5, pp. 31-56.

AMIHUD, YAKOV, and HAIM MENDELSON (1986), "Asset Pricing and the Bid-ask Spread", *Journal of Financial Economics,* 17, pp. 223-249.

AMMANN, MANUEL, and MICHAEL STEINER (2008), "Risk Factors for the Swiss Stock Market", *Swiss Journal of Economics and Statistics,* 144, pp. 1-35.

ANG, ANDREW, ROBERT J. HODRICK, YUHANG XING, and XIAOYAN ZHANG (2006), "The Cross-Section of Volatility and Expected Returns", *The Journal of Finance*, 61, pp. 259-299.

ASNESS, CLIFFORD S. (1994), "Variables that Explain Stock Returns: Simulated and Empirical Evidence", Unpublished Ph.D. Dissertation, Graduate School of Business, University of Chicago.

AVRAMOV, DORON, TARUN CHORDIA, and AMIT GOYAL (2006), "Liquidity and Autocorrelations in Individual Stock Returns", *The Journal of Finance,* 61, pp. 2365-2394.

BAKSHI, GURDIP, and NIKUNJ KAPADIA (2003), "Delta-hedged Gains and the Negative Market Volatility Risk Premium", *Review of Financial Studies*, 16, pp. 527-566.

BANZ, ROLF W. (1981), "The Relationship between Return and Market Value of Common Stocks", *Journal of Financial Economics*, 9, pp. 3-18.

BALVERS, RONALD, YANGRU WU, and ERIK GILLILAND (2000), "Mean Reversion across National Stock Markets and Parametric Contrarian Investment Strategies", *The Journal of Finance,* 55, pp. 745-772.

BARBER, BRAD M., and TERRANCE ODEAN (2002), "Online Investors: Do the Slow Die First?", *The Review of Financial Studies,* 15, pp. 455-487.

BARBER, BRAD M., and TERRANCE ODEAN (2008), "All That Glitters: The Effect of Attention and News on the Buying Behavior of Individual and Institutional Investors", *The Review of Financial Studies,* 21, pp. 785-818.

BRAUNEIS, ALEXANDER, and ROLAND MESTEL (2007), "An Event Based Approach for Dynamic Volume Return Relationships of DAX companies", Working Paper, Alpen-Adria-Universität Klagenfurt.

BRENNAN, MICHAEL J., TARUN CHORDIA, and AVANIDHAR SUBRAHMANYAM (1998), "Alternative Factor Specifications, Security Characteristics, and the Cross-Section of Expected Returns", *Journal of Financial Economics,* 49, pp. 345-373.

BRITTEN-JONES, MARK, and ANTHONY NEUBERGER (2004), "Improved Inference and Estimation in Regression with Overlapping Observations", EFA Maastricht Meetings Paper, No. 4156.

BROOKS, CHRIS (2002), *Introductory Econometrics for Finance*, New York: Cambridge University Press.

CAMPBELL, JOHN Y., SANFORD J. GROSSMAN, and JIANG WANG (1993), "Trading Volume and Serial Correlation in Stock Returns", *The Quarterly Journal of Economics,* 107, pp. 905-939.

CAMPBELL, JOHN Y. (1993), "Intertemporal Asset Pricing without Consumption Data", *American Economic Review*, 83, pp. 487-512.

CAMPBELL, JOHN Y. (1996), "Understanding Risk and Return", *Journal of Political Economy*, 104, pp. 298-345.

CARHART, MARK (1995), "Survivorship Bias and Persistence in Mutual Fund Performance", Unpublished Ph.D. Dissertation, Graduate School of Business, University of Chicago.

CARHART, MARK (1997), "On Persistence in Mutual Fund Performance", *The Journal of Finance,* 50, pp. 679-698.

CHALMERS, JOHN M. R., and GREGORY B. KADLEC (1998), "An Empirical Examination of the Amortized Spread", *Journal of Financial Economics*, 48, pp. 159-188.

CHAN, HOWARD W., and ROBERT W. FAFF (2005), "Asset Pricing and the Illiquidity Premium", *The Financial Review,* 40, pp. 429-458.

CHAN, KALOK, ALLAUDEEN HAMEED, and WILSON TONG (2000), "Profitability of Momentum Strategies in the International Equity Markets", *Journal of Financial and Quantitative Analysis,* 35, pp. 153-172.

CHEN, HONGHUI, and VIJAY SINGAL (2003), "A December Effect with Tax-Gain Selling?", *Financial Analysts Journal*, July-August 2003, pp. 78-90.

CHEN, JOSEPH (2002), "Intertemporal CAPM and the Cross-section of Stock Returns", Working Paper, University of Southern California.

CHORDIA, TARUN, RICHARD ROLL, and AVANIDHAR SUBRAHMANYAM (2000), "Commonality in Liquidity", *Journal of Financial Economics,* 56, pp. 3-28.

CHORDIA, TARUN, AVANIDHAR SUBRAHMANYAM, and V. RAVI ANSHUMAN (2001), "Trading Activity and Expected Stock Returns", *Journal of Financial Economics,* 59, pp. 3-32.

CHUANG, WEN-I, and BONG-SOO LEE (2006), "An Empirical Evaluation of the Overconfidence Hypothesis", *Journal of Banking & Finance,* 30, pp. 2489-2515.

COMISKEY, EUGENE E., RALPH A. WALKLING, and MICHAEL A. WEEKS (1987), "Dispersion of Expectations and Trading Volume", *Journal of Business Finance & Accounting,* pp. 229-239.

CONNOR, GREGORY (1995), "The Three Types of Factor Models: A Comparison of Their Explanatory Power", *Financial Analysts Journal,* May-June 1995, pp. 42-46.

CONNOR, GREGORY, and R. KORAJCZYK (1988), "Risk and Return in an Equilibrium APT: Application of a New Test Methodology", *Journal of Financial Economics,* 21, pp. 255-290.

CONRAD, JENNIFER S., ALLAUDEEN HAMEED, and CATHY NIDEN (1994), "Volume and Autocovariances in Short-Horizon Individual Security Returns", *The Journal of Finance,* 49, pp. 1305-1329.

COOPER, MICHAEL (1999), "Filter Rules Based on Price and Volume in Individual Security Overreaction", *The Review of Financial Studies,* 12, pp. 901-935.

COOPER, MICHAEL J,, ROBERTO C. GUTIERREZ JR., and ALLAUDEEN HAMEED (2004), "Market States and Momentum", *The Journal of Finance*, 59, pp. 1345-1365.

COPELAND, THOMAS (1976), "A Model of Asset Trading under the Assumption of Sequential Information Arrival", *The Journal of Finance,* 31, pp. 1149-1168.

COPELAND, THOMAS (1977), "A Probability Model of Asset Trading", *The Journal of Finance,* 31, pp. 1149-1168.

CROUCH, R. L. (1970a), "A Nonlinear Test of the Random-Walk Hypothesis", *American Economic Review,* 60, pp. 199-202.

CROUCH, R. L. (1970b), "The Volume of Transactions and Price Changes on the New York Stock Exchange", *Financial Analysts Journal*, 26, pp. 104-109.

DANIEL, KENT, DAVID HIRSHLEIFER, and AVANIDHAR SUBRAHMANYAM (1998), "Investor Psychology and Security Market Under- and Overreaction", *The Journal of Finance,* 53, pp. 1839-1886.

DATAR, VINAJ T., NARAYAN Y. NAIK, and ROBERT RADCLIFFE (1998), "Liquidity and Stock Returns: An Alternative Test", *Journal of Financial Markets,* 1, pp. 203-219.

DE BONDT, WERNER F. M., and RICHARD THALER (1985), "Does the Stock Market Overreact?", *The Journal of Finance,* 40, pp. 793-805.

DOMOWITZ, IAN, JACK GLEN, and ANANTH MADHAVAN (2001), "Liquidity, Volatility and Equity Trading Costs Across Countries and Over Time", *International Finance*, 4, pp. 221-255.

ELESWARAPU, VENKAT R. (1997), "Cost of Transacting and Expected Returns in the Nasdaq Market", *The Journal of Finance,* 52, pp. 2113-2127.

ELESWARAPU, VENKAT R., and MARK REINGANUM (1993), "The Seasonal Behavior of the Liquidity Premium in Asset Pricing, *Journal of Financial Economics,* 34, pp. 373-386.

EPPS, THOMAS (1977), "Security Price Changes and Transaction Volumes: Some Additional Evidence", *Journal of Financial and Quantitative Analysis*, 12, pp. 141-146.

EPPS, THOMAS, and MARY LEE EPPS (1976), "The Stochastic Dependence of Security Price Changes and Transaction Volumes: Implications for the Mixture-of-Distributions Hypothesis", *Econometrica,* 44, pp. 305-321.

FAMA, EUGENE F., and JAMES D. MACBETH (1973), "Risk, Return, and Equilibrium: Empirical Tests", *Journal of Political Economy,* 81, pp. 607-636.

FAMA, EUGENE F., and KENNETH R. FRENCH (1988), "Permanent and Temporary Components of Stock Prices", *Journal of Political Economy,* 96, pp. 246-273.

FAMA, EUGENE F., and KENNETH R. FRENCH (1992), "The Cross-Section of Expected Stock Returns", *The Journal of Finance,* 47, pp. 427-465.

FAMA, EUGENE F., and KENNETH R. FRENCH (1993), "Common Risk Factors in the Returns on Stocks and Bonds", *Journal of Financial Economics,* 33, pp. 3-56.

FAMA, EUGENE F., and KENNETH R. FRENCH (1996), "Multifactor Explanations of Asset Pricing Anomalies", *The Journal of Finance,* 51, pp. 55-84.

FAMA, EUGENE F., and KENNETH R. FRENCH (1998), "Value versus Growth: The International Evidence", *The Journal of Finance,* 53, pp. 1975-1999.

GALLANT, A. RONALD, PETER E. ROSSI, and GEORGE TAUCHEN (1992), "Stock Prices and Volume", *The Review of Financial Studies,* 5, pp. 199-242.

GERVAIS, SIMON, RON KANIEL, and DAN H. MINGELGRIN (2001), "The High-Volume Return Premium", *The Journal of Finance,* 56, pp. 877-919.

GERVAIS, SIMON, and TERRANCE ODEAN (2001), "Learning to Be Overconfident", *The Review of Financial Studies,* 14, pp. 1-27.

GLASER, MARKUS, and MARTIN WEBER (2003), "Momentum and Turnover: Evidence from the German Stock Market", *Schmalenbach Business Review,* 55, pp. 108-135.

GLASER, MARKUS, and MARTIN WEBER (2005), "Which Past Returns Affect Trading Volume?", Working Paper, Sonderforschungsbereich 504, University of Mannheim.

GODFREY, MICHAEL D., Clive W.J. GRANGER, and O. MORGENSTERN (1964), "The Random Walk Hypothesis of Stock Market Behavior, *Kyklos*, 17, pp. 1-30.

GRANGER, Clive W. J. (1969), "Investigating Causal Relations by Econometric Models and Cross-Spectral Methods, *Econometrica*, 37, pp. 424-438.

GRIFFIN, JOHN M., FREDERICO NARDARI, and RENE M. STULZ (2004), "Stock Market Trading and Market Conditions", NBER Working Paper 10719.

GURGUL, HENRYK, PAWEL MAJDOSZ, and ROLAND MESTEL (2007), "Price-Volume Relations of DAX Companies", *Fin Mkts Portfolio Mgmt,* 21, pp. 353-379.

HAMEED, ALLAUDEEN, and YUANTO KUSNADI (2002), "Momentum Strategies: Evidence from Pacific Basin Stock Markets", *The Journal of Financial Research",* 25, pp. 383-397.

HARRIS, LAWRENCE (1983), "The Joint Distribution of Speculative Prices and of Daily Trading Volume", Working Paper, University of Southern California.

HARRIS, LAWRENCE (1986), "Cross-Security Tests of the Mixture of Distributions Hypothesis", *Journal of Financial and Quantitative Analysis,* 21, pp. 39-46.

HARRIS, LAWRENCE (1987), "Transaction Data Tests of the Mixture of Distributions Hypothesis", *Journal of Financial and Quantitative Analysis,* 22, pp. 127-141.

HAUGEN, ROBERT A., and NARDIN L. BAKER (1996), "Commonality in the Determinants of Expected Stock Returns", *Journal of Financial Economics,* 41, pp. 401-439.

HJALMARSSON, ERIK (2008), "Inference in Long-Horizon Regressions", International Finance Discussion Papers, Number 853.

HONG, HARRISON, and JEREMY C. STEIN (1999), "A Unified Theory of Underreaction, Momentum Trading, and Overreaction in Asset Markets", *The Journal of Finance*, 54, pp. 2143-2184.

HU, SHING-YANG (1997), "Trading Turnover and Expected Stock Returns: The Trading Frequency Hypothesis and Evidence from the Tokyo Stock Exchange", Working Paper, University of Chicago.

HUDDART, STEVEN, MARK LANG, and MICHELLE H. YETMAN (2006), Working Paper Submitted to Management Science, Manuscript No. MS-00205-2006R.

INCE, OZGUR S., and R. BURT PORTER (2006), "Individual Equity Return Data from Thomson Datastream: Handle with Care!", *The Journal of Financial Research*, 29, pp. 463-479.

JAIN, PREM C., and GUN-HO JOH (1988), "The Dependence between Hourly Prices and Trading Volume", *The Journal of Financial and Quantitative Analysis,* 23, pp. 269-283.

JAMES, CHRISTOPHER, and ROBERT O. EDMISTER (1983), "The Relation between Common Stock Returns, Trading Activity and Market Value", *The Journal of Finance*, 38, pp. 1075-1086.

JEGADEESH, NARASIMHAN (1990), "Evidence of Predictable Behavior of Security Returns", *The Journal of Finance,* 45, pp. 881-898.

JEGADEESH, NARASIMHAN, and SHERIDAN TITMAN (1993), "Returns to Buying Winners and Selling Losers: Implications for Stock Market Efficiency", *The Journal of Finance,* 48, pp. 65-91.

JENNINGS, ROBERT H., LAURA T. STARKS, and JOHN C. FELLINGHAM (1981), "An Equilibrium Model of Asset Trading with Sequential Information Arrival", *The Journal of Finance,* 36, pp. 143-161.

KANIEL, RON, DONG LI, and LAURA STARKS (2007), "Investor Visibility Events: Cross-Country Evidence", Working Paper, University of Texas.

KARPOFF, JONATHAN M. (1987), "The Relation between Price Changes and Trading Volume: A Survey", *Journal of Financial and Quantitative Analysis,* 22, pp. 109-126.

KEENE, MARVIN A., and DAVID R. PETERSON (2007), "The Importance of Liquidity as a Factor in Asset Pricing", *The Journal of Financial Research,* 30, pp. 91-109.

KEIM, DONALD B. (1983), "Size Related Anomalies and the Stock Return Seasonality: Empirical Evidence", *Journal of Financial Economics*, 12, pp. 13-32.

KEYNES, JOHN M. (1930), "*Treatise on Money*", London: Macmillan.

LEE, CHARLES M. C., and BHASKARAN SWAMINATHAN (2000), "Price Momentum and Trading Volume", *The Journal of Finance,* 55, pp. 2017-2069.

LEE, CHENG, and OLIVER RUI (2000), "Does Trading Volume Contain Information to Predict Stock Returns? Evidence from China's Stock Markets", *Review of Quantitative Finance and Accounting*, 14, pp. 341-360.

LEE, CHENG, and OLIVER RUI (2002), "The Dynamic Relationship between Stock Returns and Trading Volume: Domestic and Cross-Country Evidence", *Journal of Banking & Finance*, 26, pp. 51-78.

LERMAN, ALINA, JOSHUA LIVNAT, and RICHARD R. MENDENHALL (2008), "The High-Volume Return Premium and Post-Earnings Announcement Drift", Working Paper, New York University.

LIEW, JIMMY, and MARIA VASSALOU (2000), "Can Book-to-Market, Size and Momentum Be Risk Factors that Predict Economic Growth?", *Journal of Financial Economics,* 57, pp. 221-245.

LINTNER, JOHN (1965), "The Valuation of Risk Assets and the Selection of Risky Investments in Stock Portfolios and Capital Budgets", *Review of Economics and Statistics,* 47, pp. 13-37.

LIU, WEIMIN (2006), "A Liquidity-Augmented Capital Asset Pricing Model", *Journal of Financial Economics,* 82, pp. 631-671.

LIU, WEIMIN, and NORMAN STRONG (2008), "Biases in Decomposing Holding-Period Portfolio Returns", *The Review of Financial Studies*, 21, pp. 2243-2274.

LLORENTE GUILLERMO, RONI MICHAELY, GIDEON SAAR, and JIANG WANG (2002), "Dynamic Volume-Return Relation of Individual Stocks", *The Review of Financial Studies,* 15, pp. 1005-1047.

LO, ANDREW W., and JIANG WANG (2000), "Trading Volume: Definitions, Data Analysis, and Implications of Portfolio Theory", *The Review of Financial Studies,* 13, pp. 257-300.

MANDELBROT, BENOIT (1963), "The Variation of Speculative Prices", *The Journal of Business*, 36, pp. 394-419.

MARSHALL, BEN R. (2006), "Liquidity and Stock Returns: Evidence from a Pure Order-Driven Market using a New Liquidity Proxy", *International Review of Financial Analysis*, 15, pp. 21-38.

MARSHALL, BEN R., and MARTIN YOUNG (2003), "Liquidity and Stock Returns in Pure Order-Driven Markets: Evidence from the Australian Stock Market", *International Review of Financial Analysis,* 12, pp. 173-188.

MAYSHAR, JORAM (1983), "On Divergence of Opinion and Imperfections in Capital Markets", *American Economic Review*, 73, pp. 114-128.

MCMILLAN, DAVID G. (2007), "Non-linear Forecasting of Stock Returns: Does Volume Help?", *International Journal of Forecasting,* 23, pp. 115-126.

MERTON, ROBERT C. (1987), "A Simple Model of Capital Market Equilibrium with Incomplete Information", *The Journal of Finance,* 42, pp. 483-510.

MILLER, EDWARD M. (1977), "Risk, Uncertainty, and Divergence of Opinion", *The Journal of Finance,* 32, pp. 1151-1168.

MORCK, RANDELL, BERNARD YEUNG, and WAYNE YU (2000), "The Information Content of Stock Markets: Why Do Developing Markets Have Synchronous Stock Price Movements?", *Journal of Financial Economics,* 58, pp. 215-260.

MOSSIN, JAN (1966), "Equilibrium in a Capital Asset Market, *Econometrica,* 34, pp. 261-276.

NEWEY, WHITNEY K., and KENNETH D. WEST (1987), "A Simple Positive-Definite Heteroskedasticity and Autocorrelation Consistent Covariance Matrix", *Econometrica*, 55, pp. 703-708.

ODEAN, TERRANCE (1998a), "Volume, Volatility, Price, and Profit When All Traders Are Above Average", *The Journal of Finance,* 53, pp. 1887-1934.

ODEAN, TERRANCE (1998b), "Are Investors Reluctant to Realize Their Losses?", *The Journal of Finance,* 53, pp. 1775-1798.

QUANTITATIVE MICRO SOFTWARE (2004), "*EViews 5 User's Guide*", Irvine California.

PASTOR, LUBOS, and ROBERT F. STAMBAUGH (2003), "Liquidity Risk and Expected Stock Returns", *Journal of Political Economy*, 111, pp. 642-685.

PETERSEN, MITCHELL A. (2009), "Estimating Standard Errors in Finance Panel Data Sets: Comparing Approaches", *The Review of Financial Studies*, 22, pp. 435-480.

REY, DAVID M., and MARKUS M. SCHMID (2007), "Feasible Momentum Strategies: Evidence from the Swiss Stock Market", *Fin Mkts Portfolio Mgmt,* 21, pp. 325-352.

ROUWENHORST, K. GEERT (1999), "Local Return Factors and Turnover in Emerging Stock Markets, *The Journal of Finance,* 54, pp. 1439-1464.

SCHWERT, G. WILLIAM (2002), "Anomalies and Market Efficiency", NBER Working Paper 9277.

SHARPE, WILLIAM F. (1964), "Capital Asset Prices: A Theory of Market Equilibrium Under Conditions of Risk", *The Journal of Finance,* 19, pp. 425-442.

SHEFRIN HERSH, and MEIR STATMAN (1985), "The Disposition to Sell Winners Too Early and Ride Losers Too Long: Theory and Evidence", *The Journal of Finance,* 40, pp. 777-790.

SHUMWAY, TYLER (1997), "The Delisting Bias in CRSP Data", *The Journal of Finance*, 52, pp. 327-340.

SHUMWAY, TYLER, and VINCENT A. WARTHER (1999), "The Delisting Bias in CRSP's Nasdaq Data and Its Implications for the Size Effect", *The Journal of Finance*, 54, pp. 2361-2379.

SPREMANN, KLAUS (2003), "*Portfoliomanagement*", 2. Aufl., München: Oldenbourg Verlag.

SPREMANN, KLAUS (2006), "*Portfoliomanagement*", 3. Aufl., München: Oldenbourg Verlag.

STATMAN, MEIR, STEVEN THORLEY, and KEITH VORKINK (2006), "Investor Overconfidence and Trading Volume", *The Review of Financial Studies,* 19, pp. 1532-1565.

STATTMAN, DENNIS (1980), "Book Values and Stock Returns", *The Chicago MBA: A Journal of Selected Papers,* 4, pp. 25-45.

STICKEL, SCOTT E., and ROBERT E. VERRECCHIA (1994), "Evidence that Trading Volume Sustains Stock Price Changes", *Financial Analysts Journal,* November-December 1994, pp. 57-67.

STOLL, HANS (1978), "The Supply of Dealer Services in Securities Markets", *The Journal of Finance*, 33, pp. 1133-1151.

SUBRAHMANYAM, AVANIDHAR (2005), "On the Stability of the Cross-Section of Expected Stock Returns in the Cross-Section: Understanding the Curious Role of Share Turnover", *European Financial Management*, 5, pp. 661-678.

VAIHEKOSKI, MIKA (2004), "Portfolio Construction for Tests of Asset Pricing Models", *Financial Markets, Institutions & Instruments*, 13, pp. 1-39.

WANG, CHANGYUN, and SHENGTYING CHIN (2004), "Profitability of Return and Volume-Based Investment Strategies in China's Stock Market", *Pacific-Basin Finance Journal,* 12, pp. 541-564.

WANG, JIANG (1994), "A Model of Competitive Stock Trading Volume", *Journal of Political Economy,* 102, pp. 127-168.

WATKINS, BOYCE D. (2007), "The Economic and Predictive Value of Trading Volume Growth: A Tale of Three Moments", *Applied Financial Economics,* 17, pp. 1489-1509.

WOOD, ROBERT A., THOMAS H. MCINISH, and J. K. ORD (1985), "An Investigation of Transactions Data for NYSE Stocks", *The Journal of Finance*, 60, pp. 723-739.

WOOLDRIDGE, JEFFREY M. (2002), "Econometric Analysis of Cross Section and Panel Data", Cambridge, Massachusetts: MIT Press.

YING, CHARLES C. (1966), "Market Prices and Volumes of Sales", *Econometrica,* 34, pp. 676-685.

MIX
Papier aus verantwortungsvollen Quellen
Paper from responsible sources
FSC® C105338

If you have any concerns about our products,
you can contact us on
ProductSafety@springernature.com

In case Publisher is established outside the EU,
the EU authorized representative is:
Springer Nature Customer Service Center GmbH
Europaplatz 3, 69115 Heidelberg, Germany

Printed by Libri Plureos GmbH
in Hamburg, Germany